Writing Skills Made Fun

Sentences & Paragraphs

BY KAREN KELLAHER

SCHOLASTIC PROFESSIONAL BOOKS

NEW YORK • TORONTO • LONDON • AUCKLAND • SYDNEY

MEXICO CITY • NEW DELHI • HONG KONG • BUENOS AIRES

To Sue Leahy,

a top-notch friend

Cover, interior, and poster art by Mike Moran
Front cover, interior, and poster design by Kathy Massaro

ISBN: 0-439-22266-4
Copyright © 2001 by Karen Kellaher.
Published by Scholastic Inc.
Printed in the U.S.A.

Contents

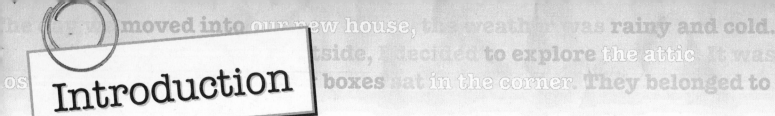

Writing Skills Made Fun: About the Series

As a writer and editor in the field of educational publishing, I frequently talk with language-arts teachers about the kinds of tools they need most. I also spend a lot of time browsing in bookstores and paging through teacher catalogs, checking out what is currently available. One thing I noticed over the past several years is that when it came to nitty-gritty writing skills, second- and third-grade teachers' needs were simply not being met. Sure, there were plenty of grammar and writing resources available to teachers of grades 5, 6, and above. But I saw very little quality material that was just right for the early elementary grades. I wrote this series to fill that "grammar gap"— and to assist you in your all-important mission of teaching the rules of writing.

As you are well aware, your job is cut out for you. According to state and national standards, by the time students enter second grade, they are expected to know and understand the basic rules of English grammar—and to consistently apply those rules to their own writing. Just take a look at some of the standards nationwide: Just take a look at some of the standards nationwide:

✳ **CALIFORNIA:** Second-graders must be able to distinguish between complete and incomplete sentences, use commas and quotation marks, and know when to capitalize letters. Third-graders in the Golden State must be able to use all four types of sentences, identify subjects and verbs, understand agreement and verb tenses, and identify and use all parts of speech.

✳ **ILLINOIS:** By the third grade, students should be able to construct complete sentences that demonstrate subject-verb agreement, use punctuation and capitalization properly, know and use the parts of speech, and demonstrate focus and organization when writing paragraphs.

✳ **TEXAS:** State standards dictate that by grade 3, "Students will recognize and demonstrate appropriate use of standard English: usage, mechanics, spelling, and sentence structure."

As you know, with tough standards come tough tests. Almost all major standardized tests for third-graders include sections on usage and mechanics. And many tests include open-ended writing sections that require students to demonstrate a working knowledge of the basic rules of grammar.

This book series, *Writing Skills Made Fun* is one way to help you meet these curriculum demands and make grammar fun. The series includes three books: *Capitalization, Punctuation & Spelling*; *Parts of Speech*; and *Sentences & Paragraphs*.

next day was sunny. Once I finished breakfast, I set out to search for the spot marked on my map. Before I had gotten very far, I heard a voice say, "I'm Kate. You must be the new kid." I said "hello." Should I

Introduction

Sentences and Paragraphs

Full-length writing assignments can seem overwhelming to a beginning writer. When asked to write a friendly letter, short story, or book report, an inexperienced writer can quickly come down with a case of the "I can't do it" blues. Help your students see that they can do it. Teach them that all good writing—no matter how long—is composed of sentences and paragraphs that follow the basic rules of grammar. Once students master the building blocks of good writing, they'll be ready to face more elaborate projects with enthusiasm.

By now your students are probably familiar with nouns, verbs, and other parts of speech. They have some experience spelling and capitalizing words correctly. With the help of this book, they will learn how best to form sentences that effectively convey ideas. They'll learn to combine sentences into paragraphs in order to present their ideas in a clear and organized fashion. The payoff, as you know, is well worth the effort. The ability to write effective sentences and paragraphs can take students anywhere. With this skill, students can convey their opinions to the editor of your local newspaper, recommend a favorite book to a classmate, or explain a scientific phenomenon. Best of all, they can write stories and reports that people actually enjoy reading!

On the pages that follow, you'll find engaging activities to help you teach students to recognize and write super sentences and paragraphs. All of the activities are interactive and kid-friendly. For example, with the So Many Sentences! Flap Book students use an easy-to-make manipulative to help learn about the different kinds of sentences and how to punctuate them. In Subject-Predicate Puzzles, they'll use their knowledge of subject-verb agreement to complete sentence jigsaw puzzles. And in Build a Paragraph Puppet, students will make a Chinese New Year Dragon by cutting out sentences and pasting them together in order to make a puppet.

You can use the activities and mini-lessons in any order you like. Check the label at the top of each lesson to see which major concepts are being explored. Other teaching tips follow.

* Distribute copies of the grammar Workshop pages (found at the beginning of each chapter) for students to refer to as they complete the activities in this book. Students can bind these pages together and add a cover to make a handy mini grammar reference book.

* Have students work on some of the activities in collaborative groups. Students will learn from and build on one another's ideas.

* Use the poster included in this book as the centerpiece of an exciting bulletin board or learning corner. See page 6 for a fun way to get started.

* Provide opportunities for students to share their work with classmates, parents, and others. For example, after students have made the So Many Sentences manipulative and discussed the four types of sentences, they can bring the manipulative home to demonstrate what they've learned.

Teaching With the Poster: "The Run-On" and "The Fragment"

In casual conversation, we don't always speak in full sentences. For example, you might say, "Ready to go?" as your class prepares to go on a field trip. Or, when recounting a vacation adventure to a colleague, you might use run-on sentences. While fragments and run-ons are acceptable in oral discourse, they are obviously not conducive to effective writing. As an adult you easily recognize the differences between spoken and written language. However, many young children tend to write in the same way they speak and think. As you introduce children to the special demands of written language, point out the importance of using complete sentences.

This poster uses humor to teach the weaknesses of run-ons and fragments. The poster contains two limericks, "The Run-On" and "The Fragment." Display the poster in a central area of your classroom, and, together, recite each poem several times. Afterward, explore the poems with your class. Give an example of a run-on that Wink might have written, and then invite students to write some run-ons of their own. Do the same with fragments: Write one or two on the board, then ask students to come up with their own. Have students exchange papers and turn their classmates' run-ons and fragments into proper sentences.

To make the most of the limericks, give students individual copies (see page 7). If you're using the two companion books in this series (*Capitalization, Punctuation & Spelling* and *Parts of Speech*), distribute copies of the rhymes in those books as well. Have students make a grammar rhyme book by binding the rhymes together and adding a cover.

Name _____

Date _____

The Run-On

A funny young fellow named Wink
Tried writing a sentence in ink.
It went on for ages,
And filled several pages.
It was a **RUN-ON**, I think.

The Fragment

Another writer named Sue
Had the opposite problem, it's true.
Her sentence did not connect
A predicate to a subject.
A **FRAGMENT** it was, through and through.

SCHOLASTIC

7

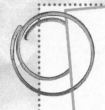

Sentence Workshop

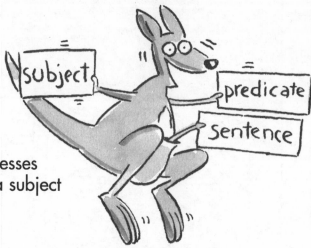

A sentence is a group of words that expresses a complete thought. Every sentence has a subject (noun or pronoun) and predicate (verb).

❋ Subjects:

A **simple** subject is the noun that tells what the sentence is about:

My <u>cousin</u> hopped up and down.

A **complete** subject is the noun plus any descriptive words that go with it:

<u>My young cousin</u> hopped up and down.

A **compound** subject is two or more simple subjects joined together:

<u>Aunt Harriet and cousin Mike</u> are coming to visit.

❋ Predicates:

A **simple** predicate is the verb of the sentence:

Jill <u>wrote</u> her essay.

A **complete** predicate is the verb plus any descriptive words that go with it:

Jill <u>wrote her essay</u>.

A **compound** predicate is two or more simple predicates joined together:

Jill <u>read and wrote</u> all night long.

Sentence Workshop (continued)

 There are four types of sentences.

A **declarative** sentence makes a statement:

The mail has arrived.

An **interrogative** sentence asks a question:

Have you seen my keys?

An **imperative** sentence gives a command. The subject of an imperative sentence is the pronoun "you," even though it is not stated:

Leave all backpacks in the hall.

An **exclamatory** sentence expresses strong feelings:

I've never been happier!

 Fragments and run-ons are not proper sentences.

A **fragment** is an incomplete thought. It is missing a subject, predicate, or both:

In the kitchen.

My brother, Joshua.

Went to the store, then the post office.

A **run-on** is a group of words that contains several thoughts and should be broken down into two or more sentences:

Hannah, who is in third grade, has never seen snow because she lived in California her whole life but now she lives on the east coast so she can't wait for winter.

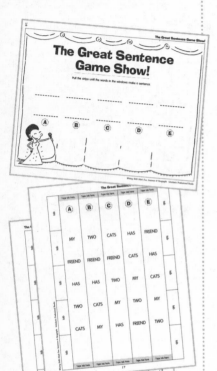

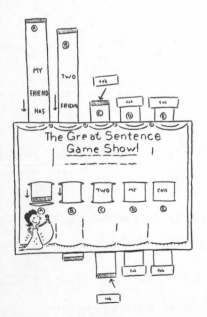

The Great Sentence Game Show! (Use with Kids' Pages 16–18.)

Forming sentences is fun when you use this creative manipulative. Designed in a game show format, this teaching tool lets students play with words until they hit the "jackpot"—a complete sentence that makes sense!

The manipulative can be used at two levels. In Game 1, beginning writers pull the paper strips to change the word order until they form one complete sentence. Game 2 offers an added challenge. Students pull the strips to mix and match a variety of subjects and predicates, forming as many sentences as they can.

You Will Need

✳ copies of pages 16–18
    (Use pages 16 and 17 for Game 1)
    Use pages 16 and 18 for Game 2)

✳ crayons or markers

✳ scissors

✳ glue stick or tape

What to Do

1 Distribute the reproducibles to students. They can color the game show page, as desired.

2 Have students cut out the game show pattern (page 16) along the outer dotted lines. Then direct them to cut along the ten small horizontal dotted lines to make slits in the page. For easy cutting, show them how to poke the tip of the scissors through the page and then snip along the rest of the line.

3 Tell students to cut along the dotted lines on the sentence reproducible (page 17 or 18), creating five vertical strips of paper. They should also cut out the ten rectangular end tabs along the margins of the reproducible, and then set the tabs aside for a moment.

4 Students then match each lettered strip to a window on the game show pattern (A, B, C, D, or E). Next, they weave each strip into the game show pattern by poking it through the slits in the paper, as shown.

5 To ensure that the strips don't fall out, have students glue or tape the ten rectangular tabs to the ends of each strip.

6 Instruct students to pull the strips up or down until a complete sentence appears in the game show windows. If they're playing Game 1, students find the proper word order and leave it on their playing boards. If they're playing Game 2, have students write down each complete sentence they make. (Challenge them to capitalize and punctuate the sentences correctly.) Compare lists at the end of the exercise.

next day was sunny. Once I finished breakfast, I set out to search for the spot marked on my map. Before I had gotten very far, I heard a voice say, "I'm Kate. You must be the new kid." I said "hello." Should I

Sentences

So Many Sentences! Flap Book

(Use with Kids' Pages 19 and 20.)

If your students sometimes need help remembering the different kinds of sentences and how to punctuate them, this flap book will be a surefire hit. The book explains the function of each type of sentence and offers several examples of each. Plus, students get a chance to add some examples of their own.

You Will Need

✱ two-sided copies of pages 19–20 (for best results, use a machine that makes two-sided copies)

✱ scissors

What to Do

1 Distribute a two-sided copy of the reproducible to each student. Instruct students to place page 19 faceup. Have them cut out the pattern along the outer dotted lines. Then have them fold the page in half along the center solid line, crease well, and place the text side faceup, as shown.

2 Have students cut along the dotted lines, creating four flaps.

3 Tell students to read the rhyme on the front of each flap, and then open the flap to reveal examples. When students have a working knowledge of the types of sentences, invite them to add an example of their own to each category.

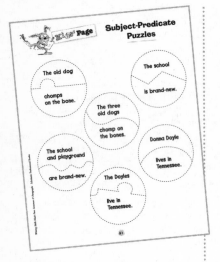

Subject-Predicate Puzzles (Use with Kids' Page 21.)

Teaching and learning subject-verb agreement can be tough. but with this jigsaw puzzle activity, your lesson will fall into place. The puzzles work well as collaborative activities, but can also be used as individual projects.

You Will Need

✳ copies of page 21 (if using as a collaborative activity, make one copy for each small group)

✳ scissors

✳ plastic sandwich bags or envelopes (one per group)

✳ construction paper

✳ glue sticks

What to Do

1 Ahead of time, stack together copies of the reproducible. Check that they are aligned and then cut out the puzzle pieces. Mix up each set of pieces and place in a plastic sandwich bag or envelope.

2 Before beginning the activity, review the basics of subject-verb agreement. Provide examples of sentences in which the subject and verb agree (*I own a goldfish; He owns a goldfish; Hillary reads a lot; Hillary and Fiona read a lot*). Also give a few examples in which the subject and verb do not agree and ask students to fix the problem (*I walks home; Chris eat ice cream*).

3 Give each group a bag or envelope containing the puzzle pieces. Point out that students will be putting two pieces together to make a circle. The interlocking puzzle pieces will form a sentence in which the subject and verb agree.

4 Have students work together to match the puzzle pieces so that the subjects and predicates agree. When they have finished, have them glue the completed circles onto a sheet of construction paper.

Sentence or Fragment?

(Use with Kids' Page 22.)

Reinforce the idea that a sentence must have a subject and a predicate by having students review a list of possible sentences. Then, distribute the reproducible. If the group of words is a sentence, students should circle S. If the group of words is missing a subject or predicate and is a fragment, students should circle F. Afterward, on a separate sheet of paper, have students use the fragments to construct complete sentences.

Repair a Run-On News Report

(Use with Kids' Page 23.)

Tell students to grab their editing pencils, because this news report is in sad shape! Distribute the reproducible, and invite students to read the run-on news report aloud. You may also wish to read it aloud yourself, allowing the words to run together. Grow a bit breathless by the end to emphasize the lack of punctuation and sentence structure. Then have students rewrite the paragraph, using complete sentences instead of run-ons. Remind them to end each sentence with appropriate punctuation (a period, exclamation point, or question mark), and to start each new sentence with a capital letter.

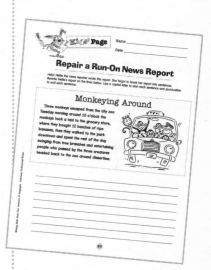

Follow up the activity by asking students to think about the importance of separating our thoughts into sentences. Ask: "How did the report sound when there were no periods separating the ideas? How did it sound once we divided it into sentences?"

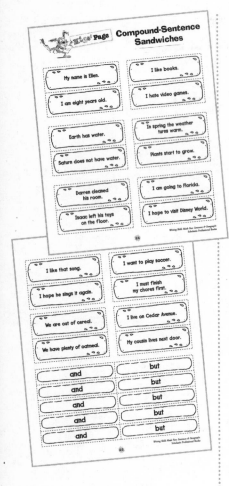

Compound-Sentence Sandwiches

(Use with Kids' Pages 24 and 25.)

Hands-on learners will love this method of exploring compound sentences. In this activity, students work together to join simple sentences using the conjunctions *and* and *but*. The complete sentences will look like hamburgers sandwiched between buns. Use them to decorate a bulletin board about sentences.

You Will Need

* copies of pages 24 and 25
* scissors
* tape

What to Do

1 Copy the reproducible. Cut out the "buns" (simple sentences) and "hamburgers" (conjunctions).

2 Divide the class into teams of two or three. Give each team a set of sentences (two halves from a bun). Also give each team a copy of the words *and* and *but* (hamburgers). Only one of these will be used.

3 Instruct students to put their two sentences together to make a longer sentence. They must decide which sentence comes first and which joining word (conjunction) to use.

4 Once students have joined their sentences, tell each team to tape together its sandwich. Then challenge them to correct any errors in punctuation or capitalization that they see.

5 Invite each team to read its compound sentence to the class.

next day was sunny. Once I finished breakfast, I set out to search for the spot marked on my map. Before I had gotten very far, I heard a voice say, "I'm Kate. You must be the new kid." I said "hello." Should I

Sentences

Sentence-Scramble Board Game

(Use with Kids' Pages 26 and 27.)

Make learning about sentences enjoyable by playing this easy-to-assemble board game. The goal of the game is to land on enough words to make a complete sentence. To secure a win, a student must get both a subject and a verb as well as some modifying words. He or she must also know how to put the words together to make a sentence.

You Will Need (for each playing group)

* copies of pages 26 and 27
* scissors
* penny
* playing pieces (different-colored buttons, colored paper circles, and so on)
* pencils

See page 26 for step-by-step directions. To prepare for the game, divide the class into groups of two or three. Provide each group with a penny, playing pieces, and pencils.

Point out to students that a sentence must make sense and not merely be a subject and verb lumped together. Explain that some players will not collect enough words (or the right words) to make a sentence and others may collect enough words to create several sentences.

The Great Sentence Game Show!

Pull the strips until the words in the windows make a sentence.

(A)   (B)   (C)   (D)   (E)

Writing Skills Made Fun: Sentences & Paragraphs Scholastic Professional Books

	Tape tab here.	Tape tab here.	Tape tab here.	Tape tab here.	Tape tab here.	
tab	**A**	**B**	**C**	**D**	**E**	tab
tab	MY	TWO	CATS	HAS	FRIEND	tab
	FRIEND	FRIEND	FRIEND	CATS	HAS	
tab	HAS	HAS	TWO	MY	CATS	tab
tab	TWO	CATS	MY	TWO	MY	tab
	CATS	MY	HAS	FRIEND	TWO	
tab						tab
	Tape tab here.	Tape tab here.	Tape tab here.	Tape tab here.	Tape tab here.	

tab	**A**	**B**	**C**	**D**	**E**	tab
tab	THE	CAR	GROW	VERY	DOOR	tab
	WHICH	CHILD	MOVED	TO	SLOWLY	tab
tab	A	FLOWERS	CARRIED	NEXT	YOU	tab
	HER	COUSIN	BELONGS	RED	HERE	tab
tab	SOME	CAT	LIVES	NEAR	BALLOONS	tab

Writing Skills Made Fun: Sentences & Paragraphs Scholastic Professional Books

So Many Sentences!

There are four kinds of sentences to explore.
Read the rhymes to find out more!

Declarative sentences state facts.
They tell you something new.
Open the paper flap to see
Just what these sentences do!

Interrogative sentences ask questions,
Like who, what, when, and where.
Look inside! We have a few
Of these sentences to share.

Imperative sentences give orders.
They tell you what to do.
Underneath this flap, there are some
Imperative sentences for you!

Exclamatory sentences show feelings
Like anger, joy, and fear.
You will find examples of
Such sentences under here.

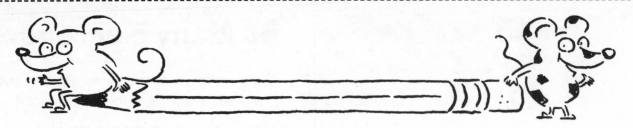

Declarative Sentences

✳ The phone is ringing.

✳ It rained all day.

✳ Mahmoud did his homework.

Write your own:

✳ _____

✳ _____

Interrogative Sentences

✳ What's your name?

✳ Who lives on the corner?

✳ Where is my bracelet?

Write your own:

✳ _____

✳ _____

Imperative Sentences

✳ Wash the dishes.

✳ Open your books, please.

✳ Don't wake the baby.

Write your own:

✳ _____

✳ _____

Exclamatory Sentences

✳ Yuck! I hate broccoli!

✳ That hurts!

✳ You can do it!

Write your own:

✳ _____

✳ _____

Writing Skills Made Fun: Sentences & Paragraphs Scholastic Professional Books

Subject-Predicate Puzzles

The old dog

chomps
on the bone.

The school

is brand-new.

The three
old dogs

chomp on
the bones.

The school
and playground

Donna Doyle

lives in
Tennessee.

are brand-new.

The Doyles

live in
Tennessee.

Writing Skills Made Fun: Sentences & Paragraphs Scholastic Professional Books

Sentence or Fragment?

Read each group of words. If they form a sentence, circle **S**. If they form a fragment, circle **F**.

1. Grace plays softball.   S   F

2. On the green field.   S   F

3. Mrs. Freeman's nephew, Jacob.   S   F

4. I have a computer.   S   F

5. School ends at 3 o'clock.   S   F

6. Driving carefully through the rain.   S   F

7. Pizza instead of hamburgers.   S   F

8. The principal said, "hello."   S   F

9. He said, "hello."   S   F

10. Is coming to dinner.   S   F

Writing Skills Made Fun: Sentences & Paragraphs Scholastic Professional Books

Repair a Run-On News Report

Help! Nellie the news reporter wrote this report. She forgot to break her report into sentences. Rewrite Nellie's report on the lines below. Use a capital letter to start each sentence and punctuation to end each sentence.

Monkeying Around

Three monkeys escaped from the city zoo Tuesday morning around 10 o'clock the monkeys took a taxi to the grocery store, where they bought 12 bunches of ripe bananas, then they walked to the park downtown and spent the rest of the day swinging from tree branches and entertaining people who passed by the three creatures headed back to the zoo around dinnertime.

_____

_____

_____

_____

_____

_____

_____

Compound-Sentence Sandwiches

My name is Ellen.

I am eight years old.

I like books.

I hate video games.

Earth has water.

Saturn does not have water.

In spring the weather turns warm.

Plants start to grow.

Darren cleaned his room.

Isaac left his toys on the floor.

I am going to Florida.

I hope to visit Disney World.

Writing Skills Made Fun: Sentences & Paragraphs
Scholastic Professional Books

Compound-Sentence Sandwiches

(continued)

I like that song.

I want to play soccer.

I hope he sings it again.

I must finish
my chores first.

We are out of cereal.

I live on Cedar Avenue.

We have plenty of oatmeal.

My cousin lives next door.

and

but

and

but

and

but

and

but

and

but

Writing Skills Made Fun: Sentences & Paragraphs
Scholastic Professional Books

Sentence Scramble

Rules and Word Cards

How to Play

1. Choose a playing piece.

2. Decide who will go first.

3. Put all playing pieces on **START**.

4. The first player tosses the penny. If it lands heads up, the player moves one space. If it lands tails up, the player moves two spaces.

5. When it's your turn, look at the word on the space where you land. Write it down on your Word Card.

6. The game ends when all players reach **FINISH**. Each player then tries to make a sentence from the words on his or her Word Card. The winner is the player who makes a complete sentence. (There can be more than one winner.)

Cut out these word cards. Give one to each player. ▶

Sentence Scramble

Word Card

_____
_____
_____
_____
_____
_____
_____
_____

Sentence Scramble

Word Card

_____
_____
_____
_____
_____
_____
_____
_____

Sentence Scramble

Word Card

_____
_____
_____
_____
_____
_____
_____
_____

Sentence Scramble

Word Card

_____
_____
_____
_____
_____
_____
_____
_____

Writing Skills Made Fun: Sentences & Paragraphs Scholastic Professional Books

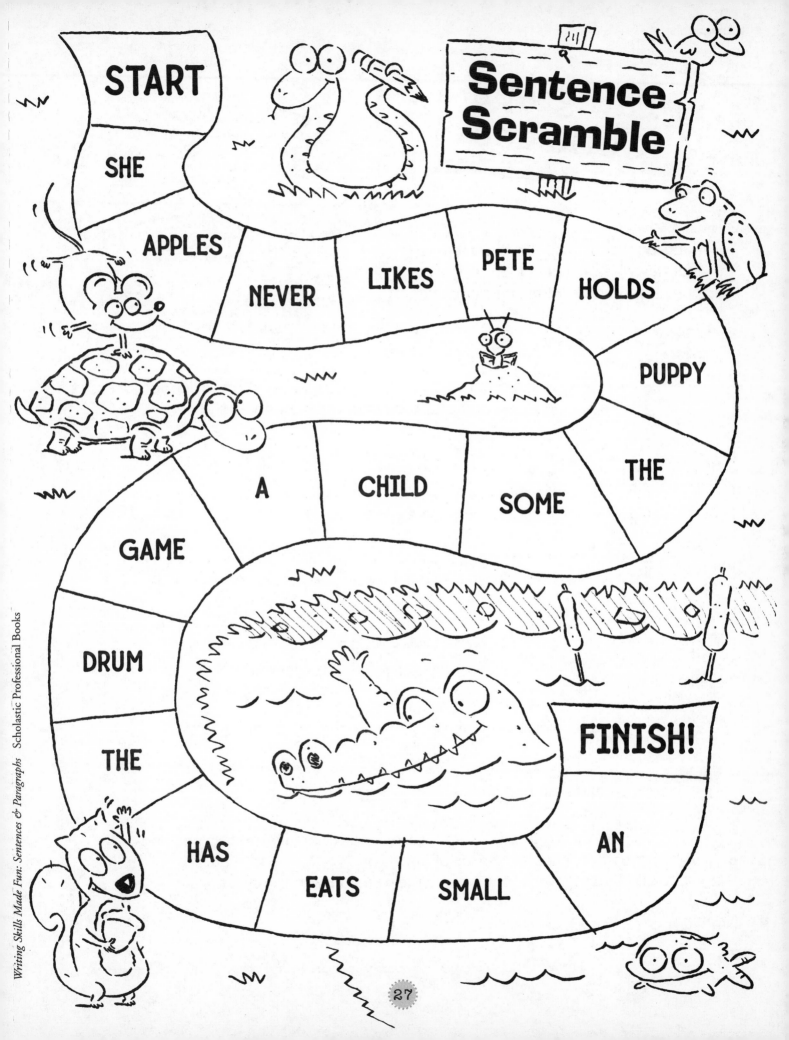

START

SHE

APPLES

Sentence Scramble

NEVER   LIKES   PETE   HOLDS

PUPPY

A   CHILD   SOME   THE

GAME

DRUM

THE

HAS   EATS   SMALL

FINISH!

AN

Paragraph Workshop

A paragraph is a group of sentences that describe the same idea. A good paragraph has several key elements:

❋ A paragraph should have a **topic sentence**, or main idea. The topic sentence tells what the paragraph is mainly about. It usually appears at the beginning of the paragraph but can also appear at the end.

❋ A paragraph has **detail sentences**, or supporting sentences. These sentences tell more about the main idea. A paragraph can have any number of detail sentences. A paragraph should not have any sentences that do not support the topic sentence.

❋ The sentences in a paragraph should appear in an **order** that makes sense. This order depends on the subject. For example, when writing a paragraph describing how to ride a bike, the writer should probably put the sentences in chronological order, starting with what the rider should do first. When writing a paragraph on why kids should help the environment, the writer might put the reasons in order of importance.

❋ A paragraph should be **indented** to show where it begins.

Here's an example of a well-written paragraph:

Our library is a great place to learn. It has computers to help you find information. It has thousands of books and magazines to read. Best of all, it has smart librarians who can help you answer any question.

Paragraph Activities

What's the Big Idea? (Use with Kids' Pages 32 and 33.)

The trademark of a well-written paragraph is an identifiable main idea. With this exercise, students will get practice locating the main idea of a paragraph. This practice will help them learn to write solid paragraphs of their own; it will also help students boost their reading comprehension skills.

Explain to students that they will become detectives in search of the main idea of each paragraph. The main idea is usually found toward the top of a paragraph, although it can also be found at the end. Very rarely is a main idea found in the middle of a paragraph. To find the main idea, students should ask themselves the following questions:

✳ What is the paragraph mostly about? Which sentence says it best?

✳ If I were going to write a title for this paragraph, what would it be?

✳ If the writer had room for only one sentence, which sentence would he or she pick from this paragraph?

Although in practice a main idea can consist of two or more sentences, the main ideas in this exercise are all single sentences. Distribute the reproducibles. Have students write the number of the main-idea sentence in the box to the right of each paragraph. Then demonstrate how to use the code at the bottom of the page to solve the riddle. If a student does not get the correct answer, "BOO-berries," he or she may have incorrectly identified one of the main ideas, or may simply have had trouble using the code. Check student work to see which is the case. Afterward, invite students to explain how they were able to locate each main idea.

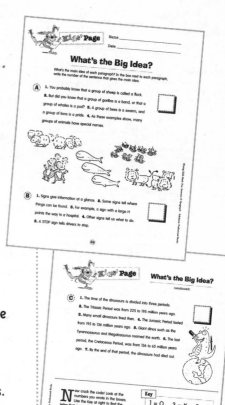

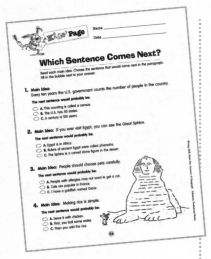

Which Sentence Comes Next? (Use with Kids' Page 34.)

In the previous activity, students practiced finding the main idea in a whole paragraph. Now challenge them to do the reverse—to identify which detail sentence best supports a stated main idea. Distribute the reproducible and have students read each main idea. Remind students to say to themselves, "This paragraph will be about...." Then ask students which of the multiple-choice sentences makes the most sense with the main idea. Have them fill in the bubble next to their answer.

Build a Paragraph Puppet

(Use with Kids' Pages 35 and 36.)

You Will Need

* copies of pages 35 and 36
* scissors
* glue sticks

To make a paragraph clear and easy to understand, a writer should put his or her sentences in an order that makes sense. For beginning writers, it can be difficult to master this skill in a first draft. Students are eager to get their ideas on paper, and the order in which the ideas occur is the order in which they are written! Encourage students to look at—and, when necessary, rearrange—sentence order when editing their work.

This hands-on activity will get students thinking about the importance of sentence order. Although the activity uses the metaphor of a Chinese New Year dragon, you can use it at any time of year. Distribute the reproducible and have students cut out the dragon segments. Then instruct them to put the sentences in the order that makes the most sense. When students feel that they have completed the task, have them tape or glue the dragon together, then tape pencils to the ends for easy carrying.

All Aboard the Topic Train!

(Use with Kids' Pages 37 and 38.)

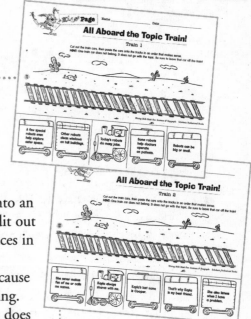

You Will Need

* copies of pages 37 and 38
* scissors
* glue sticks or tape

Sometimes even the most experienced writers let a stray thought wander into an otherwise cohesive paragraph. In this exercise, students will identify and edit out those sentences that do not belong. They'll also get practice putting sentences in a logical order to form paragraphs.

Students are often reluctant to edit sentences from their own writing because they like the way the sentence reads or they think it is particularly interesting. You might point out to students that deleting a sentence from a paragraph does not necessarily mean you are getting rid of the idea altogether. If the idea is a solid one that supports the theme of the story or report, it probably belongs in a different paragraph.

You have two versions of this activity from which to choose: one in which the main idea comes at the beginning of the paragraph, and another in which the main idea appears at the end of the paragraph. Try to use both versions at some point, since it is important for students to realize that main ideas can appear in either location. To start this activity, choose one of the two reproducibles, distribute copies, and review the directions. Provide glue sticks or tape for students to use. Then check to see whether students' trains are "on track" or "derailed" by a detail that does not belong!

Batty Paragraph Match-Up (Use with Kids' Page 39.)

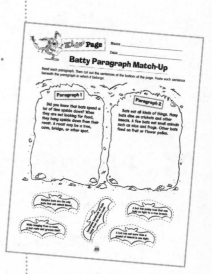

You Will Need

* copies of page 39
* scissors
* glue sticks

Here's an activity that will not only make kids better writers but also improve their thinking skills. Distribute the reproducible. Students first read two paragraphs about bats. Then they read a list of sentences and decide in which paragraph each sentence belongs. Students will cut out each new sentence and paste it beneath the appropriate paragraph.

Follow up the activity by inviting students to rewrite each paragraph with the new sentences in place. Remind them to indent at the beginning of each paragraph.

Name _____

Date _____

What's the Big Idea?

What's the main idea of each paragraph? In the box next to each paragraph, write the number of the sentence that gives the main idea.

A **1.** You probably know that a group of sheep is called a flock.

2. But did you know that a group of gorillas is a band, or that a group of whales is a pod? **3.** A group of bees is a swarm, and a group of lions is a pride. **4.** As these examples show, many groups of animals have special names.

B **1.** Signs give information at a glance. **2.** Some signs tell where things can be found. **3.** For example, a sign with a large H points the way to a hospital. **4.** Other signs tell us what to do. **5.** A STOP sign tells drivers to stop.

What's the Big Idea?

(continued)

C

1. The time of the dinosaurs is divided into three periods.

2. The Triassic Period was from 225 to 195 million years ago.

3. Many small dinosaurs lived then. **4.** The Jurassic Period lasted from 195 to 136 million years ago. **5.** Giant dinos such as the Tyrannosaurus and Megalosaurus roamed the earth. **6.** The last period, the Cretaceous Period, was from 136 to 65 million years ago. **7.** By the end of that period, the dinosaurs had died out.

Now crack the code! Look at the numbers you wrote in the boxes. Use the Key at right to find the letter that goes with each number. This will help you find the answer to this riddle:

Key

1 = O 3 = K 5 = S
2 = A 4 = B

What's a ghost's favorite fruit?

____ ____ ____ **berries!**

Name _____

Date _____

Which Sentence Comes Next?

Read each main idea. Choose the sentence that would come next in the paragraph. Fill in the bubble next to your answer.

1. Main Idea:

Every ten years the U.S. government counts the number of people in the country.

The next sentence would probably be:

○ **A.** This counting is called a census.
○ **B.** The U.S. has 50 states.
○ **C.** A century is 100 years.

2. Main Idea: If you ever visit Egypt, you can see the Great Sphinx.

The next sentence would probably be:

○ **A.** Egypt is in Africa.
○ **B.** Rulers of ancient Egypt were called pharaohs.
○ **C.** The Sphinx is a carved stone figure in the desert.

3. Main Idea: People should choose pets carefully.

The next sentence would probably be:

○ **A.** People with allergies may not want to get a cat.
○ **B.** Cats are popular in France.
○ **C.** I have a goldfish named Oscar.

4. Main Idea: Making rice is simple.

The next sentence would probably be:

○ **A.** Serve it with chicken.
○ **B.** First, you boil some water.
○ **C.** Then you add the rice.

Writing Skills Made Fun: Sentences & Paragraphs Scholastic Professional Books

Build a Paragraph Puppet

Each part of this Chinese dragon has one sentence. Cut out the parts and put them in order to make a paragraph. Color the parts and tape them together. If you'd like, tape a pencil to each end of the dragon. Hold one pencil and have a partner hold the other. Have your own Chinese New Year parade!

The Chinese New Year is one of the world's most exciting celebrations.

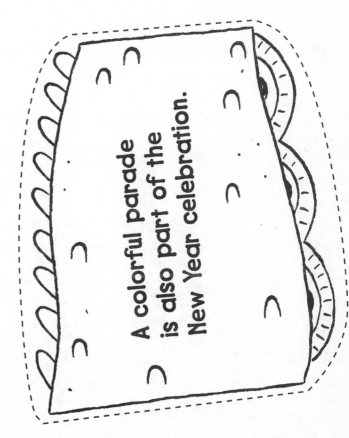

A colorful parade is also part of the New Year celebration.

These foods are supposed to bring good luck.

Build a Paragraph Puppet

(continued)

Everyone watches the dancing dragons and lions parade through the streets.

The celebration begins on the first day of the Chinese calendar and lasts 15 days.

They eat sticky rice cakes and tangerines.

To celebrate, Chinese families visit one another and share special meals.

Writing Skills Made Fun: Sentences & Paragraphs
Scholastic Professional Books

All Aboard the Topic Train!

Train 1

Cut out the train cars, then paste the cars onto the tracks in an order that makes sense.

HINT: One train car does not belong. It does not go with the topic. Be sure to leave that car off the train!

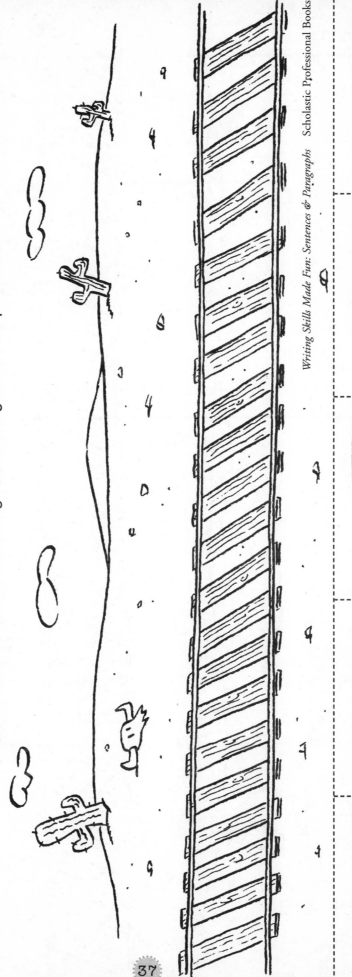

37

Writing Skills Made Fun: Sentences & Paragraphs   Scholastic Professional Books

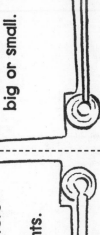

Robots can be big or small.

Some robots help doctors operate on patients.

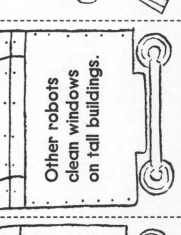

Today's robots do many jobs.

Other robots clean windows on tall buildings.

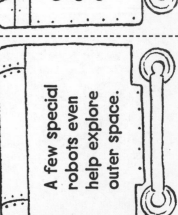

A few special robots even help explore outer space.

All Aboard the Topic Train!

Train 2

Cut out the train cars, then paste the cars onto the tracks in an order that makes sense.
HINT: One train car does not belong. It does not go with the topic. Be sure to leave that car off the train!

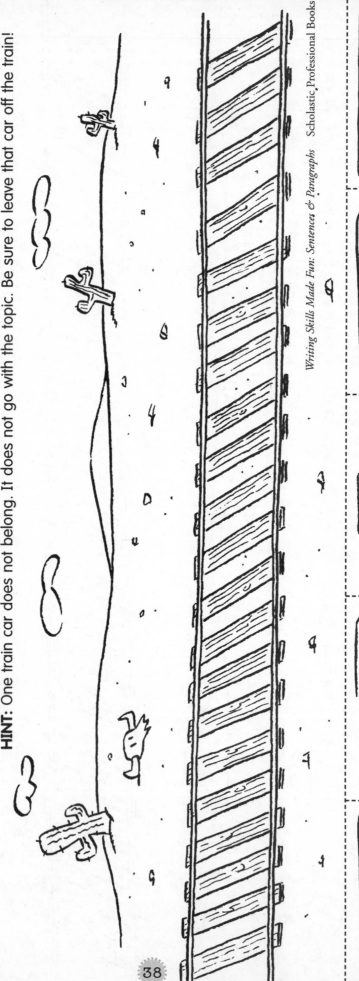

38

Writing Skills Made Fun: Sentences & Paragraphs   Scholastic Professional Books

She also listens when I have a problem.

That's why Kayla is my best friend.

Kayla's last name is Cooper.

Kayla always shares with me.

She never makes fun of me or calls me names.

Name _____

Date _____

Batty Paragraph Match-Up

Read each paragraph. Then cut out the sentences at the bottom of the page. Paste each sentence beneath the paragraph in which it belongs.

Paragraph 1

Did you know that bats spend a lot of time upside down? When they are not looking for food, they hang upside down from their roost. A roost may be a tree, cave, bridge, or other spot.

Paragraph 2

Bats eat all kinds of things. Many bats dine on crickets and other insects. A few bats eat small animals such as mice and frogs. Other bats feed on fruit or flower pollen.

Vampire bats are the only bats that eat animal blood.

Sometimes hundreds of bats hang from the same roost.

A bat has pointy toes that can hold on tight to a tree branch.

While hanging from a roost, a bat rests and grooms itself.

A bat can eat more than a pound of insects in one night.

Writing Skills Made Fun: Sentences & Paragraphs Scholastic Professional Books

The day we moved into our new house, the weather was rainy and cold.
outside, I decided to explore the attic. It was
ostly dusty boxes sat in the corner. They belonged to

Review

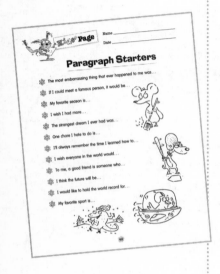

Wrap up your unit on sentences and paragraphs by engaging students in the following writing activities.

Paragraph Starters

(Use with Kids' Page 42.)

Do your students complain that they don't have anything to write about? Try some of the paragraph starters on page 42. These open-ended writing prompts make the perfect beginnings to interesting paragraphs and can be extended into longer writing assignments, if you wish.

Create a topic "lottery" by putting the paragraph starters in a hat and inviting each student to draw one randomly. Or, to motivate reluctant writers, allow each student to select a paragraph starter based on his or her interests and experiences.

Paragraph Webs

(Use with Kids' Pages 43 and 44.)

Help reinforce the structure of a paragraph by having students write original paragraphs on these paragraph webs. Web 1 sets up a paragraph in which the main idea is the first sentence. Web 2 sets up a paragraph in which the main idea comes at the end. Students should be comfortable writing both types of paragraphs.

Start with Web 1, and use this web for paragraph-writing assignments until all students are able to write an organized paragraph. You may have students write about any topic they wish or use the paragraph starters on page 42. Then introduce Web 2, and encourage students to try their hands at this upside down paragraph format. Mastering this type of paragraph may take some time.

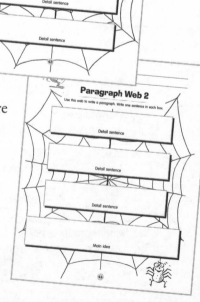

Your Turn! (Use with Kids' Pages 45 and 46.)

Have students apply all that they have learned about sentences and paragraphs by revising this poorly-written paragraph about popular toys. Remind students to consider all of the following:

✳ Is each sentence a complete sentence (not a fragment or run-on)?

✳ Do the subject and predicate of each sentence agree (go together)?

✳ Does each sentence begin with a capital letter and end with a period, exclamation point, or question mark?

✳ Does the paragraph have a main idea?

✳ Do all of the sentences in the paragraph support the main idea?

✳ Are the sentences in the paragraph in an order that makes sense?

To help students remember these criteria, distribute the checklist on page 46. You may use the checklist again with other writing assignments as a way for students to assess and improve their paragraph-writing skills.

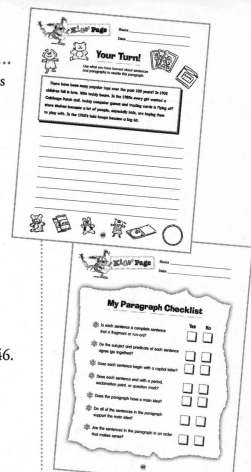

Paragraph Starters

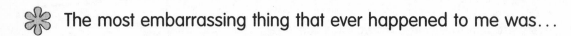

✻ The most embarrassing thing that ever happened to me was…

✻ If I could meet a famous person, it would be…

✻ My favorite season is…

✻ I wish I had more…

✻ The strangest dream I ever had was…

✻ One chore I hate to do is…

✻ I'll always remember the time I learned how to…

✻ I wish everyone in the world would…

✻ To me, a good friend is someone who…

✻ I think the future will be…

✻ I would like to hold the world record for…

✻ My favorite sport is…

Writing Skills Made Fun: Sentences & Paragraphs Scholastic Professional Books

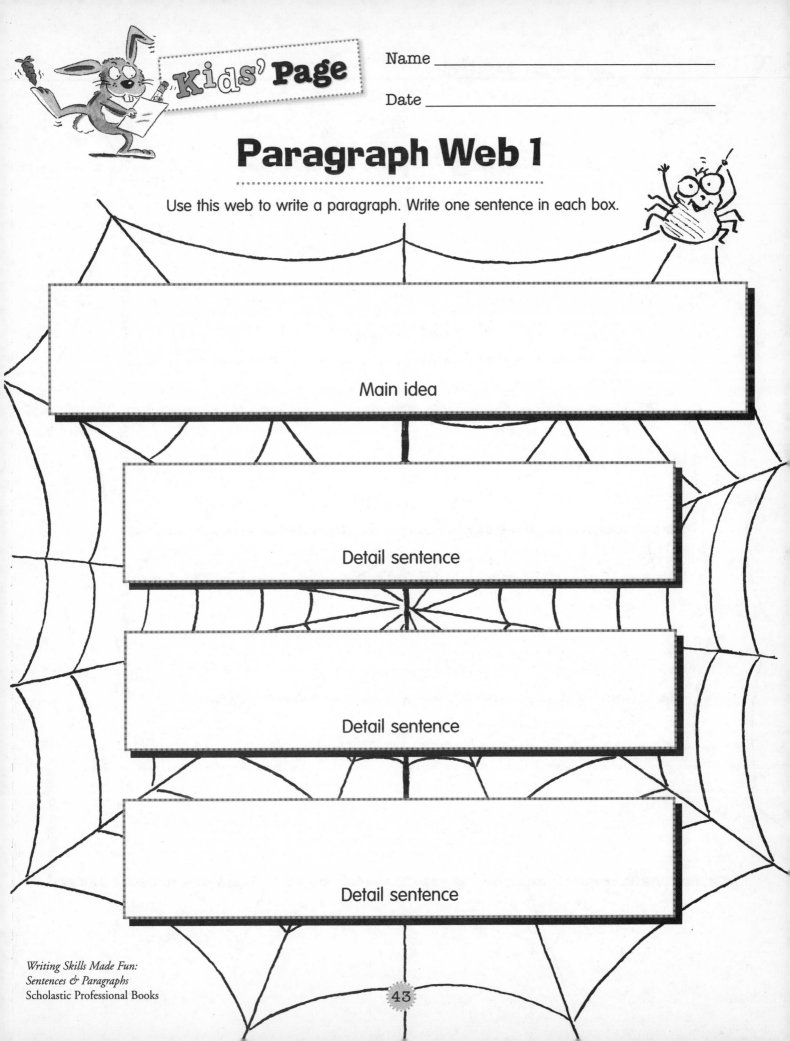

Kids' Page

Name _____

Date _____

Paragraph Web 1

Use this web to write a paragraph. Write one sentence in each box.

Main idea

Detail sentence

Detail sentence

Detail sentence

Name _____

Date _____

Paragraph Web 2

Use this web to write a paragraph. Write one sentence in each box.

Detail sentence

Detail sentence

Detail sentence

Main idea

Writing Skills Made Fun: Sentences & Paragraphs   Scholastic Professional Books

Name _____

Date _____

Your Turn!

Use what you have learned about sentences
and paragraphs to rewrite this paragraph.

There have been many popular toys over the past 100 years? In 1902
children fell in love. With teddy bears. In the 1980s every girl wanted a
Cabbage Patch doll. today computer games and trading cards is flying off
store shelves because a lot of people, especially kids, are buying them
to play with. In the 1950's hula hoops became a big hit.

_____

_____

_____

_____

_____

_____

_____

Writing Skills Made Fun: Sentences & Paragraphs Scholastic Professional Books

Name _____

Date _____

My Paragraph Checklist

	Yes	No
❀ Is each sentence a complete sentence (not a fragment or run-on)?	☐	☐
❀ Do the subject and predicate of each sentence agree (go together)?	☐	☐
❀ Does each sentence begin with a capital letter?	☐	☐
❀ Does each sentence end with a period, exclamation point, or question mark?	☐	☐
❀ Does the paragraph have a main idea?	☐	☐
❀ Do all of the sentences in the paragraph support the main idea?	☐	☐
❀ Are the sentences in the paragraph in an order that makes sense?	☐	☐

Writing Skills Made Fun: Sentences & Paragraphs Scholastic Professional Books

Additional Resources

Books

The Amazing Pop-Up Grammar Book by Jennie Maizels, illustrator, and Kate Petty, contributor (Dutton, 1996).

Elementary, My Dear: Caught 'Ya: Grammar With a Giggle for Grades One, Two, and Three by Jane Bell Kiester (Maupin House, 2000).

Grammar Puzzles and Games Kids Can't Resist by Karen Kellaher (Scholastic Professional Books, 2000).

Great Grammar Mini-Books by Maria Fleming (Scholastic Professional Books, 1999).

25 Great Grammar Poems With Activities by Bobbi Katz (Scholastic Professional Books, 1999).

Web Sites

* Have kids log on to **www.mrsabc.com** for help with spelling, punctuation, and capitalization.

* Go to **www.scholastic.com** for online writing activities, tips from authors, and more. The site features sections for teachers and students.

* Log on to **www.funbrain.com/grammar/** for exciting grammar games.

* For more suggestions on teaching grammar and other language arts topics, check out the site of the National Council of Teachers of English: **www.ncte.org/teach/**.

Answers

✱ Sentences

THE GREAT SENTENCE GAME SHOW: For Game 1, the proper word order is: "My friend has two cats." For Game 2, answers will vary.

SENTENCE OR FRAGMENT?
1. S; 2. F; 3. F; 4. S; 5. S; 6. F; 7. F; 8. S; 9. S; 10. F.

REPAIR A RUN-ON NEWS REPORT:

Monkeying Around

Three monkeys escaped from the city zoo Tuesday morning around 10 o'clock. The monkeys took a taxi to the grocery store, where they bought 12 bunches of ripe bananas. Then they walked to the park downtown and spent the rest of the day swinging from tree branches and entertaining people who passed by. The three creatures headed back to the zoo around dinnertime.

COMPOUND-SENTENCE SANDWICHES:

My name is Ellen **and** I am eight years old.

I like books **but** I hate video games.

Earth has water **but** Saturn does not have water.

In spring the weather turns warm **and** plants start to grow.

Darren cleaned his room **but** Isaac left his toys on the floor.

I am going to Florida **and** I hope to visit Disney World.

I like that song **and** I hope he sings it again.

I want to play soccer **but** I must finish my chores first.

We are out of cereal **but** we have plenty of oatmeal.

I live on Cedar Avenue **and** my cousin lives next door.

✳ Paragraphs

WHAT'S THE BIG IDEA?

A. As these examples show, many groups of animals have special names.
B. Signs give information at a glance.
C. The time of the dinosaurs is divided into three periods.

Answer to riddle: BOO berries!

WHICH SENTENCE COMES NEXT?

1. A; 2. C; 3. A; 4. B.

BUILD A PARAGRAPH PUPPET:

One order that makes sense is:

The Chinese New Year is one of the world's most exciting celebrations. The celebration begins on the first day of the Chinese calendar and lasts 15 days. To celebrate, Chinese families visit one another and share special meals. They eat sticky rice cakes and tangerines. These foods are supposed to bring good luck. A colorful parade is also part of the New Year celebration. Everyone watches the dancing dragons and lions parade through the streets.

ALL ABOARD THE TOPIC TRAIN!:

Train 1:

Train 2:

BATTY PARAGRAPH MATCH-UP:

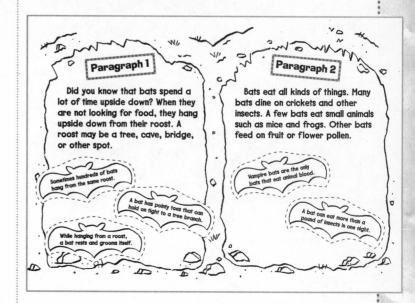

✳ Review

YOUR TURN! One way to rewrite the paragraph is:

There have been many popular toys over the past 100 years. In 1902 children fell in love with teddy bears. In the 1950s hula hoops became a big hit. In the 1980s every girl wanted a Cabbage Patch doll. Today computer games and trading cards are flying off store shelves.

THE ENDANGERED SPECIES HANDBOOK

by
Greta Nilsson

with contributions by
Michael Bean
James Buckley
Barry Groveman
and others

Photo by Andrew Young

Muriqui or Woolly Spider Monkey.

Library of Congress Card Number 82-072956
International Standard Book Number 0-938424-09-7
Printed in the United States of America
First Edition 1983

The Animal Welfare Institute
P.O. Box 3650
Washington, DC 20007

Published with assistance from The Geraldine R. Dodge Foundation and The Ahimsa Foundation.

End Sheets by Marcus Redditt entitled "Reflections: their past, our future!"
Soon these endangered species may be only reflections in time.

Animals Pictured (from left): Peregrine Falcon, Whooping Crane, Eastern Mountain Lion, Gray Wolf, Bald Eagle, Ivory-billed Woodpecker, Grizzly Bear, Barn Owl. Plants (from left): Wild Northern Monkshood, Green Pitcher Plant.

TABLE OF CONTENTS

List of Illustrations

FOREWORD

Fellow feeling is growing for the natural world and all the creatures who share it with us. But it is not yet strong enough to protect the magnificent variety of life that inhabits the earth. We are immensely fortunate to be alive now and to have the chance to save the almost incomprehensible diversity of animal and plant species which still exist. Forebodings of doom for millions of life forms are all too well-founded. Scientists who study the great forests of South America, Africa and Asia are far from having even found and named more than a small proportion of the species that still flourish in these moist havens of life.

No species can exist alone—certainly not a large mammal such as *Home sapiens*. Yet we are the species responsible for the unprecedented speed with which other species are becoming extinct. And if we don't put on the brakes at once, today's speed will accelerate to a frenzied dash, like a monstrous machine mindlessly spinning around the earth, crushing a million individual, irreplaceable forms of life which have developed over periods that go back a billion years ago or more. We will not even know what we have done because human ability to snuff out whole species so greatly exceeds our present ability to protect, study and learn from them.

It is because of this impending tragedy, which *can* be prevented, that the Animal Welfare Institute has published this handbook for students, teachers, and all concerned citizens. We hope it will help you each to do your part to head off the terrible destruction, the intolerable losses that will inevitably take place if this generation and the next do not act firmly, knowledgeably, effectively.

There is a considerable literature on endangered species, but we know of no handbook comparable to this which includes sections on
- the causes and consequences of losing wildlife;
- the rapid increase in extinctions in every class, from mammals to invertebrates to plants;
- abuse of the land;
- trade in wild animals;
- their persecution, whether purposeful or accidental, as, for example, by toxic chemicals or destructive fishing methods;
- national and state legislation and international treaties affecting endangered species;
- sketches of people who have been instrumental in preventing extinctions;
- projects for use by teachers and students;
- an annotated list of recommended films;
- a book list,
- lists of endangered and extinct species.

The projects, both for classroom use and for science fairs, continue the tradition of AWI's *Humane Biology Projects* providing suggestions for scientific study which in no way harms the animal—whether it be as rare as a whooping crane or as common as a honey bee. For kindness, care and concern must not be reserved for endangered species alone. Every animal studied must be respected and treated as the student would wish to be treated were their roles reversed. In the project on the preferences of earthworms for acidic or non-acidic moisture, the worms are returned unharmed and as comfortably plump and damp as they were found, after they have voluntarily shown their choice by crawling onto or away from the test material.

The Animal Welfare Institute subscribes to the rules for science fairs which were adopted in Canada after careful study and trial of other rules. They appear in full on page 137, and we recommend their use by all who plan to conduct or to guide a project.

While most projects have a scientific orientation some are included for art, history and language studies and for community service. The preservation of life on earth cannot be left to science and scientists alone, however much indebted we may be to them for warnings based on accurate data. There aren't enough scientists to halt the avalanche of extinctions. An informed citizenry must come to the defense of the natural world and all our fellow species on this remarkable planet. Otherwise, we will condemn ourselves to increasingly impoverished lives as the bountiful life forms, which make complex ecosystems function, are driven off the face of the earth they now adorn. As Paul Ehrlich, Professor of Population Studies at Stanford University has written, "In pushing other species to extinction, humanity is busily sawing off the limb on which it is perched." It is a strange paradox that it should sometimes be the very commercial interests who sell their products with the idea of making purchasers' lives more convenient or pleasant that are causing extinctions on an increasingly large scale, threatening the future welfare of our own species as well as all the others.

For example, South American rain forests, those treasure houses of thousands of species, are being clearcut and burned to make a temporary pasture for cattle destined to be turned into hamburgers. The ground beneath the great trees is not capable of sustaining grazing for more than a few years before it is worn out. But even if abandoned, the complex variety of trees, vines, plants and animals that make up established rain forests are incapable of regenerating because the soil is too poor. A few million hamburgers later, the land is depleted, the forest gone. Rain forests are cut for lumber, for mining and road building, too.

Such deforestation in Latin America affects not only local animals and plants but the survival of at least half the species of U.S. song birds who depend on these forests as their winter home (see page 167). And, the great whales, dolphins and other marine mammals who swim near our coasts may be destroyed by other nations whose coasts they visit on migration. Direct killing or pollution may be the cause of losses. Thus nations need to cooperate for the mutual good of all.

The project (page 188), which suggests that students correspond with their counterparts in foreign countries, could help toward bringing nations together in defense of natural diversity throughout the world.

Every student, every teacher and each friend and acquaintance here and abroad can play a part in stopping extinctions and creating the atmosphere of good will and neighborliness and, to use Albert Schweitzer's word, *reverence* toward other life forms. Such attitudes would befit us as the species with the greatest powers of destruction the earth has ever produced.

Christine Stevens
President, Animal Welfare Institute

Opening Remarks of
The Honorable James L. Buckley

Under Secretary of State
For Security Assistance, Science & Technology
At the Strategy Conference on Biological Diversity

On behalf of the State Department and the other federal sponsors listed on your program, I would like to welcome you to this strategy conference on biological diversity.

It is hard to think of a task of more fundamental importance than the one on which you will be devoting your knowledge, intelligence and judgment during the course of the next three days, because you will be dealing with the stuff of life itself.

Although the 1970's saw an extraordinary expansion of the American public's consciousness of the degree to which we depend on a sound environment, we have yet to see an equivalent understanding of the tremendous stake that future generations will have in the ability of this generation to stem the accelerating impoverishment of the globe's biological diversity.

We are still too ignorant of ultimate consequences to understand in full the urgent need to protect even the most inconspicious forms of life so that we do not diminish the rich variety of biological resources that continue to exist.

Nevertheless, the urgency is there, and we need to impress upon the public consciousness that extinction is an act of awesome finality. Extinction is one of the few processes that man cannot reverse. But if man cannot restore a species, he is nevertheless fully capable of destroying them, which he is presently doing at an astonishing rate. This century has witnessed over half the extinctions of animal species known to have occurred in recorded history; and, largely because of the vast scale on which tropical rain forests are being cut around the world, it is estimated that by the year 2000 upwards of a million additional species—about 20% of those now in existence—may become extinct. Yet on this threatened biological diversity depends in significant degree the fundamental support system for man and other living things.

As living creatures, the more we understand of biological processes, the more wisely we will be able to manage ourselves. Thus the needless extermination of a single species can be an act of recklessness. By permitting high rates of extinction to continue, we are limiting the potential growth of biological knowledge. In essence, the process is tantamount to book-burning; but it is even worse, in that it involves books yet to be deciphered and read.

Unfortunately, this is a fact that is not as yet sufficiently understood. Therefore, if we are to generate the necessary support for the task ahead, we will need to remind the public that fully 40% of all modern drugs have been derived from nature; that most of the food man eats comes from only about twenty out of the thousands of plants known to be edible; and that even those currently being cultivated require the preservation of large pools of genetic material on which plant scientists can draw in order to produce most useful strains or restore the vigor of the highly inbred varieties that have revolutionized agriculture in our times.

Recent well publicized break-throughs in genetic engineering may be what is required to focus public attention on the explicit interest each one of us has in seeing that the global stock of irreplaceable genetic material isn't squandered. This may help us focus attention on the practical need to conserve our biological resources. But we must also impress upon the public that this is inherently an international problem requiring an international approach.

A significant portion of the biological resources that today require the most urgent protection are located in undeveloped nations that do not have the resources to do the job alone. Demands generated in the industrialized world can add to the pressures with which such nations must cope, witness the impact of the Japanese appetite for lumber on Indonesian forests. Migratory birds and marine life can only be protected through international cooperation.

There are other areas where our knowledge of ecological cause and effect is still too uncertain to enable us to reach firm conclusions as to the extent of our own self-interest in what happens to plant and animal life half a world away. What, for example, is the modulating role—if any—that is played by the world's biota on global weather patterns; which is another way of saying, what might be the impact of the destruction of Brazilian rain forests on the production of wheat in Kansas some fifty or one hundred years from now? We don't know. But because the possibility of such an impact is not entirely implausible, it causes this conservative, at least, to urge caution; it being a conservative's and a conservationist's instinct to be careful about disturbing systems which seem to have been working reasonably well for an aeon or two.

In any event, as a long-time champion of the snail darter and furbish lousewort and other equally obscure but endangered species, I am especially pleased that this conference has attracted so distinguished a group of participants.

You more than most understand the special meaning for our times of Edmund Burke's reminder that the men and women of any generation are but "temporary possessors and life-rentors" who "should not think it among their rights to cut off the entail, or commit waste on the inheritance," lest they "leave to those who come after them a ruin instead of a habitation."

We need your insights and your guidance, not only as to the nature of the problems we face, but as to the practical, achievable measures we must be prepared to take both at the national and international levels to preserve our biological diversity; measures by which we can best protect our natural inheritance against the waste that this generation of temporary possessors has proven itself so capable of committing.

The Strategy Conference on Biological Diversity
Washington, D.C.
November 16, 1981

ACKNOWLEDGEMENTS

Numerous individuals and organizations have generously given me editorial advice, technical information, photographs and illustrations. Special thanks go to Dr. David Johnston of George Mason University's Biology Department who volunteered to edit the manuscript and contributed many valuable suggestions. Other helpful comments were made by Virginia Knoder and Christabel Gough.

Donations of photographs and drawings have been invaluable, and the Animal Welfare Institute is very grateful. The beautiful paintings and drawings from *The Doomsday Book of Animals* that enhance this book were made available through the generosity of the author, David Day, and the publisher, Viking Press. Other donors of photographs and illustrations include Mary Bloom, Janis Carter, the Cincinnati Zoo, A.F. Coimbra-Filho, Dr. Jared Diamond and *Science* journal, John Domont, Richard Ellis, the Fauna Preservation Society, Florida Game and Fresh Water Fish Commission, Larry Foster, Dr. Michael W. Fox, Greenpeace, Hancock House publishing company, Dr. Erwin Hauer, the Houghton Library of Harvard University, the International Crane Foundation, Jack Jarvie, Dr. Carl G. Jones, Mason Keeler, Norris Klessman, Lion Country Safari, the Los Angeles Police Department, the Los Angeles Zoo, Jean Lynn, R.H. Martin, David Matilla, Dr. Russell Mittermeier, Tui de Roy Moore, Narca Moore-Craig, Cynthia Moss, the National Gallery of Art, the National Marine Fisheries Service, the New York Botanical Garden Library, Margaret Owings, Dr. Roger Pasquier, the Patuxent Wildlife Research Center, the Peregrine Fund, John Perry, Jonathan Pollock, S. Price, Dick Randall and Defenders of Wildlife, the *Russian Red Data Book*, Patrick Rose of the Florida Audubon Society, Nan Rollison of the U.S. Fish and Wildlife Service, Hope Ryden, Eric Schwartz, Martha Swope, Dr. Merlin Tuttle of Bat Conservation International, Linda Tyrell, the U.S. Customs Service, Brett Whitely and the Embassy of Australia, Richard Willson, the World Wildlife Fund and Andrew Young.

Raymond T. Rye II of the Smithsonian Institution and Michael Brett-Surman of George Washington University provided information on dinosaurs, and scientists from the U.S. Office of Endangered Species, Dr. George Drewry, Dr. Kenneth Dodd, Dr. Ronald Nowak, and Dr. Paul Opler were very helpful in answering myriad questions. Bill Sheppard of the Arkansas Natural Heritage Commission and Tom Owens of the Washington State Nongame Program furnished reports and data on state programs. Joan Fordham and Dr. George Archibald of the International Crane Foundation gave a wealth of information on that organization. Dr. Shirley McGreal of the International Primate Protection League added comments and corrections to the text.

Many scientists, specialists and teachers contributed to the section on projects for students. Richard Block of the University of Michigan suggested many projects and contributed lists of films on endangered species. Thanks also to Dr. Marjorie Anchel, Peter Batten, Margaret Campbell, Dr. Dewey Caron, Dr. Scott Derickson, Dr. Lee R. Dice, Dr. Robert Fagen, Dr. Vagn Flyger, Dr. Roger S. Fouts, Martita Goshen, Mac Adam City High School, Dr. George Middendorf, Andrew Orlans, Ken Runyon and Denise Trindall.

Barry Groveman's chapter on the enforcement of California's strong Endangered Species law and Michael Bean's questions and answers on the Endangered Species Act bring the legislative aspects of endangered species protection to life.

The careful attention to detail and imagination of artwork done by Marcus Redditt and Esta Belcher add much to this book.

For the sponsorship of this book, I want to thank the Animal Welfare Institute and its President, Christine Stevens. Staff members Maria Gulino, Felicity Luebke, Fran Lipscomb and John Gleiber made my task easier by providing research materials, data, photographs and editorial comments.

Greta Nilsson

Vanishing Wildlife
Causes and Consequences

International Crane Foundation

Whooping Cranes *by Owing Gromme.*

Dinosaurs and Dodos

The **Iguanadon**—*Dinosaurs faded out over a period of millions of years.*

Does the fact that dinosaurs became extinct long before humans existed on the planet mean that all extinctions are natural events? Why should we be concerned about animals becoming extinct if it is a natural phenomenon?

These are questions frequently asked by skeptics. In fact, enormous differences are known between the extinctions of the dinosaurs and those of recently disappeared species. We do not know with certainty what caused the dinosaurs to pass into oblivion, although many theories have been proposed. We do know that the dinosaurs reigned on earth for over 130 million years (humans have existed only about 4 million years). We also know that literally hundreds of dinosaur species existed, and that their extinctions did not happen suddenly, but gradually. Dinosaurs "faded out" over a period of millions of years. The Ornithischia, for example, one major group of dinosaurs, had an enormous number of living species, at the beginning of the Cretaceous Period, 135 million years ago. The Ornithischia slowly died out over the next 60 million years, with fewer and fewer surviving species in the order, until the last of the line became extinct some 64 million years ago. The recent debate over the causes of dinosaur extinctions center on the final demise of the group which occurred quite suddenly.

It is difficult to grasp the reality of their immensely long sojourn, some species existing for only one hundred thousand years, some for millions of years. The diversity of dinosaur species, which is an indication of their successful adaptations to a wide variety of habitats and climates, decreased gradually. And as they decreased—at a rate of about one species disappearing every thousand years—other reptiles, birds and mammals proliferated. As the dinosaurs were replaced with other animal species, the overall numbers of animals and the diversity of animal life did not change dramatically. The chart on page 3 shows this gradual evolutionary process.

In the course of nature, most animal bones, which form the basis of the fossil record, decay into nothingness. Those that are found were preserved under extraordinary conditions such as mud slides, tar pits, or sedimentary strata.

Even if we know only one-tenth of the animals once resident on our planet, the dinosaurs' extinction rate is still about 50 times slower than that of today's wildlife.

The Recent Picture: A Rapid Increase in Extinctions

Over the past 350 years, some 109 bird species have become extinct. * Birds are fairly representative of vertebrate species, in terms of their rates of extinction, although there are many more bird species than mammal, reptile or amphibian species. At least 8,600 bird species exist today, compared to 4,100 mammal, 2,600 amphibian, and 6,500 reptile species. When the incidence of extinctions of birds is analyzed over 50-year periods since 1600, the

* The list of extinct birds can be found in the Appendix On the whole it was drawn from publications of the International Council for Bird Preservation.

increasing number of extinctions becomes dramatic. Between 1600 and 1800, a 200-year period, only 25 birds were lost, while between 1800 and 1950, a period of only 150 years, 78 birds became extinct.

This acceleration of extinctions has now reached the rate of two birds every three years, and should it continue, one bird species will be lost every year by the year 2000. Scientists allow a period of 50 years—more or less—from the last sighting of a species, unless there are thorough searches in the wild, before it is declared extinct. If there have not been searches, this period may be extended. An additional 18 birds fall into the category of "probably extinct" and may have to join the roster of the extinct over the next 20 years. The graph on page 5 shows this alarming increase.

The causes of all these extinctions are not known with certainty, since many were resident on remote, rarely visited islands, but we do know that the majority—63% or more—were exterminated either directly by man, such as the Passenger Pigeon and the Dodo, or by conditions caused by man, through habitat destruction, or competition and predation from introduced rats, cats, dogs, and livestock.

Mammals, reptiles, amphibians, and fish have also shown rising extinction rates, as well as population declines pushing an increasing number of species each year into the endangered category. For the invertebrates and plants, which form the base of ecological systems, extinctions are even more dramatic. Ecologist Norman Myers

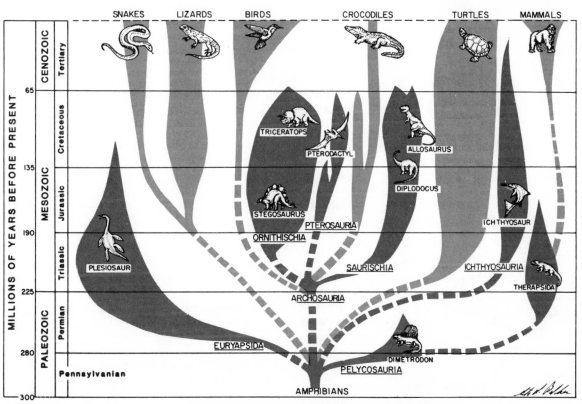

Chart by Esta Belcher

DINOSAURS APPEAR AND RECEDE

Ornithischia and Saurischia, the true dinosaurs, and other early reptiles faded out gradually as modern life forms evolved. Dashed lines indicated presumed lineages. Some scientists believe that birds are derived from Saurischian dinosaurs.

calculates that the extinction rate for *all* species—plants and animals—may be approaching one species per day due almost entirely to the activities of man.[1] Such estimates may be overly pessimistic, but clearly, the increase in extinctions is alarming. It is with this perspective that we can see the present situation as an *unnatural* event, not linked to climatic changes, meteors, or volcanic eruptions, but a result of changes wrought in earth's environments by man, and also by direct extermination.[2]

The Geography of Extinction

Over the past 350 years, at least 80% of mammal, bird, reptile, and amphibian extinctions have taken place on islands. (See table "The Geography of Extinctions"). The loss of any species is tragic, but these extinctions were doubly unfortunate because a majority of the species were distinctive and unusual, products of thousands or millions of years of evolution in isolation. Few have left close relatives. Of the 109 bird species which have become extinct since 1600, 91 were island dwellers. Until 1844 when the last Great Auk* of North America was killed, all known bird extinctions had occurred on islands (and even the Great Auk had become confined to a few islands off Newfoundland).

The colonization of islands by wildlife, primarily birds, but also by some reptiles and mammals, is a fascinating saga. Those islands located fairly close to continental land masses are usually inhabited by species from the neighboring mainland, and frequent arrivals of birds of the same species tend to prevent unique species from evolving.

It is extraordinary how land birds become resident on islands remote from continents. Many may have been carried by hurricanes or storms, or become disoriented in migration and, no doubt, thousands of birds die at sea. Lone birds may be successful in reaching a landfall with food sources, but for lack of a mate cannot reproduce.

Rails on Islands

Rails, compact and stocky water birds ranging in size from four inches in length to the chicken-sized Takahe of New Zealand (an endangered species once thought extinct), are among the most characteristic birds of oceanic islands. Almost all islands in tropical latitudes have endemic** usually flightless rails, or fossil evidence that rails once lived there.

Anyone who has searched for rails knows that they spend most of their time on the ground, and are elusive birds stepping delicately on their long, spindly legs in and out of marsh vegetation. When frightened, they usually do not take wing, but disappear into a matted mass of reeds. They are, in the words of S. Dillon Ripley, the eminent ornithologist, "loath to fly."[3] When they do fly for short distances, it is rather feebly, with legs dangling down. How could they have reached islands thousands of miles distant from the mainland? It appears that rails do not have ancestral migration routes as is the case with most birds but disperse in many directions. Once

Drawing from the Doomsday Book of Animals

The **Laysan Rail** was a victim of exotic species introduction and war.

*When a species is mentioned such as the Great Auk or Takahe, the name or names are capitalized. General terms such as rails, referring to more than one species, are not capitalized.

** Endemic describes species existing only in a particular region or island. The Wake Island Rail was endemic to that island, living nowhere else.

aloft, they can be strong fliers who turn up in unexpected places. North American Purple Gallinules, rather large and colorful rails, have flown to tiny Tristan da Cunha Island halfway between South America and Africa in the South Atlantic;[3] European Corncrakes, another type of rail, have landed exhausted on ships in the Indian Ocean, or even off New Zealand.[3]

Fully thirteen species of unique island rails, many of them flightless, have become extinct over the past 350 years, and a large number of the remaining species are endangered.[4] Rats, pigs, and mongooses have caused extinctions, and in one case, rabbits destroyed the vegetation of Laysan Island, home of a rail of that name. This little rail had been transported by biologists to nearby Midway Island after introduced rabbits devegetated Laysan. It flourished there until World War II when the island became a naval base. The navy personnel were entranced by this bird, utterly fearless and agile, in spite of its flightlessness, springing into people's laps or onto the mess table in search of crumbs of food. Unfortunately, it

The Rising Rate of Bird Extinctions

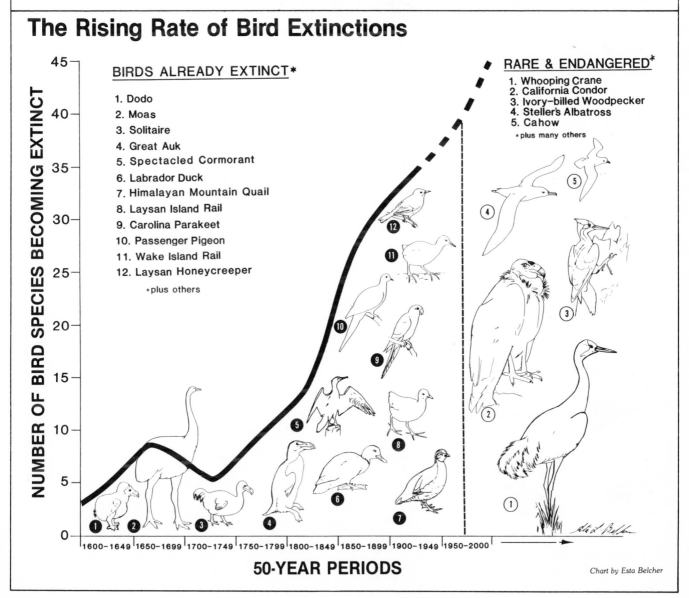

NUMBER OF BIRD SPECIES BECOMING EXTINCT

BIRDS ALREADY EXTINCT*

1. Dodo
2. Moas
3. Solitaire
4. Great Auk
5. Spectacled Cormorant
6. Labrador Duck
7. Himalayan Mountain Quail
8. Laysan Island Rail
9. Carolina Parakeet
10. Passenger Pigeon
11. Wake Island Rail
12. Laysan Honeycreeper

*plus others

RARE & ENDANGERED*

1. Whooping Crane
2. California Condor
3. Ivory-billed Woodpecker
4. Steller's Albatross
5. Cahow

*plus many others

50-YEAR PERIODS

1600-1649 | 1650-1699 | 1700-1749 | 1750-1799 | 1800-1849 | 1850-1899 | 1900-1949 | 1950-2000

Chart by Esta Belcher

The Geography of Extinction

Species Extinct Since 1600	Islands	Species Threatened with Extinction
	Islands	
	Indian Ocean Islands	
	Aldabra I.	1 bird
3 mammals	Christmas I.	3 birds
4 birds, 1 mammal	Madagascar	20 birds, 14 mammals, 3 reptiles
20 birds, 7 reptiles	Mascarene Is.	11 birds, 2 mammals, 6 reptiles
1 bird, 1 reptile	Seychelles Is.	7 birds, 4 amphibians
	Pacific Ocean Islands	
1 bird, 1 mammal	Bering I.	
3 birds	Bonin Is.	
2 birds	Caroline Is.	4 birds
3 birds	Chatham I.	3 birds
	Cook Is.	1 bird
1 bird	Fiji Is.	3 birds, 2 reptiles
4 mammals	Galapagos Is.	3 birds, 4 reptiles
2 birds	Guadalupe I.	
15 birds	Hawaiian Is.	16 birds
1 bird	Kermadec Is.	
3 birds	Lord Howe & Norfolk Is.	2 birds
	Marianas Is.	4 birds, 2 mammals
	Marquesas Is.	3 birds
3 birds	New Caledonia	3 birds
1 bird	New Hebrides	1 bird
10 birds	New Zealand & Auckland	14 birds, 1 reptile, 3 amphibians
1 bird	Philippine Is.	1 bird, 4 mammals, 2 reptiles
	Rapa I.	1 bird
2 birds	Ryukyu Is.	1 bird, 2 mammals
1 bird	Samoan Is.	1 bird
7 birds	Society Is.	2 birds
1 bird	Solomon Is.	1 bird
1 bird	Tuamotu Is.	2 birds
1 bird	Wake I.	
1 bird	Pacific Area	
	Atlantic Ocean Islands	
1 bird	Ascension I.	1 bird
	Bermuda	1 bird
1 reptile	Canary Is.	2 birds
1 reptile	Cape Verde Is.	1 bird, 1 reptile
1 bird	Sao Tome I.	
1 bird	St. Helena I.	
1 bird	Tristan da Cunha	1 bird
	Caribbean Islands	
	Aruba	1 reptile
1 bird	Bahamas	1 mammal, 5 reptiles
2 mammals	Barbuda	
1 bird, 7 mammals	Cuba	3 birds, 3 mammals, 2 reptiles
	Dominica	2 birds
11 mammals	Dominican Republic & Haiti	1 bird, 3 mammals
	Grenada	1 bird
1 reptile	Guadeloupe	
1 bird, 2 mammals, 3 reptiles	Jamaica	1 mammal, 1 reptile
2 mammals, 3 reptiles	Martinique	
7 mammals	Puerto Rico	3 birds, 1 amphibian, 3 reptiles
2 mammals, 1 reptile	St. Lucia	2 birds
1 mammal	St. Vincent	1 bird
1 reptile	Virgin Is.	2 reptiles
1 reptile	West Indies	1 bird

Species Extinct Since 1600	Continents	Species Threatened with Extinction
3 mammals	Africa	18 birds, 35 mammals 2 amphibians, 5 reptiles
3 mammals, 1 reptile	Europe–Near East	3 birds, 4 mammals, 3 amphibians, 1 reptile
4 birds, 1 mammal	USSR–Asia	41 birds, 62 mammals, 3 amphibians, 11 reptiles
9 birds, 1 mammal	Mexico & Latin America	65 birds, 48 mammals, 1 amphibian, 14 reptiles
4 birds, 3 mammals	U.S. & Canada	7 birds, 11 mammals, 14 amphibians, 6 reptiles
1 bird, 8 mammals	Australia	10 birds, 22 mammals, 2 amphibians, 3 reptiles
	Worldwide	1 bird
2 mammals	**Oceans** *	16 mammals, 7 reptiles

* The species listed here are animals such as whales and sea turtles. Seals are listed under the islands or continents where they breed.

Totals by Class of Animal

The percentages refer to totals by category. For example, 17 Mainland mammals have become extinct, comprising 27% of all mammal extinctions.

	Mammals				**Birds**			
	Extinct since 1600		Threatened with Extinction		Extinct since 1600		Threatened with Extinction	
	No. of Species	Percent	No. of Species	Percent	No. of Species	Percent	No. of Species	Percent
Mainland	17	27	182	78	18	17	144	23
Island	45	70	35	15	91	83	128	46
Ocean	2	3	16	7			1	1
Totals	64	100%	233	100%	109	100%	273	100%

	Reptiles				**Amphibians**			
	Extinct since 1600		Threatened with Extinction		Extinct since 1600		Threatened with Extinction	
	No. of Species	Percent	No. of Species	Percent	No. of Species	Percent	No. of Species	Percent
Mainland	1	5	39	49	1	100	26	79
Island	19	95	32	41			7	21
Ocean			7	10				
Totals	20	100%	78	100%	1	100%	33	100%

Totals by Region

	Extinct since 1600		**Threatened with Extinction**	
	No. of Species	Percent of all Extinctions	No. of Species	Percent of all Threatened Species
Mainland	37	19	391	63
Island	155	80	202	33
Ocean	2	1	24	4
Totals	194	100%	617	100%

Sources on Extinct Species: extinct mammals: HRH Prince Philip and James Fisher. 1970. Wildlife Crisis. Cowles Book Co., and Day, David. 1981. The Doomsday Book of Animals. Viking, and Allen, G.M. 1972. Extinct and Vanishing Mammals of the Western Hemisphere. Cooper Square Publishers, Inc. Extinct Reptiles and Amphibians: Honegger, Rene. 1981. List of amphibians and reptiles either known or thought to have become extinct since 1600. Biological Conservation. 19(2):141-158. Jan. and Day, David. 1981. The Doomsday Book of Animals. Viking.

The major sources for information on extinct birds were the International Council for Bird Preservation (ICBP). 1965. List of Birds Either Known or Thought to Have Become Extinct Since 1600. and Red Data Book, *Aves,* Vol. 2. Smithsonian Institution, 1980. Also Greenway, James C., Jr. 1967. Extinct and Vanishing Birds of the World. Dover. and Day, David. 1981. The Doomsday Book of Animals. Viking.

Threatened Species: All were derived from the IUCN Red Data Books, Vol. 1 *Mammalia,* Vol. 2 *Aves* (published by ICBP) and Vol. 3 *Amphibia* and *Reptilia.*

perished soon after 1942 when rats from a naval landing craft apparently ate the little rail's eggs and preyed on its young. A few of the rails had been returned to Laysan Island when rabbits were removed, but the vegetation had not recovered sufficiently, and the birds did not survive.[3] The endemic rail of Wake Island became another casualty when the island was occupied during World War II by the Japanese, who apparently used it for food, and destroyed its habitat.[5]

Fully 155 species of mammals, birds and reptiles which once inhabited islands are now extinct. The table on pages 6 and 7 shows the patterns of extinction by geographical area.

Hawaiian Islands

The Hawaiian Islands lost 15 bird species, including many colorful and fascinating honeycreepers and other unique birds of species existing nowhere else. Its varied wildlife and plants have been greatly reduced and nearly all remaining honeycreepers, other native birds, the endemic bat subspecies, and some 800 native plants are endangered. Happily, sometimes species thought extinct are rediscovered. One of the most beautiful Hawaiian birds, known as Bishops O'O' after its call, was last sighted on the island of Molokai in 1904. Cadmium yellow feathers, in tufts near the ears and under the wings, stand out against glossy black plumage. These feathers were used by Hawaiian royalty for headdresses and capes, but the major cause of its disappearance was thought to be the introduction of pigs and rats that destroyed its habitat. In May 1981, its existence was confirmed by Stephen R. Sabo who saw it on the island of Maui in a remote forest reserve. This very rare bird's existence is still threatened by the same exotic species.

New Zealand

New Zealand's two major islands and outlying islands were home to the moas, giant flightless birds which, prior to the settlement of the islands by the Polynesian Maoris, numbered some 25 species, the largest measuring over 12 feet. The last of the moas was killed off by white settlers in 1785. Among the 10 New Zealand bird species to become extinct since 1600 was the Huia, a bird that may have represented the most unusual adaptation to a restricted environment of any known bird species: the male and female had beaks of different size and shape, leading early naturalists to assume that they were separate species. They used their beaks to seek different food sources. The male's shorter bill was able to chop and break up rotten bark in search of insects, while the female's longer bill probed crevices for insects that the male could not reach.[3] The forests of New Zealand were cut by settlers, livestock and rats introduced, and possibly disease was brought by mynah birds transported by Europeans.[5] An added final pressure was the sudden fashion for their long black tail feathers started by the Duke of York, future King George V of England, around the turn of the century. The Duke, presented some feathers on a visit, wore them in his hat, and launched a fashion in England which resulted in hundreds—646 birds in one month alone—of Huias being killed.[5] The last Huia was seen in 1907.[5]

Many species of animals have become extinct for reasons similar to those which exterminated the Huia. Island animals are more vulnerable than mainland species since they occupy limited habitats, and many are—or were—flightless birds, or, slow-moving animals, unable either to flee the human predator, or adapt to changes he made in their environment.

The islands which were the scene of the greatest number of animal extinctions were once a zoological treasure house.

The Mascarene Islands: The Dodo and Fellow Inhabitants

The story of the Mascarene extinctions holds lessons for the future, and encapsulates the major pressures that have brought about animal extinctions, pressures which are continuing to operate today.

Of all extinct birds, perhaps the most famous, and for some, a synonym for the word extinction, for others the word stupidity, is the Dodo, *Raphus cucullatus,* once native to the island of Mauritius in the Indian Ocean. The Dodo became extinct in the late 17th century, some 100 years after its discovery by Europeans. For many years, the very existence of the Dodo was questioned by many scientists. Most species of animals encountered at that period became known through the accounts of travelers. Europeans were sailing the oceans in search of commodities, from East Indian spices and tea to seal skins, timber and slaves. In most cases, when remote islands were visited, their wildlife was exploited for food, and domestic animals were released for availability as future provisions when ships stopped there. The domestic animals usually multiplied and often overran islands within fifty years or less. Pigs rooted in forests, cattle overgrazed, and goats ate all types of vegetation, creating environmental havoc. Sometimes dogs were also brought to islands, and these have been destructive as well, preying on flightless birds and tortoises. Rats that swam from ships colonized the majority of islands, killing small birds, eating their eggs and young, and even becoming tree-climbing, adding to their threat to native wildlife.

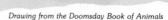

Drawing from the Doomsday Book of Animals

*The **Huias** were unique: males and females had different beaks to feed on different types of food.*

Dodo. *A sketch from Lewis Carroll's Alice in Wonderland.*

Drawing by Sir John Tenniel

Drawing from the Doomsday Book of Animals

*It is thought that the Dodo was able to digest the seeds of the **Calvaria tree.** The defecated seeds then sprouted.*

Mauritius is one of the Mascarene Islands, lying 500 miles east of Madagascar in the southern Indian Ocean. The other two major islands of the group are Reunion and Rodrigues; though quite separated from one another, all three are fairly large (about 120 square miles each) and of volcanic origin. Their mountains were once covered by lush tropical forests.[6] Mauritius was first visited by Portuguese sailors in the early 1500's, who found the island uninhabited. They brought pigs and macaque monkeys with them, which they released.[6] Dodos were still abundant in 1598 when Dutch merchant ships began to arrive to provision their ships. The enormous Dodos, weighing some 50 pounds, covered with grayish downy feathers and flapping small, useless wings, were easily killed for food. In 1602, a Dutch sea captain describes the bird as having tough flesh except for the breast and belly meat which were considered quite tasty.[7] The name "Dodo" is apparently derived from the early Dutch sailors—Dodars may be a composite of dodoor, meaning sluggard, and dodaers, a lubber.[8] In fact, its original Latin name was *Didus ineptus,* indicating its inability to flee humans or defend itself. Animals are frequently judged stupid if their natural defenses against humans are inadequate, and vicious if they are able to defend themselves. In truth, the Dodo was the final product of thousands, perhaps millions of years of evolution in isolation on an island with no land predators. At some early date birds, perhaps only a pair, had landed by chance on Mauritius and become resident. One theory as to the kind of bird from which the Dodo evolved held by Tim Halliday, an Oxford University zoologist, in *Vanishing Birds* is that it was a type of tooth-billed pigeon which can still be found in New Guinea and Pacific islands.[8] David Day, in his impressive book on extinct animals, concurs in this opinion.[5] There is a marked resemblance in that both the tooth-billed pigeons and the Dodo have a curious hooked beak, although the Dodo's was far more massive (fully nine inches long!). Whatever its ancestry, the Dodo became flightless, as did many island birds, in its predator-free environment. Its feathers lost their sheen and aerodynamic properties, and came to resemble the down of nestling birds. In its gizzard, the sailors butchering it found stones, whose purpose did not become clear until 300 years after its extinction.

In 1973, Dr. Stanley Temple, an American ornithologist working to preserve Mauritius' remaining Kestrels (which numbered less than 10 at that time), made a remarkable discovery about the Dodo. He noticed that a beautiful tree native to the island called *Calvaria major,* was reduced to 13 old and dying specimens, all over 300 years old. They were still producing apparently fertile seeds each year, but none germinated, even under nursery conditions. Because no young trees were located, it occurred to Dr. Temple that no seeds had germinated since the 17th century when the Dodo became extinct, because the stones in the Dodo's gizzard might have been able to abrade the thick shell covering the *Calvaria* seeds. Dr. Temple fed some of the seeds to turkeys, which have similar digestive systems, and of ten seeds recovered from feces or regurgitation, three sprouted when planted.[9] These were probably the first seeds of *Calvaria* to germinate in 300 years! So little is known of ecological relationships between animals and plants that thousands of such examples of possible co-evolution have doubtless been destroyed in the past. One species may doom others that depend on it as it fades to extinction.

Photos by Carl G. Jones

*(top) The beautiful island of **Mauritius** was the scene of the Dodo's and many other species' extinctions.*

*(middle) The entire population of the **Mauritius Pink Pigeon** numbers less than 50 birds.*

*(bottom) The **Mauritius Kestrel** has been reduced to a population of only 15 individual birds.*

Settlement of the island by the Dutch in 1644 was followed by the establishment of a penal colony and systematic clearing of the forests in order to plant crops.[8] The last account of the living Dodo was provided by a British captain who found its flesh "very hard" and the species became extinct in 1681.[6] A few Dodos had been brought to Europe and caused quite a sensation when exhibited in London. None were kept as zoological specimens, save for one skin of a captive Dodo that had died, and even it was almost destroyed when a specimen collection was burned to destroy vermin. A few bones and a skull were all that remained and many began to doubt that there ever had been a Dodo; in the 19th century, excavation on the island revealed hundreds of bones of Dodos, and its existence was verified.[8] The bones found on Mauritius evidenced a very long residence by the ground-dwelling Dodo, a species well adapted to its environment, and successful in exploiting plants as food, resulting in a huge body size. If not for the arrival of humans for which it had no defenses, it would still exist.

Mauritius, Reunion and Rodrigues have long been separated from each other and from Madagascar by such great distances that each island's birds developed into distinct species. Similar to the Dodo, Solitaires on Reunion and Rodrigues also became extinct. The endemic wildlife of these islands has been decimated in the past three hundred years. Twenty full species of birds and 8 reptiles were exterminated, as were races or subspecies* of many others.[6,10] Giant tortoises once inhabited the islands and like the Dodo were killed to provision ships and settlers. Huge flightless parrots, four kinds of owls, two flightless rails, two flightless pigeons, starlings and parakeets, large gecko lizards and skinks all lived on the islands. Travelers described a ring-necked parakeet, a fody (a colorful songbird which is a type of weaver), and another species of Dodo on Reunion Island, but to date no bones have been found of these birds.

The extinct and endangered species of the Mascarenes are shown in the list below—an amazing tally for so few islands.

Today, the islands' remaining wildlife is teetering on the brink of extinction—11 bird species, 2 mammals and 8 reptiles are listed by the International Union for the Conservation of Nature's (IUCN) *Red Data Books* of threatened and endangered species and the International Council for Bird Preservation (ICBP). Five of the endangered birds have populations that are tiny and fragile: the Rodrigues Fody is reduced to 120 individual birds; the Rodrigues Brush Warbler, 40 to 60; the Mauritius Pink Pigeon 50, of which 30 are in captivity; the Mauritius Kestrel numbers only 15, and most endangered of all, the Mauritius Parakeet now has a total population of only five birds.[4] They are among the most endangered birds in the world.

Mascarene wildlife must compete for survival with the growing human population. Two islands—Mauritius and Reunion—alone now have a combined human population of over 1,330,000.[11] There has been massive destruction of the original lush tropical forests on the islands, mainly to clear the land for agriculture. Sugar

* A subspecies is a geographically defined aggregate of local populations which differs taxonomically from other subdivisions of the species. The races of humans are the most familiar example of subspecies. Subspecies develop in response to the different environments in which they find themselves, and exhibit genetic differences. Sometimes animals of different subspecies vary so dramatically in color or size, for example, that a lay person would assume them to be separate species. Each subspecies represents a unique genetic assemblage and its preservation is important.

cane is a major crop produced for export. Of the three major islands, Rodrigues has suffered the greatest forest loss: 99% has been cleared.[12] Because of the clearing and unregulated hunting, it has also lost the greatest number of species: 13 birds and reptiles of Rodrigues are extinct. Mauritius' forests have been reduced by 93%, and Reunion's by 61%.[12] The wholesale loss of the native plants and

Mascarene Wildlife

The year of extinction precedes the species. Latin names are listed in Appendix in the List of Extinct Species.

Extinct Species

Rodrigues Island

Birds
1691 Leguat's Owl
1693 Rodrigues Pigeon
1730 Rodrigues Blue Rail
1730 Rodrigues Little Owl
1730 Flightless Night Heron
1760 Rodrigues Parrot
1791 Rodrigues Solitaire
1832 Leguat's Starling
1875 Rodrigues Parakeet

Reptiles
1800 Rodrigues Tortoise
1840 Vosmaer's Giant Tortoise
1874 Rodrigues Gecko
1917 Newton's Day Gecko

Reunion Island

Birds
1669 Bourbon Pink Pigeon
1669 Bourbon Parrot
1746 Reunion Solitaire
1834 Mascarene Parrot
1862 Bourbon Crested Starling

Reptiles
1773 Reunion Giant Tortoise

Mauritius Island

Birds
1638 Broad-billed Parrot
1675 Van den Broecke Rail
1681 Dodo
1700 Mauritius Owl
1830 Mauritius Blue Pigeon
1837 Scops Owl

Reptiles
1600 Gadow's Giant Tortoise
1650 Mauritian Giant Skink
1894 Mauritius Tortoise

Endangered Species

Mammals
Rodrigues Flying Fox

Birds
Rodrigues Brush Warbler
Rodrigues Fody

Reptiles
Rodrigues Day Gecko

Birds
Reunion Petrel
Reunion Cuckoo—Shrike

Reptiles
Dumeril's Boa

Mammals
Mauritian Flying Fox

Birds
Mauritius Kestrel
Pink Pigeon
Mauritius Parakeet
Mauritius Cuckoo—Shrike
Mauritius Paradise Flycatcher
Mauritius White-eye
Mauritius Fody

Reptiles
Serpent Island Gecko
Round Island Day Gecko
Macabe Forest Skink
Round Island Skink
Round Island Boa*
Round Island Keel-scaled Boa

*Probably extinct—only one individual left

Sources: This list was compiled from the following sources: Curry-Lindahl, Kai. 1972. Let Them Live. A Worldwide survey of Animals Threatened with Extinction. Wm. Morrow & Co.; Day, David. 1981. The Doomsday Book of Animals. Viking.; Greenway, James C., Jr. 1967. Extinct and Vanishing Birds of the World. Dover; Honegger, Rene. 1981. List of amphibians and reptiles either known or thought to have become extinct since 1600. Biological Conservation, 19(2):141-158. Jan.; IUCN Red Data Books. Vol. 1: *Mammalia;* Vol. 3: *Amphibia* and *Reptilia.* Morges, Switzerland; International Council for Bird Preservation. 1980. Red Data Book—Vol. 2: *Aves.* Smithsonian Institution Press; HRH Prince Philip, and James Fisher. 1970. Wildlife Crisis. Cowles Book Co., Inc.

animals, and the bleak future of the remaining forests on Mauritius prompted Dr. Temple, who has continued to work to preserve these islands' fauna, to suggest that some of its endangered birds be transferred to Reunion, since that island has, relatively speaking, the largest percentage of its original forest cover.[12]

Bird Extinctions Where and Why

Much has already been said of the 109 birds that have become extinct since 1600. When the list is examined for both causes and geography, several conclusions can be reached although for about 36%* of bird extinctions, the causes remain obscure. Many of these birds were collected by scientists, given species' names, described in scientific literature, and then never seen again by subsequent visitors to the area. In some cases, the causes became evident when rats** and other exotics were observed on islands in numbers sufficient to have destroyed them. In others, habitat destruction had occurred since discovery of the species.

About 22% became extinct as a result of introduction, usually on islands of rats, cats, goats, pigs, sheep and cattle. Cats were brought by settlers to some islands, and in one case, a single cat owned by a lighthouse keeper on a tiny islet off New Zealand is blamed for the extinction of an endemic bird—the St. Stephen's Wren. Cats also killed a large number of Hawaii's native birds, as did rats and dogs.[5] One major effect of livestock is destroying habitat by removing vegetation and stomping on seedlings. Of all livestock species the most destructive has been the omnivorous goat, of which one of the Galapagos Islands has a population of over 100,000.

These unfortunate population explosions are generally blamed on the animals rather than on the people who released them. Domestic animals should never be abandoned or set free to fend for themselves, and if they over populate, they should never be killed by painful methods. The animals we have domesticated remain the responsibility of our species.

The role of habitat destruction is sometimes difficult to separate from the exotic species problem for island birds, but an estimated 20% of bird extinctions can be traced to habitat destruction alone. Some mainland species have had their habitats totally destroyed and naturalists surveying for their presence have had to conclude that they were extinct. Most of these birds had occupied very restricted areas, and their rarity was not fully appreciated at the time of their discovery. The Magdalena Tinamou, Brown-banded Pitta, and Cherry-throated Tanager of South America were all known only from one or two specimens taken on their discovery in forest areas that were later destroyed.[4]

Two South American birds, the Brasilia Tapaculo, found on the site of the present capital city of Brazil, and Tumaco Seedeater of Colombia, had their entire known habitats covered by cities.[4]

The world's largest woodpecker, the handsome black Imperial Woodpecker of Mexico, has not been seen since 1958 and is feared extinct. Forest cutting and shooting are the primary causes. Another species, the Helmeted Woodpecker of southeastern Brazil and neighboring areas of Paraguay and Argentina has not been seen

The Fody of Rodrigues Island in the Mascarenes, where 99% of the forests have been cleared, is highly endangered.

Photo by Carl G. Jones

---

* This and other percentages of extinctions and endangered status are rough estimates arrived at by examination of numerous sources on this subject, cited in the references.
** Norway, brown and black rats, originating in Eurasia, escapees from ships.

since 1954. Most of its forest habitat has been cleared.[4] The Glaucous Macaw, a large, bluish grey bird from this same region was fairly common in 19th century aviculture collections in Europe, but it seems to have disappeared with habitat destruction a possible cause. The destruction of forests in South America is also blamed for the extinction of the Olive-headed Brush-finch, known from only 25 specimens, and the Brown-banded Antpitta, both rare birds of Colombia, not seen since 1911.[4] There are probably many more birds of the world which have recently become extinct as a result of forest clearance, but to date, research on the status of rare birds in the wild has been poorly funded.

The habitat destruction which removes millions of acres of both tropical and temperate habitats yearly has emerged as the major threat to birds and all vertebrates. The speed with which it is accomplished—an acre of ancient tropical forest can be leveled by saw and bulldozer in less than an hour—may cause the demise of many species of birds within the next 20 years. In the case of birds of very restricted range, special attention is needed, for these birds are as vulnerable as island species to possible extinction. Likewise, newly discovered species are usually of limited distribution, and their range and population should be ascertained as soon as possible to prevent their disappearance. This danger is recognized by scientists and conservationists, but often, funds are not available to conduct surveys and acquire sufficient habitat.

The direct killing that exterminated the Dodo also was responsible for at least 18% of all bird extinctions since 1600. Another victim was the Passenger Pigeon, best known of North American extinct birds, and perhaps the most abundant bird in the world just 150 years ago. Its story has been told many times, but one can never hear it without shock. 1914 was the year when both the Passenger Pigeon and the

Drawing by Esta Belcher

Farmers shot **Carolina Parakeets** by the hundreds as they flocked about their fallen comrades. The species became extinct in 1914.

colorful Carolina Parakeet became extinct. Both species ended their days as single birds in the Cincinnati Zoological Gardens and the last individuals died within a month of each other.[5] The Carolina Parakeet (*Conuropsis carolinensis*) was the only native parrot in the United States, a small greenish bird with long graceful tail and bright yellow and orange head. Like the Passenger Pigeon it was widespread in eastern United States and once formed flocks of hundreds which roosted in hollow trees in mature forests. It fed on a variety of nuts, fruits and seeds. The felling of forests by settlers removed some of its habitat, but the major cause of its extinction was direct persecution by farmers who saw it as a pest to their crops and orchards. Large numbers were shot and the Parakeets tended to flock around their fallen flock members, a behavior that might have served them to scare off predators, but which proved fatal in the face of guns. John James Audubon, renowned naturalist and bird painter, who warned that they were becoming rare as early as 1831, described the shootings:

". . .the Parakeets are destroyed in great numbers, for whilst busily engaged in plucking off the fruits or tearing the grain from the stacks, the husbandman approaches them with perfect ease, and commits great slaughter among them. All the survivors rise, shriek, fly round for a few minutes, and again alight on the very place of most imminent danger. The gun is kept at work; eight or ten, or even twenty, are killed at every discharge. The living birds, as if conscious of the death of their companions, sweep over their bodies, screaming as loud as ever, but still return to the stack to be shot at, until so few remain alive, that the farmer does not consider it worth his while to spend more of his ammunition. I have seen several hundreds destroyed in this manner in the course of a few hours, and have procured a basketful of these birds at a few shots. . ." (quoted in *Audubon's America*, edited by D.C. Poattie, 1940, Houghton Mifflin Co., Boston)

Such slaughters of wildlife were commonplace in the 19th century, whether for sport, trade, or in the name of crop protection, and the results were extinctions, and innumerable cases of near-extinctions of birds, mammals and even fish. The abundant wildlife of America, unfamiliar with guns, presented an opportunity to the new settlers of wilderness areas to kill without restrictions, unhampered by the protective game laws of their European homelands.

The striking black and white Labrador Duck of the eastern U.S. and Canadian coasts was another victim of market hunters. It was probably always a rare species which could not stand hunting pressure, and details of its extinction may never be known. The last specimen was shot in 1875.[5] The beautiful Pink-headed Duck of India, extinct by 1944, succumbed to over-hunting and over-collecting for museums. It was a rare bird before its decline and, unfortunately, conservation measures came too late to save it.

Hunting has not been eliminated as a cause endangering birds, and an estimated 11% of birds listed by the ICBP *Red Data Book* are imperiled by hunting in their country of origin. Often, hunting is very difficult to control even when laws are passed protecting species. A perennial problem among hunters of many areas is their perception of the prey species' abundance. In North America game birds are monitored for population size, and hunting seasons are curtailed when populations drop—at least in principle. In many parts of the world, however, localized subsistence hunting can have a devastating impact on rare species, and hunters are often unaware that the prey species is not abundant. Some birds have been victimized by persecution. The role that predatory birds play in maintaining the balance of nature by keeping rodent populations in check is often unrecognized, and many are shot on sight.

Disease has played a role in the extinction of birds, although it has been hotly debated as to how great a threat it has been. The birds of Hawaii were swept by several diseases introduced by exotic species of insects—bird malaria and bird pox—and many birds were found with tumors, growths, oozing ocular discharges, and other symptoms of these diseases near the turn of the century. It is likely that disease did play a role in both New Zealand and Hawaii, and when added to other threats, it qualified as a contributing factor to about 1% of bird extinctions. Today, disease presents about the same degree of threat, and could assume greater proportions if chance introduction of certain highly contagious bird diseases such as some viral strains or Exotic Newcastle Disease should occur in the habitat of an endangered bird.

Other causes of bird extinctions have been the collection of birds for the pet trade, a rather recent threat, and incidental kill accompanying war or other devastating human activity. The Paradise Parrot of Australia, though rumored to still exist, has not been seen since 1927, and a major cause of its decline was its collection for the pet and aviculture interests, accompanied by livestock overgrazing in its habitat. The pet trade has been a factor in bird declines as a result of the recent rise in the capture of wild birds for commercial sale. Some 7½ million birds are captured every year in tropical countries and many populations have declined as a result of over-collection.

New causes have emerged to threaten birds such as environmental pollution, mainly pesticides, and human disturbance of nesting birds, which were once quite isolated. These will be discussed in a later chapter.

Mammal Extinctions Where and Why

About two percent of all mammals living in 1600, or 64 species, are now extinct. Seventy percent of these occurred on islands. Over half, or 37 species, were rodents and insectivores, and the remainder were bats and large mammals. Of the 45 island mammals that have disappeared, three-fourths were Caribbean species.

When one thinks of the wildlife of the Caribbean, colorful tropical birds such as the Bananaquits that feed in hotel or suburban gardens, or sea birds planing over the blue water come to mind. The past history of West Indian animal extinctions, however, shows that many islands, especially the larger ones, Cuba, Puerto Rico, Haiti and Jamaica, had a rich variety of native rodents and shrew-like insectivores. Large rodents the size of small groundhogs had evolved into different species on various islands, perhaps transported by Carib Indians who depended on them as a major food staple. In Pleistocene times when sea levels were low, ancestors of these and other large animals are thought to have colonized the southern islands from Latin America. Remains of giant sloths have been found on Puerto Rico, and a rodent almost the size of a Black Bear once inhabited Anguilla and St. Martin.[13] Most of the 34 species of mammals made extinct in this area since 1600 were small, however. Rice rats inhabited the larger Antillean islands of St. Lucia, St. Vincent, Barbuda and Martinique along with brown and white muskrats. Hutias, large rodents that resemble South American Agoutis, were once

Photo: New York Zoological Society

*Hutias are rodents found only in the West Indies. The **Bahaman Hutia** shown here is, like other surviving species, threatened with extinction.*

found in a variety of species on Cuba, Hispaniola, Puerto Rico and Jamaica. At least five species of hutias are extinct and the few that remain are highly endangered. This area also lost several bat species. As noted before, most extinctions occurred when Europeans colonized the islands, cut forests, and introduced rats, livestock and mongooses, although some of the early extinctions are blamed on native Indians—both Carib and Arawak tribes who hunted the larger mammals heavily. Two species were lost on Martinique—a muskrat and a rice rat—when Mt. Pelee erupted in 1902. This is a rare example of a modern extinction by natural causes.

Four other small island mammals were rice rats of the Galapagos Islands, each a separate species belonging to its own island. One species had been first described by Darwin, who surmised that the rodents had been brought by ships at a much earlier date.

One extinct rodent, the Gull Island Vole, was native to a tiny island off New York's Long Island, and became extinct soon after its discovery in 1898 when a portion of the island was cleared for fortifications.[14]

Hunting and trapping caused the extinction of about 22% of all extinct mammals, with large mammals being the major victims.

Trapping destroyed the North American Sea Mink *(Mustela macrodon),* a species larger than the remaining mink species, it lived along the coasts of Maine and New Brunswick in Canada. It was very heavily trapped for the fur trade which paid high prices for its large, thick pelt, and dogs were even used to locate it in rocky crevices along the shores, where it sought refuge. The last Sea Mink was trapped in 1894.[14] The Falkland Island Fox, *(Dusicyon australis),* a wolf-like canid of the Falkland Islands off the southern coast of South America, was killed by both settlers and trappers sent from John Jacob Astor's fur trade company. This tame island species was eliminated by 1876.[14]

Two hoofed mammals of South Africa, the Blaauwbok, or Blue Buck *(Hippotragus leucophaeus)* and the Quagga *(Equus quagga)* were driven to extinction by Dutch settlers who waged a relentless campaign to rid the region of native animals so that agricultural crops and livestock could be raised. The Blue Buck was an antelope restricted to an area in the old Cape Colony which later became Zwellendam province. A large and graceful antelope related to the Roan, it became extinct within 80 years of its discovery. The last six animals, seen in 1796 after the species was presumed extinct, were shot over the next three years and their skins sent to Holland.[5] The Quagga, a zebra-like animal with stripes only on the front part of its body, was the only zebra found on the Cape Colony veldt and was shot by the thousands for food and its hides by Boers of the 19th century. It had even been imported to Europe and was used for a time in the 1830's as a harness animal in London. These Quaggas were probably gelded stallions, zebras being notorious for intractability when attempts have been made to domesticate them.[5] Some were tamed by the Boers and used to warn them of approaching dangers to their livestock at night; in spite of the Quagga's apparent usefulness to the Boers, it was totally eliminated in the wild by 1878, and the last captive Quagga died in the Amsterdam Zoo in 1883.[5]

Also victims of overkill were the ancestors of domestic horses and cattle in Europe. The Tarpan, parent of the breeding stock of European horses, was obliterated by the 19th century in the wild in Europe, and the massive Auroch, ancestor of domestic cattle, had

Drawing from the Doomsday Book of Animals

The zebra-like **Quaggas** were exterminated by South African settlers.

been killed off much earlier, in the 17th century.

The Schomburgk's Deer native to southeast Asia is now considered extinct; since the one shot in 1932, none has been seen.[5]

The Steller's Sea Cow (*Hydrodamalis stelleri*) was an enormous marine mammal 24 to 30 feet long, similar to the Dugong and manatees that barely survive today. It was larger, however, and swam in cold arctic waters of the Bering Sea enduring temperatures that would kill its closest relatives. Slow and sluggish, the sea cows were killed off only 27 years after their discovery. They were first seen by the shipwrecked crew of the explorer Vitus Bering in 1741 in the vicinity of Bering Island in the Commander Islands off the east coast of Kamchatka peninsula of Asia. The Sea Cows were tame and easy to spear and harpoon by ship crews who killed most of the population, calculated at only about 1,500 since the species was discovered.

This species, like many whales and porpoises today, showed extreme protectiveness toward its fellows and strong bonds between mates. The naturalist Georg Wilhelm Steller, after whom the species was named, described their behavior on being harpooned. "...Some of them tried to upset the boat [when another Sea Cow was struck] with their backs, while others pressed down the rope and endeavoured to break it, or strove to remove the hook from the wound in the back by blows of their tail, in which they actually succeeded several times. It is most remarkable proof of their conjugal affection that the male, after having tried with all his might, although in vain, to free the female caught by the hook, and in spite of the beating we gave him, nevertheless followed her to the shore, and that several times, even after she was dead, he shot unexpectedly up to her like a speeding arrow. Early next morning, when we came to cut up the meat and bring it to the dugout, we found the male by the female, and the same I observed on the third day when I went there by myself for the sole purpose of examining the intestine."[5]

On Madagascar, many lemurs had been killed off by the Malagasy, the most recent extinction occurring about 1930 of the Giant AyeAye, relative of the highly endangered remaining AyeAye, one of the world's strangest and most intriguing animals.

Of the remaining 4,100 mammal species, 233 are threatened with extinction.[15] Most are larger mammals, 182 from mainland areas, 35 from islands and 16 marine mammals. The problem of habitat destruction is now greater than hunting, threatening about 32% of endangered mammals. Hunting remains a threat, however, nearly as great as in the past. It adds to the plight of many animals. The continued over-utilization of fur animals, the senseless killing of the great whales, the slaughter of elephants and rhinoceroses for ivory and horn, and the heavy toll on primates of the commercial trade for research laboratories and zoos are all evidence of our heedless slaughter of wildlife. The preponderance of large mammals on the endangered list points to an amazing change which will occur in the earth's mammal fauna if endangered large mammals all become extinct over the next few decades. Clearly, we are exterminating a majority of the remaining large mammals on the planet.

Reptile Extinctions Where and Why

The major cause of extinction for the 20 species of reptiles that have disappeared since 1600 has been the effects of exotic species—predation on native reptile species and competition for food, along with destruction of their island habitats by introduced livestock. Virtually all extinct reptiles inhabited islands. Giant tortoises similar to those remaining on Aldabra Island in the Indian Ocean once inhabited the larger islands of the Seychelles and the Mascarenes— Rodrigues, Mauritius and Reunion. These tortoises were used as food by settlers of the islands—in 1759 and 1760 30,000 tortoises were killed to feed domestic pigs on Rodrigues.[6] When one island's tortoises were killed off, another's became exploited. Four species of these giant tortoises were slaughtered to extinction—three from the Mascarenes and one from the Seychelles Islands to the north.

Six reptiles of West Indian islands—lizards and snakes—succumbed to the effects of livestock grazing and to predation by introduced mongooses and cats. A seventh was eliminated by a hurricane, and two other lizard species disappeared from unknown causes in the Caribbean region. Often mongoose predation was accompanied by direct killing for food or sport, and livestock grazing on these islands has destroyed their habitats. The mongoose, ironically, was imported into many islands to control introduced snakes which in turn had been introduced to control rats. . .an endless chain of ecological nightmares created by man. George Laycock's very interesting and readable book, *The Alien Animals,* is a discussion of the effects of exotic species on environments and animals worldwide, devotes an entire chapter to "The Conquering Mongoose," so pervasive have been its effects.[18] The destruction of habitat alone has been a minor cause for the disappearance of reptiles if separated from the exotic species problem. Only about 5% of reptile extinctions can be traced to habitat destruction as a primary cause. At present, however, it represents a major threat, endangering some 21% of species listed in the *Red Data Book.*[17]

Unfortunately, reptiles are among the world's most heavily utilized animals for commercial purposes. Most sea turtles—survivors from prehistoric times—are now threatened or endangered from direct killing for their meat, oil, eggs, leather and tortoise shell. Most of the world's tropical islands and shores have been used for nesting by these reptiles, and it is during their only visits to land to lay eggs that the majority are killed. Considering their enormous original ranges, it is amazing and tragic that the populations of these great reptiles have been so drastically reduced. Killing of sea turtles and crocodiles by native peoples in tropical countries has been responsible for reducing some populations, but the major cause that has placed them in precarious status is the commercial marketing of their products. Turtle soup and steaks enjoyed by gourmets in European, Japanese and American restaurants, expensive shoes and luggage made from crocodile and alligator, turtle oil used in cosmetics, these essentially luxury items, bought eagerly by importers, have resulted in huge slaughters pushing some 34 species of reptiles into endangered or threatened status. Direct killing has always played a major role in the extinction of reptiles; at present, it represents the major threat.

The second most important threat to reptiles is habitat destruction, which mainly affects island species. Goats and other livestock overgraze, while feral dogs and mongooses prey on young turtles and lizards. The destruction of habitat from all causes has pushed about 21% of endangered reptiles into threatened status and predation accounts for another 16%. Some reptiles are confined to a restricted range, which makes them vulnerable.

The zoo and pet trades account for another estimated 8% of major causes threatening reptiles, and for some species this trade is critical,

Leatherback Turtles are the largest of all sea turtles, over 6 feet long. Once abundant, they are now endangered in most parts of their range.

Extinct and Disappearing Species— The Causes

*The endangered **Galapagos Tortoise** of Pinzon Island has evolved a very long neck to reach vegetation of low trees.*

Causes	Extinction Percentage Due To Each Cause	Endangered or Threatened Percentage Due To Each Cause
Mammals		
Hunting—subsistence, commercial & sport . .	23%	29%
Habitat Destruction	19%	32%
Exotic Species Introduction	20%	17%
Capture for pet, zoo & research trades	0%	2%
Predator Control	1%	8%
Incidental Kill (road kills, etc.)	0%	2%
Natural Causes	1%	?
Unknown	36%	10%
	100%	100%
Birds		
Habitat Destruction	20%	60%
Exotic Species Introduction	22%	12%
Hunting—subsistence, commercial & sport . .	18%	11%
Capture for pet, zoo & falconry trades	1%	9%
Disease	1%	1%
Pollution & Pesticides	0%	1%
Human Disturbance	0%	2%
Incidental Kill	1%	1%
Unknown	37%	3%
	100%	100%
Reptiles		
Hunting, mainly commercial	32%	44%
Exotic Species Introduction	42%	24%
Habitat Destruction	5%	22%
Capture for zoo or pet trade	0%	8%
Incidental kill (drowning in fish nets, etc.) . . .	0%	1%
Unknown	21%	1%
	100%	100%
Amphibians		
Habitat Destruction	100%	66%
Restricted Range	0%	16%
Exotic Species Introduction	0%	9%
Hunting—subsistence	0%	5%
Toxic Chemical Pollution	0%	4%
	100%	100%

Sources: These figures are estimates determined from examination of available information; (see sources in References List). They are open to discussion and the likelihood exists that more extensive information will emerge to clarify existing data. The major purpose of this table is to place in perspective the causes of the past and those of the present that threaten species, so that we can better learn from past mistakes and cope with new threats as well.

as taking of snakes, tortoises, and lizards for the pet trade is increasing. The U.S. Fish and Wildlife Service made a series of arrests involving the illegal sale of some 10,000 reptiles in 1981, the major markets being collectors and zoos in Europe and Japan.

For a few species, over-collection of specimens, mainly for scientific or teaching purposes, is a factor in their decline. The Bimini Boa of the Bahamas, for example, is critically endangered from collecting by amateur herpetologists along with habitat destruction.[17] Legislation regulating the collecting of reptiles and amphibians is far less stringent than that which applies to birds and mammals in the United States. Guidebooks for field study of reptiles and amphibians give how-to advice for collecting. Encouragingly, many scientists nowadays show more genuine conservation concern which results in fewer specimens taken, and more attention paid to wild status and habitat protection. Also, regulations are becoming stricter as an increasing number of reptiles and amphibians receive federal or state protection in the United States and in Europe.

Amphibian Extinctions Where and Why

Amphibians have fared better than other vertebrates. Only one species, the Israel Painted Frog (*Discoglossus nigriventer*) has disappeared in recent times. It once inhabited large marshes and portions of Lake Huleh in northern Israel. The marshes were drained after Israel became a nation, and the frog disappeared sometime between 1940 and 1956.[16]

At present, 33 species of amphibians are threatened with extinction worldwide, according to the *Red Data Book*. However, this figure may be too conservative, and the list is undergoing revision. Of the 33 species, only seven are island species (21%), and the remaining are confined to continental areas, many in the United States and Latin America. The major threat to amphibians is destruction of their swamp, river, lake, marsh, and wet woodland habitats. About 16% are confined to small areas making them vulnerable to any changes in their environment. The wetlands of all continents have been destroyed at a very great rate over the past century, usually prior to filling and planting for agriculture. Only recently are their values in flood control, as nurseries for fish, and as highly diverse ecosystems being appreciated.

As semi-aquatic species, amphibians are highly susceptible to pollution of their habitats by toxic chemicals and an increasing number are becoming affected by the insidious entry of these lethal agents into rivers, wetlands and lakes.[17]

A few amphibians, the larger frogs and salamanders for example, are killed by local peoples for food. In some areas, such killing results in declines of these species. Exotic species of frogs or other amphibians have been unwisely introduced into parts of the world where they have out-competed native species.[17]

While most of us think of amphibians as tiny salamanders or frogs measuring three or four inches, in reality they can, like the Chinese Giant Salamander, reach weights of 70 pounds and lengths of five feet. This salamander, whose status has not been studied carefully in the wild, was traditionally a valuable food resource of the people of western China. Others such as the Lake Lerma Salamander, are confined entirely to restricted areas. This salamander has declined steadily as its sole habitat has been drained, and it has suffered from hunting by local people as well. The smallest endangered amphibian may be the Golden Coqui frog of Puerto Rico, less than one inch

Drawing by Huang Zhujian, reprinted from the Oryx

Chinese Salamanders *can reach five feet in length. They have been heavily hunted for food.*

long. Its entire habitat is confined to a few acres of bromeliads, the tropical plants in which it lives. It is the only New World frog to bear live young, rather than lay eggs, and is considered a zoological rarity of great importance.

Fish and Invertebrates

Of the 20,000-plus fish species, an increasing number are becoming endangered. On a worldwide basis, however, the problem is in its early stages of study.

While most of the conservation attention has been given to dwindling vertebrates, primarily mammals and birds, ecologists are reminding us of the key role played in ecosystems by invertebrates and plants. They form the base of food chains upon which vertebrates depend. Some great whales feed exclusively on plankton and small shrimp called krill. Many food crops are pollinated by insects. The invertebrates in danger of extinction will be a subject of importance for research and conservation programs in the 1980's and beyond. Already, much is being done on that front in the United States.

The Future

What can we learn from past extinctions that could save some endangered animals? Lessons of the past should be a key to avoidance of future mistakes, but it is obvious that many of the same elements are still causing extinctions. The major difference is an increasing awareness of these very factors, alerting conservationists and scientists alike, and a growing knowledge of the complex ecological systems on earth. One facet not usually touched upon is the fact that certain vertebrates are more likely than others to become endangered because of behavior, habitat preference or other factors. Listed below are some of these potentially vulnerable forms—a list that will grow longer as we learn more about endangered species' preservation and prediction.

The Vulnerable Species

1. Flightless birds and slow-moving animals are helpless in the face of hunting pressure. Many of the species listed in the IUCN *Red Data Book* fall into this category. If such animals, whether or not now listed, are not given total protection, they will be quickly exterminated by unregulated hunting.

2. Large animals have been vulnerable since the Pleistocene to overhunting. Large mammals and reptiles have suffered the greatest losses in this century due to both hunting and the pressures of expanding human populations moving into former wilderness areas. Such species require relatively large habitats to survive.

3. Altruism, or care for wounded or fallen members of one's own species, highly admired as a human trait, has been fatal to many animals—the Steller's Sea Cow, the Passenger Pigeon, and the Carolina Parakeet are examples. This behavior served to preserve bonds between animals and to scare off predators in their evolutionary history. Wolves, whales and otters have been easier to kill in large numbers because of this trait.

4. Animals that are long-lived and have low reproductive rates, the latter term indicating species that do not breed until a relatively advanced age and have few young, are also vulnerable. These animals have evolved with a fairly low natural mortality and cannot afford artificial losses in their numbers. Although few of the now extinct animals were ever studied in the wild, enough is known of related species to guess that certain animals fell into this category.

*The flightless **Rheas** of South America are vulnerable to hunting, and have declined in many areas.*

*The calls of the **Ivory-billed Woodpecker** once resounded in southern forests. The old trees it required have been cut and no sightings have been made of this bird for many years.*

The Steller's Sea Cow, for example, was closely related to manatees and Dugongs which have few natural enemies, do not breed until aged 7 to 10 years old, and have only one young every five years. Many large birds such as condors, eagles, and the larger parrots have low reproductive rates with stable populations under natural circumstances. Sea turtles and tortoises may be the ultimate example of this category of animals. Biologists are learning that many of these reptiles, which have been known to live to be over 150 years old, may not breed until they are at least 25.

5. Vulnerability through restricted habitat has been a major cause of extinctions. Island animals for the most part have small total populations confined to areas that may measure only a few square miles. Species on mainland areas can also be restricted to very limited areas. The Slender-billed Grackle (*Cassidix palustris*) once inhabited a single marsh near Mexico City which was filled about 1910 spelling extinction for this bird. Many endangered species fall into this category.

6. A related vulnerability is over-specialization of habitat. The American Ivory-billed Woodpecker, now probably extinct, required old growth forests with many dead and dying trees as habitat, and these forests were among the first to be cut by settlers. The endangered Kirtland's Warbler of midwestern U.S. needs jackpine forest for feeding and nesting that is 8 to 22 years old on well-drained, sandy soil. This habitat must now be artificially maintained to prevent its extinction. The Palila, a Hawaiian honeycreeper, is dependent on the mamane tree, which has declined as a result of cutting and destruction of seedlings by introduced game species and livestock.

The species that simultaneously suffer from several of these factors can be quickly eliminated. The Steller's Sea Cow, for example, was large, altruistic, confined to a small area, and probably had a low reproductive rate.

Obviously, in view of the killing potential of humans, their rate of increase and ability to destroy the natural world, *all* wildlife is vulnerable on a long-term basis.

Diversity

Recent books are acquainting us with the enormous diversity of life on earth and the imminent threats that have placed some 20% of all living things in danger of extinction over the next 20 years.[1] The earth may have as many as 10 million species, and if, as the more pessimistic ecologists predict, 20% are lost by the year 2000, 2 million species could become extinct.[1] Most of these species are plants, which may number some 8 million, with insects and other invertebrates numbering several million, of which only a small percentage have been described scientifically.

The areas of the world most under threat at the present are tropical forests and coral reefs, which together harbor the largest diversity of plant and animal species on earth. Species diversity increases in tropical latitudes. While some 700 bird species breed in the United States and Canada, the figure for Mexico alone is about 1,000, and for the rest of Central and South America, at least 2,780.[1] Similarly, Canada has 22 species of snakes, the United States 126, and Mexico 293.[1] The Great Lakes of North America contain 172 fish species in an area of 197,000 km², while Lake Tanganyika in Africa, with only 34,000 km², has 214 species of fish.[1] In a single square kilometer of Freetown, Liberia, around 300 species of butterfly have been recorded, more than in the whole of the eastern United States.[1] The

Amazon region of South America has the richest diversity of plant and animal species in the world, possibly totalling one million. Of these 1,800 are birds, more than one-fifth of all birds on earth, and 2,000 are fish, ten times as many as in all of Europe and eight times the number in the Mississippi River system.[1] With this in mind, the significance of accelerating (and alarming!) forest destruction in that region, with 100,000 square kilometers of forest removed each year for agriculture and livestock, becomes clear: literally thousands of species are being lost in the process.

Few species have been studied for their potential use in agriculture and medicine and the disappearance rate is so great that potential new crop plants or cures for diseases are lost before research can take place.

The very biological stability of the planet is tied to species diversity which is being undermined on a worldwide basis. We are, in effect, pulling out the rug from under ourselves by destroying our life support systems.

Drawing by Marcus Redditt

Sloths *are denizens of tropical Amazonia, vulnerable to extinction because they are very slow-moving, and because their forest habitats are being destroyed.*

Unlearned Lessons From the Past

Abuse of the Land

ISLAND OF NATURAL WONDERS

Imagine a huge island over one thousand miles long in a blue tropical ocean. Forests cover vast areas interspersed with swamps where giant crocodiles eight meters long wait quietly to prey on pygmy hippopotamuses, or chimpanzee-sized primates. Land tortoises, which dwarf even those surviving in the Aldabra and Galapagos islands today, lumber about the forest floor. In the trees and in dryer parts of the island live an astounding variety of primates—over 30 species of lemurs varying in size from the world's smallest primate, the mouse lemur (it could fit in a teacup), to a fierce-looking carnivorous lemur looking like a cross between a Koala and a cow, yet with long, sharp teeth.[1]

Giant white elephant birds—probably the heaviest birds ever to have lived on earth, plod along forest trails and through savannah grasses. There are seven species of these birds—the largest, *Aepyornis*, resembles an ostrich, but is far more massive in build, weighing some 1,000 pounds. It stands 10′ high, lays eggs 13″ long that weigh some 47 pounds. Over 200 other kinds of tropical birds known nowhere else fly in dark forests and wade in still marshes.

Primitive spiny mammals, tenrecs, resembling European hedgehogs, but closely related to no other mammals, scurry in forest underbrush; when frightened, they roll their quilled forehead over their eyes like a cap, leaving only a small pointed nose protruding. One type of tenrec lives in cold mountain streams, swimming with webbed feet and flattened tail.

One hundred and fifty kinds of frogs leap in green shadows, and 32 kinds of chameleons creep invisibly about; the largest, two feet long, can capture mice and birds, while another measures only an inch and a half long.[2]

Trees and other plants exist in a variety unparalleled, a botanical paradise. Relics of plants long extinct on mainland areas, unique desert trees, and orchids of every imaginable shape and color bloom throughout the island. Along the west coast, a deciduous forest stretches the length of the island, and penetrates most of the central highlands, while the eastern regions are covered in a dense, humid rainforest. In the extreme southern area a unique desert environment prevails, harboring *Didierea*, strange cacti-like plants which form long spiny, twisted shafts rising 30 feet into the air.

Such was the island of Madagascar in the year 400 A.D. prior to the arrival of the Malagasy people of Asia. That such a huge land mass went uninhabited by humans for so long is truly remarkable. *Had humans reached Madagascar earlier, it might not have evolved its amazingly diverse, yet vulnerable fauna.* The island probably separated from Africa about 100 million years ago—what fauna and flora inhabited this island-continent at that time can only be surmised. Some 180 million years ago it is thought that Africa and South America were united into a giant continent, which might explain the similarity of many plants, snakes related to boas, iguanid lizards and perhaps even the curious tenrec, whose nearest relative is the solenodon, a small insectivore now restricted to a few West Indian islands.[1] According to the continental drift theory Madagascar

Drawing by Marcus Redditt

Smallest of all primates, the diminutive **Mouse Lemur** *hides in tree holes during the day, and is only active at night.*

*Drawing by
Esta Belcher*

*Towering nearly ten feet and weighing over a thousand pounds, the **Elephant Bird** became extinct in Madagascar in the 17th century.*

moved slowly away from Africa over a period of some 30 million years, and became colonized by lemurs and other animals that may have floated across the channel when it was not as wide as it is today. Vegetation mats broken away from the African coast, or even tree trunks which had been uprooted farther inland and were swept down coursing rivers to the sea, could have served to convey them. Birds and insects arrived from Africa, Asia and the Pacific, and bats colonized the island as well. No large carnivore arrived, however. The largest mammal predators from Africa were civets, among them the primitive cat-like Fossa.

Flightlessness, fearlessness, gigantism, survival of relict species—all occurred in this evolutionary laboratory uninfluenced by man.[2] Nowhere else has evolution been allowed to run its course without man's intervention in such a large area, and for such a long period.

The Madagascar of today is still a remarkable place. Twenty-one lemur species still survive, along with the tenrecs, Fossa, and many native reptiles, amphibians, birds and plants. Gone forever, though, are all seven species of elephant birds, a pygmy hippopotamus, which was quite different from the species surviving in Africa today, the giant tortoise, a unique species of fish, ten species of lemurs—all but one larger than the living species—along with 90% of its forests, and 70% of all its vegetation.[3] Most of these extinctions occurred within several hundred years after the arrival of the Malagasy people from Indonesia in about 500 A.D.

All but the largest elephant bird species disappeared before Europeans discovered the island in the 17th century, probably from a combination of hunting, egg-collecting and forest burning. The fabulous elephant bird, which some think inspired the fable of the roc, a bird said to be able to lift an elephant into the sky, lingered on. Its size and talons protected it to some extent, but by the 17th century, it had become very rare and retreated to remote swamps. Sieur Etienne de Flacourt, a Frenchman sent to establish a colony on Madagascar, landed on the southeast coast in 1648, and was told of a huge, white bird which the people of the region were unable to capture, and which was found only in the "most deserted places."[4] He never saw the bird, nor did any European to our knowledge. The last of the elephant birds occupied an impenetrable swamp forest and only when the forest was burned by the Malagasy about 1649, was the great bird finally vanquished.[5] Its bones have been found throughout the island, and an expedition in 1967 even unearthed an unbroken egg, which, when x-rayed, revealed an embryo, somehow preserved over hundreds and perhaps thousands of years.[6]

The Prosimians

The 10 extinct lemur species were probably exterminated by man. Archaeologists have found their bones with earthenware jars. Axheads made from a now-extinct flightless bird had split their skulls.[1] Lemurs as tall as men must have startled the Malagasy immigrants and gave rise to legends still told among these highly superstitious people. Some lemurs were thought sacred, ancestors of man, and these managed to survive until the present.

The lemurs belong to a group known as "prosimians," fascinating because they represent a stage in early primate evolution, though later than other prosimians since they are beginning to be monkeys—sociable, with long, agile limbs, flexible toes and fingers—yet with foxlike faces, and long noses evidencing their acute sense of smell.[7] Lemurs, or prosimians similar to them, once lived on many continents. Today, they survive only on Madagascar and the nearby Comoro Islands. A few other lemur-relatives are found elsewhere—the big-eyed bushbaby of Africa, the long-fingered tarsier, and Slow Loris of Asia. Most probably, early lemurs of large continental areas could not compete with the more aggressive monkeys and apes which displaced them, and perhaps even preyed on them.

Of the 21 remaining lemur species, 12 are listed by the *Red Data Book* in various status categories, five as endangered. Subspecies of two other lemurs are also listed—some 60% of all lemurs are threatened with extinction. Forest destruction continues to take 40 to 50 square miles per year as the food demands of the eight million people use up more and more of the remaining forest. The agriculture system is based on slash and burn, or cutting of all vegetation prior to burning and plowing. Each year one quarter of Madagascar burns.[1] Planting of rice and other crops and grazing for the island's 10 million zebu cattle deplete the thin tropical soil. In a few years after the forests are cut, the land becomes barren and hard, and large sections of it wash away with the rains. Much of central Madagascar now resembles a moonscape, with some of the most severe erosion found anywhere in the world. The dry deciduous forests were first to disappear, because these are less likely to regenerate than the wetter eastern forests. When the forest in one area is gone, and the cleared land no longer productive, more forest is cut. Whittling away of the forest in this fashion has been going on for centuries, but the rise in human population from about one million in the early part of the century to its present eight million has brought about an acceleration of the process.[7] Even with increased agricultural development, the government must still import rice to feed its people.[7]

The Indri

The largest lemur is the Indri, nearly tailless, heavy, but graceful, in panda-like black and white fur; it survives in a few reserves on the east coast. Once very common in the eastern forests near the capital, visitors remarked that it was impossible to travel far without hearing their eerie calls ringing out; they have disappeared from the capital region along with the forests. One naturalist, Faith McNulty, set out to look for the Indri with her Malagasy guide, Emmanuel Folo, an ardent lemur conservationist. Her island tour was sponsored by Defenders of Wildlife. She was lucky enough to see one hugging a tree and staring curiously at her for several minutes until it became bored and bounded away; she and her guide heard their beautiful dawn song:

"The sound came first from the top of our hill and was answered from another. It was a chorus of high voices, not shrill, but silvery, that rose and fell through a series of liquid notes. It was closer to the human voice than any sound I have ever heard from an animal, but at the same time it was inhumanly high and thin . . . Millions of years ago indri had greeted the dawn of a young world with a song like this. Now to my ears, the beauty of the sound had a touch of tristesse suitable to the setting of their sun."[7]

The Indri is one of the few lemurs whose killing is considered taboo by the Malagasy, but the old taboos are breaking down, and now, like all lemurs, it is killed with blowguns, snares, guns or even clubs. In some cases, religious leaders are encouraging such killing. One

Photo by Jonathan Pollack

Indri live in pairs, one male with one female. They usually cling to vertical trunks and reach out their long, hooked hands to pull in leafy branches for food. They live only in the eastern rainforest of Madagascar.

lemur scientist met a Catholic priest who killed several Indris, roasted them, and served them to his congregation.[7]

Indris have never survived in captivity long enough to breed. In the wild, Indri pairs have only one young every three years,[1] one of the slowest breeding rates of any animal. Other lemurs, likewise, fail to survive in captivity. Avahis and sifakas, other threatened species, usually die almost immediately upon capture. On one occasion, some Malagasy brought an endangered sifaka they had captured to lemur biologist, Dr. Alison Jolly, hoping for a reward. It was dragged half-choked by a vine around its neck, with one arm dangling loose below the elbow, a jagged bone protruding; blood oozed down its white fur, and it gasped for air through a muzzle smashed by a flung stone.[1] Dr. Jolly expressed horror at its condition and refused to pay them any reward. She then amazed them by telling them it was a unique sifaka, found only there in that small part of Madagascar. They were incredulous—not in Tananarive (the capital city)? not in France? not in America? they asked.[1] To the Malagasy, their lemurs are familiar animals, easy to capture and valuable as food. Malagasy schools teach only about European animals, therefore unfortunately many people have assumed that their lemurs are unimportant.

The Ayeaye

The strangest lemur of all is the Ayeaye, so unique that it is assigned to its own family. When first discovered, scientists classified it as a squirrel, and certainly its long bushy tail, and short-legged body might give one that idea. In 1863, after anatomical studies, the Ayeaye was revealed to be a lemur, in spite of incisor teeth that never stop growing, and other unlemur-like characteristics. A nocturnal animal, whose ears are sensitive enough to hear the movement of insects under tree bark, the Ayeaye uses its long spidery, clawed fingers to peel off bark, and reaches into holes with its extra-long middle finger.[7] It fills the ecological role of a woodpecker. While primarily insectivorous, Ayeayes eat fruit as well, and they can bite holes into coconuts and scrape the meat out with the middle finger.[8] Their cries, strange sounds like two metal sheets being rubbed together, are apparently territorial warnings to other Ayeayes which answer the calls. When approached by an observer or when a light is flashed in its huge, reflectant yellow eyes, an angry cry is emitted, sounding like "Ron-Tsit", repeated rapidly many times in succession.[8] Truly, there is no animal like the Ayeaye.

To many Malagasy, the Ayeaye is the embodiment of evil. When one is sighted, there is nothing to do but burn one's house down, kill the Ayeaye and move away.[1] If a witch doctor can obtain the long middle finger of the Ayeaye, the Malagasy believe it can be used to ward off the evil.[7] So persecuted that it disappeared from its eastern range, it was thought extinct until rediscovered by Dr. Jean Jacques Petter in 1957.[7] When surveyed in 1963, it was on the verge of extinction and Dr. Petter persuaded the World Wildlife Fund to aid in a survey, live capture and transfer to the island of Nossi Mangabé, an area of about five square kilometers, off the northeast coast.[7] Nine Ayeayes were trapped and released on the uninhabited island which was declared a refuge. No one surveyed the population for a decade, until a film crew from a wildlife program, on a search for the species in 1976, saw its leaf nests and some bright reflecting yellow eyes shining back at them. (This was shown on the "World of Sur-

*The strange **Ayeaye**, a nocturnal lemur that feeds on insects and fruit, is so endangered that its population may number less than 20 animals.*

Photo by R.H. Martin

Ring-tailed Lemurs *are the most gregarious of all lemurs, traveling about in boisterous, friendly troops.*

vival" television program in 1977.) Later, foresters located five more of their leaf nests.

Dr. Ian Tattersall, an eminent primatologist, found an Ayeaye dead on the main island in 1974 with a wire pulled tight around its neck.[7] Even on Nossi Mangabé its future is not secure, because such a small reserve may not provide adequate habitat on a long term basis, and the islet is constantly buffeted by salt spray coating all the vegetation.[1]

Other endangered lemurs include two species of mouse lemur, the Mongoose Lemur, three of the four subspecies of Sportive Lemur, four subspecies of Black Lemur, two species of gentle lemur, two of the dwarf lemur, Verreaux's Sifaka, Perrier's Sifaka and the Western Woolly Avahi. Only a few, including the boisterous and sociable Ring-tailed Lemur are not listed by the *Red Data Book*. Because of the forest destruction, however, virtually all lemurs are endangered and may disappear eventually.

In some areas of Madagascar, notably on Nossi Bê, an island off the northwest coast, lemurs are fully protected by taboo. Here Black Lemurs, one of the most beautiful lemur species, are fed by the villagers and they have become tame and confiding. The gentle, curious stares of lemurs have left an indelible impression on many people, and their extinctions would be tragic, not just for biological reasons, but also because of their unique and delightful qualities.

Perhaps lemurs thought to be extinct still exist. An amazing story was recounted by a retired forester, who said that in 1932 or 1933 in the eastern forest he saw a creature even larger than the Indri, but tailless, with black and white fur, a far heavier build and a flat, black face like a gorilla. After staring at the forester for a few minutes, the creature leaped away using its hands for support. Even more recently, a man encountered by primatologist Alison Jolly in Madagascar a few years ago, recounted that he had been given a young lemur of a type he had never seen before. This lemur had very dark fur, walked on its hindlegs, one foot after the other, rather than hopping like the Sifaka, and had a flat face different from the pointed muzzles of living lemurs.[1] After only two months this lemur died, and its skeleton was buried in an unknown place.[1]

From Elephant Birds to Vangas

Until recently, the amazing lemurs overshadowed the remarkable birds of Madagascar. Apart from the spectacular extinct elephant birds, four entire families of birds are unique to the island. The most dramatic of these may be the vangas, which evolved into 12 forms, probably from a single ancestral species similar in their evolution to Darwin's finches or the Hawaiian honeycreepers. One vanga has a very long, down-curved bill used to probe insects in tree crevices. The smallest, the Red-tailed Vanga, uses its tiny bill to capture beetles, caterpillars and grasshoppers. The Sickle-billed Vanga lives on insects, but also preys on frogs, tree lizards and chameleons, with its hawklike bill.[9] Pollen's Vanga and Bernier's Vanga are both endangered.[10] Twenty native birds have been listed by the *Red Data Book,* some with unfamiliar names—mesites, monias, ground rollers, and newtonia. One species of endemic bird became extinct about 1930, the Madagascar Coucal, *Coua delalandei.* This cuckoo-like bird was restricted to a small islet off the east coast where it was trapped and hunted.[3] The last one was reported shortly before 1930, and despite large sums of money offered to local hunters, no additional specimens were found.[3] Hunting was probably the major

Drawing from the Doomsday Book of Animals

The **Madagascar Coucal** became extinct about 1930. It was the largest of the 10 endemic coucal species.

The Patterned Tortoises

cause of extinction, but forest destruction also contributed. It was the largest, some 22 inches long, of the 10 endemic coucal species.

Two other birds are probably also extinct, not having been seen since about 1930—the Madagascar Serpent Eagle, and the Fanovana Newtonia. One of the foremost experts on eagles, zoologist Leslie Brown, considered the Serpent Eagle one of the four most endangered birds of prey in the world (along with the California condor, Philippine (monkey-eating) Eagle and the Mauritius Kestrel.)[11] This eagle was once found in the humid eastern forests, most of which have been cleared, and recent searches have been fruitless. Only one specimen of the flycatcher, Fanovana Newtonia, exists. Discovered in 1931 in Fanovana forest in eastern Madagascar, it has not been seen since.[10]

Another endemic eagle, the Madagascar Sea Eagle, is on the verge of extinction, numbering only a few pairs. It was common until the end of the 19th century near coastal regions and inland lakes and rivers. Human persecution in the form of shooting has been the sole reason for its precipitous decline.[10] By 1978, only one breeding pair was known.[10] Should it disappear, it will follow the pattern of extinction in Madagascar—the largest animals have all become extinct.

Shooting has been a major factor in the decline of other Madagascar birds as well. The Madagascar Crested Ibis, a colorful and unusual endemic with a heavy, pheasant-brown body, long iridescent green crest, down-curved beak and short red legs, has also declined greatly from shooting. It has the unique distinction of being the only bird in Madagascar that has received official government "protection." This protection, however, consists of a regulation that a small fee must be paid in order to hunt or capture it; in practice this rainforest and savanna ibis has been avidly hunted.[10]

The Madagascar Teal has been reduced to less than 100 birds and perhaps less than 60. When a group of 60 birds was found on Lake Masama in western Madagascar in 1970, and written about in an ornithological journal in Europe, a group of European "sportsmen" went to the lake and killed more than 25% of the population.[3] In 1973, another group of these teal was seen on Lake Bemamba; this may be the last remaining population, if it has not already been eliminated, since a recently opened airstrip nearby on the west coast provides access for hunters to the once remote area.[10] Other endemic waterbirds are threatened: the Madagascar Pochard,[10] Meller's Duck,[13] the Malagasy Pond Heron,[12] and the Malagasy Heron,[12] although only the pochard is listed by the *Red Data Book*. Unregulated hunting by foreign sportsmen and natives, and reduction or elimination of wetland habitats by lowered water tables combine to destroy these birds.

The arid regions at the northern and southern ends of the islands are home to two large and dramatically patterned tortoises, both endangered. In the north, the Madagascar Tortoise varies in color from tan with narrow black lines delineating delicate hexagonal patterns to specimens with patterns richly outlined in black. Reduced by early trade when it was shipped by the thousands to the nearby Comoro Islands to use as meat for settlers from the 17th century onward, it is now on the edge of extinction.[14] Its population, lowered by the trade that ended in the 19th century, never recovered its numbers due partly to the continued take by villagers for pets, and to the massive destruction of its habitat. Several captive breeding centers, begun as early as 1971, have so far failed to produce young tortoises, but recent success with the Radiated Tortoise, the southern species, gives some hope that the species may be aided by captive breeding.[14] But the wild population appears to be doomed since its habitat is continuing to deteriorate, and collection for pets continues.[14]

The related but geographically widely separated species is the beautiful Radiated Tortoise which inhabits the dry lands of the extreme south where the strange *Didierea* plants twist into the sky. This tortoise has similar, but more lacy striated black patterns on its yellowish shell, and unlike the northern tortoise, it has diamond patterns on the underside of the shell.

The Radiated Tortoise was also killed by the thousands for food; weighing from 20 to 30 pounds each, they were shipped to the Comoro Islands and elsewhere until about 1930. In 1922 alone, 22,000 of these tortoises were exported.[1] Recently, its major threat comes from the pet trade which has collected thousands more for international sale. It is popular because of the striking shell patterns. It has a far larger range than the Madagascar tortoise, and its population is not as critically depleted as that of the latter species. There are hopeful signs that the Malagasy government may protect the Radiated Tortoise stringently. Export and collection are prohibited on Madagascar, and recently a forester caught a man with 40 tortoises for sale, and put him in prison.[1] The tortoises were individually tagged for future identification and released. The U.S. prohibits commercial importation of Radiated Tortoises as do several European countries. In fact, a New York man was arrested in 1977 attempting to smuggle 33 Radiated Tortoises through JFK airport in New York City. He was fined $1000. The Spider Tortoise and The Tree Boa are also considered rare by the *Red Data Book* and the Convention on International Trade in Endangered Species of Wild Fauna and Flora (CITES).

Photo by R.H. Martin

Radiated Tortoises *have become endangered as a result of killing for their meat and collection for the pet trade.*

Madagascar's Periwinkles and Other Flora

Drawing by New York Botanical Garden Library

*The **Madagascar Periwinkle** has exceptional medicinal value in treating various types of leukemia.*

For the island's plant and invertebrate species, no comprehensive endangered species list has been drawn up, nor for its fish and amphibians. Only one plant, the Leathery Periwinkle, has been listed by the *Red Data Book of Plants*. Should an inclusive list be drawn up of the plants and invertebrates which are endangered, it would undoubtedly be very extensive.

The interdependence of the plants and animals on Madagascar is highlighted by the extraordinary story of lemurs pollinating many endemic plants. Six species of lemurs, and perhaps others, feed on the nectar of various plants, and serve as the major pollinators of these plants.[16] Madagascar's bats are not flower-pollinators, and lemurs have filled this role. It is thought, in fact, that one of the contributing factors to the decline of nocturnal primates in the past has been the evolution of bats which became more efficient at obtaining nectar.[16] Many of Madagascar's flowering plants produce unusually large flowers with strong odor, and copious nectar. Lemurs are attracted to feed on them.[16] Insect pollinators service many of the world's plants, and flowers, but it is now known that some mammals play a significant role in pollination. This ecological interdependence may date back to Paleogene times.[16]

Among the hundreds of endemic plant species is a flowering plant which has proved to be a true medical treasure. Some 20 years ago, it was discovered that the Madagascar Rosy Periwinkle, a cousin to the endangered Leathery Periwinkle, can be used as a very effective treatment for blood cancers, primarily childhood leukemia.[1] Long esteemed as folk medicine for a variety of ills, this periwinkle was found to stop cancer cells dividing; now it is processed to separate vincristine sulfate compound from the other constituents for worldwide medical use.[1] The family of Dr. Paul Ehrlich, author of *Extinction*,[26] endured a personal tragedy that would probably have been prevented had the medical properties of the Rosy Periwinkle been discovered a few years earlier. Dr. Ehrlich's father died of Hodgkin's Disease in 1955 after 13 years of suffering.[26] This disease is a leukemia-like disorder of the lymphatic system. Two chemicals derived from the Rosy Periwinkle have proved effective in treating it, saving thousands of lives. Fortunately the Rosy Periwinkle grows easily in greenhouses and other climates, and has become established in other parts of the world.[1]

NATURE'S RETREAT

Madagascar's story is one of ecological collapse and gradual extermination of its life forms. Is it relevant to the endangered species problem elsewhere in the world? One's first response might be that its experience is as far from the rest of the world as it is geographically remote. However, the extreme extent of destruction of nature seen on Madagascar is mirrored in many parts of the world. And it is from the extremes that the underlying trends become clear. Often ecological and faunal changes are gradual, so gradual that they go almost unnoticed until it is too late.

We are in the beginning stages of assessing the enormity of the destruction of the natural world and its effects on the world's wildlife. Some 1,000 vertebrate species are listed in the IUCN's *Red Data Books*. Surveys to determine status of wild animals have taken place for only a small percentage of vertebrates. Mammals and birds have been the focus of most such research for several decades, and yet we still can see only the tip of the iceberg. For example, the damage being done to the rainforests of Amazonia, Africa and Southeast Asia has not been fully assessed. Even in the U.S., status surveys of *all* vertebrates have not been carried out.

Two research projects published in the past two years show the current state of knowledge about the extent of environmental deterioration on a global scale and its effects—potential and realized—on wildlife. The IUCN, in cooperation with its affiliate, The World Wildlife Fund, and the United Nations Environment Programme (UNEP), recently conducted an ambitious study to assess the status of the world's environment. After years of consulting scientists, governments, agencies, educators, and conservationists, it produced *World Conservation Strategy,*[17] and a book based on it in layman's terms, *How to Save the World.*[18] The Council on Environmental Quality of the United States government published the other major report— *Global 2000*[19]—an assessment of the state of the environment and projections of what the condition of the earth's air, water, soil, forests, wildlife and human population numbers will be in the year 2000. The latter report emphasizes human needs and the former nature's. If taken together, they provide, at least in part, the major environmental problems and suggested solutions. Both are unqualified in their conclusion that we are faced with extremely critical and in some cases urgent situations in need of immediate action. Some of their conclusions and findings on habitat destruction are startling.

Human Population

In 1650, when Dodos were still common on the island of Mauritius, the world's humans totalled about 500,000,000, much less than India's present population. Two hundred years later in 1850, the number had doubled to a billion. Since then it has taken shorter periods for the human population to double; at present the doubling time is every 37 years! The similarity between the astronomic rise in human population and the extinction rate is not accidental.

Human population increases are the number one social, economic, health and environmental problem facing the world, according to Larry Gordon, President of the American Public Health Association. They are the underlying causes for the extinction of many plant and animal species, and Gordon notes along with many ecologists, that continued destruction of plant and animal species may distort the future course of evolution and genetic diversity on the planet.

Expanding populations make enormous demands on the environment. The present population of over four billion people has so crowded the planet that nature is being obliterated and millions of people die yearly of starvation. Much of the intensive forest cutting over the past decades has been to clear land for agriculture to feed the growing number of humans. The highest rates of population growth are in tropical regions of Asia, Latin America and Africa, where environmental deterioration has been most severe.

Rivers are becoming increasingly polluted from human waste since in many parts of the world sewage treatment systems have not been constructed. Starving people, hunting animals and gathering plants for subsistence, cutting trees for fuel and establishing settlements in wilderness areas are causing a further retreat of nature. Desertification is increasing.

By the turn of the century the *Global 2000 Report* estimates there will be almost six billion people on earth. Over the next 900 years, if

World Population Growth, 500 B.C.–A.D. 2000

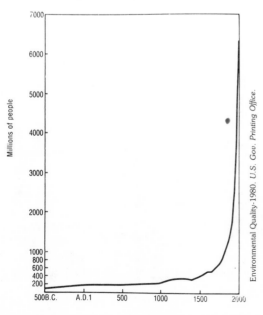

Millions of people

Environmental Quality-1980. U.S. Gov. Printing Office.

growth continues at this rate there will be 60 billion people, or 100 persons per square yard on earth's surface, land and sea, according to Dr. Paul Ehrlich's book *The Population Bomb*. Nature on our fragile planet could not tolerate a human population even a fraction that size as we are discovering.

Forests

Photo by Andrew Young

The world's rainforests will disappear altogether in 85 years if the present rate of 43,000 square miles destroyed per year (or 50 acres per minute) continues.[18] Most of the world's species reside in rainforests, with lowland forests containing the largest diversity. These lowland areas are being destroyed at an even greater rate. The diversity of the rainforests of Amazonia is distributed in patches. Millions of years ago, a lake covered most of the region and as it dried up, it left small, isolated pockets of plant and animal life. Species evolved in these patches almost as if they were on islands. This pattern produced the thousands of unique plants and animals which are often restricted to tiny forest tracts. This explains why forest destruction can be devastating even when on a small scale. A tropical bird species may occur in only a few square miles of rain forest and nowhere else. Up to 20% of Brazil's rainforest has already been destroyed. Agricultural development has not been successful because of the thin, poor soil in most of Amazonia, but commercial forest cutting and mining are expected to increase. Scientists are racing to save patches of the forest, and catalog some of the myriad wildlife and plant species before they are lost forever. In Southeast Asia much of the damage has already been done. Over 66 million acres of Indonesia are officially classified as denuded by uncontrolled cutting, and over the next 20 years, demand for hardwood is expected to triple.[18] Much of the forest clearing is carried out to establish cattle ranches, and these have required heavy applications of herbicides to keep scrub from becoming established. The ancient rainforest does not return, however. Some of the tropical rainforests are many millions of years old. Forests in Borneo have the same kind of trees growing today as in the late Pliocene period.[18] The forests of southeast Asia contain over 25,000 species of plants, 49% of which are

Photo by Douglas R. Shane, World Wildlife Fund

*Fifty acres of **tropical forest** are destroyed every minute, year round, threatening thousands of species.*

*The amazing bower of the **Yellow-fronted Bowerbird** has piles of yellow, blue and green fruit on a moss platform surrounding a stick tower—all constructed by the male to lure the female.*

*The habitat in southeastern Brazil of the beautiful little **Golden-Lion Marmoset** has been almost totally destroyed.*

found nowhere else, and of the 660 bird species of the Malay peninsula, 444 are restricted to the rainforest.[18] The IUCN found that for the most part, these forests are being destroyed in such a way as to prevent their regeneration: "if tropical rainforests are exploited with scant regard for their characteristics, as generally they are, they cannot renew themselves."[18] The forests of Malaysia, Indonesia, the Philippines and New Guinea are among the most species-rich in plants in the world, but those of the Philippines and Malaysia are expected to have vanished completely within a decade.[18]

The remarkable birds of paradise and bowerbirds of New Guinea and northern Australia were depleted in the past by hunting for their spectacular plumes. They are all protected at present, although some illegal killing still occurs. Their major threat lies in the destruction of their tropical rainforest homes, which are being cut in many areas and replanted with fast-growing eucalyptus or pine, trees not compatible with the habitat needs of these species. One very rare bowerbird, searched for in the wild on a dozen occasions, was finally found in the remote Foja Mountains of western New Guinea in 1979 and 1981. This beautiful bird, the Yellow-fronted Gardener Bowerbird, numbers a few thousand or less, and its elaborate mating ritual was observed by its discoverer, Dr. Jared M. Diamond of the University of California. The male bowerbird of this species arranges sticks in a pile around a tree fern or sapling, forming a tower up to 3½ feet high on a circular moss platform with a raised rim. It clears the adjacent area of debris, and places separate piles of blue, green and yellow fruit to attract the female. (The blue fruit came from a previously unknown plant.) Making varied, loud calls even while holding a blue fruit in its beak, which contrasts boldly wth its brilliant yellow head and back feathers, the Yellow-fronted Bowerbird perches near its elaborate bower performing for the drabber female. The constructions of bowerbirds are so elaborate that when explorers first encountered them they were assumed to be manmade. Each species has variations on the construction, some building bowers with pass-through tunnels, others concentrating on accumulating a vast array of objects—usually all of one color—to attract females. The birds of paradise are cloaked in dazzling feathers with tails that are often many feet long. They produce a large number of strange calls and display their feathers in dramatic courtship dances. These latter birds are listed on Appendix II of CITES, but the bowerbirds have no international protection. The fascinating new-found Yellow-fronted Gardener Bowerbird deserves Appendix I status on CITES and inclusion on the U.S. Endangered Species list. The loss of these remarkable birds would be a major one, should their primeval forests be destroyed.

The overall future of forests worldwide is hardly more hopeful. Only 22 years ago, forests covered over one fourth of the world's land surface.[19] Today, they cover one-fifth, and in 22 years, *Global 2000* predicts they will be reduced to one-sixth of the land area.[19] Much of the destruction is carried on by one-half the world's peoples who are under pressure to stave off hunger and find fuel are cutting forests for firewood and forcing their livestock to overgraze.[18] India has 678 million people occupying a land mass one-third the size of the United States. To meet their fuel demands, the forests are cut in ever-widening swaths. In Nepal, most of the original forests of moist hill pines and oak-rhododendron have been stripped, and every ridge in the middle Himalayas is being intensively farmed.[20]

Photo by R. Mittermeier

Photo by A.F. Coimbra-Filho

Photo by A. Young

*Forest destruction threatens primates of southeastern Brazil. At top, the **Muriqui** or **Woolly Spider Monkey,** most endangered South American primate, whose total known population is only 100. The **Brown Howler Monkey,** above left, whose booming voice carries for miles, may soon be silenced by extinction in the wild. Above right, the tiny **Buff-headed Marmoset** has disappeared from most of its former range.*

Forest wildlife in Asia, Africa and, most recently, Latin America, has declined as the forests dwindled. Almost all native deer in Asia are now threatened, as are many primates, all the large and most of the small cats, and many of the continent's beautiful pheasant species.

In 1978, the IUCN calculated that there were about 90 vertebrate species threatened with extinction that were dependent on forest habitats.[21] Most (68 species) were found in tropical rainforests.[21] Further research has revealed an additional 48 species and subspecies of birds in South America threatened by forest destruction.

In Southern Brazil, only 2% of the original coastal forest remains, most of it in degraded form, adding up to an area only half the size of Yellowstone National Park. In these remnant tracts survive the last wild Golden Lion Marmosets and four other species of these tiny and beautiful primates, along with other endangered monkeys: the Masked Titi, Brown Howler Monkey and Woolly Spider Monkey. The IUCN Primate Specialist Group, funded by the World Wildlife Fund, has begun an emergency program to save these animals. Research on status is nearly complete and efforts will be made to rescue these marmosets and monkeys in the small forest patches that are slated for destruction, and relocate them in protected areas or place them in captive breeding programs. In the same region of southeast Brazil, no less than 36 bird species, almost all endemic to the area, are threatened with extinction.[10] Among these birds are parrots, four kinds of colorful hummingbirds, woodpeckers, antwrens, cotingas, a hawk, an eagle, a tiger-heron and a merganser. One hummingbird, the Klabin Farm Long-tailed Hermit, was only recently discovered on a 4,000 hectare tract of privately owned forest in Espirito Santo.[10] The survival of this bird and others will depend on whether reserves, some of which have already been established, will be sufficiently large for their needs. Two birds of the area have already disappeared, and it is difficult to be optimistic that in the long term the rest will survive. Such is the result of destruction of the precious tropical forests.

Drylands

The savannas and scrub woodlands of Africa and other dryland areas are turning to desert at a fairly fast rate, mainly as a result of livestock overgrazing and wood-gathering. As satellites spin around the earth, they photograph the changes in the earth's surface, even those on a relatively small scale. From satellite data we know that in recent years, between 23,000 and 27,000 square miles per year have become desert.[18,22] Much of this area is in the Sahel region of Africa. Drylands are particularly susceptible to livestock grazing. Much of the Near East and the Sahara region was once grassland, and slowly turned to desert as it was degraded by livestock and human overpopulation.[22] The Negev Desert supported as many as 3 million people in classical times. This population was reduced to 300,000 by the 1800's, and today the land is an almost uninhabited rocky desert.[22]

The Sahel region southwest of the Sahara is now the scene of such desertification. In Upper Volta, Chief Issoufi Alimonzo remembers, "There were once elephants and giraffes and lions here. The father of my father saw them. When his forefathers came to this place 300 years ago, there were so many trees you couldn't see the lake."[22] Today, the region is bare of the trees once harvested to sell as fuel in the cities of the region, and surrounding countries of the Sahel are experiencing similar devegetation. Large mammals have disappeared from North Africa as a whole, and many dryland gazelles and antelope are on the verge of extinction. The Rio de Oro Dama Gazelle of Spanish Sahara, the majestic Scimitar-horned Oryx, Addax, Dibatag and several other gazelle species of the Sudan region are all endangered from desertification and, in some areas, from unregulated hunting.[10]

In Israel, conservationists are attempting to reintroduce species long extinct there, and are replanting the desert. They have released Nubian Ibexes, Arabian Oryx, Addax, Somali Asses, Ostriches, and after a dangerous expedition to Iran, a few Mesopotamian Fallow Deer were smuggled out of that country with aid from the Prince Abdor Riza. Introductions of Oryx have also taken place in Oman and Jordan.

Wetlands and Aquatic Ecosystems

Wetlands are also being destroyed at an unprecedented rate. The statistics on losses are not as complete as for forest destruction, however. The freshwater wetlands in most European countries and North America have been filled in gradually for centuries, usually under the assumption, often erroneous, that the land would make prime farmland. The benefits of wetlands in preventing floods by retaining runoff water for slow release during the year have only recently been learned—too late for about 50% of wetlands in the United States. In spite of recent victories such as the establishment of the Coto Doñana reserve in Spain which shelters a vast and beautiful array of waterbirds, otters, and other wetland animals, only about 5% of Europe's major wetlands (both coastal and freshwater) have any protection.[18] The Hermit Ibis is now extinct in Europe as a result of marsh drainage, and the Dalmatian Pelican is endangered by this destruction.

Two of the largest remaining freshwater marshes in the world, both in Africa—the Sudd swamp of Sudan and the Okavango swamp in Botswana—are threatened with development. A massive canal cutting through the Sudd linking the White Nile with the Nile is nearly complete. It will drain a large portion of the 7,500 square-mile wetland, and ecological consequences such as disruption of the water table, decreased rainfall in the region, and a decline in many aquatic species are predicted. In addition, the canal will act as a barrier to the migration of several antelope species—Tiang, Reedbuck, Mongalla Gazelle, and Nile Lechwe—a further reduction in the amazing variety of African gazelles and antelopes.

The majority of birds endangered by marsh drainage are those dependent on freshwater ecosystems. Some 31 species and subspecies of birds listed by the *Red Data Book* have declined as a result of freshwater marsh drainage.[10] Those species that use freshwater marshes as a prime habitat, such as rails, rather than for occasional feeding are doubly vulnerable. Thirteen species and subspecies of rails are listed as endangered by the *Red Data Book*.[10] Other freshwater birds in decline are many species of storks, ibises, cranes, and numerous ducks, mergansers and grebes. Numerous amphibians and reptiles are dependent on freshwater wetlands and ponds, and their filling and pollution threaten them.[10]

Coastal wetlands in estuaries are usually filled when cities are built near these fertile marshlands. These are prime locations for ports since they are situated at the mouths of rivers, useful for transportation. The National Estuary Study done in 1970 by the U.S. Fish and

Photo by the New York Zoological Society

*A massive canal through the Sudd swamp in the Sudan threatens the migration of the **Reedbuck**.*

Photo by John Domont

Bald Eagles *are being introduced along the coast of Georgia where the marshes have been preserved by conservationists.*

Wildlife Service calculated that 23% of the nation's estuaries are severely degraded and another 50% are moderately degraded. The eastern port cities of Boston, New York and Philadelphia filled the majority of the estuarine marshes surrounding them in the 19th century. It is over the past 20 years, however, that a progressive loss of 500,000 acres has occurred along American coasts, a result of dredging and filling for industry and housing. Every year, 165,000 acres of estuary in the Gulf of Mexico are destroyed; this constitutes almost 3% of the region's entire coastal area.[18]

The world's fisheries have already been harmed by filling of these salt marshes that serve as nurseries for shrimp, crabs and about two-thirds of all saltwater fishes caught commercially. The beautiful coastal marshes of Georgia were under threat in the late 1960's when it was discovered that large deposits of phosphate, which could be mined for fertilizer, lay under them. Dr. Eugene Odum, professor of ecology at the University of Georgia, and author of the first major text on that subject,[23] was able to prove to legislators that the long-term gain from these marshes as nurseries for commercial and sport fisheries far exceeded the short-term profits that would accrue from permanently destroying them by mining. His research has also shown that coastal marshes are among the most productive of all ecosystems in terms of species diversity and biotic richness. The endangered Bald Eagle has recently been reintroduced along Georgia's coasts to take its place again in this remarkable habitat.

Elsewhere in the world, coastal marshes are destroyed with impunity. In Sri Lanka, the productive mangroves along estuaries are cut for firewood exposing the underlying mud and leaves to direct sunlight.[18] This destroys shrimp and crab habitat and means a loss both of wildlife and potential food for a hungry world.[18] This same phenomenon is occurring in India where 16,000 square kilometers of coastal mangrove, an area larger than the state of Connecticut, have disappeared since the turn of the century. Marine invertebrates, fish, crocodiles, otters, turtles, dugongs and waterbirds have all suffered from the mangrove loss.

Herbicides were dumped on an estimated 124,000 hectares of mangrove in South Vietnam during the Vietnam War, and these areas have remained for the most part devegetated.[24]

Industrial pollution has been the major culprit in destroying the once vast and productive marshes of the Wadden Sea in northern Europe. Direct mortality has been high to Sandwich Terns and eider ducks caused by heavy industrial pollution emanating from the Rhine River.

Some progress has been made in protecting wetlands with the ratification of the Ramsar Convention,* now with 32 member countries. Under this convention, wetland sites of special merit, usually one or two per country, are listed in inventories. Unfortunately, protection of the areas is not mandated under the Ramsar Convention, but some 216 sites are now listed totalling an area equivalent to Belgium and Holland combined, and protection has been accorded some of these wetlands.[25]

Coastal wetlands and navigable waters in the United States are regulated by the U.S. Army Corps of Engineers which issues permits for dredging and filling.

*See International Legislation.

Dams

A majority of U.S. rivers south of Alaska have been dammed and/or polluted over the past 100 years. The water pollution of heavy industry has been reduced from the past as a result of water pollution control. Some of the Great Lakes, thought to be dying a decade ago, have improved in water quality although much remains to be done. Acid rain, pesticides, dioxin, PCBs, and other pollutants are entering water systems worldwide causing fish mortality, interfering with reproduction in birds and other wildlife. They may be even more dangerous than previously known pollutants (see section on Unintended Victims).

When a dam is built, resident wildlife in the flooded area usually fails to survive. Dams impede the passage of spawning fish, and turn fast-flowing rivers into placid lakes, habitats to which many fish species cannot adjust.

Darters are the most colorful American freshwater fish, exhibiting a rainbow of hues—brilliant blues, oranges, yellows, greens, and browns, often iridescent. They sport names evoking their color or origin: Amber, Freckled, Bluestripe, Yazbo, Slackwater, Watercress, Okaloosa and Maryland are some of the endangered darters. Scores of species of these little fish, usually less than three inches long, are listed by various states of the Southeast and Midwest and by the federal Endangered Species Act as endangered. They are fish of clear, fast-flowing rivers and streams. The dam and channelization projects of the Tennessee Valley Authority (TVA) utility, the Army Corps of Engineers, the Bureau of Reclamation and various state agencies have ruined their habitats in a growing number of rivers and streams.

The most famous is the three-inch Snail Darter (*Percina tanasi*), object of such heated debate that it precipitated changes weakening the Endangered Species Act. The species was discovered on the Little Tennessee River in 1973 above the Tellico Dam site after construction of this major dam by the TVA had begun. The dam would destroy the fast waters the fish required to survive, yet construction continued after the TVA reversed preliminary injunctions, brought by conservationists and irate Tennessee residents being evicted from their land, to delay the dam. By the time the Snail Darter was scientifically described, proposed and listed under the Endangered Species Act, the dam was nearly complete. There is evidence that construction was speeded up when word of the fishes' discovery became known, in order to prevent conservationists from halting the dam, the rationale being that when costs had passed a certain level, it would be considered uneconomic to stop construction. Once the little fish was listed as endangered, a prolonged two-year court battle began when the Environmental Defense Fund and other groups sued the TVA under Section 7 of the Act which prohibits federal agencies from activities which would harm endangered species. Lower court rulings prohibited closing the dam, but in 1978, the Supreme Court ruled that the dam be closed in order to protect the Snail Darter. Conservationists pointed out that besides the threat to the Snail Darter, this dam had major drawbacks—it inundated lands sacred to the Cherokee Indians, displaced hundreds of residents, and submerged much farmland. Its recreational and electrical generating benefits would not be cost efficient. The dam builders have many friends in Congress, however, and they rushed to the defense of the Tellico Dam as soon as the Supreme Court decision was handed down. By the end of 1978, amendments to the En-

Drawing by Esta Belcher

*The tiny **Snail Darter**, threatened by the building of a dam in Tennessee, caused a major controversy resulting in weakening of the Endangered Species Act.*

dangered Species Act had been passed requiring that all future proposed species be accompanied by critical habitat requirements. This meant that in order to list a native species, its precise habitat with geographical limits defined had to accompany proposals for listing. Under the critical habitat rules, few of the species previously listed would be able to meet these criteria since the exact locations of all individuals are not usually known with certainty. In the case of migratory species, territories can cover thousands of square miles.

Also, an economic impact study was mandated and public hearings were to be held prior to final listings—all within two years of the original proposal. Moreover, an Endangered Species Committee composed of government officials was created which was empowered to make exemptions allowing a species to become extinct if the costs, real and to society, were deemed too great to permit its preservation. Nicknamed the "God Committee", its first action was to rule on the Snail Darter's possible exemption from provisions of the Endangered Species Act. To the dismay and outrage of those who expected a different decision, it ruled in favor of the Snail Darter. At this point, an amendment to a water projects bill was pushed through Congress unread by the few members in attendance, which specifically exempted the Tellico Dam from provisions of the Endangered Species Act as well as all other environmental laws.

The Snail Darter survives because it was transplanted into other parts of the Little Tennessee River and a few of its tributaries. It was also found in a new site on the South Chickamauga Creek in Tennessee in 1980 by Dr. David Etnier of the University of Tennessee, who had originally discovered the species. Since then, a few other populations have been found in the Tennessee River and the Sequatchie River. These discoveries showing the Snail Darter to be more widespread than originally thought are optimistic signs for its survival. They demonstrate also that knowledge of the fish fauna of these areas, and probably of many other areas, is fragmentary. Surveys have often been done by dedicated biologists on their own time, rather than by the TVA.

In addition, the Snail Darter story serves as a warning that political and industrial interests which do not appreciate the importance of saving species can, without the support of the American people, legalize extinctions.

A 1980 survey indicated that a majority of Americans favored protecting wildlife, whether endangered species or not, even at the cost of forgoing additional jobs, housing, or other developmental projects.[26]

Almost ignored in the controversy is the fascinating ecology of the Snail Darter. In their natural state, the fast clear rivers of the southeast had beds of mussels (clams), spaced at intervals along the river bed which aided in cleansing the water by straining it through their gills. These mussel beds serve as submerged islands in the river bottoms, supporting numerous types of life. Fish congregate around the beds and many species of mussels depend, in turn, on the fish to complete their life cycle: embryonic mussels parasitize specific fish by attaching to their outside surface by which they are transported to new areas where they detach and colonize stream beds.[27] In turn, the fish are fed upon by larger fish, otters, mink, and fish-eating birds. The shoals or mussel beds attract snails also, which feed on the detritus and algae, another cleansing system. The Snail Darter eats some of these snails and embryonic mussels may parasitize it as well.

These mussels, some as large as dinner plates, were once abundant in the Ohio, Tennessee, Cumberland, Alabama, and Cahaba Rivers; over 1,000 species, evolved over millions of years, once occurred here.[27] The richest of all known beds, Mussel Shoals, occurred in Alabama on the Tennessee River, where some 70 species were found. The Wilson Dam, completed in 1924, completely submerged Mussel Shoals, and later covered it with 15-20 feet of muck, causing the extinction of at least half the mussel species and five of the seven large river snails.[27] By 1967, there were 9 dams on the Tennessee River leaving only 22 miles of free-flowing water. The last undammed river in Tennessee, the Duck River, was dammed in 1975. It contained the greatest diversity of snail species left in the Tennessee-Ohio River system.[27]

To compound the damage, the dam builders usually channelize rivers downstream from dams, turning curves into straight lines, clearing streamsides, and worst of all, dredging the river bottoms and depositing all mollusks and crustaceans in lifeless piles along the banks. What is left is a sea of mud in a ditch devoid of life.

Malacologist Dr. George M. Davis concludes that these projects, combined with acid drainage from strip mining, erosion and pesticide run-off from agriculture, have caused the extinction or endangerment of 40-50% of all this mollusk fauna.[27]

When the Endangered Species Act listed seven species of endangered mollusks from these rivers, mainly the Duck River where the Columbia Dam was under construction, the TVA brought a law suit against the Department of Interior.[28] The suit was dismissed by the U.S. District Court which declared in 1978: "The urgency [of protecting endangered wildlife] is declared by Congress. This Court, the Secretary [of Interior], and others cannot add to or subtract from the procedures set out in the Endangered Species Act."[28]

Besides the biological impoverishment resulting from dam construction, many potential food sources for humans are lost—clams, crayfish, and fish, for example. The justifications for more dams are becoming feebler by the year, but federal subsidies for water projects (at present, 253 projects are in progress, with estimated budgets of $40 billion) are lobbied in Congress by representatives from the states in which construction jobs would be created, and they have been remarkably successful.

Dam construction is disrupting ecosystems worldwide. In Sri Lanka, elephant habitats and migration trails are being inundated, and in Brazil and Paraguay, giant dams have flooded hundreds of thousands of acres of tropical forest. In Zambia, dams are destroying the habitat of the Lechwe, a threatened semi-aquatic antelope. These statuesque animals feed on grasses in the flood plain of the Kafue River moving from one spot to another as flood waters recede.[29] The Lechwe social behavior is tied to the flood plain as well—males occupy and defend small territories on a breeding ground in the flats next to the river, where they confront each other with displays of tearing at the ground, head-high poses, and mock charges. Lambs are born in the high grasses surrounded by water which shield them for many days after birth.[30] The dams will turn this entire region for miles into a series of lakes, extirpating many fish and bird species, and jeopardizing the future of this graceful antelope.[30]

Many other habitats are disappearing worldwide at a rate which must be arrested to prevent future extinctions.

The **Lechwe** antelope is threatened by dam building.

Photo by Zoological Society of San Diego

Trade in Wild Animals

Trade in wildlife—both live animals and the grisly products made from them—is the second most important cause, after habitat destruction, pushing species toward extinction. The slaughter and capture are all the more tragic and appalling because almost all such activities are for the luxury trade or for products for which substitutes exist. Whale oil is no longer needed as an industrial lubricant, nor are furs needed for warmth. Here too are practiced the cruelest methods of killing and capture: steel jaw leghold traps and wire neck snares mangle and torture their victims to produce pelts for "fun furs"; harpoons cause great agony as they plunge into whales; frightened live animals are crowded into cramped, dirty cages and transported to pet shops and laboratories, suffering high mortality along the way. Man's inhumanity to animals reaches an extreme in the wild animal trade.

THE GREAT WHALES

Whales are revealing their intelligence and amazing communication abilities to scientists in one part of the world, while in another they are being ruthlessly slaughtered for pet food, lipstick and oil.

These remarkable mammals are the largest animals on earth, larger even than any of the dinosaurs.[1] Once they swam in enormous numbers in all oceans, communicating in complex sounds thought to carry over distances as great as between Antarctica and Alaska.[1] These beautiful and eerie "songs" can be high pitched

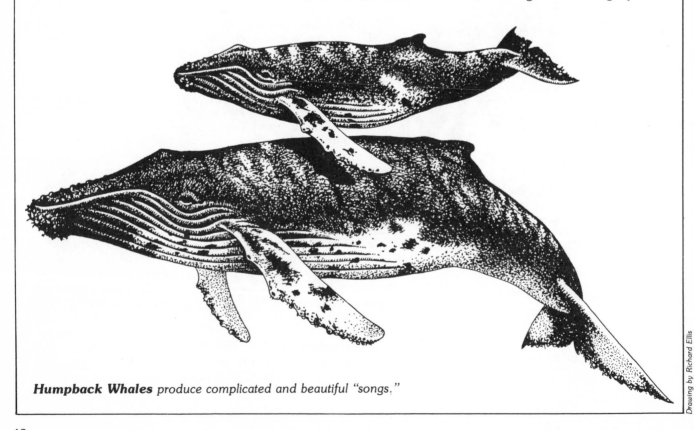

Humpback Whales *produce complicated and beautiful "songs."*

Drawing by Richard Ellis

pings, clicks or the long violin-like notes of the Humpback Whales. Whale biologists analyzing Humpback songs have found that they are as complicated in composition as Homer's *Iliad*.[1] We are just beginning to learn some of their meanings, but it is clear from preliminary studies of their apparent language that whale intelligence is great. Unfortunately, whales now may not be able to receive communications from other whales which are more distant than a few hundred kilometers; their communication is interfered with by the noise of ships' motors, sounds which must be as painful to whales' ears as the roar of trucks to humans'. In the words of Carl Sagan, "We have cut the whales off from themselves...But we have done worse than that, because there persists today a traffic in the dead bodies of whales. There are humans who hunt and slaughter whales and market the products for lipstick or industrial lubricant. Many nations understand that the systematic murder of such intelligent creatures is monstrous, but the traffic continues, promoted chiefly by Japan, Norway and the Soviet Union. We humans, as a species, are interested in communication with extraterrestrial intelligence. Would not a good beginning be improved communication with terrestrial intelligence, with other human beings of different cultures and languages, with the great apes, with the dolphins, but particularly with those intelligent masters of the deep, the great whales?"[1]

Slaughter to Commercial Extinction

The decimation of the great whales has been going on for centuries, one species after another hunted to commercial extinction, i.e. to levels so low that it is no longer profitable to hunt them. As early as the eighth century the Basques of northern Spain hunted the Atlantic Right Whale for meat and whalebone. It was so named by English whalers because it was "right" for their purposes, easy to kill, peaceful and slow-moving, feeding in shallow coastal water on plankton and krill, which it strained through its baleen plates. Also this whale yielded large quantities of oil and whalebone, and floated when dead.[2]

The Atlantic Right Whale was eliminated from its European coastal feeding areas by 1700, and whalers began pursuing it as far west as Newfoundland.[2] By 1800 it had become commercially extinct in European waters and the New England colonists likewise nearly eliminated the western Atlantic population by the end of the 18th century.[2] Killing of this beleaguered species continued from whaling stations off Ireland and the Hebrides which managed to catch between 10 and 18 a year in the early 1900's, until the whalers could find no more by about 1910. It is not surprising that after 700 years of persecution, this whale has not recovered its numbers, nor has it returned to its ancestral feeding grounds along the Bay of Biscay. This species remains the most endangered of all whales, especially in the eastern Atlantic where there have only been a few sightings since whaling stopped. Tragically, in 1967, a mother whale and her calf were killed by whalers near the island of Madeira. The population along North America's Atlantic coast seems to be recovering very slowly and may number a few hundred now.[4]

Whalers then pursued the Pacific Right, Atlantic Sperm and Bowhead Whales until they, too, neared extinction, following a pattern still prevalent: when one species or population of whale becomes depleted, whalers pursue another, less valuable species until it also reaches commercial extinction.

Drawing by Richard Willson

This picture shows the war on whales still carried out by Japan and the U.S.S.R. with helicopters, airplanes, ships, radar, ASDIC, and bombs that detonate inside the whale.

The greatest change in whaling has been in the efficiency of the whaling ships in pursuing and killing their victims. In 1865 an explosive bomb to be fired into a whale's body from a cannon mounted in the bow of ships was invented in Norway.[2] Its deadly power was soon turned on the rorquals (Humpback, Blue, Fin and Gray Whales) which had been difficult for whalers to take prior to the development of the explosive harpoon because they were swift and strong swimmers.[2] Also they had less blubber making them less valuable.[2] The new explosive harpoons, although deadly, did not kill instantly. They were used to slaughter off coastal Pacific whales. When these became depleted, the whalers turned to those whales still found in great numbers in Antarctic waters. Vast numbers of Blue, Humpback, Fin and Sei Whales migrated to the Southern Ocean each summer to feed on the krill and fish which abounded.

In 1903, the first "floating factory" whaling ship sailed from Spitzbergen, Norway. These ships, when moored near a land base, could process whales brought alongside by small killer boats. The initial victims of these new ships were the Antarctic Humpback Whales that congregated each summer near the Antarctic Peninsula, especially near South Georgia Island. The factory ships were joined by some older vessels and exploitation was severe. About 70,000 Humpbacks were killed in the years 1909 to 1913, and by World War I, the Humpbacks were almost extinct in these waters.[3]

The toll of Antarctic Whales taken in the early 20th century was staggering: over 122,000 whales were killed between 1909 and 1927.[4]

Factory ships were developed in 1925 that had rear slipways through which whales were winched onto the ships. Whales could be killed in the open ocean, and pulled onto the deck for flensing and rendering, freeing the vessels from confinement to sheltered waters.[3] With this development, the fate of the vast populations of Blue and Finback Whales of the Antarctic was sealed. First the Blue Whales, largest of all whales, reaching 100 feet in length, were killed off. The Blue Whales tended to congregate close to the pack ice, convenient for both the factory ships and moored vessels. Over 15,000 a year were taken in the 1920's, with a high of almost 30,000 in 1930.[2] By the 1930's the Blue Whales were becoming depleted. An armada of floating factories and killer boats sailed the Antarctic. By 1934, the average length of Blue Whales killed had dropped to 79 feet, and 41% of all females caught were immature.[2] These great whales do not reach sexual maturity until females attain a length of 78 feet. The 1937 International Agreement for the Regulation of Whaling reduced the limit to 70 feet for Blue Whales, thus failing to conserve the breeding females.[2] By 1965, the average length of the whales caught had declined to 73 feet.[5] Not until the Blue Whales were reduced to about 6% of their original numbers in 1965, were they finally accorded protection by the International Whaling Commission (IWC).[5]

The decimation of the Finback Whales followed that of the Blue Whales in the Southern Ocean, during the 1930's. After World War II, these whales remained the focus of exploitation. About 30,000 a year were taken even as late as 1959 and 1960, just before the population collapsed. The severe depletion of the Antarctic Finback Whales by the mid 1960's resulted in the redirection of the whalers to the much smaller Sei Whales.

In spite of many years of protection, many large whale

species—Blue, Humpback, Right, and Bowhead—have remained endangered. The failure of most whale populations—only the Gray Whale has recovered somewhat from exploitation—to rebound quickly, if at all, is not fully understood, but their life histories are certainly part of the explanation. Blue Whale females, for example, are thought to become sexually mature only when they reach ten years of age.[6] Gestation lasts 12 months, and the 21-foot-long calf stays with its mother for eight months; when weaned the calf is about 45 feet long.[6] Female Blue Whales can live as long as 45 years.[5] Whales knew few enemies in the sea before man and they evolved no defenses that could have protected them from the cruel harpoon tearing through their flesh, or compensated for sudden losses in their numbers. Also, entire populations in many areas were completely eliminated. Some species, after heavy losses, began to mature to breeding age somewhat sooner, but this has failed to compensate for the extremely high kill.

If a calf was struck the mother did not desert it, and her attempts to save it usually cost her her own life. Gray Whale mothers were so brave that they actually attacked whaling ships when their calves were struck. Captain C.M. Scammon, who slaughtered hundreds of these whales in their Baja California breeding grounds in the 19th century, called them "devil fish" because they fought so staunchly to protect their young. In 1935, the killing of mothers and calves was finally prohibited. In the 1950's a whaling fleet operated by the Greek shipping magnate Aristotle Onassis illegally killed numerous female whales nursing their young. The floating bodies of the babies were found. Peruvian authorities impounded his ships and fined him.

The Cruelty of Whaling

The suffering that harpooned whales endure was described by an eyewitness on an Australian whaler in 1977:

The harpoon seemed to pass right through it, which can happen, and the second explosion took longer. The whole event this time seemed in slow motion. The whale dived, and a great green cloud burst up to the surface. Blood turns green underwater at 50 feet. . . or was this some of its intestines? It came up on the starboard side, its huge head, a third of its total body size, shaking itself, and then it gave out a most terrible cry, half in protest, half in pain, and then it dived again. They loaded the next harpoon, the killer, but could not get a shot at it as it twisted and turned, hurting itself all the more. Finally, the lookout in the crow's nest shouted down that it was coming up dying. Its mouth was opening.[7]

No method exists to kill whales instantly.

The cold harpoons used by native peoples and by Japanese, Soviet, Icelandic, Norwegian and Brazilian whalers to kill thousands of Minke Whales are cruel instruments of death, sometimes taking an hour to kill. In 1981, a major humane victory was won. The cold harpoon, which had been banned for use on all but Minke Whales, was banned for all commercial whaling effective the end of 1982. The decision, the result of the effective lobbying by the conservation countries led by the Australian delegation, is a major one. It means that humaneness is now an issue to be considered in whaling, and the IWC has undertaken the responsibility to insure that methods are not unnecessarily cruel. Unfortunately, Japan, Norway and Iceland filed a formal objection to the cold harpoon ban, followed by the U.S.S.R. and Brazil.

A dying Blue Whale beached itself on the Peruvian coast in February, 1978. This young female had been illegally harpooned by whalers from a Japanese-owned whaling station, 100 miles up the coast.[8] As described by Craig Van Note in his exposé *Outlaw Whalers:* "A 150-lb. harpoon had been fired into the side of the whale . . . after penetrating three feet, a massive grenade at the tip of the harpoon exploded, tearing the whale's internal organs to a bloody pulp with jagged, fist-sized metal fragments. In her agony, the . . . whale tore at the heavy barbs that had expanded from the sides of the harpoon. Wrenching her 75-ton body, she pulled free from the harpoon and heavy rope that run back to the catcher boat. With a gaping wound in her side, the whale dove deep to success-fully escape her pursuers. But the terrible wound caused massive hemorrhaging and each succeeding day the whale grew weaker. Finally, she could not hold herself up to the surface to breathe. So she swam ashore through the surf, sliding to a halt on the coarse sand at Conchan. There Peruvian conservationists gathered to witness the final hours of life of the blue whale. She lay on her side,

Sizes of Whales—Compared with Other Animals

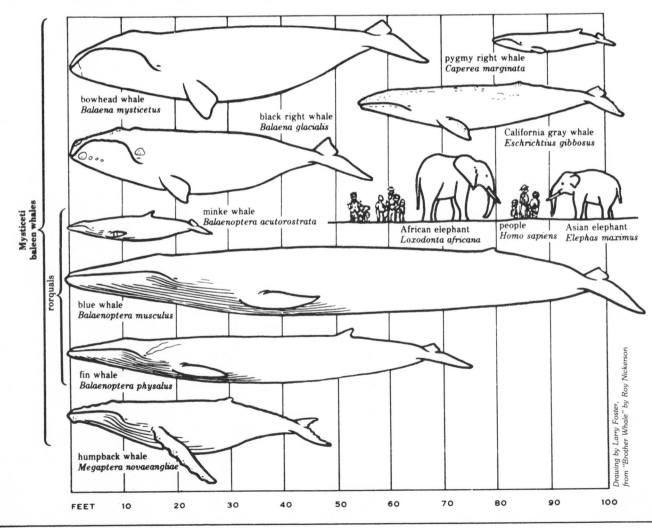

Mysticeti baleen whales

rorquals

bowhead whale
Balaena mysticetus

black right whale
Balaena glacialis

pygmy right whale
Caperea marginata

California gray whale
Eschrichtius gibbosus

minke whale
Balaenoptera acutorostrata

African elephant
Loxodonta africana

people
Homo sapiens

Asian elephant
Elephas maximus

blue whale
Balaenoptera musculus

fin whale
Balaenoptera physalus

humpback whale
Megaptera novaeangliae

FEET   10   20   30   40   50   60   70   80   90   100

Drawing by Larry Foster,
from "Brother Whale" by Roy Nickerson

with the harpoon-wound facing shore, gasping for breath. Comments Felipe Benavides, who has fought to drive the foreign whalers from Peru's shores for 30 years: 'This young whale was one of the most beautiful creatures I have ever seen. Watching her die was one of the saddest experiences of my life.'"[8]

Pirate whalers have killed many protected species, and these non-IWC unregulated ships have been linked to whaling interests in Japan and Norway. The notorious *Sierra* whaler killed thousands of Fin Whales in the Atlantic before it was rammed in 1979 by the *Sea Shepherd*, a ship manned by activists supported by the Fund for Animals organization. Later in port, it was sunk by a mine.

The brutal business of whaling is regulated by the International Whaling Commission (IWC) which was formed after World War II to provide conservation and set quotas on whale kills based on advice from their Scientific Committee. The Commissioners are delegates from both whaling and non-whaling nations, until recently mainly the former. Unfortunately, because whaling nations were in effect policing themselves, quotas set have been far too liberal, and the IWC has

Even the enormous Brontosaurus was smaller than the Blue Whale, largest animal ever to have lived on earth.

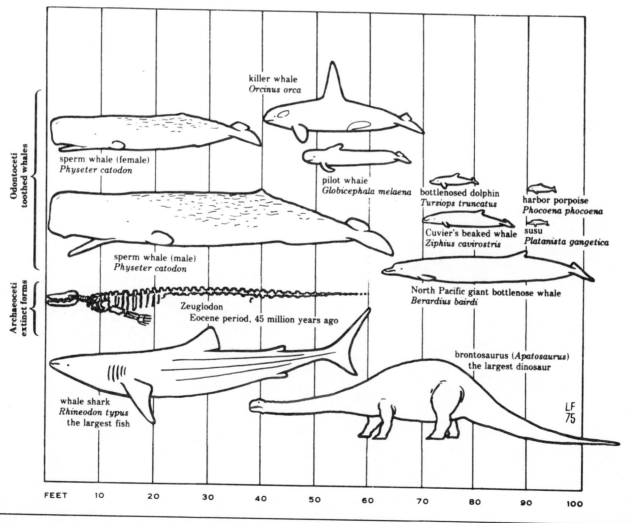

no means to enforce them. In addition, a country may file an objection to a quota and thereby choose to ignore it.

It is ironic that Japan, which kills more whales than any other country, was launched into the whaling business after World War II by the Supreme Command Allied Powers (SCAP) which saw this as a means of increasing the Japanese food supply.[10] The whale oil was taken by SCAP in return for supplying diesel fuel and the meat was processed for the use of the Japanese.[10] This whaling for meat has continued to this day and encourages other countries' whaling because Japan imports large quantities of whale meat. In the early years, quotas were not allocated to individual countries, which resulted in a first come, first served basis, depleting whales all the more. Protection of Humpbacks in the Antarctic was revoked when the IWC was first formed and this led to their commercial extinction by the early 1960's.[10] Japan and the U.S.S.R. take 61% of the whales caught by IWC whalers. Since Japan buys the entire Soviet and Icelandic catches of whale meat, it provides the major incentive for whaling to continue.

The Campaign to Save The Whales

The Japanese and Russian fleets dominated all pelagic whaling from the 1960's on with their huge factory ships. Whaling concentrated on the Pacific and Southern Ocean where Soviet and Japanese fleets depleted Fin, Sperm and Sei Whale populations.

To stem the tide, conservationists pressed for protections on the national and international levels. U.S. Secretary of Interior Walter Hickel placed eight great whales on the U.S. Endangered Species list banning import in the face of much opposition, since one U.S. company was still whaling and large amounts of whale products were imported. In 1971 the U.S. Secretary of Commerce terminated U.S. commercial whaling. Also in 1971, the Congress passed a resolution

*Felipe Benavides deplored the death of a protected **Blue Whale** that had been illegally harpooned.*

Photo by Greenpeace USA

48

calling on the Secretary of State to negotiate a ten-year moratorium on commercial whaling. In 1972, the United Nations Conference on the Human Environment unanimously voted a similar resolution which was later adopted by the UN General Assembly. Only days later, the IWC rejected the U.S. proposal for a ten-year moratorium with only 4 of the 16 member nations voting in favor. Instead, they voted a quota of 45,000 whales. In 1974, effective in 1975, the IWC adopted the so-called "New Management Procedure" (NMP) under which whale populations were allowed to be reduced to 54% of the estimated original population. Compromise and tedious negotiations resulted in some victories for conservationists with protection of depleted stocks. Even so, it is obvious that the "maximum sustainable yield" methods used to determine whale quotas greatly overestimated the whales' capacity to sustain such high losses. These errors were reflected in declining quotas. In the 1979 IWC meeting, a factory ship moratorium, applying to all species but Minke Whales, was passed.[3]

Another victory for conservationists was the Indian Ocean Sanctuary. Proposed by the Seychelles, it is now secure for all whales, and there may soon be other such sanctuaries. The U.S. does not allow whaling within 200 miles of its coasts, which offers another protection.

Whale Quotas 1973-1981 *

1973	45,673
1974	42,473
1975	33,936
1976	28,050
1977	23,500
1978	19,526
1979	15,656
1980	14,523
1981	14,070

Source: Review of the 33rd International Whaling Commission Meeting, U.S. House of Representatives, Committee on Foreign Affairs, Hearing, Sept. 22, 1981, U.S. Government Printing Office.

*The 1982-83 pelagic and coastal quota was set at 12,371 whales and the 1981-82 quota was raised by 450 whales to 14,520.

At the 1982 meeting of the International Whaling Commission a resolution was passed to set zero quotas for all whales killed for commercial purposes beginning in 1986. Though strongly debated, the resolution passed by the overwhelming majority vote of 25 to 7 with 5 abstentions. Spain was the only whaling country to vote in favor of the cessation of whaling. The others: Brazil, Iceland, Japan, Korea, Norway, Peru and the Soviet Union voted against the resolution. Unfortunately, Norway, Peru, Japan and the Soviet Union have filed formal objections. These objections may be rescinded, but if not, these countries will not be bound by the IWC decision.

The species now legally killed under IWC quotas are the small 25-30 foot Minke, Bryde's and some populations of Fin and Sei in the North Atlantic and Sperm Whales in the Northwest Pacific.

The little Minke Whales, only ¼ the length of Blue Whales, are bearing the brunt of whaling—11,762 were caught in 1979, 12,017 were allowed as the 1981-82 quota, and 10,423 as the 1982-83 quota.

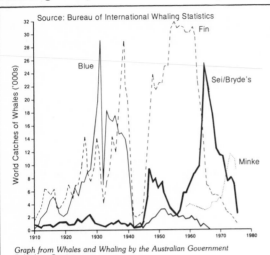

Source: Bureau of International Whaling Statistics

Graph from Whales and Whaling by the Australian Government Publishing Service

World Catches of Whales

The Fin Whale stocks of the North Atlantic still being exploited are showing signs of commercial extinction. The proportion of undersized Fin Whales caught by Spanish whalers rose from 5% in 1978 to 29% in 1980. In 1981, a Spanish parliamentary committee voted to end whaling and to support the moratorium; however, the whaling company nearly succeeded in undermining this decision by asserting that only if aboriginal whaling were ended at the same time as commercial whaling would the parliamentary decision apply. On the preliminary vote in the IWC's Technical Committee, the Spanish Commissioner voted against the cessation, but on the final vote in Plenary, he voted yes.

Aboriginal whaling under IWC rules includes that by Greenland Eskimos, the Alaskan Inuit, and Soviet native peoples. The Alaskan Eskimo kill of Bowhead Whales has been a subject of heated debate at IWC meetings. The Scientific Committee recommended a zero quota in 1977, which was adopted, but later altered at a special meeting to a quota of 12 landed or 18 struck. In 1980, a total of 18 landed or 26 struck, whichever came first, was approved: for 1981-83, a bloc quota of 45 landed or 65 struck and lost was voted. The Alaskan Eskimo Whaling Commission, formed in 1978, now enforces the regulations. The highly endangered Bowheads need protection. They are threatened by oil spills as well as by whaling.

The Gray Whale, the only great whale to have made a recovery from whaling, now numbers about 15,000 in the Pacific Ocean and it is taken by the Soviets on its wintering ground. The IWC allowed a quota of 179 whales to be caught in 1981-82 allegedly for native peoples; however, photographic evidence gathered by environmentalist Paul Watson indicates that the Soviets are feeding this whale meat to furbearers on ranches rather than using it for native consumption only, as IWC regulations require. The quota set for Greenland Eskimos for 1982-83 is 10 Humpback Whales, six Fin Whales, and an undetermined share of the 444 Minke Whales in the West Greenland area. Norway and Iceland have a commercial take from this quota, too.

The IWC will continue to set quotas for the 1984-85 and 1985-86 pelagic and 1986 coastal seasons for commercial whaling, following which, zero quotas come into force unless a whaling nation has filed a formal objection to the 1982 resolution. Although the IWC has no effective sanctions to enforce its decisions, the United States does.

Section 8 of the Fisherman's Protective Act, the "Pelly Amendment" permits the President to embargo any and all fisheries products from countries whose nationals have engaged in taking a marine resource in such manner as to "diminish the effectiveness of an international fishery conservation program." In 1979 an additional sanction was voted into law—the Packwood-Magnuson Amendment. This amends the Fishery Conservation and Management Act to cut fish allocations by half on certification by the Secretary of Commerce that a nation has violated the provisions of the Pelly Amendment. If the nation persists, all fishing rights are cancelled. In 1981, Japan's allocation allowed it to catch nearly half a billion dollars worth of fish within the U.S. 200-mile zone—a powerful economic incentive to adhere to IWC decisions.

Achievement of an international ban on the commercial whaling that has decimated whale species and populations worldwide shows what can be done to protect endangered species when informed citi-

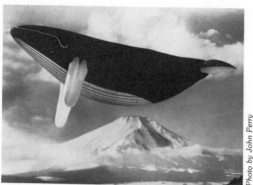

*"Flo", a huge balloon designed by John Perry, demonstrates for the **Save the Whales Campaign** in Japan.*

Photo by John Perry

zens take determined action together. The whale became the symbol of the Stockholm Conference on the Human Environment in 1972 when the moratorium resolution was passed and conservationists asked one another, "If we can't save the whales, how can we hope to save other, lesser creatures?" Ten years later the non-binding United Nations Environment Program's resolution became a binding IWC resolution which nations must take seriously. Those ten years were filled with intense campaigning for whales: diplomacy, demonstrations, boycotts of products from whaling countries, advertisements in the world press, confrontations with whalers on the high seas, undercover investigations of pirate whaling, and significantly, the whales spoke for themselves through the recordings made by Roger Payne, "The Songs of the Humpback Whale" which moved from a scientific recording through mass sales by Capitol Records to distribution in an issue of *The National Geographic*. The ten million copies of this record constituted the largest single pressing of any record ever made.

The symbol of the Stockholm Conference points the way for thousands of other endangered or threatened species that must be protected from extinction.

FUR
A History of Endangering Species

The history of the fur trade past and present, is evidence that no animal, no matter how abundant, is immune to possible extinction should its pelt become valuable to the fur trade. A pattern develops as fur pelt prices rise, and as trappers find fewer valuable pelts, these pelts become more avidly sought out. Commercial extinction can result fairly quickly if animals with valuable pelts are killed in a totally unregulated manner. Animals whose populations numbered in the millions and whose ranges extended over entire continents have been reduced to near extinction within the space of a few decades, as has recently been demonstrated by the trade in spotted cats. For those animals unfortunate enough to be naturally rare in the wild for ecological or geographical reasons—the Falkland Island Fox and the North American Sea Mink, for example—total extermination came easily and quickly when their pelts were in demand by the fur trade.

Prior to the 20th century, a long list of furbearers were nearly eliminated by the fur and hide trade. In North America, the Bison, Beaver, River and Sea Otters, Marten, Fisher and Kit Fox disappeared from most of the continent by the end of the 19th century. Today, the Beaver has made a comeback, largely as a result of reintroductions, but the other species have greatly reduced distributions and numbers.

Fur Seals

Fur seals worldwide were bludgeoned on shores where they bred, from the Aleutian Islands to the Antarctic. The Guadalupe Fur Seal and the Philippi Fur Seal have not recovered their numbers significantly. The Guadalupe Fur Seal, once found throughout the Baja California coastal region and the southern California coasts, was twice considered extinct (1895-1926, 1928-1949).[1] Rediscovered on Guadalupe Island in 1926 by two fishermen, several seals were sent to the San Diego Zoo in 1928.[2] After a quarrel between one of the fishermen who discovered the seals, and the Director of the San Diego Zoo, the former stormed off to Guadalupe Island in 1928 to kill the entire herd; he killed every seal he found and sold the skins in Panama, where he was killed in a barroom fight.[2] Not until 1949 was the species seen again off southern California. In 1954 a small colony was found on Guadalupe Island, hiding in caves along the

*Still very rare, the **Guadalupe Fur Seal** was nearly eliminated altogether by the fur trade in the 19th and early 20th centuries.*

shore.[2] They were accorded protection by Mexico, and by the U.S. Marine Mammal Protection Act of 1971, but numbers have only recently (1977) climbed to a high of 1,000.[1] Its fur is still considered valuable, and poaching is a threat.[1] This fur seal is presently listed on Appendix I of the Convention on International Trade in Endangered Species of Wild Fauna and Flora (CITES) and remains protected from harvest.[*]

The Philippi Fur Seal also remains very rare and continues to be illegally killed. In 1978, the government of Chile decreed protection for all seals found in Chilean waters in recognition of the sharp decline in the Philippi Fur Seal and the Southern Fur Seal in this region.[3]

Chinchillas

In the 20th century, Latin America's wildlife has suffered more dramatic declines as a direct result of the fur and hide trade than any other region on earth. Exploitation of fur seals and chinchillas began well before the 20th century. Chinchillas, small Andean rodents with silky grey fur, were imported into the United States in gradually decreasing numbers from 1862; between 1862 and 1891, 872,953 chinchilla pelts were imported from South America.[1] In the early 20th century, the demand for their fur increased, as furbearers declined elsewhere, and in 1905 alone, 217,836 pelts were registered exported by one city, Coquimbo, in Chile; by 1909 the figure had dropped to 27,936 and the price was $500 for a dozen pelts.[2] By 1930, pelts of the Peruvian or royal Chinchilla, the most prized

[*]CITES has been ratified by 77 countries. It regulates the international trade in wildlife and wildlife products, including furs. It is explained in the International Legislation chapter in detail. In essence, species listed on Appendix I are endangered and commercial trade is prohibited except under permit for scientific or breeding purposes. Species listed on Appendix II are either threatened, or likely to become so if trade reaches high levels, and export permits are required. Appendix III lists species protected by individual countries. Permits are granted for trade only after a Scientific Authority in each country advises a Management Authority that export will not be detrimental to the survival of the species.

type, had risen to $200 per pelt and European markets had instructed agents to obtain pelts "at any price".[3] Numbers of this once abundant rodent plummeted and while its original range in the Andes mountains included Peru, Chile, Argentina and Bolivia, it became commercially extinct by the late 1920's and two of the three races are presumed extinct.[2] The remaining population in northern Chile is highly endangered; in the 1930's the species was taken from Chile and Bolivia to be raised in captivity for the fur trade. Due to lack of protection of the remaining wild chinchillas in Chile, the species may disappear altogether in the near future.[2]

Vicuna

Vicunas were strictly protected by the Incan nobles who sheared their fine wool. In recent times, however, they were killed in large numbers for the international market in luxury cloth.

Photo by W.L. Franklin Courtesy of World Wildlife Fund

Another Andean mammal, the graceful Vicuna, a close relative of the domestic llama, had been protected by the Incan chiefs who used its fine wool for royal garments. Traditionally, it was sheared rather than killed for its wool, and at the time of the Spanish conquest numbered two million.[4] The Spanish slaughtered thousands of Vicunas and the species was killed over the years for its wool until it finally received protection by Peru in 1920. Between 1950 and 1970, about 400,000 Vicunas were killed despite legal protection. By 1966 total population of Vicunas in South America had dropped from an estimated 650,000 in 1957 to 8,000 in Peru, 1,500 in Bolivia and a scattered remnant numbering about 100 in Chile and Argentina; it was totally extinct in Ecuador.[2] A pact between Peru and Bolivia in the late 1960's and later ratified by Argentina and Chile, declared a 10-year moratorium on the killing of Vicunas; the herds increased to approximately 60,000 in Peru, where 80% of Vicunas remain. In 1979, the Peruvian government resumed killing Vicunas almost immediately after the 10-year moratorium had elapsed, and several thousand were slaughtered to generate income from the sale of their wool.[4] Many conservationists objected, since numbers are still less than 4% of their original population, and killing the Vicunas is unnecessary since shearing the wool is possible. The Peruvian government transferred 1,000 in 1980 and plans to transfer more Vicunas to new areas from their overcrowded reserves.[5] Due to its listing on Appendix I of the CITES, international trade is not legally possible. Proposals were put forth by Peru and Chile to allow international trade by downgrading the Vicunas from Appendix I to Appendix II at the CITES meeting in 1979, but these were defeated.

Spotted Cats

The South American spotted cats were killed for their fur at ever increasing rates from the 1940's. Jaguars, the largest wild cats in Latin America, were killed in the greatest numbers in the 1960's; in 1968, 13,516 pelts were imported into the U.S. alone and numbers of this magnificent animal, which requires large areas of habitat, fell precipitously throughout Latin America. It became extinct in El Salvador, and very rare in most other parts of its range. Its commercial import into the United States was not banned until 1972 when it was listed on the Endangered Species Act; smuggling of pelts has continued to the present. The smaller cats, Ocelot and Margay, were far more abundant in nature due to their smaller habitat requirements and the fact that unlike the Jaguar, they do not prey on livestock, which would cause them to be directly persecuted by ranchers. Over 100,000 skins per year of Ocelot were imported by the U.S. alone between 1965 and 1969[6] and numbers equally high were imported into Europe.[7]

By 1970, U.S. imports dropped to 87,645 Ocelots and various

Pet and trophy hunting are pushing the **Snow Leopard** *toward extinction.*

Photo by the Zoological Society of Cincinnati

South American countries enacted export bans as the Ocelot disappeared from vast regions. Figures for the Margay, a spotted cat smaller than the Ocelot, were not itemized by the U.S. Department of Commerce, but are presumed to be as high as those of the Ocelot. Import bans were enacted in 1972 for the United States and by 1975, when CITES came into effect, legal trade in all three species was restricted. However, trade in these small spotted cats has continued. In 1977, Peru exported the pelts of 7,233 Ocelots, and over 18,000 pelts were imported by European countries from various South American nations; world trade in Ocelot is now estimated at over 30,000 by the IUCN TRAFFIC Group.[8] Brazil, a country which legally banned the export of all wildlife in 1967, continues to export large numbers of wild cat pelts (75,262 in 1977).[8]

In Asia several species of large cat, the Tiger, largest of all wild cats, the Snow Leopard, the Clouded Leopard, and Leopard have all been reduced to near extinction by hunting for fur and trophies, plus massive habitat destruction. These species have been listed on Appendix I of CITES, but illegal trade continues to reduce their numbers.

Retail sale of coats from endangered wild cats has been restricted by the CITES, but some countries still sell them openly. In Japan, a survey of Tokyo department stores in January, 1981, revealed the following endangered spotted cat coats for sale:

Clouded Leopard	$25,750-$124,270
Tiger	$94,750
Snow Leopard	$33,000
Ocelot	$23,795-$32,400
African Leopard	$72,000
Asian Leopard	$32,500-$50,000

Source: Milliken, Tom. 1981. Wildlife Shopping in Tokyo—1981. IUCN TRAFFIC Bull. Wildlife Trade Monitoring Unit. Vol. 3(3/4):43-46. May/August

The unabashed sale of these endangered species products has shocked conservationists around the world. In March 1982 CBS-TV showed the modeling of a Snow Leopard coat in a Tokyo store. Japan has not taken reservations on any of these species. Open sale of Appendix I species two years after the country joined CITES strongly suggests that Japan is not enforcing the treaty which prohibits importation for commercial purposes of Appendix I species.

Otters

The otters of South America have been nearly exterminated by the fur trade. The Giant Otter, largest otter species, has declined to near extinction in Brazil and Peru. Exports decreased from over 2,000 to 210 by the late 1960's. Three other otter species, the La Plata Otter of Brazil, Paraguay and Argentina, the Southern River Otter of Chile and Argentina and the Southern Marine Otter of the Pacific coasts of Chile and Peru have all been so exploited that they are listed by CITES on Appendix I as endangered species. Over 45,000 otters per year were imported by the U.S. from South America from 1965-1969, primarily from Brazil and Columbia.[6]

In Europe and the United States otters have become greatly reduced by fur trapping. The Common Otter of Europe is listed on CITES Appendix I. In the United States, fur trapping played a major role in eliminating this animal from the central part of the country. The last River Otter in Kansas, for example, was killed in 1904, causing biologist E.R. Hall to observe, "The short glossy fur of the river otter has commanded a high price for many years—so high a price that trappers took the very last individual in our state."

African Wildlife

Photo by Neal Johnston, Los Angeles Zoo

Black and White Colobus Monkeys of Africa were heavily slaughtered in the 1920's for fur coats, and even today, tourist curios such as rugs are sold which were made from fur of these rare monkeys.

In the 19th and early 20th centuries, the Black and White Colobus Monkey of Africa was imported in large numbers into the U.S. and Europe. This monkey became rare and remains so. A coat of this monkey species was advertised in Japan in 1980 for $6,000.

The Barbary Leopard of North Africa, while protected since 1948, has nevertheless declined greatly from pelt-hunting during the past two decades.[10] This race of the Leopard is perhaps the most critically endangered form of the species in Africa. Leopards, which once ranged over most of the continent have been greatly reduced over the past twenty years by hunting for pelts. The Leopard was listed on the U.S. Endangered Species Act in 1972, and prior to that date the U.S. had imported over 4,000 skins from Africa in 1968 and 1969. Illegal trade continues, despite its listing on CITES Appendix I, and its pelt is now worth $2,000.[11]

Hunting of Africa's wildlife for hides, meat and trophies, combined with habitat destruction and the introduction of livestock, have since 1900 reduced the large mammals by at least 75%.[10] Many of the gazelles, antelopes and especially zebras, have been killed for their hides which were sold as novelty items and for rugs to tourists. These animals are often poached in national parks by means of cruel wire snares which are hidden in brush. When the animal thrashes about to escape, the wire works deep into the flesh of the leg, on occasion nearly severing the limb; traps and poison are also used to kill Cheetah, Leopard and other furbearers.

Cheetahs have become Africa's most endangered cat species. Found mainly in savannah country where they rely on great speed to chase small antelopes, their numbers have recently shown a catastrophic decline. Although numbers of Cheetah pelts imported into the U.S. and Europe in the 1960's reached less than 10,000, the natural rarity of the species, and habitat disturbance combined with these killings to eliminate it in almost all its range outside of national parks.[10] Illegal trade in Cheetah pelts continues. In 1979, 319 Ethiopian Cheetah skins were seized in Hong Kong.[11] In 1980 and 1981, Cheetah skins were openly sold in South African markets.

Platypuses and Kangaroos

One of the strangest of all mammals is the Platypus, looking like a combination of a mole and a beaver with a duck's bill. Not only is its appearance unusual, but it and the echidnas are the only mammals to lay eggs instead of giving birth to live young. This Australian rarity was nearly obliterated by fur traders. Before it received protection in 1906, more than a million Platypus pelts were taken annually and sewn into rugs. Today, it is a rare species confined to clear streams in Queensland. The Koala also nearly became extinct from the fur trade of the 1920's when millions were killed for fur coats. Both species are dependent on continued protection. The kangaroos are now bearing the brunt of killing for the animal product trade.

Australian kangaroos were considered pests for settlers colonizing Australia, and a bounty was placed on them in most areas. In one state alone, 26 million scalps were delivered for bounty in the forty years prior to 1917. During the first half of the century, 3-4 million skins per year were marketed.[12] In the 1960's, a market was created for kangaroo meat abroad, and wholesale shooting of kangaroos took place in most states.[12] Protests of the barbarity of the slaughter

Drawing by Esta Belcher

The **Red Kangaroo** *(top) is listed as threatened under the U.S. Endangered Species Act but is now being hunted again. Kangaroo "joeys" die when their mothers are shot.*

were heard worldwide and by 1973, imports of three species of kangaroo (Red, Western Gray and Eastern Gray kangaroos) were banned when these species were listed as threatened under the U.S. Endangered Species Act. The large kangaroos declined greatly during this period of intensive shooting, and much cruelty to the kangaroos took place: females were shot and pelted while their joeys and young climbed on their bodies. Hunting with spotlights took place and many kangaroos were wounded and left to die.[13] The ban on U.S. imports has recently been lifted. The 1982 quota in Australia was over 3 million kangaroos, an unprecedented figure. The meat is being marketed again as well, and some was illegally imported into the U.S. before the import ban was lifted. The inhumaneness of the killing is reported even worse than the 1960's, with kangaroos purposely crippled to keep the meat fresh until slaughter, and joeys stomped or bashed to death. Protests are being lodged with the Australian government and the U.S. Fish and Wildlife Service to reimpose the ban.

Trapping Pressure

An example of what trappers call **"wring-off."** *The desperate animal escapes at the price of gnawing off his own foot.*

Within the past ten years, trapping has intensified greatly as fur markets boomed and pelt prices rose astronomically. The popularity of the "long hair furs" such as Raccoon, Bobcat, Lynx, Coyote and Gray Wolf has resulted in unprecedented trapping of these animals.

The animals commanding the highest pelt prices at present exist in nature in numbers far lower than hares, rabbits, mice, deer and caribou upon which they depend for survival. All predators, in fact, need fairly large habitats commensurate with their food supply. Territory requirements for some species are enormous. Each African Cheetah, a species in grave danger of extinction, requires at least 30 square miles.[18] The Grizzly Bear of northern Alaska claims a territory of 100 square miles, and River Otters in Oregon approximately 70 square miles of habitat.[19] Over half of the mammals exterminated in Africa, Asia, Europe and North America have been large, wide-ranging predators—bears, wolves, foxes and cats.[20] The vulnerability of wild cats and otters to overtrapping caused the inclusion of all species of these animals on CITES.

All of these predators have a low natural mortality in the wild, are usually long-lived and reproduce fewer offspring than their prey species. Some large carnivores such as Tigers and most bear species spend two entire years with their offspring before breeding again.

In Europe, the Lynx preys on both hares and deer and is the only large cat predator. It has been reduced greatly in numbers and forced into ever more remote regions, occupying less than ¼ of its original range.[15] The life cycle of these predators has direct bearing on the effect of trapping on their populations. The young Lynx of Europe stays with its mother for one full year, learning to kill prey; and if its mother is killed, even when it is 6 months old, it will usually die. At nine months of age it still has milk teeth and undeveloped claws and is dependent on its mother for food.[15]

In a recent long-term biological study of Canadian Lynx published in the *Journal of Wildlife Management*,[16] it was revealed that during periods of hare decline almost no Lynx kittens survive until their first year due to the scarcity of food supply, and that for three to four years recruitment of kittens remains near zero. For adult Lynx as well, survival is difficult during these periods of hare decline, and researchers found that food supply dropped 20% below that required to maintain body weight.[16]

In examining the effects of heavy trapping on Lynx when in these periods of decline, the researchers concluded, "intensive trapping could result in local extirpations of Lynx during years when recruitment is absent."[16] The geographical range of Canadian Lynx decreased during previous periods of heavy trapping in Lynx decline in the mid-1920's, 1930's and 1940's. Kittens of Canadian Lynx, like the European Lynx, are dependent on their mother for one full year.[16] This study recommended the closure of Lynx trapping for three to four years coinciding with hare decline in each ten-year cycle, since trapping pressure was found to be directly related to pelt price, which rose to all-time highs while Lynx populations plunged to lows during 1975–1976 and disappeared altogether from parts of Alberta due to heavy trapping.[16] Researchers also found that Lynx remained in leghold traps an average of two to three days in the study area in Alberta, Canada, before trappers arrived, and most trappers found them still alive after this long period.

The steel jaw leghold trap, instrument of death for 80% of wild furs taken in the U.S., is extremely cruel. It holds the animal's paw

The young **Lynx** *is dependent on its mother for a full year, and dies if its mother is trapped.*

Photo by the Zoological Society of San Diego

Bobcat dead in double steel jaw leghold traps. Note protruding bones.

Photo © Dick Randall, Defenders of Wildlife

tightly, usually cutting off circulation which can cause gangrene and often breaking bones when it slams shut. Many animals are so frantic to escape the trap that they chew off their own paws. Trappers in many states do not have to check their traps for days on end, while the animal suffers pain, trauma, hunger and thirst. There are even cases of trappers failing to return to check traps until the snow cover melted, revealing animals that had taken weeks to starve to death.

Regulating the Trade

Endangered species legislation offers great hope for many species now being decimated by the fur trade. It should be remembered that there is some inconsistency in interpretation of "endangered" and "threatened" categories. Some authorities and governments designating species assign animals to the endangered category only when on the brink of extinction, while other authorities determine a species to be endangered as soon as its population becomes depleted and losses far exceed natural recruitment. There are numerous species that are endangered, but not to be found on any list due to inadequate biological research or bureaucratic inertia. A time lapse may also occur between decline, when rapid, and protection.

Numerous seizures of smuggled pelts have been made by enforcement agents. Such seizures can be prosecuted under several United States laws including the Lacey Act and the Endangered Species Act.

A seizure was made in Hong Kong in January, 1979, of 319 Cheetah skins, 31 Leopard skins, 560 Genet skins and 36 Serval skins which had been smuggled from Ethiopia in a container labelled "Mink".[22] Prices of endangered wild cats have risen greatly since the CITES treaty went into effect. Black market Tiger skins are now worth $3,000 in Hong Kong.[22] In England in January, 1979, a store was fined for offering three Leopard skins for sale.[22] Four Tiger skins and two Leopard skins were seized at Hong Kong airport in February, 1979, each carrying the head and intended as trophies.[22]

CITES has been in effect only a few years, and enforcement procedures are still less than perfect. Each country which is party to the Convention issues a report on imports and exports of CITES species annually. Since all wild cats are listed either in Appendix I or II, listing in CITES reports of all wild cat pelts is required.

The CITES Secretariat has uncovered numerous cases of smuggling. In late 1980, it discovered that a Frankfurt, West Germany trader had been using illegal documents to import 40,000 Ocelot skins and 140,000 skins of otters and other endangered species from Paraguay. By cross-checking the trader's permits with Paraguayan authorities, the CITES officials found that the permits had never been issued. A number of skins were from animals not native to Paraguay, and it is thought that they had been smuggled into that country from neighboring Brazil, Argentina or Bolivia.

Enforcement varies from country to country, but to date, the combined effect of the U.S. Endangered Species Act and CITES has succeeded in stopping almost all imports into the United States of the endangered spotted cats, and Vicuna. Ads for these species are virtually unknown.

Certain identification problems exist with species bearing a close resemblance to one another. Many fox and wolf skins are very similar, as are otter species, other than the Sea Otter. Less difficulty is presented by readily distinguishable pelts such as Tiger, Cheetah, Leopard, and Vicuna. Identification difficulties exist also with sub-

Drawing from the Russian Red Data Book

*The regal **Cheetah** has declined to endangered status from fur trapping and habitat loss.*

Photo by A. Wright, World Wildlife Fund

These Tiger and Leopard skins were seized from an Italian trader at the Calcutta airport.

species, or races of endangered animals. In some cases, only portions of total populations of species are listed as endangered; for example, the Spanish subspecies of the European Lynx, the Mexican subspecies of the Bobcat, and the San Joaquin (California) subspecies of the Kit Fox are listed on CITES or the U.S. Endangered Species Act. When such trade is prohibited, but trade in other subspecies of the same animal is allowed, identification of skins is often possible only by an expert. In some cases even experts cannot distinguish these pelts from other pelts of the same species since differences may be exhibited only when skull or total body skin can be examined. A recent case involved the Leopard Cat, one subspecies of which is listed on Appendix I of CITES, (*Felis bengalensis bengalensis*). The 1979 International Fur Fair held in New York City, exhibited pelts of the Leopard Cat. Two representatives of the Animal Welfare Institute called enforcement agents, and the pelts were confiscated, but prosecution of the case was not carried out since experts were unable to conclusively identify these pelts by subspecies.

Identification problems will persist as an enforcement difficulty, although the manual being prepared for enforcement officials, which identify pelts and skins of CITES species, will aid in this area.

Furriers and Endangered Species

The International Fur Trade Federation in 1970, at the instigation of the International Union for the Conservation of Nature (IUCN), recommended a voluntary total ban on trade in the skins of 5 vanishing species: Clouded and Snow Leopards, Tiger, Giant Otter, and La Plata Otter, and a 3-year ban on Leopard and Cheetah. Members of the Furriers Joint Council of New York, and its affiliate, the Amalgamated Meat Cutters and Butcher Workmen of North America, pledged not to cut or fashion the skins of endangered species. The New York furrier Georges Kaplan announced in 1968 that he would no longer deal in endangered species.

Vogue and *Country Life* magazines in Britain agreed not to advertise endangered species, as did *The New York Times*.

In 1970, the Mason Act of New York state was enacted which banned the sale of Leopard, Snow Leopard, Clouded Leopard, Cheetah, Tiger, Ocelot, Margay, Red Wolf, Vicuna, Polar Bear, Mountain Lion (Cougar), and alligator and crocodile products. The fur industry took the bill to court as unconstitutional. The Court of Appeals made a sweeping decision upholding the bill, which then passed in Delaware, California, Connecticut, Pennsylvania, Illinois and Massachusetts, although the latter state weakened the Act in 1979.

In spite of continued smuggling of endangered species, and the imperfect enforcement of CITES, one can realize with satisfaction that there is a growing awareness of the need to protect endangered species, and a vast improvement in legislative protection in the past few years. In the United States, open sale of endangered species is almost unknown. In the late 1960's, the ad below appeared in a literary magazine, an ad which would be illegal today:

"Untamed . . . the Snow Leopard. Provocatively dangerous. A mankiller. Born free in the wild whiteness of the high Himalayas only to be snared as part of the captivating new fur collection . . . styled and shaped in a one-of-a-kindness to bring out the animal instinct in you."[25]

THE REPTILE PRODUCT TRADE
Sea Turtles

*Baby **sea turtles** struggling out of their shells face an uncertain future.*

Photo by Andrew Young

Huge sea turtles have been laboring up the beaches of tropical shores for 50 million years, digging deep holes with their flippers, and depositing their slippery eggs before making their way back to the sea. The adult turtles had few enemies, except sharks which occasionally attack their flippers. Even today the great turtles are enigmas. How do they find their way over thousands of miles of open sea to return to the same beach on which they hatched? Where do they spend their first years of life? Scientists are very slowly unraveling some of their secrets. For example, it is now thought that they may not nest until they are fifty years old. If true, this would make them the slowest reproducing of all known animals and would explain their inability to recover when slaughtered by the thousands by commercial exploiters.

Of the seven species of sea turtles, the four most heavily exploited are the Green, the Hawksbill, and the two types of Ridley—Kemp's or Atlantic, and Olive or Pacific. The other sea turtles are also endangered, some because of excessive egg taking by natives, some by drowning in shrimp nets, others by construction on their nesting beaches, or a combination of these.

Hunting of the sea turtles has been relentless. In the 1970's the Hawksbill Turtle, killed mainly for its shell which is made into trinkets and jewelry, has been nearly eliminated throughout its range, which once encompassed most of the tropical seas. Shells of over 250,000 of these turtles were sold yearly in 1976 and 1977;[1] and in 1978 the numbers doubled.[1]

Dr. Archie Carr, a biologist who has spent a lifetime studying sea turtles, is pessimistic about the future of the Hawksbill. Natives are scouring every reef and beach in the Caribbean for these turtles whose shells sell for as much as $70. Even in remote areas Carr has visited, the Hawksbill has disappeared.[2]

The Green Turtle, major subject of Dr. Carr's fascinating book, *So Excellent a Fishe,*[3] has a history of exploitation that goes back hundreds of years. The Bermuda Assembly passed an act in 1620 to outlaw the killing of young turtles because they had been decimated in the surrounding waters even by that early date. The Assembly commented,

> In regard that much waste and abuse hath been offered and yet is by sundrye lewd and impudient psons inhabitinge within these Islands who in their continuall goinges out to sea for fish doe upon all occasions, And at all tymes as they can meete with them, snatch & catch up indifferentlye all kinds of Tortoyses both yonge and old little and greate and soe kill carrye awaye and devoure them and to the much decay of the breed of so excellent a fishe the daylye skarringe of them from our shores and the danger of an utter distroyinge and losse of them.[3]

Until recently, Green Turtles were killed mainly by natives who caused local population declines, but did not threaten the species as a whole. The market for its meat for steaks and soup, and for its oil which is used in cosmetics, as well as for its shell, which is only a little less valuable than the Hawksbill's, and even for its neck and flipper skin, tanned for leather, has brought about its decimation. Its most remote nesting beaches have been discovered, and female turtles slaughtered as they lay their eggs, or congregate offshore. Even baby turtles are killed and stuffed to be sold as souvenirs.

The Ridley Turtles are also nearing extinction. There were once huge nesting aggregations of Kemp's Ridley Turtles on the Caribbean coast of Mexico. Over 40,000 female turtles were seen to come ashore on one beach alone, crowding one another for space and presenting a spectacle that evoked past eons of time when reptiles ruled the earth. A few days of slaughter over several consecutive years reduced the enormous "arribádas" or mass arrivals to only 500 turtles by 1978. Finally this remnant population which is estimated at less than 8,000 (including males) has been given official protection, and armed guards protect the remaining turtles when they come ashore to nest. Some of the eggs have been transplanted to Padre Island in Texas to re-establish them where they once nested. On Pacific shores, the Olive Ridley also nested in "arribadas" in Mexico and Ecuador, and between the two countries, 150,000 adult turtles were killed each year in 1976, 1977 and 1978, reducing them to straggling remnants of their former abundance.

The U.S. Endangered Species Act extended protection to the Hawksbill and Kemp's Ridley Turtles as early as 1969, thereby shutting off legal imports. It was not until 1977, however, that some restrictions were imposed on the international trade. All species of sea turtles were added to the CITES Appendix I in that year, banning commercial trade by party nations. The U.S. banned imports of all wild turtle products in 1977 to comply with CITES, limiting imports to the "farmed" turtles raised at the Cayman Turtle Farm in the Caribbean and a few other commercial operations that specialize in Green Turtles. Unfortunately, these legal steps did not stop the trade. Many nations party to CITES continued importing and exporting sea turtle products, either by ignoring the Convention or by taking reservations* on sea turtles. France and Italy both tan large amounts of sea turtle leather, and reservations were lodged. Ecuador exported 139,900 kg of skins of Olive Ridley Turtles, well after they had become party to CITES, claiming that sea turtles were classified under their Fisheries Department which was exempt from the Convention.[1] Hawksbill and Green Turtle shells were exported by Indonesia, Malaysia, India, Pakistan, the Seychelles, Panama, and Nicaragua—all member nations—between 1977 and 1979.[1] West Germany provided a major market, and smaller amounts were imported by the United Kingdom. In all, between 118,014 kg and 132,932 kg of shell were traded in the three years from 1977 to 1979, which represented over 100,000 turtles. 146,518 kg of skins of an estimated 73,259 Olive and Green Turtles were also traded— all in contravention of CITES.[1] In 1981, Ecuador finally banned the export of turtle skins.

The U.S. Endangered Species Act finally listed the Green, Olive Ridley and Loggerhead Turtles in 1979—seven years after they had been proposed—when the Environmental Defense Fund threatened a law suit over the issue. Imports of the "farmed" Green Turtles were cut off and recovery programs were initiated for U.S. populations of these turtles.

The farming of Green Turtles has been the focus of controversy. To date, the largest turtle enterprise, Cayman Turtle Farm (CTF), is still not self-sufficient in that until recently all the eggs were gathered from the wild. The Farm has stopped gathering wild eggs, and reports some captive breeding, but a closed system consisting entirely of captive-raised turtles is many years away, if indeed it is ever feasible. Cayman Turtle Farm has sold large amounts of meat— some 130,000 kg in 1977, and 54,000 kg in 1979. Until the U.S.

Drawing by Esta Belcher

*Among the most venerable species on earth, **Green Turtles** are struggling to survive the massive killings for meat, shell and oil.*

---

*A reservation indicates that the country gives notice it will not enforce the CITES regulation on that species.

*This **Green Turtle** has just been caught and is awaiting slaughter.*

Photo by Jean Lynn

Endangered Species Act listed the Green Turtle in 1979, this country provided the major market for CTF meat. After the listing, CTF still attempted to export meat to the U.S. The matter was settled by litigation which determined that the Cayman Turtle Farm's turtles could not be imported under provisions of the U.S. Act because they were not captive-bred and constituted a drain on wild populations of turtles. The CTF has pressured the U.S. since then to reopen imports, the latest attempt being a petition presented by a West Coast legal firm in January, 1982 which requested unlimited imports of farmed turtle products. The CTF was suspected of repacking and relabelling wild-caught turtle meat with its own emblem in 1979,[1] and such activity would be very difficult to control. Monitoring is almost impossible, especially if turtle farms are established in other parts of the world. Other negative aspects of the trade in farmed turtle meat include the fact that so little is known about the life history of the Green Turtle that farming efforts are operating without adequate biological information. Such trade also encourages the killing of wild turtles to supply the demand created. One might well ask why these fascinating animals should be killed to supply the tables of thoughtless diners in gourmet restaurants?

The meat of Olive Ridley Turtles continued to be imported into the United States even after it was banned in 1977 mislabelled as other kinds of turtle. 110,000 pounds of smuggled meat from Mexico were seized in the two years after the ban was imposed. The largest seizures were made in August, 1980—some 106,000 lbs. of meat smuggled in from Mexico to various dealers in the U.S. from an estimated 8,800 Ridley Turtles seized. Until he turned it over to the Government in 1981, the Mexican turtle fishery was run exclusively by one man, Antonio Suarez, who owned three processing plants.[1] Not only has Mr. Suarez been indicted for smuggling hundreds of pounds of turtle meat into the U.S., but his purchases of turtles from fishermen in Mexico usually exceeded the government quotas.[1] In 1978, one of Suarez' plants took 50,000 Olive Ridleys, 90% of which were females. This was 16,000 turtles more than the quota permitted.[1] The Government quotas are far higher than the turtle populations can support, so catches in 1979 and 1980 fell precipitously.

In the decade of the 1970's the heavy exploitation of these sea turtles pushed them to commercial extinction in most parts of their ranges. The Kemp's Ridley Turtle is the most endangered, and the others whose original ranges were far larger, are now approaching similar status. Should trade continue—both illegal and between non-CITES countries—at this rate, there is a distinct possibility that these turtles will become extinct in the wild within 10 years. One of the largest remaining markets is Japan. Although it became a member of CITES in 1980, Japan took 9 reservations, including all three commercially exploited sea turtle species (Olive Ridley, Green and Hawksbill).[4] An IUCN researcher shopping in Tokyo in January, 1981 found tortoiseshell eyeglass frames priced at $1600-$4140, turtle skin handbags for $215, and stuffed baby turtles at $150-$400 each.[4]

Only if the markets are closed completely, and wild populations protected from all commercial killing, will the depleted sea turtle populations be able to recover, and their slow rate of reproduction may mean that recovery will take many years.

Crocodiles, Lizards and Snakes

Virtually all the large crocodiles and alligators (20 species) have been decimated by hide hunting over the past 20 years, and are now listed on Appendix I or II of CITES. The South American crocodiles and caimans were so abundant in the early 1960's that millions were killed for export to Europe and the U.S. Their hides are fashioned into shoes, handbags and suitcases for the luxury trade. Elsewhere, crocodiles in Africa, Asia and Australia came under similar pressure, as did the American Alligator. In fact, the depletion of wild crocodiles which occurred by the early 1970's caused the trade interests to turn to turtle skin, continuing their record of massive over-exploitation.

Hunting of the crocodiles and alligators took place during the day as crocodiles tend to form large groups sunning themselves on the banks of rivers. One Colombian conservationist noted that in 1956, it was easy to see 200 adult caimans on the banks of the River Ariari and elsewhere in Colombia, but now they have practically disappeared.[5] In two weeks of recent searching, he and his assistant did not see a single caiman.[5] This in spite of the fact that Colombia has banned exports of crocodile hides for many years. The illegal trade has flourished with Paraguay, the largest South American exporter at present. In 1980, the CITES Secretariat discovered that a Frankfurt, West Germany trader had imported under false documentation, some 200,000 caiman skins from Paraguay.[6]

In Tokyo, crocodilian products are considered status symbols, and high prices do not seem to daunt customers. A single handbag in 1981 sold for $6,250, one belt was priced at $500, and a key holder of crocodile skin was priced at $125.[4] Exorbitant profits such as these keep the market in endangered species alive. The Japanese took a reservation on Saltwater Crocodiles when they joined CITES. Their imports of crocodile products have been considerable (162,727 kg in 1979 alone[4]).

The market in American Alligator has recently been reopened on a quota basis as a result of the species' recovery from the massive slaughter of the 1950's and 1960's, and marked hides are now allowed to be exported and sold within the U.S. There is always the danger that the demand will exceed the supply causing poaching to begin again.

Crocodilians have an important ecological role to play in nature. They affect populations of the fish they prey on and, in times of drought, dig waterholes that save the lives of numerous animals. Their disappearance has resulted in ecological imbalances in many parts of the world.

The luxury leather trade has pushed literally dozens of species toward extinction, and it shows no signs of altering course. Lizard and snakeskin products are now taking the place of turtle and crocodilian leather in the luxury trade. Handbags, wallets and shoes from these reptiles can be seen in department and shoe stores in this country as well as Europe and parts of Asia. The Boa Constrictor, all Python snakes, and Asian monitor lizards, among others, had to be listed on CITES, mainly as a result of their depletion from the skin trade. Others are sure to follow.

A tough California law restricting the sale of reptile products (it also prohibits ivory sale—see next chapter) resulted in the seizure of more than $58,000 worth of crocodile and snake shoes and accessories in December, 1981. Seven fashionable Beverly Hills stores were raided by state officials, startling the owners of Neiman-Marcus, Lanvin of Paris, Hermes Boutique and others whose inventory included the

Photo by Ch. Zuber, World Wildlife Fund

Stuffed caimans *for sale to tourists in Guadeloupe. Hide hunting has reduced most crocodiles to endangered status.*

products of many endangered reptiles. This law, if passed by other states, would be a major deterrent in slowing this trade.

The endangered reptile species of tomorrow can be seen in the advertisements and luxury shops of today. Consumers rarely realize the volume of skins used for commercially popular items. In 1979, for example, Indian Customs officials seized 150,000 snake skins being illegally exported. Millions of these reptiles are being killed worldwide to supply the market.

WILD PETS
Cage Birds

The 1970's brought about two trends, both of which affected the continued survival of rare species of the world, in contrasting ways. First, the keeping of wild animals as pets became more popular than ever before, and collectors, aviculturists and zoos eagerly sought out specimens. If the species were considered rare or endangered, they became more valuable and desirable, in direct proportion to their rarity. Second, conservationists succeeded in enactment of legislation and treaties which set some limits on the pet trade.

In the past 13 years, 6,448,608 birds have been imported into the U.S. alone, of which an estimated 75% were wild caught. World trade in wild birds is estimated at at least 7½ million per year.

In view of the enormous number of wild birds involved in the cage bird trade, it is not surprising to discover that for some species, the drain has resulted in declines, often precipitous, in populations, as well as range reductions of an increasing number of birds.

Many of Australia's brightly colored parrots and parakeets have declined due to overtrapping for aviculturists. The Orange-bellied (*Neophema chrysogaster*), Turquoise (*Neophema pulchella*) and the Splendid Parakeets (*Neophema splendida*) are considered endangered under the U.S. Endangered Species Act. The Paradise Parrot (*Psephotus pulcherrimus*) listed on Appendix I of CITES and endangered on the U.S. Endangered Species list, may well be extinct in the wild.[1] The Golden-shouldered Parrot (*Psephotus chrysopterygius*) is one of the most coveted of all the parrot family—it is worth $300 to the trapper, and collectors are willing to pay as much as $10,000 to obtain one of these rare birds. Subject of an an aptly titled article, "The Parrot with a Price on its Head,"[2] this species and a subspecies known as the Hooded Parrot, remain in high demand. In spite of legal protection, and CITES Appendix I listing, continued losses from illegal trapping and habitat destruction have reached such proportions that *Parrots of the World* author, Joseph Forshaw considered its extinction to be a possibility should present trends continue.[1]

Photo by Helen Snyder, Fish and Wildlife Service

*Capture for the pet trade played a role in endangering the **Puerto Rican Parrot.** There are less than 30 birds left in the wild.*

Caribbean Amazon parrots, too, have suffered from over-collecting for the pet and zoo trade. The magnificent Imperial Parrot of Dominica is endangered mainly as a result of over-capture. It is worth $1000 to anyone who wounds one in the wing for capture, a sum which may represent a year's income to natives of this island. Red-necked, St. Vincent, St. Lucia, Puerto Rican and Bahaman Parrots—all endangered species—likewise are highly coveted by collectors. Unfortunately, there are some collectors who consider themselves bird lovers, but who are willing to acquire a rare species whether or not it has been legally imported; these latter indiviuals are responsible for the removal from the wild of many endangered species for which they are willing to pay exorbitant prices.

The recent craze for parrots in the U.S. has resulted in the importation of thousands of parrots—almost a quarter of a million in

1980 alone—most of them wild-caught. The Red-fronted Macaw (*Ara rubrogenys*), a species whose entire population may number only a few thousand living in a few mountainous provinces of Bolivia, has been imported in increasing numbers by the pet trade. In 1980, 141 were imported, and many are being shipped to Europe, too. This species as well as the Gray-cheeked Parakeet and the Scarlet Macaw, are all threatened by the cage bird trade, but to date receive no protection from the U.S. Endangered Species Act.

Many endangered parrots, cockatoos, and other tropical birds are in great demand, and if legal import is not sanctioned, illegal import is often carried out.

Investigation by the British Customs revealed that one of the largest bird import firms in the country, owned by a Gordon Cooke, had successfully smuggled a pair of Spix Macaws into England in 1977 labeled as Blue-headed Macaws, which are not on any endangered species list.[3] He sold the pair to a U.S. collector for $10,000.[3] It is not known how the birds were imported into the U.S., since the species is on Appendix I of the CITES and endangered on the U.S. Act, but perhaps the same mislabeling strategy was employed. Mr. Cooke was arraigned on six charges of importing endangered species (the Spix Macaws were only one of the protected species he illegally imported); on conviction, he was jailed for six months for making fraudulent Customs declarations, fined £100 and sentenced to three months on the other charges.[4] Only one pair of Spix Macaws has bred in captivity in a Brazilian zoo. In 1978, there were 13 birds known to be in captivity in Europe and the U.S., but no captive breeding programs or stud-book exist to encourage captive breeding.[5] An ornithologist, Robert Ridgely, who conducted surveys of the macaws and parrots of Latin America in 1976, 1977, and 1979, noted that the Spix Macaw is restricted to groves of *Mauritia flexuosa,* a type of palm, and is scarce and apparently nomadic in this habitat; it is found only in portions of four states in eastern Brazil, and there is no reserve to protect it. Ridgely concluded that the major threat to the survival of the Spix Macaw is its high value as a cage bird, which results in its being smuggled out of Brazil into Paraguay for export abroad.[6]

The Black Palm Cockatoo, which is protected throughout its range in New Guinea, Indonesia and Australia, has been regularly smuggled into the U.S. David Wee, a Singapore dealer, gave careful instruction to a customer:

> Dear Sir:
>
> Your cable acknowledge and thank you. The Black Palms, this we have them for you and is ready for immediate shipment.
>
> In your cable, you mention payment by letter of credit, this we could accept, but on condition that you just write four heads live cockatoos and not Black Palm Cockatoo, as we cannot export this birds out legal, as this is protected birds, also in your UK Import Permit you just put live Cockatoos . . . Thank you and inform us as we are keeping this Palms for you.
>
> Yours faithfully,
> David Wee

This letter was received by a British aviculturist who turned the letter over to authorities.[7]

In 1979 and 1980 alone 27 Black Palm Cockatoos were confiscated from three wildlife importers as they were being smuggled into the U.S.

*These **baby parrots** were being sold in a Mexican border town. It is illegal to remove parrots from the nest in Mexico.*

Photo by Linda Tyrrell

Rare and endangered species are occasionally advertised openly. In 1979, a New York City chain of pet stores offered a Black Palm Cockatoo for $4,500. The ad offered "any species of parrot available immediately. Time needed for endangered species."[8] A wholesale pet dealer in Florida's price list for June, 1979 contained ads for an endangered species (Razor-billed Curassow—$599), and several protected species (Baby Male Eclectus Parrot—$800; Baby Hand-feeding Bare Eye Cockatoo— $1,000; and Male Adult Leadbeater Cockatoo—$3,750).

While birds seem to be the most popular among wild pets there is a growing market for snakes and tortoises, many of them endangered or protected species.

Reptile Pets

At one time zoos were the major buyers of rare and endangered reptiles, and many zoos felt they had to obtain "one of everything." In 1977, a major case broke involving the smuggling of a large number of endangered reptiles by U.S. pet dealers. Species included the Fiji Iguana, a beautiful emerald green lizard, very rare in the wild, Green Tree Pythons and Johnson's Crocodiles from Asia. In all, about 350 endangered reptiles were shipped from their native countries through Zurich to New York where documents were altered by entering non-endangered species' names. Most of the reptiles were sold directly to zoos. However, 75 of the unsold reptiles froze to death when they were left out in the open on a cold November night by the dealer. To hide the evidence, he buried them. Agents from the Fish and Wildlife Service and Customs later exhumed the animals which led to a long investigation resulting in a grand jury indictment in 1977. Zoos which had purchased reptiles from the dealers included some of the largest in the United States.

The market for reptiles has grown exponentially in the years since 1977. A major undercover case conducted by the Fish and Wildlife Service revealed the illegal shipment of some 10,000 native American as well as foreign reptiles, mainly to private collectors in the U.S. and abroad. Under investigation in 1981 were 175 customers, all of whom purchased endangered or protected reptiles from the Atlanta Wildlife Exchange. The Fish and Wildlife Service estimates that illegal traffic in native reptiles may involve as many as 100,000 specimens a year.[9] Some of the endangered and protected reptiles included San Francisco Garter Snakes, Jamaica Boas, Indian Pythons, Eastern Indigo Snakes, New Mexico Ridge-nosed Rattlesnakes, Rosy Rat Snakes of Florida, Rosy Boas, Gopher Snakes, and King Snakes from California. Exorbitant prices are charged by dealers for these rare species. A Texas Indigo Snake, a protected species, can sell for $300 or more and some of the rarer species sell for well over $1000.

The reptile market continues to thrive, and dealers' lists regularly include rare and endangered species which they mark with a note— "Endangered Species permit needed." Since commercial traffic is prohibited in endangered and CITES Appendix I species, one can well wonder how the dealers acquired these reptiles. One dealer, Midwest Reptile Sales, Inc. has a price list which goes on for 10 pages with hundreds of species available, many rare and endangered.

In Europe there is a sizeable market for tortoises, most of which are imported from Greece, the Mideast and North Africa. The Royal Society for the Prevention of Cruelty to Animals investigated this

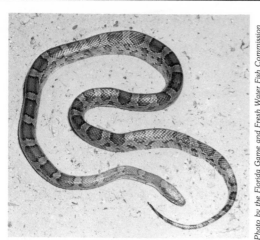

Photo by the Florida Game and Fresh Water Fish Commission

Snakes have become popular as pets, causing many species such as the protected **Rosy Rat Snake** *to be illegally captured and smuggled to collectors.*

trade and found that it was driving several species to near extinction. Moreover, there was a mortality rate of over 80% in the first year of captivity.[10] The number of tortoises involved was astounding—almost 2 million Spur-thighed Tortoises (*Testudo graeca*) entered the United Kingdom between 1965 and 1977. Over 350,000 Hermann's Tortoise and 119,000 Horsfield's Tortoise were imported during the same period. Of these 2,468,820 tortoises, an estimated 1,975,056, died within one year.

A study done in Morocco showed a decrease in abundance of these tortoises of 86% over the last 80 years, and the IUCN *Red Data Book* lists the Mediterranean Spur-thighed Tortoise (*Testudo graeca graeca*) as vulnerable and depleted because of the pet trade.

Chameleons are popular pets in the United States. They are not well suited to captivity, however, having specialized requirements for temperature, moisture and nutrition, and they usually perish within days of purchase. Over 80,000 chameleons were imported from Kenya in the years 1978 to 1980. This trade is controlled by Jonathan Leakey, son of the late anthropologist, Dr. Louis Leakey. Dr. C. Kenneth Dodd, Jr., a herpetologist with the U.S. Office of Endangered Species, visited collecting areas in Kenya, and described the conditions of the animals awaiting export:

> "The lower part of the cage was filled with dead and rotting chameleons, and many of the live animals were very thin or moved with unnatural spastic movements. The cage had a very strong odor of rotting animals. The collector told me that the animals are not fed.."*

The live pet trade involves many other types of animals, including millions of tropical fish, and many types of mammals. The rare species attract the highest prices and are the most sought after, thereby increasing their rarity.

The Pet Industry and Endangered Species

The pet trade has reacted to the recent increase in arrests and investigations of illegal trafficking by raising funds for their lobbying organizations. In the U.S., the Pet Industry Joint Advisory Council is the largest. Its ads say "Stop adverse federal, state and local regulation from putting us out of business." A recent editorial in the trade magazine *Pet Business* (Jan. 1982) alleged: "overzealous Interior and Customs Agents can be seen swarming over our industry, guns drawn, handcuffs ready, as if Elliott Ness had returned to television."[11] The editorial claimed that the recent arrests in the major reptile case were a "handful of questionable suspects."

Even more serious is the "hit list" of the pet trade as represented by three major organizations in the U.S. and Europe. This list includes 28 species which the pet industry wants to have deleted or downgraded in status on CITES lists.[12] The Radiated Tortoise of Madagascar (see Island of Natural Wonders) is recommended by the pet industry for downgrading to Appendix II which would open up trade. Several parrot species, the Vinaceous Amazon, Spix Macaw, and Bahama Amazon, among others, are recommended for deletion or downgrading.[12]

Other Wild Collectibles

• The beautiful arctic Gyrfalcon nesting in its remote aerie can have its young plucked away for sale to an Arab sheikh for $25,000 or

*Dodd, C. Kenneth, Jr. 1982. Kenya's Kinyonga may be in trouble. *Defenders*, June, 57(3):19-25.

more, to be added to a princely collection of hundreds of hunting falcons. Peregrine Falcons are equally coveted by falconers, and conservationists had to install a radar detector on one of the few remaining nests in California to prevent the chicks from being stolen by falconers after repeated attempts, sometimes successful, at theft. Falconry is rising in popularity to the dismay of many conservationists.

• Avid butterfly collectors increased the rarity of some species by their willingness to pay thousands of dollars for specimens. Biologists attempting to preserve the endangered Prairie Sphinx Moth found only in a tiny area in Colorado, have been tailed by collectors and forced to drive hundreds of miles out of their way to avoid disclosing the moths' location. Collectors will pay $750 for a single specimen of this moth. Some species fetch $2,000 or more. The dramatic birdwing butterflies of New Guinea were added to CITES after collectors depleted wild populations.

• Some 5,000 species of sea shells can be purchased in shops in Florida, and a worldwide network of dealers supplies collectors by mail with rare specimens. The U.S. alone imports 4 million kg of shells every year, and even some common species are becoming depleted. A rare Glory of the Seas shell or Golden Cowrie can sell for thousands of dollars, and dramatic foot-long Triton shells have been so heavily collected that they have disappeared from many coral reefs. Some biologists have suggested that the spread of the coral-eating Crown-of-Thorns starfish which is threatening many reefs can be traced to the disappearance of the Tritons which prey on these starfish. Corals are likewise being removed from reefs for jewelry and novelty items—500,000 kg of coral are imported into the U.S. each year, and much of it is obtained by dynamiting coral reefs in Sri Lanka, and the Philippines.

• Cactus rustlers are uprooting these desert plants on such a scale that the family *Cactaceae* has been added to CITES. Some European collectors were recently caught with over 5,000 rare cacti they were attempting to smuggle out of Mexico. The trade is of such proportions that many species are in imminent danger of extinction.

• Exotic animals are sold with little restriction in the United States. Large animals are auctioned off to the highest bidder at regular sales. At one auction held in Missouri in 1981, 3,500 animals, including Bactrian Camels, Hartmann's Mountain Zebras, Bengal Tigers, Leopards—all endangered species—and many CITES Appendix II animals including wild cats, Guanacos, Lions, otters, wolves and African antelopes were sold. Many of these animals end up in shabby roadside zoos, private game preserves, trained animal acts, and even slaughtered for the exotic meat business. As Jim Mason, a writer who attended this auction, reported in a recent *Vegetarian Times* (#54), the inhumanity and lack of restrictions on these auctions are shocking. The conditions under which many animals were kept were extremely inhumane—two bobcats were caged in a ten-gallon drum with wire mesh on the open end, without drains, food or water. Many of the hoofed animals were injured or sick, and had not received veterinary care.

A number of species are on their way toward endangered status through over-commercialization. Just by consulting endangered species lists, one cannot be certain a species is currently endangered.

Photo by U.S. Fish and Wildlife Service

Collectors have illegally uprooted and stolen many types of rare cacti. This **Bunched Cory cactus** *is listed as threatened by the U.S. Act.*

There is a long lapse between status surveys and official listing, and often bureaucratic inertia delays or even prevents such listing. To be absolutely sure that you are not causing species to decline, avoid buying wild animals and plants as pets or products made from wild animals.

ENDANGERED SPECIES – THE CALIFORNIA APPROACH TO LAW AND ENFORCEMENT

By Barry C. Groveman
Los Angeles Deputy City Attorney
Office of City Attorney
Special Prosecution Unit

*Baby **African Elephants** stay with their mothers who, along with female relatives, protect them fiercely for five years or more.*

Photo by Cynthia Moss, African Wildlife Leadership Foundation

Currently hundreds of species of plants and animals worldwide are threatened with extinction. Many of these are listed on the federal endangered species list of individual states. While several factors are involved, a major danger is the ruthless and systematic commercial exploitation of many animals.

Widely publicized facts contained in respected publications, such as *National Geographic,* indicate the seriousness of this growing problem. A most dramatic example is the diminishing elephant population in many African countries, such as Uganda, where poachers can earn incredible sums compared to what would otherwise be their yearly incomes, because of the high prices created by western markets. In some instances the price of elephant ivory has reportedly been as high as $90 a pound, which provides an enormous profit from an elephant with tusks weighing 100 pounds each. It's easy to understand how the largest national park in Uganda saw its elephant population diminish from 8,000 animals in 1966 to roughly 160 by 1976, and now to near extermination. Similar heartbreaking statistics extend to many endangered animals and span many areas of the world. This tragedy poses a threat to continued tourism in countries where wildlife is a significant natural attraction, while destroying beautiful, serene and docile animals who now die in agony at the hands of hunters and poachers.

Negotiations by many nations have led to treaties and conventions dealing with the specific issue of trade to endangered species. In the United States as well as many other countries, such trafficking or trade is illegal. Goods manufactured from endangered species can be seized at ports of entry and impounded. Currently thousands of seized items are in U.S. Customs and U.S. Fish and Wildlife Service warehouses. While many states do not even attempt to regulate trade in endangered species, a few, California in particular, have enacted stringent laws to protect endangered species and wildlife. This California law, which appears to be the strongest in the United States, is more restrictive than the federal law. "The California Endangered Species Act," was enacted in the early '70's and subsequently amended to its present form. The law, contained in section 653(o) of the California Penal Code, provides:

"Endangered species; Importation or possession for sale unlawful (a) It is unlawful to import into this state for commercial purposes, to possess with intent to sell, or to sell within the state, *the dead body,* or any part or product thereof, of any alligator, crocodile, polar bear, leopard, ocelot, tiger, cheetah, jaguar, sable antelope, wolf (*Canis lupus*) zebra, whale, cobra, python, sea turtle, colobus monkey, kangaroo, vicuna, sea otter, free-roaming feral horse, dolphin or porpoise (Delphinidae), Spanish lynx, or elephant. [emphasis added]

"Any person who violates any provision of this section is guilty of a misdemeanor and shall be subject to a fine of not less than one thousand dollars ($1,000) and not to exceed five thousand dollars ($5,000) or imprisonment in the county jail for not to

*The **Ivory** Room at Mombasa. The high prices paid for ivory have had tragic consequences for elephants.*

Photo by World Wildlife Fund

exceed six months, or both such fine and imprisonment, for each violation."

Even the strongest law is ineffective unless aggressively enforced. Such programs have emerged in California in cities such as Los Angeles, San Diego, and San Francisco. One of the most vigorous efforts has been waged by the Los Angeles City Attorney's Office. A specialized prosecution unit concentrating on major issues of environmental protection has been set up. The unit, three attorneys, one law clerk, and a support staff of two, was created eight years ago under the then newly-elected City Attorney Burt Pines. It was designed mainly to prosecute air pollution violators and gradually increased to include hazardous waste and then endangered species and wildlife. About two years ago, becoming aware of the increasing trade in endangered species within the City of Los Angeles, the Environmental Protection Unit began to initiate many of its own investigations into the source and illegal trade of these animals within the city.

One of their first cases was *People v. Rose Kirby*, Case No. 31112284, which dealt with a small retail jewelry store which was selling items made from elephant ivory. In order to prosecute for a violation of the Endangered Species Act, Penal Code 653(o), the ivory carvings had to be shown to be made from elephant ivory and also had to be shown to have been imported into the State of California subsequent to the enactment of Penal Code Section 653(o) on June 1, 1977. The latter was not difficult since this shipment of ivory had been traced from Hong Kong to California (in 1979) through Hawaii and had cleared customs in Hawaii where federal agents marked it with invisible powder. The U.S. Fish and Wildlife Service agents knew that if these items were offered for sale in California they would be in violation of California law. By marking the items with powder, it could be proven that these items had entered the State of California subsequent to enactment of the 1977 law. When the ivory arrived in California, federal agents advised local authorities that the shipment had entered the State. The ivory was traced to the retail store in question where undercover agents observed it was being offered for sale. Agents, posing as buyers, handled the items in a way that would allow the invisible powder to rub off on their hands. After leaving the store and checking their hands under a black light, they knew that the ivory offered for sale was the same ivory that had entered the state within the statutory time frame. The ivory was seized and criminal charges were filed. The difficulty in proving this case, however, turned upon the ability of the prosecution to prove to a jury of 12 people that the ivory was from a *dead elephant,* as required by the statute. The defense posed several arguments, claiming that it was theoretically *possible* for the elephant to have been drugged while the tusk was removed or for the tusk to have been shed from a live elephant. Since two of the 12 jurors believed that it was *possible* for ivory to have been taken from a live elephant in this manner despite the high cost and impracticality of such a practice, the jury was hung and no decision was rendered. The store did, however, discontinue the sale of items made from elephant ivory.

Even if heavy equipment were available and time did not matter, the process of removing an elephant's tusk would be extremely difficult since the tusk is actually imbedded in the elephant's skull. Experts believe that the elephant must die or suffer greatly if its tusks are removed, particularly since the valued part of the tusk is close to the base of the skull and must literally be yanked or hacked out. Films produced by wildlife associations in Kenya show that poachers often kill the elephant, hide it, and come back days later to remove more easily the tusks from the decaying animal. To perform major surgery in the African bush to get ivory from a living elephant is out of the question.

Other cases later emerged with more positive results, such as the *People v. Richard's Shoes*, Case No. 31172279, and *People v. Howard & Phil's Western Wear*, Case No. 31172281. In both cases information was received that these large boot and shoe retailers were offering items for sale that were comprised wholly or in part of python skin or elephant ear. Undercover investigations were made of all these stores and positive identification was made of the questioned skins. Once sufficient evidence was gathered to establish probable cause that Penal Code Section 653(o) was being violated, all the items from the stores were seized and the stores were later prosecuted successfully. The convictions resulted in very large fines and unique conditions of probation which required the store owners to advertise in local newspapers in support of the Endangered Species Act.

The trend of successful prosecutions continued as numerous retailers were caught and found guilty of selling products made from endangered species. Perhaps the most significant prosecution thus far in this area was the case of *People v. Stanley Galleries, Inc.*, Case No. 31201777. This case involved the offering for sale of approximately 300 items of intricately carved elephant ivory with an estimated retail value of $1 million. Many of the pieces were true works of art. Once again, based upon an investigation initiated by the Environmental Protection Unit, undercover police officers and agents of the State Department of Fish and Game entered Stanley Galleries, Inc., in the Los Angeles Hilton Hotel and identified the items for sale as elephant ivory. Since the ivory was discovered in the store and was not traced from a port of entry into California, there was uncertainty as to whether these items had been in California prior to the enactment of Penal Code Section 653(o). It appeared unlikely, however, that a shop dealing almost exclusively in the sale of ivory would not have turned over any of its inventory in four years. Because of the considerable value of the items and the concern that unwarranted removal of these delicate items could irreparably damage the defendant's business and create a substantial liability to the City of Los Angeles, novel warrants were prepared which in effect froze the items in the store for approximately 72 hours during which time the owner was allowed to provide documentation showing that these items had been in California prior to 1977. The warrants indicated that if the owner was unwilling or unable to provide such documentation, then the items would be seized and removed. At the expiration of the 72-hour time limit no documentation was forthcoming and statements made by the owner through his attorneys indicated that no reasonable amount of time would facilitate the production of the necessary documents. Accordingly, all the items of elephant ivory were removed from the store through a careful and tedious process that took over 11 hours. Also seized were numerous documents and bills of sale reflecting sales to private buyers and providing clues as to the origin of this large quantity of ivory. It was suspected that large amounts of ivory were coming from a well-known New York ivory wholesaler. Cooperation was sought

Photo by Los Angeles Police Department

An ivory carving seized by California law enforcement officials.

and received from the New York State Department of Environmental Conservation. Agents from that Department entered the suspected wholesale outlet in New York and requested voluntary production of documentation of any ivory sales to Stanley Galleries, Inc., in Los Angeles. The proprietors of the wholesale outlet in New York, unaware of the pending investigation in Los Angeles, freely volunteered this information since the sale of ivory is not banned in New York. Copies of these documents were sent to Los Angeles proving, beyond a reasonable doubt, that a large amount of the ivory had in fact been shipped into the State of California subsequent to the enactment of Penal Code Section 653(o). Thus the case was practically complete and there was now no time for any documents to be forged which would otherwise establish that the ivory had been in California prior to the enactment of the California law. At the same time, based upon facts presented by the Los Angeles City Attorney's Office, an investigation was begun by the San Francisco District Attorney's Office into a large wholesale outfit in San Francisco, related to the wholesale store in New York, that allegedly had also sold large quantities of ivory to the Los Angeles based Stanley Galleries, Inc.

Photo by Fish and Wildlife Service

*Thousands of **products made from endangered species** are confiscated yearly by U.S. Fish and Wildlife Service and Customs officials from tourists and others who contribute to species' rarity with their purchases.*

Further documentation and evidence gathered in San Francisco provided the remaining pieces of the puzzle, establishing that virtually all the ivory in the Stanley Galleries, Inc., store had arrived in California subsequent to the enactment of the California law. These swift investigations and their resulting evidence, along with the possibility that additional charges might be filed based upon crimes being investigated by the San Francisco District Attorney, i.e., a conspiracy involving several corporations, led to a quick resolution in the Stanley Galleries, Inc. case. The proprietors of Stanley Galleries, Inc. were eager to cut their losses and put an end to this episode. Thus, Stanley Galleries, Inc., entered pleas of nolo contendere to numerous counts of Penal Code Section 653(o) and agreed to cooperate with the San Francisco District Attorney. In return for their cooperation and upon recommendation by the prosecution, the sentence imposed by the court upon Stanley Galleries, Inc., was lenient, yet served as an effective punishment and as a deterrent to others. Most significant, however, were the unique conditions of probation that utilized punishment as a way of providing a public service. The court ordered the company to forfeit the entire inventory, an estimated $1 million of elephant ivory, to the Board of Recreation and Parks for use in educational displays at the Los Angeles Zoo and for use in an exhibit to be constructed at the Los Angeles International Airport. This exhibit will be constructed prior to the 1984 Olympics scheduled to be held in Los Angeles and will focus on California law dealing with endangered animals. In addition, the defendants were placed on 18 months probation upon the condition that they pay a $5,000 fine, contribute an additional $3,000 to the construction of the endangered species exhibit for the Airport, and provide $1,500 for advertising, in major news periodicals, in support of the California Endangered Species Act.

The Stanley Galleries, Inc., case was reported to be the largest seizure and prosecution for elephant ivory in United States history.

The types of cases discussed above are not unique to California. They are symptomatic of a burgeoning problem spreading throughout the United States. The markets for endangered animal products will continue to flourish in those states that do not have adequate laws and aggressive enforcement programs to check the ruthless commercial exploitation of and trade in endangered animals.

While it may not be completely realistic to expect strong, uniform laws and vigorous enforcement in states across the United States will completely eliminate the market for endangered animals, it is reasonable to believe that significant efforts in this direction will protect many of nature's precious animals threatened with extinction. Through tougher laws, aggressive enforcement and public education, the incentives for useless slaughter and commercial exploitation can and will be outweighed by the disincentives of punishment and public censure.

Overhunting and Persecution

Over the centuries, man's hunting has been responsible for a number of extinctions. Ice Age hunters eliminated the cave bear and cave hyena in Europe, and in America, the mastodon, mammoth, giant sloth and other large mammals are thought to have been exterminated by Pleistocene hunters. The Moas, Elephant Bird, Carolina Parakeet, Passenger Pigeon, and many others have succumbed in more recent times to overkill. Today's endangered species list still contains examples of excessive hunting. Most wildlife killing which endangers animals is for commercial purposes, but in many parts of the world, meat and sports hunting is virtually wiping out species. Many animals subject to heavy hunting in the past have not returned to their former abundance in spite of protection. Trophy hunting has also affected wildlife because the targets are often rare species, either rare from hunting or from other causes.

Trophy Hunting

During the late 19th and early 20th centuries sports hunting was at its height. Wealthy European and Indian big game hunters competed with one another for trophies and big kills. Many Indian maharajahs and British hunters took what Vinzenz Ziswiler, in his interesting

Tigre royal lithograph by Eugène Delacroix

National Gallery of Art

book *Extinct and Vanishing Animals,* describes as "a morbid pleasure in killing."[1] Lord Ripon, an Englishman who died in 1923, was credited with killing 500,000 game birds and mammals—about 67 creatures for every shooting day of his life![2]

Mainly confined to Africa today, Lions once inhabited most of west Asia, and parts of eastern Europe. The Romans killed hundreds in gladiatorial spectacles, having to import most from North Africa, so rare had they become even at that early date. Gradually, Lions were eliminated from the western parts of their range. By the thirteenth century, they disappeared from the Near East, and by 1800 they had been shot out of Iraq. Iran and Pakistan followed suit.[2] By the mid-19th century, Asian Lions were confined to India, but were still widespread.[2] British Colonial officers traditionally took a Lion pelt proudly back to England, and a single hunter boasted of shooting 300 Indian Lions in 1860.[3] Under such pressure, Lions disappeared from all of India save the Gir Forest in the southwest by 1884.[3] In 1900, protection was finally extended when their populations had been reduced to less than 100 animals.[2] Today, the Gir Forest Lions number only about 180, limited by the steady deterioration of the forest from overgrazing by livestock and tree cutting.[3] The habitat became protected in 1971, and their population is now stable.[3]

Trophy hunting *has been a factor making many rare species even rarer.*

The most prestigious trophy for maharajahs and colonial hunters was the Tiger, largest of all cats. One maharajah shot at least 1,000 Tigers in his lifetime, while another complained that his total bag of Tigers was only 1,150.[2] Tiger hunts were a royal pastime—hundreds of native "beaters" drove the frightened Tiger toward a hunter who was perched safely atop an elephant. The number of Tigers killed by these two maharajahs equalled the total population of Tigers in India by the late 1960's.

Since Tigers require large territories, at least ten square kilometers, their natural density is very low. Even so, they probably once numbered 50,000 in India alone, and their range once extended throughout most of Asia. One biologist calculated that 117,000 Tigers could live on Sumatra, 31,000 on Java, and 560 on Bali under ideal circumstances.[1] Yet the World Wildlife Fund recently calculated that the total world population of Tigers did not exceed 5,000.[4] The Bali race is now considered extinct, and on Java, only three to five Tigers remain.[4] The combined effects of massive logging and other habitat loss, persecution from livestock owners and farmers, and continued trophy and fur hunting have reduced the Tiger population to a tiny remnant of its original numbers.

In the stark deserts of the Arabian peninsula, wildlife is not abundant: the animals struggle just to survive in the harsh environment. When Arab sheikhs began hunting Oryx, gazelles and Ostriches in jeeps and trucks, mowing down the animals with repeating rifles and shotguns, the result was predictable. From World War II onward, these macabre and senseless raids took place, even involving the use of planes and helicopters for spotting. Sometimes animals were pursued until they dropped from exhaustion. In 1955, some 482 cars took part in a hunt, during the course of a "royal good-will tour" in northern Arabia, and every living animal seen was gunned down.[2] The Arabian Ostrich was a casualty of these forays—the last wild Ostrich was seen in 1966 and this subspecies is now extinct. The Syrian Wild Ass also succumbed to over-hunting. It became clear to conservationists alarmed at these massacres that the Arabian Oryx

Photo by World Wildlife Fund/OKAPH

Elephants *are being killed to manufacture tourist curios such as these grisly wastebaskets made from their feet, ivory jewelry and other trinkets.*

would be the next animal to become extinct if quick action were not taken. Ian Grimwood, sponsored by the Fauna Preservation Society and the IUCN, undertook an expedition in 1962 to capture some of the last wild Oryx for captive breeding. In eastern Aden, they managed to capture four Oryx, and the herd was augmented from private game farms and zoos by another eight animals, which were all transported to the zoo in Phoenix, Arizona. The Oryx adjusted easily to the desert climate of the American Southwest. This project saved the species from extinction, because the last three Oryx ever seen in the wild were killed in 1972 in southern Oman.[3] Today, the captive herd is flourishing at three zoos in the U.S., and some of these stately animals have been reintroduced in protected preserves in Israel, and in 1982 in Oman and Jordan. The delicate Arabian and Sand Gazelles still survive in this region in very reduced numbers— endangered from excessive mechanized hunting according to the *Red Data Book*.[3]

The vastness of the Sahara has been the scene of similar carnage. The Addax, a large and statuesque antelope, is in the words of the IUCN, "in danger of extinction from ruthless hunting over much of its range."[3] Army and big game hunters have been pursuing the Addax, Scimitar-horned Oryx, Pelzeln's Gazelle, and the Slender-horned Gazelle of North Africa in jeeps gunning them down with machine guns.[3] This activity intensified in the late 1970's.

In the Abou Telfane Game Reserve in southern Chad, the last Greater Kudus were seen being destroyed in 1976. Helicopter crews were shooting the animals with rockets, and the same method was used to kill elephants.[5]

Perhaps the most famous massacre of recent times was carried out by Idi Amin's troops in Uganda. The African Elephant population dropped from 30,000 in 1973 to 4,000 in 1978, and a 1980 census found less than 2,000 animals in all of Uganda.[6] Uganda's national parks are still littered with animal carcasses, poacher's camps and meat-drying racks. Dr. Eric L. Edroma, Director of the Uganda Institute of Ecology, described the scene as "horrifying, pathetic and sad."[6] All elephants in Uganda had been given legal protection in 1975, and all hunting had been banned in 1979,[6] laws which the President flouted, opening up the country to wholesale slaughter. (See "People Who Make a Difference" for a portrait of Paul Ssali, one of the few Ugandan park wardens who attempted to stem this tide.)

A recent survey of Americans found that most approved of hunting for meat, but 80% condemned trophy hunting. Several European countries have placed a blanket ban on the importation of CITES Appendix I species trophies. The United States has not done this. For many trophy hunters, the most sought after animals are often endangered species, especially fine specimens—those that should be left to maintain the genetic strength of the species.

In 1978 the Safari Club International filed an application with the Department of Interior to import trophies of 1,120 endangered animals.

The application list included the following animals:
    25 Argali Sheep
    10 Shapo Sheep
    50 Urial Sheep
    10 Eld's Brow-antlered Deer

*A baby **Orangutan**. The Safari Club International requested a permit to kill orangutans as trophies, along with many other rare and endangered species.*

Photo by Smithsonian Institution

- 10 Hog Deer
- 10 Marsh Deer
- 10 Musk Deer
- 10 Pampas Deer
- 10 Persian Fallow Deer
- 10 Swamp Deer
- 15 Clark's Gazelles
- 25 Dorcas Gazelles
- 5 Rio de Oro Dama Gazelles
- 5 Slender-horned Rhim Gazelles
- 15 Swayne's Hartebeests
- 5 Pyrenees Ibex
- 15 Black-faced Impalas
- 150 Lechwes
- 10 Seladangs
- 100 Mountain Zebras
- 20 Markhors
- 10 Northern White Rhinoceros
- 40 Bobcats (endangered Mexican subspecies)
- 20 Black-footed Cats
- 10 Tiger Cats
- 100 Cheetahs
- 40 Jaguars
- 20 Jaguarundis
- 150 Leopards
- 5 Clouded Leopards
- 10 Snow Leopards
- 40 Margays
- 50 Ocelots
- 25 Tigers
- 15 Black Colobus Monkeys
- 5 Red and Zanzibar Colobus Monkeys
- 5 Gorillas
- 5 Orangutans
- 50 Slender-snouted Crocodiles

Source: Notice by the Fish and Wildlife Service in the Federal Register, Vol. 43(23):53121, December 12, 1978.

After a public outcry the Club withdrew its application, but in 1982 it was successful in its long battle to allow importation of leopard trophies.

Hunting articles in magazines frequently glorify the pursuit of endangered species. One such article in 1981 encouraged the hunting in Mexico of Puma, Jaguar, Ocelot and "crested Guan" or Horned Guan, all endangered species.[8] It noted parenthetically, "However, United States laws prohibit bringing in skins."[8]

Conservationists are protesting the opening of Mongolia to trophy hunters: it is a country with a strong history of wildlife conservation.[9] The total population of Snow Leopards in Mongolia is estimated at less than 300,[3] but it is now a game animal under new regulations. One West German and two U.S. hunting firms are now offering trophy hunters the opportunity to shoot this magnificent animal for a $50,000 premium.[9]

The Argali Sheep is also endangered, yet is now a game species in Mongolia. Both the Argali Sheep and the Snow Leopard are listed on CITES, the Snow Leopard being in the restrictive, endangered

Recently, a large number of rare **Lammergeiers** *have been killed by driving a nail into the head of the live bird for the taxidermy market in West Germany.*

category of Appendix I species. Two American hunters encountered by a reporter in Mongolia did not expect any trouble in bringing back their Snow Leopard trophies[9] in spite of both international regulations and the listing of these animals on the U.S. Endangered Species list.

In 1980, the Klineburger World Adventure Club Hunting Report presented a plan to open up the Himalayan regions of India to trophy hunting. Twelve huntable animals were listed that are all on CITES Appendix I.

Some birds are hunted as trophies and mounted. An endangered Peregrine Falcon, captive bred at Cornell University's facility in Ithaca, which has produced over 200 Peregrines for reintroduction to the wild, was killed by a hunter in New Jersey in 1975. He had it mounted by a taxidermist complete with legbands and radio transmitter designed to trace the bird's movements after release. Someone reported him; the incident made national news, and eventually the State of New Jersey reached an out-of-court settlement for $2,000 which was donated to the Peregrine Fund at Cornell.[10]

Even more lugubrious is the trade in Lammergeiers, large birds of prey listed on CITES Appendix II, which have become very rare in their vast range which once extended from southern Europe east to Tibet and south to eastern Africa. In 1979, 200 Lammergeiers were imported into Germany from China.[11] The birds had been caught alive and then killed by driving a nail into the back of their heads.[11] This preserved the birds as prime specimens for German taxidermists who mount them and sell them for very high prices.[11] The bodies of 300 Black Vultures were also imported into Germany from China under exactly the same circumstances; this may represent a growing trend for stuffed and mounted birds of prey.

Meat Hunting

The hunting of animals for subsistence has made some inroads on wildlife in the past, but not on today's massive scale. Within the last 20 years the human population explosion, coupled with the use of automatic weapons, has had very serious consequences on the wildlife of Asia, Africa and Latin America, especially where large numbers of people live off the land. In Southeast Asia deer and related species are under heavy siege from local hunters. The guerrilla wars in Laos, Cambodia, and Thailand in the past few years have aggravated the danger since entire bands of hundreds of soldiers live off the land, killing any wild animal that can provide a meal. The Kouprey, a large wild bovid, native to this region, was on the verge of extinction prior to recent hostilities. Biologists have been unable to enter the area of southern Laos and western Vietnam to ascertain whether it still exists. The major range of Fea's Muntjac, a heavy-set deer of Burma and Thailand whose flesh is considered a great delicacy by natives, lies in an area where armed insurgents are hunting local game.[3] Other deer which are highly threatened by meat hunting are Kuhl's Deer found only on Bawean Island north of Java, the Calamian Deer confined to two Philippine Islands, and races of the beautiful Sika Deer in the Ryukyu Islands and China.[3] The Formosan Sika Deer has been totally exterminated in the wild by hunting and exists only in captivity. The amazing variety of deer and other ungulates in Asia is being reduced to scattered remnants mainly because of uncontrolled hunting.

Likewise in Latin America, species of deer, tapirs and peccaries are under constant pressure from hunters, especially with recent road building which provides access into previously remote wilderness areas. Among the most endangered by these activities are the South Andean Huemul deer, North Andean Huemul, the Marsh Deer, Northern Pudu, and Central American Tapir.[3]

All species of Sirenia or sea cows are threatened by intense hunting for their meat. The Dugong was once widely distributed from the western Pacific to the Red Sea, but wherever these large, slow-moving and helpless mammals occur, they are killed with impunity by fishermen. They inhabit sheltered, shallow coastal areas, like the Manatees of Africa and the Western Hemisphere, placing them in frequent contact with humans. The Dugong, Caribbean Manatee, Amazonian Manatee and the West African Manatee are protected in many parts of their range and listed on CITES, but this protection is inadequately enforced. In Florida, manatees were greatly reduced by hunting in the 19th and early 20th centuries, but the major threat today to the remaining 1,000 animals is human disturbance and injury from motorboats.

For fully 30 species of birds in the *Red Data Book*, hunting is a major threat reducing their numbers.[12] For many others, shooting is a lesser, but still significant threat. Asian pheasants, whose beauty and variety of plumage are legendary, are relentlessly hunted; eight species are close to extinction. The pheasants stay in family groups in one small area for several months at a time, and even when under constant fire, they do not disperse, so whole families are shot at the same time.

Rheas of South America make easy targets for hunters on the treeless pampas, and one endangered race, the Puna Rhea, although protected, is still avidly hunted by people in dune buggies near mining centers.[12] Other large game birds of South America are critically depleted from over-hunting. The Red-billed Curassow of Brazil, Razor-billed Curassow, Horned Guan, Utile Chachalaca, White-winged Guan and Trinidad Piping Guan are among these endangered birds.

Numerous wild pigeons are endangered by hunting as are two species of West Indian parrots (the Red-necked and Imperial Amazons of the island of Dominica). The Helmeted Hornbill, a very large tropical Asian species, has an outsized bill with horny casque atop which natives carve into curios for sale to tourists. The Hornbills are also hunted for meat and feathers.

The largest woodpecker in the world, the Imperial Woodpecker, inhabited the remote pine forests of northwest Mexico until the very recent past. These huge, black woodpeckers needed large territories—255 square km per pair—since they fed only on insects in ancient, dead pines. They have been shot on sight by Mexicans for many years. A group of ornithologists looking vainly for the species in the mid-1970's was told that the birds made a very good meal. The last ones were probably shot in the early 1970's, and heavy logging has removed many of the old nesting and feeding trees, although the habitat is still largely intact.

When protective legislation was enacted in the United States to prevent the massive slaughters commonplace in the 19th and early 20th centuries, some wildlife species recovered quickly—the Pronghorn Antelope, Bison, and most ducks and geese, for example. For others, a critical low point was reached in their population, and recovery has been glacially slow. The national bird of Hawaii, the Hawaiian Goose, or Nene, numbered 25,000 prior to heavy hunt-

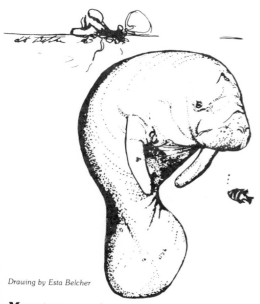

Drawing by Esta Belcher

Manatees *are slow-moving marine mammals still heavily hunted for meat.*

The **American Bison** numbered 50 million in the Great Plains before hunting nearly caused its extinction.

Photo by Lion Country Safari

ing. By the 1940's it was down to 50 birds and in spite of strict protection, it has increased to only about 1,000 birds.[12] Eskimo Curlews once gathered in immense flocks in the 19th century before migrating from the Canadian tundra to South American pampas each fall. As they flew through the Great Plains and the Eastern seaboard, hunters shot hundreds of them at a time, usually leaving them in piles to rot, or selling them in markets by the barrel. The Curlews were thought extinct for many years. Groups of one to three have been seen since the mid-1950's by bird watchers, ever on the lookout for this highly endangered bird. In 1981, biologists saw a flock of 26 birds in Texas, the largest number observed in recent history, giving some hope that the species might be recovering.[13]

The Whooping Cranes, too, were heavily hunted during the same period, and these beautiful birds declined to a low of 15 individuals in 1941.[12] Like the Eskimo Curlews, Bison and other animals, the Whooping Cranes had flourished in greatest numbers on the prairies of the West, scene of some of the worst wildlife slaughters. After 40 years of protection, and very substantial expenditures on conservation and breeding programs, Whooping Cranes still number only about 100 birds.

Open prairies once covered half of the North American continent offering wildlife little cover to hide from hunters. Other casualties were the still rare Greater Prairie Chickens, plump targets for meat hunters, and the Trumpeter Swans whose prairie breeding population was totally eliminated by hunting. Several mid-western states have reintroduced Trumpeter Swans, and Prairie Chickens survive in the remnants of grassland habitat. These birds were slaughtered mainly for meat hunting, but feather hunting and the sheer pleasure of killing all entered in.

Predator Prejudice

Predators were considered vermin by American settlers, and most colonies passed laws such as that in South Carolina enacted in 1695, "An Act for Destroying Beasts of Prey," which mandated that all Indian braves be required to yearly bring in one wolf, panther or bear skin, or two Bobcat skins; if he failed to do so, he would be "severely whipped" but if more than one skin was provided, he would receive a reward.[16] Later, settlers themselves systematically eliminated the Gray and Red Wolves, Cougar and Black Bear. All but the Black Bear were extinct in eastern United States by the early 1800's. Grizzly Bear and wolf hunters were considered heros for extirpating these predators in the Great Plains. The Plains Wolf, almost white in color, was usually trailed by packs of Coyotes who fed on the remains of its kills. The Grizzly Bear, strongest and largest American predator, fought back bravely when shot, but was not able to withstand the pressure from generations of hunters. Both these animals disappeared from the Great Plains in the 19th century. Shooting decimated the wildlife panorama of the Great Plains which once rivaled that of East Africa. Today it is hard to imagine that the fields of corn and wheat now covering this region were once grazing land for herds of Bison fifty million strong, that giant Grizzly Bears, Pronghorn antelope, deer and wolves wandered boldly, and clouds of birds darkened the sky filling the air with their music.

Three centuries of killing predators in the United States have resulted in the near extinction of the Gray Wolf and Grizzly Bear in the lower 48 states and the total extinction of the Red Wolf in the wild. The Grizzly Bear, reduced to remnant populations in Yellow-

Photo by Metro-Goldwyn-Mayer

*Predator destruction programs have reduced the **Grey Wolf,** which once lived throughout most of the United States, to a few scattered populations.*

stone National Park and Montana, seems still to represent an irresistible target to hunters who convinced the Interior Department to permit hunting of Montana's Grizzlies when the species was listed as threatened. South of Canada, the Gray Wolf persists only in tiny numbers in remote parts of Montana, Wyoming, and Washington; about 1,000 live in northern Minnesota, and a few in Wisconsin. Listing the Grizzly Bear and two Gray Wolf subspecies even in their critically depleted numbers on the U.S. Endangered Species Act required threatened law suits by The Fund for Animals and other conservation organizations. In 1982, the Interior Department is considering removing the Minnesota Eastern Timber Wolf from the list altogether. Years of protest from livestock producers have resulted in a weakening of support on the part of the Interior Department for the Eastern Timber Wolf.

The early predator destruction programs carried on by colonists were continued by the U.S. government from 1931 on when an act was passed by Congress authorizing a wide spectrum of control measures. Poison was the major tool used, and it was liberally spread over most of the West for the next 40 years. Thallium sulfate, strychnine, Compound 1080 and cyanide in great quantities were distributed around the country, killing not only wolves, bears and Coyotes, but foxes, weasels, ferrets, and eagles—any animal that ate the poisoned bait. All these poisons except cyanide, which kills quickly, are cruel in the extreme—poisoned animals could take hours to die from Compound 1080, and sometimes days after ingesting thallium sulfate; strychnine causes the most intense pain. Water supplies were sometimes accidentally poisoned, killing humans, dogs and livestock. The violent vomiting that occurred with the deadly convulsions spread more poison that remained toxic for a year or more. Compound 1080, the sheepmen's favored poison, has the added threat of secondary poisoning—an animal dying from this poison can poison another animal that eats its flesh. This secondary poisoning resulted in heavy losses of magpies, crows, ravens, eagles and other creatures which scavenge some of their food.

The poisoning was augmented by trapping, which is equally indiscriminate in its victims, and these predator control programs were especially intensive in the 1950's. There are many documented cases of mutilation and torture of trapped predators by the trappers. Their campaign went far beyond the protection of livestock; they sought out wolves and bears in remote wilderness areas where no livestock grazed, with the express purpose of obliterating predators to the last animal. This irrational prejudice was supported by state and federal legislation through subsidies and bounties and at the height of the government predator control programs in the 1950's, hundreds of trappers and poisoners combed the countryside, randomly placing poison and traps even in areas where endangered species were known to live.

Native American Indians revered the wolf and Grizzly Bear, and the notion that these animals were innately destructive, even to deer and antelope, was the antithesis of their wisdom.

Scientific studies came later, but even in 1940, Adolph Murie, one of the greatest American biologists, found wolves to be a positive element in their environment. In his remarkable study, *The Wolves of Mount McKinley,* he concluded after years of patient observation, "It appears that wolves prey mainly on the weak classes of sheep, that is, the old, the diseased, and the young in their first year. Such

Photo by Mary Bloom

Komondor sheep dogs *have proven very effective in protecting sheep, yet many livestock owners continue to use non-selective and cruel methods of predator control.*

predation would seem to benefit the species over a long period of time and indicates a normal prey-predator adjustment in Mount McKinley National Park."[14] Dr. Murie also observed the close bonds among wolves, and noted that his main impression of the wolf was the remarkable friendliness among members of the pack. His conclusions were borne out by later biologists. The predator hunter of today is only able to use livestock losses as a rationale to kill predators, and even these have been greatly exaggerated by livestock growers. Many die-hard trappers, however, are totally uninformed about the wolf's ecology, and some state Fish and Game Departments still conduct predator reduction programs.

The federal Animal Damage Control Division of the Fish and Wildlife Service persists in its deadly work. Coyote pups are killed in the den, and some 50,000 leghold traps are used. Predators are shot from land and airplane. Alternatives such as guard dogs and taste aversion chemicals such as lithium chloride which make predators sick on eating meat laced with them, but are not lethal, have not been considered viable alternatives by the tradition-bound control agents. Federal trappers have traditionally failed to substantiate the causes of livestock losses, and independent studies have shown losses to predation to be far lower than those claimed by sheep farmers. Predator control programs are conducted on about 18 million acres of federal land, and state and county agents cover millions more.

Conservationists seeking limits to the uses of poisons on federal lands achieved a major victory when President Nixon issued an Executive Order in 1972 banning thallium, 1080, strychnine and cyanide for predator control on federal land. It was modified during the administration of President Ford when the M-44, which shoots the fast acting poison sodium cyanide into the mouth of a predator that tugs on the stick-like mechanism, was allowed on a limited basis. Experimental use of Compound 1080 in sheep collars was permitted under President Carter. Sheepmen have continued to pressure the government to allow use of Compound 1080, one of the worst predator poisons, which kills slowly with great suffering. They successfully lobbied the Reagan administration to rescind the 1972 ban in 1982. Legally, Compound 1080 is still banned by the Environmental Protection Agency (EPA) for predator control, but sheepmen have pressed the EPA into an extensive review of the ban on 1080. The EPA did field research in the 1970's which established conclusively that Compound 1080 and strychnine used either in predator or rodent control are highly toxic to nontarget wildlife. Strychnine used to kill rodents proved lethal to birds which fed on the rodents, even in low concentrations.[*] The EPA had planned to cancel and suspend *all* uses of these chemicals based on this research, but political pressure prevented this action, and now threatens to reverse the clock to a return to the widespread use of poisons.

The Red Wolf Extinct in the Wild

For one species, the predator control program spelled extinction in the wild. The Red Wolf (*Canis rufus*), smaller than the Gray Wolf, once lived in the forests of southeastern United States. From colonial times, Red Wolves were trapped, shot, and poisoned, and caught in

[*]Environmental Protection Agency, 1976. Issuance of a RPAR for products containing strychnine—Action memo 25 pp.

Photo by U.S. Fish and Wildlife Service

*Smaller than the Grey Wolf, the **Red Wolf** is now extinct in the wild as the result of predator control programs and hybridization with the Coyote.*

The Swift Fox

pits where trappers often hamstrung them. This wolf, which had both red and black color phases, is the only wolf surviving to modern times that actually evolved in North America. This species and its ancestor, *Canis edwardii,* were once residents of southern forests as far north as the present state of Pennsylvania since the middle Quaternary.[16] The Grey Wolf is thought by taxonomy specialist Dr. Ronald Nowak of the Office of Endangered Species, to have evolved much later, in the early Pleistocene, and migrated into North America from the Old World.[16] Feeding mainly on rabbits and rodents, the Red Wolf was not a threat to settlers, yet it was systematically trapped out of its range.

It was not until 1962 that this wolf's highly endangered status was realized, and no conservation action to aid the species in the wild took place for another 11 years. By 1970, only a tiny fraction of its original numbers survived in one county in southwestern Louisiana and adjoining areas of northeastern Texas.[17] As these wolves were reduced or eliminated, Coyotes moved into their territories and hybridized with pure Red Wolves. This hybridization spelled the Red Wolf's final demise in a wild state, and even the last remnant populations became diluted by the late 1970's. A live-trapping program to capture the last, pure-blooded specimens with the objective of eventual release in Coyote-free areas began in 1973 in Texas, funded by the Endangered Species Act.[17] Many of the animals captured turned out to be hybrids (determined by head X-ray), and most were in very poor health from mange, heartworm, and other parasites.[17] Their last struggle to survive in the wild was obviously a difficult one. After five years of live-trapping (padded traps and tranquilizer tabs on the traps were used in an effort to avoid injuring the animals), and shipping the Wolves to Point Defiance Zoo in Tacoma, Washington, the total number of adult wild-caught Red Wolves was 30.[17] In 1979, Curtis Carley of the Red Wolf Recovery Team announced quietly in a status report, "Recent findings indicate that the only extant subspecies (*C.r. gregoryi*), once occurring from eastern Texas to eastern Mississippi, for all practical purposes is extinct in the wild."[17] Their last area of residence was no longer wilderness, having been invaded by agriculture and residential development.[17] The captive Red Wolves have bred at the zoo in Tacoma, and several trial attempts have been made to reintroduce the species on islands off the Carolinas. This unique animal may live to wander southern forests again, as reintroduction plans are still afoot, but it can never fully reoccupy its former range.

In the short-grass prairie of the Great Plains, another canid has suffered from predator control. Smallest of all wild dogs, the beautiful, tawny Swift Fox (*Vulpes velox*) weighs only about five pounds, and feeds mainly on small rodents and rabbits. Originally found in the broad strip of short-grass prairie that stretched from Saskatchewan to Texas, the northern race (*Vulpes velox hebes*) of this little fox has been reduced to endangered status, gone from over 90% of its range. The naturalist Ernest Thompson Seton commented on its vulnerability, "Harmless to man and mankind's interests; and yet he is going fast with all the other innocent and lovely wild things. Yes, faster than most, for he is the least cunning of our foxes—so guileless that he readily takes the poisoned baits used nowadays for killing coyotes." In fact, almost none were seen from the early 1920's to the late 1950's.[18] Since then, there have been isolated sightings, and small numbers are known to survive in southwestern Kansas, Nebraska, Montana, Wyoming, and North and South Dakota.[18] Some areas of unplowed prairie provide refuge and the fox has been able to colonize roadsides next to fields and prairie dog towns.

Even though the northern Swift Fox is listed by the Endangered Species Act and by several state laws, predator prejudice continues to take its toll. A family of Swift Foxes in Kansas, being observed and photographed by Glenn Chambers in 1977, was killed by two farmers who poured gasoline in the den entrance and set fire to it. The male fox, provider of all the food for the vixen and pups, was found in a ditch a few yards away, his rib cage ripped out by a high-velocity bullet; the vixen had escaped the burning den with two of the pups, but the farmers shot her as she watched over them.[18] Other Swift Foxes continue to be taken in Animal Damage Control traps. Eight were killed and seven caught and released in just one recent year—1977, according to the ADC unpublished reports. But release from a steel jaw leghold trap is likely to spell death later from gangrene, starvation or infected wounds. Nebraska has conducted an in-depth study of the Swift Fox, and there is some room for cautious optimism that increased public attention to this little fox will result in closure of all trapping wherever the fox is known to occur, and protection of its habitat.

The Black-footed Ferret

Poisoning of prairie dog towns is thought responsible for eliminating the Black-footed Ferret from the Great Plains. Always elusive, this long-bodied, low-slung member of the weasel family is primarily nocturnal, and few people had ever seen one, even prior to the massive poisoning campaigns. A large number of specimens were taken, however, 88 from west Kansas alone, in the late 19th century. Almost all specimens were taken prior to 1931, and subsequently, millions of acres of prairie dog towns were poisoned at the request of farmers and livestock growers. Black-footed Ferrets were seen in 1964 for the first time in nearly a half-century in Mellette County, South Dakota, creating quite a stir, and launching the first study in the wild ever undertaken.[19] The South Dakota Cooperative Wildlife Research Unit study produced a wealth of information, as well as the first and to date, finest photos ever taken of these mysterious animals.[19] Sightings in Mellette County were quite common in the late 1960's, and some Ferrets were killed by road traffic. Still, in spite of the extreme rarity of the species, adequate funds were not available to purchase habitat. A few Ferrets were seen on the Pine Ridge Indian Reservation of the Oglala Sioux, and five animals were taken into captivity by the Fish and Wildlife Service from this part of South Dakota. Because no sanctuary had been provided, poisoning continued, carried out on the Pine Ridge Reservation in 1973, and there have been no sightings in South Dakota in recent years.

Faith McNulty's moving book recounting the plight of the Black-footed Ferret and the prairie dog, *Must They Die?*, published in 1971, made the public aware of the massive poison campaigns and the continued killing of Ferrets in spite of their listing on the Endangered Species Act.[20] In 1973, a Black-footed Ferret and Prairie Dog Workshop was held at South Dakota State University pooling known information on historic sightings (no recent ones had been made) and life history. It suggested coordinated efforts to aid these species.[21] The Ferrets in captivity at the Fish and Wildlife Service's

Photo by U.S. Fish and Wildlife Service

*The recent discovery of a small number of **Black-footed Ferrets** in Wyoming gives hope that this very rare species may yet be saved from extinction.*

Patuxent Wildlife Research Center all died off by 1979, and the young produced by captive breeding did not survive.

With hopes waning that any Black-footed Ferrets survived in the wild, many conservationists began to consider the species extinct.

One zoologist began investigating sightings reported in western Wyoming, an area not originally thought to have Ferrets. Tim Clark's research began in 1973, and over the next years he distributed some 9,000 self-addressed post cards to government officials, schools, colleges and ranchers with pictures of Ferrets and requests for sightings. Articles were written for newspapers and a reward was offered for the sighting of a Black-footed Ferret. Nearly 250 sightings were reported, of which about half were discarded because of lack of sufficient information or misidentification.[22] Of the remaining, some 90 were considered positive, and indicated that there were Ferrets in many parts of the state other than the southeast.[22] Thirty-four of these reports were of dead animals—10 had been caught in Coyote traps, two in Badger traps, one was shot, one was road-killed, one drowned in a stock tank, and the others are thought to have been poisoned.[22] The majority of reports showed Ferrets in close association with White-tailed Prairie Dog towns in sagebrush-grass habitat.[22] The Fish and Wildlife Service continued research in Wyoming in 1978, surveying over 200,000 acres of public land.[23] In 1979, two recent skulls were found and dogs were trained to locate Ferret scent in prairie dog towns.[23] In 1981, Black-footed Ferrets were located by researchers, and in October of that year a young male Ferret was captured and fitted with a tiny radio transmitter so that biologists could track its movements.[24] Since then, other Ferrets have been seen in the area, and Dr. Clark and his associates have counted 58 Ferrets, of which 36 were born in 1982. This time, it is hoped that the prairie dog town will be protected from trapping, poisoning and shooting, and the Ferrets safeguarded. In other states, New Mexico and Texas for example, dogs are also being used to locate Ferrets by scent, so far without success.

The Thylacine

In Tasmania, a marsupial resembling a dog, the Thylacine, or Tasmanian Wolf, suffered a similar fate to that of the Red Wolf. Settlers systematically killed Thylacines, which were once widespread on the island. In prehistoric times, Thylacines were found in mainland Australia and even New Guinea, but it is thought that competition with dingos brought by the aborigines when they entered Australia, caused the Thylacines to disappear.[3] Most of the predator control campaigns conducted by Tasmanian settlers took place between 1888 and 1914, when the Thylacine suddenly became very rare. None were seen after one was killed in 1930.[3] Thylacines finally received legal protection, with heavy penalties for killing them under any circumstances. In 1966, an immense reserve of 647,000 hectares was set aside in hopes that the species still existed there, and all cats, dogs, and guns were prohibited from the reserve.[3] Dr. Eric R. Guiler, who has searched for the Thylacine for many years, launched an intensive hunt a few years ago, setting up 15 movie cameras on animal trails where the animal was rumored to have been seen. As of 1981, however, no Thylacines had set off the cameras.[25]

The lesson of the Thylacine might be applied to other very rare species, for which the right conservation action was taken too late.

Black-footed Ferrets, for example, still have no sanctuaries set aside, and the poisoning of prairie dog towns, even in areas where

Drawing from the Doomsday Book of Animals

The **Thylacine,** *in spite of protection and searches in the huge reserve set aside for it in Tasmania, is probably extinct.*

they have been seen, continues. Trappers are under orders to inspect prairie dog towns for signs of Ferrets such as the long furrows they make near their dens, before poisoning, but such signs are not always present even where Ferrets are found. The continued use of leghold traps presents the constant danger that a Ferret be trapped, as 12 were in Tim Clark's study. So often in the past, we have acted too late to save a species from extinction, and decisions made now will decide whether the Black-footed Ferret, Swift Fox and others follow the path of the Thylacine and Red Wolf.

Persecution

Persecution takes many forms. Fishermen have persecuted seals, otters and sea birds such as the Osprey in many parts of the world. The Japanese Sea Lion is now nearly extinct from shooting by fishermen, yet still has not received official protection.[3] The Mediterranean Monk Seal has been driven from most of the shores of that sea and North African coasts.[3] Resort and industrial development have contributed to its decline, but fishermen have been a major element. At present the total population of this seal is estimated to be less than 1,000 animals.[3] In 1981, Greek fishermen threatened to kill off all the remaining Monk Seals on Greek shores if they were not paid compensation for the fish the seals would eat. The Fauna and Flora Preservation Society in London raised the money—several thousand dollars—after public appeal in the newspapers. The Common Otter is now endangered in many parts of Europe from trapping and deliberate persecution by fishermen and hunters. Chasing otters is considered great sport in some countries, and a breed of dog, the Otter Hound, was developed to pursue and kill these playful animals. Some of this prejudice was brought to the United States by European settlers, and even today many fishermen shoot River Otters on sight, contributing to their rarity. Scientific research has established that otters do not deplete game fish, but prey instead mainly on the slower-moving species of fish, which are often predators of game fish and their young. Thus otters actually benefit game fish populations.

The attitude that seals and other fish-eaters are depriving humans of food is prevalent in many parts of the world, and has recently caused abalone fishermen in California to illegally shoot Sea Otters. This point of view has influenced the state of Alaska to request authority from the Marine Mammal Commission to kill many thousands of seals and Sea Otters. Many Alaskan fishermen, who net some of the largest fish catches in the world, still resent the number taken by the seals and other marine mammals in their waters even though many of these are non-commercial species of fish not sought by the fishermen.

Birds of prey have been shot for centuries, either because they made a large target, or because they were suspected of killing chickens or livestock. They are now protected in North America by the Migratory Bird Treaty Act, and The Bald and Golden Eagle Protection Act. Especially large penalties are imposed for killing Bald Eagles, Golden Eagles, and Peregrine Falcons. In spite of this, hawks, Ospreys, falcons and eagles are shot by the hundreds each year. Shooting is a major cause of death in Bald Eagles.

The California Condor, America's largest bird, with a wing span of nine feet, has been a major victim of persecution. It once soared over western cliffs searching for carrion, and in the Pleistocene, the Condor ranged eastward as far as Florida. Lewis and Clark saw them in

Photo by U.S. Fish and Wildlife Service

Many **Sea Otters** are killed illegally each year off the California coast by abalone fishermen.

Photo by Fred Sibley, U.S. Fish and Wildlife Service

*The giant **California Condors** number less than 30 birds in the wild.*

1806 at the mouth of the Columbia River in Washington state, and in the 19th century, they bred as far south as Baja California, Mexico. Though not abundant, the Condors were certainly numerous until shooting, poisoning and egg collecting nearly eliminated them altogether. They are very long-lived, surviving up to 50 years, and have only one chick every two years. In spite of legal protection from shooting, restrictions on poison use, and Endangered Species Act listing, the giant Condors dwindled in the 20th century. The cause seems to be a high mortality of adults, but it is not known whether from illegal shooting or other causes. The Fish and Wildlife Service failed to take any action to stem the decline until very recently. At present, they number less than 30 birds. The Fish and Wildlife Service gave final approval in 1980 to a plan calling for capture of the wild birds for captive breeding and radio-tracking. This plan provoked a fiery debate; opponents were led by Friends of the Earth organization, which claimed that the birds would be injured or die of shock on capture, and that the Fish and Wildlife Service had not paid sufficient attention to protecting the birds' habitat.

The Condors' remaining habitat consists of a 45,000 sq. km area in the southern California foothills of the Sierra Nevada mountains.[12] A portion of this area in the Los Padres National Forest has been declared a Condor refuge, but adjoining areas are still open to mining and tree harvesting.

Tragedy struck the first handling of wild Condors in spring, 1980. Two chicks, one quite young and the other some weeks older, were discovered in separate cave nests by biologists. First one, and then the other chick were handled by biologists, weighed and sampled for parasites and blood. The first and younger chick was unaffected by the handling, but the older chick, after almost an hour of handling, in which it repeatedly hissed and jabbed at the researcher, suddenly died.[26] Later, it was revealed that shock caused its death. The incident was filmed and later shown on national TV news.

The state of California cancelled the recovery program almost immediately after the chick died, and a long period of re-evaluation and controversy began. In 1981, one Condor chick was successfully raised in the Sespe Condor Refuge while another chick hatched outside the refuge apparently died when newly hatched (observations were made at a distance).[27] By July, 1981, the state of California reached an agreement with the Fish and Wildlife Service to allow capture of nine Condors.[28] The original plan of the Service had involved blanket approval to capture and/or mark all remaining Condors over an indefinite time period. Immediate plans call for three of the Condors to be kept in captivity for breeding, including a mate for Topatopa, the only Condor now in captivity. Two additional birds are to be captured and radio transmitters attached to their wings.[28] Opponents continue to argue against the program, and Friends of the Earth has published a book, *The Condor Question, Captive or Forever Free?* representing their case for a program emphasizing habitat protection.[29]

Friends of the Earth has some prestigious scientists on its side, notably Dr. Paul Ehrlich of Stanford University, who recently authored the book, *Extinction*, mentioned elsewhere in this book. The pro-capture side includes the National Audubon Society and the International Council for Bird Preservation. Meanwhile, one of two known Condor nests of 1982 failed when the parents became involved in a squabble, pushing the egg off the side of the cliff. The birds laid a second egg in April, 1982 but unfortunately, this too, was broken. In August, 1982, the surviving chick was captured for captive breeding.

In any case, the program is under extremely strong scrutiny, as it should be, and John Ogden, the National Audubon Society biologist assigned to the program, remarked in 1982, "We all know that if just one bird is killed or badly injured, that could mean the end of the program."[30]

Without doubt, the California Condor has suffered at the hands of man. One has only to read the early issues of *The Condor* ornithological journal to be appalled at the numerous cases reported of unabashed egg stealing by collectors and outright cruelty to these birds. One Frank S. Daggett in 1901 reported shooting a Condor, wounding it in the wing, and then when it fell to the ground shooting it three more times, still not killing it. Finally he clubbed it and shot it yet again before the valiant bird died.[31] Many Condors were shot and their carcasses left, adding to the known 288 birds killed as museum specimens, collected between 1881 and 1910.[12] Shootings continued for many years, and may still take place. The words of William Leon Dawson evoke the hope that only a few of these great birds be captured for captive breeding, and that the program must never prevent the remaining Condors from surviving as wild creatures, ". . . for me the heart of mystery, of wonder, and of desire lies with the California Condor, that majestic and almost legendary figure, which still haunts the fastnesses of our lessening wilderness."[29]

*These magnificent lifesize sculptures of **California Condors** were created by Dr. Erwin Hauer of Yale University.*

Unintended Victims

Pesticides

When the pesticide DDT* was developed in the 1940's, it was hailed as a boon to mankind. Spraying of swamps to control malaria began on a large scale, first in the United States, and later worldwide. Farmers began using the chemical to spray their fields to kill insect pests of many types, and home gardeners sprayed it on vegetables and fruit trees.

By the late 1940's, DDT's lethal effects on wildlife became apparent. In one typical case, Clear Lake, a beautiful area in northern California, was sprayed several times over a period of years to control gnats that residents found annoying. Soon after the sprayings began, over one hundred Western Grebes living on the lake died. These beautiful waterbirds are known for their dramatic courtship ritual in which they paddle over the water, skimming rapidly across its surface in unison. The grebes had accumulated high concentrations of DDD, a close relative of DDT, that had been sprayed. Chemists began to piece the puzzle together. Plankton in the lake was analyzed and found to contain about 5 parts per million (ppm) of DDD, far more than the water itself. Fishes eating the contaminated plankton had built up concentrations from 40 to 300 ppm, and carnivorous fishes had the highest accumulations—one Brown Bullhead had 2,500 ppm. These accumulations had built up over a period of months or years; the DDT family of pesticides does not break down into component parts when released into the environment, but is stored for years in increasingly lethal amounts in the tissues of plants and animals. California Gulls in Clear Lake had concentrations of over 2,000 ppm. Meanwhile, the Western Grebe colonies dwindled from over 1,000 pairs before the first spraying to about 30 pairs by 1960. And even the last Grebes nested in vain, for no young were produced.

The American chemical industry expressed little interest in the wildlife losses, and developed other pesticides of the same chorinated hydrocarbon family, many of which were far more toxic than DDT. Methoxychlor, chlordane, lindane, dieldrin, toxaphene, aldrin, heptachlor, and the most deadly of all, endrin, were ominous names that appeared on the market.

With the heavy application of these powerful poisons came a rain of death—thousands of song birds died and massive fish kills were reported. Endrin was hazardous at only 5 ppm, and lethal to wildlife at 10 ppm. Not until 1962, however, did the public as a whole become aware of the severity of the situation. In that year, a quiet, scholarly Fish and Wildlife Service biologist named Rachel Carson wrote a book, *Silent Spring,* that become a landmark, the beginning of the environmental movement.[1] *Silent Spring* carefully and eloquently chronicled the pervasive and lethal effects of these chemicals. Contamination of water, soil, plants and animals was threatening our life support system, and killing some of the earth's most beautiful and delicate animals. Rachel Carson acquainted the

Photo by A. Wetmore, U.S. Fish and Wildlife Service

Breeding populations of the beautiful **Western Grebe** *were eliminated by DDD use on Clear Lake, California.*

*short for dichloro-diphenyl-trichloro-ethane

Peregrine Falcons have suffered drastic declines mainly as a result of DDT which interferes with their reproduction.

Photo by Mike Smith, U.S. Fish and Wildlife Service

public with the chlorinated hydrocarbon pesticides, as well as others that were also having devastating effects on wildlife—organophosphates, mercury and arsenic pesticides, and organic carbamates.[1] In the U.S. alone, production of synthetic pesticides had soared from 124,259,000 pounds in 1947 to almost seven hundred million pounds in 1960, more than a five-fold increase.[1]

The more highly toxic of these chemicals caused immediate wildlife deaths, and many of the less toxic chlorinated hydrocarbons had pernicious side effects, interfering with animal reproduction. Between 1950 and 1963, Frank Graham Jr. chronicled the deaths of 10 to 15 *million* fishes in the lower Mississippi River caused by endrin use and runoff from Velsicol Chemical Corporation's plant at Memphis, Tennessee.[2] The Corporation denied any responsibility and claimed that the fish died of dropsy, a disease that is never epidemic in fishes.[2] As the Ehrlichs wrote in *Extinction,* "The pesticide industry, which was then and remains today one of the least socially responsible businesses, promoted the notion that trying to control the use of pesticides was a communist plot! They fought bitterly against imposition of any controls on pesticide manufacturing or usage. Controls have been steadily increased since the mid-1960's, however, without the dire consequences predicted by industry spokesmen."[3]

Dramatic declines took place in the population of birds at the top of their food chain: the hawks, eagles and other fish- and meat-eating species. In New York State, Peregrine Falcons once nested in cliffs along the Hudson River. Richard and Kathleen Herbert studied these birds for 30 years, and made 1,200 visits to eyries between 1949 and 1959.[4] To their surprise and sadness, they witnessed the decline to final disappearance of these birds that had been resident along the Hudson River from time immemorial. The Herberts had admired the regal and dignified falcons, fastest of all birds of prey, flying over their domain, the beautiful Hudson River valley north of New York City. Beginning in 1949, the Herberts noticed very unusual nesting behavior by the Peregrines. Eggs were abandoned, and second, third, and even fourth attempts were made to nest, each clutch failing because of egg breakage or abandonment.[4] Year after year the Peregrines returned to their cliff ledges to lay eggs, and one can imagine their frustration at rearing no young after sitting on eggs for months at a time. One male disappeared when he was about 20 years old, a female when she was about 17, and another male was last seen when he was at least 18 years old.[4] It appears that the Peregrines kept trying to nest until they finally died off, one after another, of old age or other causes. The last of the Peregrines of the Hudson River Valley was seen by the Herberts in 1961.[4]

Derek Ratcliffe, a British ornithologist, had observed Peregrines in Great Britain suffer a similar decline, and other biologists and naturalists saw them die out elsewhere in Europe and North America. The Herberts had been mystified, suggesting possible explanations such as harassment and shooting, disturbance by road construction, predation by Great Horned Owls, and even bad weather. Ratcliffe, however, believed the answer lay in the pesticide DDT. In 1963 he suggested it as the culprit, having noticed that pre-DDT eggs laid by Peregrine Falcons in England had thicker shells than those being laid during the 1960's.[5] In fact, many of the eggs Ratcliffe examined were so thin-shelled that they cracked when the birds incubated them.[5]

*In Siberia, **Red-breasted Geese** have declined in response to the disappearance of **Peregrine Falcons,** who are thought to have protected their nests from predators.*

Drawing from the Russian Red Data Book

Scientific research followed that confirmed Ratcliffe's theory. Birds of many species fed DDT had impaired reproduction, laying thin-shelled eggs, or hatching young that died at an early age.[6] DDE, a break-down of DDT, is usually the chemical detected in tissues and eggs. Some species of birds show a higher sensitivity to DDT than others, with most birds of prey, pelicans, and herons much more vulnerable to even low concentrations of DDT or dieldrin than ducks, chickens or gulls.

The Peregrine Falcon was once found nearly worldwide in suitable habitat, one of the few birds to have such a wide distribution. By the early 1960's, the species had declined to near extinction throughout most of Europe and North America. A survey of Peregrines in the eastern United States, Canada and Greenland had been carried out in the late 1930's and early 1940's by Dr. Joseph Hickey. Over 400 eyries were located, of which 275 were in the eastern U.S., and Dr. Hickey estimated that 350 pairs of Peregrines occupied the region east of the Mississippi River.[7] When Dr. Hickey's tracks were retraced in 1964, researchers found at least 146 of these historic eyries, and *not a single one* had nesting Peregrines.[7] In 1975, when DDT had been banned for 3 years, another survey was undertaken, and the results were the same, "There were no breeding pairs or occupied eyries observed in the eastern United States, although there was still suitable nesting habitat."[7] For the eastern Peregrines, the ban on DDT had come too late, all the resident birds having apparently died off.

In the western United States declines came later, in the early 1970's. DDT use was not as concentrated here, and Peregrines probably picked up the pesticide from prey species eaten while on migration and wintering in Latin America, where even today, this pesticide is heavily used. By 1979, only about one-fourth of the Peregrines that nested in the western half of the continent in the early 1970's survived. Elsewhere, declines have mirrored DDT use. Wherever use is heavy in breeding, migratory and wintering areas, declines of Peregrines follow. Non-migratory Peregrines living in areas of low pesticide use, such as the Peale's subspecies of British Columbia and the Aleutian Islands have suffered least, declining very little. Some examples of declines were compiled by the International Council for Bird Preservation in 1979.[8] The Alaskan and Canadian tundra Peregrines, for example, once numbered 2,200 pairs, and today they total less than 250 pairs.[8] In parts of Europe, declines have been up to 95% of the 1940's populations, and the species no longer nests in Belgium, Denmark, or Hungary.[8] Little is known of Peregrine populations in South America, Africa, southeast Asia, or parts of Australia.[8]

The decline of the Peregrine Falcon in Siberia brought about a parallel decline in a species that is dependent on it. The beautiful, dainty Red-breasted Geese nest only in a restricted and inaccessible region of northern Siberia. The Geese form small colonies of 3 to 20 nests around the nests of Peregrine Falcons. Nesting on the ground makes them vulnerable to predation by foxes, Skuas and other predators. It is thought that the presence of the Peregrines nearby shields them from such predation. The Peregrines seem to have other prey available, and usually do not choose birds as large as geese. With the decline of the Siberian Peregrines from DDT has come a precipitous decline in Red-breasted Geese.

Recent events have brightened this bleak picture. For the first time in decades, Peregrine Falcons are again breeding in the eastern U.S. Cornell University's captive breeding project, The Peregrine Fund, can claim the credit. In the early 1970's, Dr. Heinz Meng, a biology professor in New Paltz, New York, was successful in breeding Peregrine Falcons in captivity, a feat that had defied zoos and research facilities. Only a few other cases of captive breeding of this proud and difficult species had taken place, and these had been poorly documented instances in Europe in the 1940's. Once the key factors were learned, Cornell University's program, headed by Dr. Tom Cade, began to produce large numbers of Peregrines by captive breeding. The purpose was release into their previous United States range, and in 1975, the first captive-bred Peregrines were set free at various sites in the northeast. Without their parents to protect them from predators such as Raccoons and Great Horned Owls, the young birds are quite vulnerable. The Peregrine Fund places the chicks on platforms in protected boxes, watched over by biologists who place food out for them, and keep an eye out for predators until they fledge.

The young birds have for the most part survived, and learned to hunt for themselves, no small feat for a species whose parents in the natural state spend weeks showing chicks how to select prey, swoop on it at speeds up to 200 mph, and grasp it in their talons.

One Peregrine, called the Red Baron, took up residence on Sedge Island in the southeastern coastal marshes of New Jersey, near to the platform he had been released from three years before. In 1978, the Peregrine Fund placed five chicks in the same box. Instead of considering the five youngsters unwelcome invaders of his territory, he adopted them. Immediately moving to the front of the box, he "bowed and 'echiped' loudly before his new brood. We were confident that these young falcons would learn the ways of a wild Peregrine from an expert, and so they did," observed the Peregrine Fund researcher.[9] From then on the Red Baron brought food every day, feeding the young through the bars for 10 days until their release. He faithfully cared for them when they fledged until they struck out on their own.

The following year, three pairs of captive-bred birds released in previous years paired off and gave signs of nesting near the release towers. The Red Baron had found a mate, and the pair produced three eggs. Unfortunately, two of the eggs disappeared, and one was found cracked on the ground underneath the tower. The other two pairs did not succeed in raising young either, and it was not until 1980 that the release program had its true proof of success. The Red Baron and his mate nested at a tower behind security fences of the American Telephone and Telegraph Company at Manahawkin and raised three young; another pair of released Peregrines nested at a release tower in the Brigantine National Wildlife Refuge not far from Atlantic City.[11] These nestings marked the first time since the 1950's that the Peregrines fledged their own young east of the Mississippi River.[11] DDT residues and other chemical contaminants that interfere with their reproduction have finally reached a low enough level in prey to allow the falcons to lay eggs with shells thick enough to survive incubation without breaking.

In 1981, four pairs of released Peregrines successfully bred and raised young in the wild—three in New Jersey and one pair at a historic eyrie on a natural cliff face in New Hampshire.[12]

The Peregrine Fund is a cooperator in another breeding facility for introduction of Peregrines in the western states. This center is located

Photo by R. Watts courtesy of The Peregrine Fund

Scarlett, one of the Peregrine Fund's captive-bred birds, looks on while Rhett feeds foster young.

in Fort Collins, Colorado, and has about 24 female Peregrines. Together the two breeding centers produce over 100 baby Peregrines each year. Since the program began, and through the 1981 season, 740 captive-bred young have been raised to fledging and 605 Peregrines have been released to the wild by the two facilities. Releases have taken place in many of the historic Peregrine eyries, and attempts have been made to reestablish them in several eastern cities where they nested in the 1930's, preying on pigeons and starlings. In Baltimore, a released falcon took up residence at the U.S. Fidelity and Guaranty building a few years ago. The falcons usually chose buildings housing banks or insurance companies in the days when they nested in cities, and today, seem drawn to the same buildings. Urban releases have usually taken place on government buildings, such as the Department of Interior building in Washington, D.C., but the Peregrines go elsewhere. The falcon in Baltimore was named Scarlett, and she set up housekeeping on the 33rd floor window ledge of the building, but the first spring, no mate appeared. The Peregrine Fund, on being told of her presence there, released several males about two years of age nearby. First tries failed, but in 1980, Scarlett accepted a male from Cornell who was quickly dubbed "Rhett." They were introduced to each other too late in the season for mating, so Cornell provided four chicks which they succeeded in raising.[11] Tragedy struck in November, 1980 when Rhett was found dead near a grain elevator in Baltimore.[12] He had fed on a pigeon that contained the cruel poison strychnine.[12] This was the second instance of released Peregrines being killed by this poison which is used in many urban and rural areas, endangering both wild and domestic animals. Scarlett was provided with five young in 1981 which she raised alone.[12]

Another threat to Peregrines is nest robbing. Peregrine chicks have been stolen from nests by falconers in many areas. In California, falconers took chicks from one of the few remaining nests at Morro Rock on the coast for several successive years in the early 1970's despite nearly 24-hour surveillance by volunteers. Although several of the snatchers were apprehended, the stolen birds were never recovered. Defenders of Wildlife and the National Audubon Society finally had to install an electronic alarm system around the nest to detect any trespasser. It was successful, and in 1974, four falcons fledged from the nest. With the rise in popularity of falconry, there is increased pressure on Peregrine Falcons.

Peregrine Falcon breeding centers have been established elsewhere now. The Santa Cruz Predatory Bird Research Group in California released 35 Peregrines to parts of the West in 1981, and Macdonald Raptor Research Centre at McGill University in Canada bred Peregrines for the first time in 1981. Releases have taken place in Canada by the Canadian Wildlife Service's breeding facility.

Surveys are active in Greenland where a stable population of about 12 pairs of Peregrines nest. In Scotland, the recovery of Peregrines has been excellent, with 39 breeding pairs in 1980.[11] Derek Ratcliffe estimates that throughout Britain pre-1940, there were about 800 occupied territories; by 1963, the number had dropped to about 350, but numbers had increased by 1971 to an estimated 470 pairs. In 1978, 540 territories were estimated to be occupied. Their recovery is well on the way.

Other rare birds of prey whose numbers have been reduced by pesticides are also being bred in captivity for release. The Bald Eagle,

*This **Bald Eagle** is resident in British Columbia. Our national symbol is staging a comeback in response to the banning of certain pesticides.*

America's national bird, has declined drastically in most of the lower 48 states. Its diet of fish has made it especially vulnerable since pesticides and many other contaminants tend to concentrate in aquatic ecosystems. Only about 1000 pairs of Bald Eagles still breed in the U.S. south of Alaska. By the late 1960's, it was gone from the Great Lakes as a breeding bird, and only one breeding pair each remained in the northeastern states of New York and New Jersey. Florida once had the highest population of eagles south of Alaska, but their populations decreased in the 1950's by about 90%. Within the past ten years, however, Bald Eagles have rebounded to pre-DDT numbers in Florida. Elsewhere, they have returned to many parts of the northeast and the Great Lakes, but they are still absent from most of the southeast. Since they do not migrate to Latin America in the winter, but congregate in open waters in the U.S., they have been able to recover more easily than migratory populations, such as the *tundra* and *anatum* subspecies of the Peregrine Falcon, and other migratory birds. It is still not clear where the captive-bred Peregrines spend the winter, but some seem to be remaining in the U.S. Captive-raised Bald Eagles, produced mainly at Patuxent Wildlife Research Center of the Fish and Wildlife Service, have been released in New York, Georgia and Tennessee. In New York, these eagles have bred in the wild. In some areas of the country where Bald Eagles have not succeeded in producing eggs which did not crack, young from other areas are transplanted into the nest for them to raise.

The Osprey, too, has repopulated much of its historical range in the eastern United States. Although pesticides have taken a toll, it is still found throughout Eurasia and the southern coasts of South America, as well as in North America.

Some water birds have been acutely sensitive to pesticides, while others seem to maintain their populations. The Oriental White Stork is an endangered subspecies of the European Stork, familiar to all because of the story told of its bringing babies. The Oriental White Storks have been totally exterminated in Japan as a result of widespread use there of mercury pesticides which caused reproductive failures.[8] The European White Stork has fared somewhat better, but it has disappeared from much of Europe because of water pollution, draining of marshes, and disturbance. They still nest on roofs of some country villages, although they sometimes have to fly farther for frogs and small fish to feed their young, and superhighways now come closer to their once quiet domains. Pesticides and shooting in their African wintering grounds continue to reduce their numbers.

The Hermit Ibis, once a breeding bird throughout much of Europe and the Mediterranean region is now an endangered species, largely as a result of pesticide use. It survives only in Turkey, where 13 pairs still nest, and in Morocco where 250 birds remain.[8] Six hundred Hermit Ibis were found dead in the late 1950's from pesticide use.[8]

The species which may be the most sensitive of all birds to DDT and other chlorinated hydrocarbon pesticides is the Brown Pelican. Louisiana once harbored 50,000 of these birds and declared the Brown Pelican the state bird. By the early 1960's the huge colonies had vanished, and not a single pelican nest was found in the state after the 1961 season. Colonies in Texas, South Carolina and California declined drastically in the 1960's and early 1970's. Only in Florida did the Brown Pelican maintain its numbers, about 7,000 breeding pairs.[13] Research by the Fish and Wildlife Service showed

Photo by Mason Keeler

Photo by Zoological Society of San Diego

Once common in Europe and Asia, **White Storks** *have disappeared in many areas, and have been eliminated in Japan after heavy use of mercury pesticides.*

that only 2.5 ppm of DDE in Brown Pelican eggs can spell reproductive failure.[13] During the years when the pelicans were dying off there were massive fish kills in the Mississippi River attributed to pesticide use, and the colony on Anacapa Island off the California coast was known to have high concentrations of DDT, mainly derived from effluent discharged by Montrose Chemical Corporation's manufacturing plant at Los Angeles.[13] After a lawsuit and local government pressure, Montrose finally halted the dumping, although it still manufactures DDT for export.[13] The Louisiana die-off was attributed to endrin run-off from Velsicol Corporation in Tennessee, which caused massive fish kills, primarily of the Brown Pelican's major food item, the menhaden.

The state of Louisiana began introducing Pelicans taken from Florida in the late 1960's to rebuild populations, and at first numbers began to increase. Then in 1975, another die-off occurred, when more than 300 of the 465 birds imported from Florida died of lethal amounts of endrin in their brains.[14] This time, the heavy use of endrin on cotton crops to the north, with residue transported by the Mississippi River was blamed.[14] Velsicol's run-off had been stopped in the early 1960's. Transplants continued, with about 100 Florida Pelicans introduced into Louisiana each year, and although the populations are still not sizeable—only about 300 Brown Pelicans were breeding in Louisiana in 1980—there is room for optimism since endrin use has decreased markedly as a result of insect resistance. In California, South Carolina and Texas, Brown Pelicans are increasing yearly. The residues in the off-shore waters of California in bottom sediment are still issuing amounts of DDT, and it may be many more generations until they regain their original numbers, but in South Carolina, there are now 5,000 pairs, up from 1,100 in 1969.[15] Only about 0.3 ppm of endrin decreases productivity in most birds, and 0.8 ppm is lethal to most species. Pelicans which died in 1975 in Louisiana had from 0.3 to 0.7 ppm of endrin, as well as dieldrin, toxaphene, DDE and BHC (benzene hexachloride), accumulated from the fish of the Gulf, which in turn picked it up from their prey or plant species. The species has been listed as endangered by the U.S. Endangered Species Act since 1970, and soon, populations which have rebounded may be taken off the list.

Birds are not the only animals to be affected by pesticides. Bats, many of which feed on insects and thereby ingest sublethal amounts of pesticides which the insects have absorbed from spraying, have declined in many areas. The Carlsbad Caverns of New Mexico once harbored 8 million Mexican Free-tailed Bats that would fly from the cave each night in great rustling clouds. By 1974, only 200,000 of these bats remained in the Cavern and a scientific study began to establish the cause. Researchers found that the bats' bodies contained large accumulations of DDT, and its break-down product DDE. The chemical was stored in the body fat of the bats, and during migration, when fat was used up, the bats probably died from lethal release of the pesticide in their systems. The bats migrated in winter to Mexico, where it is thought they picked up much of this DDT. Preliminary studies of bats showed that they were more sensitive to DDT poisoning than other mammals.[16] Another colony of Free-tailed Bats in Arizona numbered 25 million individuals in 1963, but by 1969, it had decreased to 30,000.[17]

Since bats are long-lived like the Peregrine Falcon, they are able to accumulate toxic chemicals over a period of years, slowly building up to lethal levels. Some species of bats live as long as 21 years.[17] A number of dead and dying bats were found in Sonora, Mexico in 1968; post-mortem examinations showed they had 6 ppm of DDT and DDE in body fat. The use of DDT continues in Mexico, endangering many species of mammals and birds that winter there. A colony of 250,000 bats can consume 4 tons of insects per night, making them one of nature's major insect controls, and a severe loss to natural systems if they die out. The routine use of dieldrin killed Gray Bats found dead in caves in Missouri in 1975.[18] Although both dieldrin and aldrin were banned by the Environmental Protection Agency in 1974, existing stocks of these chemicals were allowed to be sold and used. Most bats that die are lost because they roost over water, or die in places remote from their caves, so the exact extent of pesticide-induced mortality in bats may never be known. Gray Bats are an endangered species, and pesticide use may be one of the major causes for their decline.

The toll of heavy DDT applications has been high. Along with mosquitos, many beneficial insects are killed, including natural enemies of the mosquito. In the early 1970's DDT was sprayed on a marsh in the Himalayan kingdom of Sikkim to control malarial mosquitos. This area was also the habitat of six hundred different species of butterflies, including some of the world's rarest species.[19] The sprayings nearly eliminated the butterflies.[19]

Butterflies have been killed by the millions from pesticide spraying, and their plant habitats have been heavily sprayed with herbicides. They have undergone dramatic declines in areas of heavy pesticide use. To identify and preserve rare and endangered butterfly and moth species, the Xerces Society has been formed. It was named after the Xerces Blue Butterfly, the first North American butterfly species to become extinct in modern times. In fact, many species have become too rare to support collecting. Some butterflies play a role in pollinating plants, by fertilizing the flowers when they move from plant to plant, feeding on nectar. The Yucca Moth is the only pollinator of the desert Yucca plant, and its disappearance would cause the plant's extinction.

Scientists are now learning that some butterflies migrate using the same flyways that birds use, a mystery for scientists who are wondering whether birds or butterflies first established the flyways.[20] The Monarch Butterflies migrate hundreds or even thousands of miles each winter to congregate in warmer climates. In northern Mexico the wintering area of eastern Monarch Butterflies was located a few years ago. Butterflies gather by the millions in a few acres of forest where they cling to tree trunks in a semi-torpor, coating the trees in dazzling color. These butterflies are very vulnerable to destruction of their habitat, and in fact timber cutting has reduced their wintering range. Pesticide spraying in the area could eliminate the entire population.

The specter of death brought by chlorinated hydrocarbon pesticides has been lifted to a great extent by the suspension or cancellation of many of these chemicals in the United States. Aldrin, chlordane, DDD, DDT, dieldrin, heptachlor, lindane, and toxaphene are now strictly controlled. The use of endrin on tobacco has been cancelled, but it is still used for other purposes in spite of years of protests from environmentalists. We are reminded, however, that this is one earth. The very same chlorinated hydrocarbons are still being used in developing countries, affecting North American birds

Photo by Merlin Tuttle, Bat Conservation International

The pesticide dieldrin has been responsible for killing endangered **Gray Bats.**

as well as tropical wildlife, and entering the ocean food chain. Pesticide use worldwide increased by 50% between 1971 and 1973, and it is expected to rise by 9% each year.[22] In 1977, 4.1 *billion* pounds of pesticides were used worldwide, causing environmental damage and wildlife losses on an ever-increasing scale. In the U.S. alone, some 100 companies profit from this multi-billion dollar industry, some of the largest producers being Allied Chemical, Du Pont, Hooker Farm Chemicals, Monsanto, and Shell Chemical. Half of all pesticides used in developing countries are chlorinated hydrocarbons because of their lower cost.[22]

In Africa, a 1981 study showed some recent effects of DDT use. Zimbabwe uses 1,000 tons of DDT each year, and sampling of Fish Eagle eggs has shown half of them to have shells that are 10% thinner than normal because of DDT.[23] Fish Eagles resemble American Bald Eagles, and have a similar diet. They may also suffer declines parallelling that of our national symbol. When eggs decrease in thickness by 10% they have little chance of hatching, and these birds may cease breeding in the area where DDT is used within a decade.[23]

Many of North America's birds that migrate to Latin America have shown recent declines as well, indicating a need to extend environmental laws and restrictions on pesticide use worldwide. The U.S. is often the source of DDT and other pesticides now banned for domestic use which are exported by the ton to developing countries.

The insect pests that pesticides have been used to destroy have shown a great genetic flexibility, many of them becoming resistant to DDT and related chemicals. Of 25 insect pests examined in a Council on Environmental Quality study, 21 have been found resistant to one or more pesticides: 16 to DDT, 16 to organophosphates, and 10 to cyclodines.[22] In California, where pesticide use is very heavy, 17 of the 25 species of insect pests were found resistant to one or more types of insecticides; of these resistant insect pests, many are malarial mosquitos.[22] One species has become resistant to all major chemical insecticides.[22]

Acid Rain

While pesticides are disrupting ecological systems, killing predator and prey alike, some chemicals are obliterating all life forms where they are introduced. Oxides of sulphur and nitrogen created from the burning of fossil fuels—coal, oil and gas—are being released into the atmosphere where they react with other substances in the air to form sulphuric and nitric acids. Rain and snow become contaminated by these acids. In many parts of Europe and North America, the rain is so acidic that numerous species of freshwater animals would be killed instantly if they were exposed directly to this water.[24] Millions of tons of oxides are spewed into the atmosphere each year, and the net effect of acid rain is the gradual killing of thousands of lakes and streams. About 250 lakes in the Adirondacks are now devoid of fish and lakes in Ontario eastwards to Nova Scotia are gradually becoming lifeless as well. In Scandinavia and Great Britain, the phenomenon began in the 1920's and has become so severe that Atlantic Salmon streams and thousands of lakes are now empty of all aquatic life. Invertebrates, microscopic plankton and higher plants are eliminated as well, and in fact their disappearance may bring about that of the fish. Recently, scientists have found the effects of the acids spreading to surrounding plant and animal life. Lichens and

*Acid rain has caused mortality in **Spotted Salamanders.***

Spotted Salamanders are disappearing in regions where acid rain falls, and tree deaths which have been epidemic in these areas may also be traced to acid rain.[25]

The implications of acid rain for endangered species are very significant. Should this phenomenon spread, as it seems to be doing, recently discovered in the American West, for example, extinctions are sure to occur in large numbers.

PCBs

Other toxic chemicals produced by industry are posing major threats to ecosystems in many parts of the world. PCBs, or polychlorinated biphenyls, are chemicals used in refrigeration, insulation systems and related areas. They are not biodegradable and are posing a threat to wildlife nearly equal to that of the DDT family of pesticides. The latter chemicals break down after a period of 25 or more years, but there is no evidence that PCBs ever decompose. Mammals are particularly susceptible to PCBs which have caused birth defects, reduced fertility and caused abnormal behavior in the mother. Female Harbor Seals in Washington State that had high concentrations of PCBs aborted their young, or killed them by throwing them against the rocks soon after birth. Laboratory tests have shown reproductive malformations in monkeys, mink, birds and fish having PCB concentrations of 100 ppm or more. The chemical is released into water by industry and can be dispersed by air currents. It falls in precipitation in large quantities—1,400 pounds of PCBs rain into Lake Michigan each year. There have been counts as high as 2000 ppm in some Great Lakes birds and at those levels it is lethal to humans. This chemical is suspected of causing the decline of Striped Bass from the Atlantic Coast and interfering with reproduction in many species of fish. The manufacture of PCBs is now banned in the United States, but it has become pervasive in the environment.

These toxic chemicals are only the tip of the iceberg, a small percentage of contaminants being released into the environment, producing effects on wildlife that scientists of the future will document unless controls are put into action in the immediate future. In the U.S., a new superfund has been authorized with money from chemical companies to pay for toxic chemical disposal, a first step toward control.

Other chemicals are known to have a harmful effect on wildlife:
    heavy metals (lead, mercury and cadmium)
    dioxin (a contaminant in herbicides)
    2,4-D, 2,4,5-T (herbicides)
    arsenic
    chemical warfare agents such as "yellow rain"
    PBB, or polybrominated biphenyl (a fire retardant)
    all radioactive compounds, above all plutonium, the most
      toxic substance known

These chemicals have changed genes, caused birth defects, cancer and direct mortality both to animals and to humans. There are thousands of synthetic chemicals being released to the environment that may be combining with one another to produce new and deadly compounds.

Fisheries and Incidental Kills

Sea Turtles

Known for the large size of their heads, the Loggerhead Sea Turtles have been swimming tropical ocean waters for many millions of years. Their "beaks" aid them in feeding on mollusks and crustaceans which they crush in their mouths. Weighing hundreds of pounds, they lumber with difficulty on their only land voyages—the annual laying of eggs in sandy beach nests. The Loggerheads escaped much of the slaughter that decimated the Green, Ridley and Hawksbill Sea Turtles, because their shells and meat were considered less valuable. Until recently, their major problem involved the development for resorts or houses of the shores where they laid their eggs. They disappeared from many ancestral beaches in the southeastern coastal areas of the United States, and the Fish and Wildlife Service designated them a threatened species on the U.S. Endangered Species Act.

The development of shrimp fisheries in the Gulf of Mexico and Caribbean spelled further declines for the Loggerheads. When shrimp nets came into use, hundreds of turtles were caught up in them as they were pulled behind the boats, drowning before the nets were drawn up. Large numbers of drowned sea turtles began washing up on the shores of Florida and neighboring states, alarming conservationists. When counts were made, it was discovered that about 2000 Loggerheads were being drowned each year by shrimp nets. The Recovery Team set up by the Endangered Species Act urged the shrimp trawlers to develop technology to permit the turtles to escape from the nets, but years went by before a net modification was finally invented. The Turtle Excluder Device was developed by the National Marine Fisheries Service of the Department of Commerce and was tested in 1981. This device is a modification of the funnel net used by shrimpers that allows turtles to escape through a passageway held open by a metal cage sewn into the net, like a basketball hoop. Deflector bars in the net push the turtles upward toward the opening, allowing them to escape. Shrimp are not heavy enough to trigger the bars and an open netting keeps them inside.

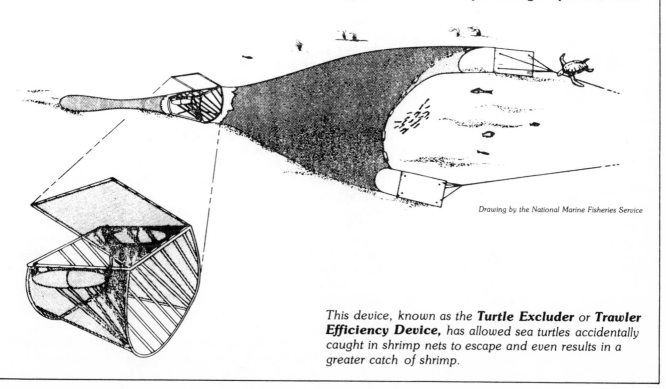

Drawing by the National Marine Fisheries Service

This device, known as the **Turtle Excluder** or **Trawler Efficiency Device,** has allowed sea turtles accidentally caught in shrimp nets to escape and even results in a greater catch of shrimp.

Horseshoe crabs also escape upwards. The Turtle Excluder or Trawler Efficiency Device has the added benefit of allowing a greater catch of shrimp because there is less drag on the nets. It costs only $200 to modify existing nets. By early 1982, there were about 10 or 15 of these Excluder Devices in use, and government regulations are needed so that all shrimp boats will be equipped promptly.

The Loggerhead Sea Turtles have been discovered in a hibernating condition in East Coast channels off Florida, buried in the bottom. Unfortunately, the shrimp trawlers are causing mortality for these turtles as well, by routing them from the bottom. The turtles have been dislodged by the hundreds over the past few years, and do not survive the trauma of being forced out of hibernation. They overwinter in the mud to escape colder temperatures. When prematurely dragged from the bottom, they were observed by Dr. Archie Carr and others to die even if released alive by the shrimpers. Dr. Carr was told by a shrimper captain of seeing some 150 to 200 Loggerhead Turtles floating offshore, having been scooped from the bottom. The turtles looked sick, and made no attempt to escape by diving or swimming when the boat approached.[26] "Some were blind, many had lost their flippers, and there were areas of bare bone on their heads and shells. Dense growth of long filamentous algae were attached to the submerged shell and throat surfaces of many of them, indicating that the turtles had spent considerable time floating in the photic surface water."[26] Carr surmised that these turtles had been dragged from the bottom when the temperature of the water had become too low to permit resumption of normal activity, and afterwards they had drifted aimlessly, unable to feed, and without energy to evade shark bites. "There was little doubt that the plight of these turtles was terminal."[26] In a two month period in 1978, 56 Loggerheads were taken by experimental trawl drags in the Port Canaveral Ship Channel off Florida, and it appears that hundreds are dying from this winter trawling.[26] These channels could be put out of bounds for shrimp trawlers during the winter months, or other devices developed to avoid this mortality. When the mortalities of the two types of shrimp trawler incidental catches are added to the decreasing nesting habitat, the future of the Loggerheads in U.S. waters is uncertain.

Whales

Sometimes whales are trapped in fishing gear, and in the northwestern Atlantic incidents involving whales—entrapments and collisions with fishing vessels—increased more than 150% in 1979 from 1978.[27] The most commonly trapped whale in this area is the highly endangered Humpback Whale. Seventy percent of incidents involve this species, causing injury and occasional death to the whales, and damage to fishing gear.[27] Fishermen, according to the Sierra Club, have been defiant in resenting the situation; "There are too many whales in this area and they feed on the same thing we catch, so there's competition," said Billy Lee, skipper of a fishing and salvage boat in the region.[27] "They should find a way to keep them [the whales] out of here," Lee added. "They're going to have to start killing them in a couple of years or they'll overpopulate themselves." Whale experts explain, however, that far from overpopulating, the whales are compelled to feed inshore due to overfishing offshore by Russian factory ships.[27]

Dolphins

Endangered species in the making are other victims of incidental kills by fishing nets in many parts of the world. A fisheries expert, Dr. William Perrin of the National Marine Fisheries Service, documented in 1969 the drowning of an estimated 250,000 dolphins per year in tuna nets in the Pacific.[28] The huge purse seine nets used by the tuna boats enclosed entire schools of dolphins which drowned as the nets were drawn up. The ironic aspect is that the tuna boats locate schools of tuna by spotting the dolphins, since Yellowfin Tuna tend to swim under these mammals.[28] Years passed before any action was taken to reduce dolphin mortality and some *six million* of these intelligent animals perished before nets were developed allowing most of the dolphins to escape. Still, mortality remained high in the 1970's, and enforcement of regulations under the Marine Mammal Protection Act was so slow that various environmental organizations led by the Environmental Defense Fund and Friends of Animals filed suits against the National Marine Fisheries Service and won four different court cases. Improved regulations were issued in 1977 to reduce dolphin deaths. Dolphins have come to associate the tuna boats with danger, and now flee at high speed when they spot a boat. The tuna boats pursue, sometimes over a period of hours, exhausting and causing injury or death to pregnant females, young and less fit individuals. The 1981 allowable kill was 20,500 by U.S. fleets, a big improvement over the massive mortalities of the past. The total killed in 1981 fell below the quota—15,584 dolphins drowned. Even so, at that rate, 3.51 dolphins are killed each time a tuna net is set, and .36 for every ton of tuna that is caught. Other countries fishing for tuna with purse seine nets have also adopted the modifications to reduce dolphin mortality, but a few have not. Many Mexican and Peruvian boats still use unmodified nets, killing thousands of dolphins needlessly. The United States prohibited importation of tuna from these nations in 1982. Although dolphin mortality has dropped considerably, the total killed by the 11 nations fishing for Yellowfin Tuna using modifications and the two not using them is still very serious. The exact figure is not known. Development of technology to achieve zero mortality is urgently needed, and work is being done on aggregating devices and on using hydrophones to locate schools of tuna.

Seals

The U.S. National Marine Fisheries Service grants exemptions by permit under the Marine Mammal Protection Act to both American and foreign fishing vessels to take large numbers of seals incidentally with fish. "Take" in this context means kill, and research is needed to determine the real extent of this mortality.

Sea Birds

For sea birds caught accidentally in fishing nets, there is no legal protection, not even a permit system which would regulate this extremely destructive activity. The International Council for Bird Preservation has found that since 1952, nearly ten million Pacific sea birds have been killed in Japanese gill nets fishing for salmon! The annual mortality is about 266,500 birds drowned in the nets.[29] Three species of seabirds that have been most affected by this kill are the Thick-billed Murre, Horned Puffin and Tufted Puffin.[29] Approx-

***Dolphins** are among the most intelligent mammals. They have been drowned by the millions in tuna purse seine nets. Only recently have net modifications reduced mortality.*

imately 44% of all Horned Puffin young produced each year, or 11,650 birds are killed, and over 51,000 Tufted Puffins die annually. Ornithologists aboard these ships in 1978 and 1979 observed fifteen species of seabirds being caught by the ten-mile long gill nets.[30] Salmon gill-netting in the Atlantic has caught an estimated 88% of the 350,000–500,000 Thick-billed Murres drowned yearly. Their nets are set fairly close to shore. If the ships set their nets farther offshore, much of the seabird mortality would be avoided. But the best solution would be for Japan to prohibit this gill-netting.

The Brown Pelicans of Florida escaped serious declines from pesticides, but many are killed each year as a result of injuries they receive from accidental snagging on fish hooks. The Pelican's beak or pouch often gets snagged as it strikes at a lure or tries to grab bait. Even minor injuries can result in infection and death according to Ralph Heath, founder of the Suncoast Seabird Sanctuary in Indian Shores, Florida, which treats many wounded Brown Pelicans, some of them with as many as eight fish hooks embedded in their flesh. Sometimes a hook will slash an open wound in the Pelican's pouch that is so large the bird cannot swallow and it starves to death. Many Pelicans die when they snag their bills on trotline hooks, and others die after becoming hopelessly entangled in fishline that has been cut off and thrown in the water. One Pelican had a hook embedded in both feet preventing it from swimming, and causing it to starve to death. Ralph Heath and his co-workers have saved the lives of many of these birds and recommend that anyone who hooks a seabird by accident try to catch it gently in a hoop net, and bring it to Suncoast Seabird Sanctuary or a veterinarian, rather than cutting the line or trying to remove the hook. The Sanctuary has published a pamphlet "Help for Hooked Birds"* with instructions for the care of these birds.

Many birds that are too seriously wounded to be released, live and nest at the Sanctuary. There is no netting over the top of the Pelican enclosures, so any bird well enough to fly off is free to do so—and to return for a fish dinner at will. Brown Pelicans raised at the Sanctuary are helping to repopulate areas where they were extirpated.

Drawing by Esta Belcher

*Fish hooks ensnare hundreds of **Brown Pelicans,** causing injuries often resulting in their death.*

*Heath, Ralph T., Jr., Pete Van Allen, and Dr. Harold Albers. "Help for Hooked Birds" available from Suncoast Seabird Sanctuary, 18328 Gulf Blvd. Indian Shores, Florida 33535

Motorboats and Other Vehicles

Manatees

In the clear springs and rivers of Florida, the last remaining Caribbean Manatees swim slowly about, searching for aquatic vegetation and quiet resting areas. Into this peaceful scene roar high-speed motor boats, oblivious to the gentle sea cows. The propellers rip gaping wounds in the backs of the Manatees as the boats tear through the waterways.

These 2,000 pound mammals tend to hang just below the water's surface out of sight of boaters, and they are too ponderous to move aside in time. Many Manatees die of the wounds, so many that it is a major cause of mortality to the 1,000 remaining Florida animals.

Almost all Manatees have a series of scars on their backs from past encounters with motorboats. Others die from being crushed in automatic flood control gates. In 1980, 67 dead Manatees were reported from all causes, and in 1981, 105 Manatees were found dead, over 10% of the population. Of these, many had starved to death in the winter, chilled into torpor by the cold waters, and 21 were victims of motorboat propellers.[31] The species clearly cannot sustain such losses. It is long-lived, and has only one young every three to five years, having evolved with a very low natural mortality.

The state of Florida enacted the Florida Manatee Sanctuary Act in 1978 which declared the entire state a refuge and sanctuary for the Manatee. In thirteen wintering areas, boat speeds are regulated, and parts of Crystal River, where the majority of Manatees congregate in winter, are now reserves where boats and people are not allowed.[32] The Nature Conservancy is seeking to purchase 14 islands in the Crystal River. The islands had been slated for residential development which would have brought people and boats disturbing and injuring the Manatees.

The Florida Power and Light Co. has thermal discharges issuing from several of its plants which have saved the lives of many Manatees during cold winters, and the company has established boat-free areas for the animals during the winter when they congregate around the outlets. In 1982 the company sponsored a Manatee Awareness Workshop drawing many environmentalists and even some boaters who were ordered to attend the workshop when ticketed for speeding in areas marked for slow speed to protect the Manatees.[33] Governor Robert Graham of Florida has gotten involved in the plight of the Manatee as well and formed a Save the Manatee Committee with fund-raiser Jimmy Buffet publicizing the urgent need for boaters to slow down.[33]

Dredging in Port Everglades, where Manatees winter, was permitted under strict rules protecting the animals. The dredging company installed a radar which can detect the slow-moving mammals and if one is spotted, the project comes to a halt until the Manatee moves away, which can take up to 30 minutes.[34] Measures such as these may help turn the tide for these gentle, 2000-pound creatures, so that they may share the rivers with man in peace.

The visible scars on the back of this **Florida Manatee** *are proof of its many painful encounters with boat propellers, a major cause of mortality for these endangered mammals.*

Photo by Patrick Rose, Florida Audubon Society

Key Deer

Florida is the scene of other collisions with endangered species as well. Cars that speed along the main highway that cuts through the Florida Keys often hit the tiny Key Deer as they step daintily across the road. These little deer were rescued from the brink of extinction when they numbered only 50 in 1947. In 1971, they had increased to about 700, aided by the purchase of the National Key Deer

Refuge of 7,332 acres and strict protection from illegal shooting.[35] But in that year alone, 52 Key Deer were struck and killed by automobiles, and in the 24-year period from 1947 to 1971, 590 of these two-foot tall deer were killed by cars, trucks and buses.[35] By 1980, numbers had decreased to 350 to 400, as a result of continued road-kills and destruction of habitat by resort development on the Keys.[35] Between 1968 and 1973, 75% of known mortalities occurred from cars, in spite of warning signs and a 35 mph speed limit within most of its range.[36] Recently discs* that reflect oncoming car lights have been installed on posts next to the highway going through the Key Deer Refuge. Since the installation of these reflectors, no road-killed deer have been documented along this stretch of highway.

Florida Panther

Farther north in the Everglades region the tawny Florida panther is one of the rarest species in the state, with a population of less than 20 animals. It has been federally protected by the Endangered Species Act since 1967, but these rare animals too, have been occasionally struck by cars. In 1981 alone three panthers were killed in south Florida; the third was a pregnant female.[37]

*Swareflex Reflectors, Strieter Corporation, 2100 18th Ave., Rock Island, Illinois 61201.

Photo by Hope Ryden

*Smallest race of the White-tailed Deer, the tiny **Key Deer** are often killed by road traffic as they attempt to cross the Key Highway in Florida.*

References

Dinosaurs and Dodos, pages 2 to 24

Vanishing Wildlife — Causes and Consequences

1. Myers, Norman. 1979. *The Sinking Ark.* Pergamon Press, N.Y.
2. Ehrlich, Paul, and Anne Ehrlich. 1980. *Extinction.* Random House, N.Y.
3. Ripley, S. Dillon. 1977. "Bird that is loath to fly but roams afar all the same." Smithsonian. March. Vol. 7(12):89-93.
4. International Council for Bird Preservation. 1965. *List of Birds Either Known or Thought to Have Become Extinct Since 1600.* Special Supplement to *IUCN Bulletin* No. 16, July/September, 1965; ICBP. 1980. *Red Data Book of Endangered Birds of the World.* Smithsonian Inst. Press, Washington, D.C.; King, Warren B. 1981. The World's Rarest Birds. *International Wildlife.* Vol. 11(5):13-19.
5. Day, David. 1981. *The Doomsday Book of Animals.* Viking Press, N.Y.
6. Curry-Lindahl, Kai. 1972. *Let Them Live. A worldwide survey of animals threatened with extinction.* Wm. Morrow & Co., N.Y.
7. Greenway, James C., Jr. 1967. *Extinct and Vanishing Birds of the World.* Dover, N.Y.
8. Halliday, Tim. 1978. *Vanishing Birds of the World.* Holt, Rinehart, and Winston, N.Y.
9. Anon. 1978. The Tree That Needs the Dodo. *Oryx.* Nov. 14(4): 292-293.
10. HRH Prince Philip, and James Fisher. 1970. *Wildlife Crisis.* Cowles Book Co., Inc., N.Y.
11. Kamm, Henry. 1975. For One Island, French Legacy is Riches, for others, Poverty. *The New York Times,* Dec. 22.; Tiny Mauritius Seeks Amity with All World. *The New York Times,* Dec. 29.
12. Temple, Stanley A. 1981. Applied Island Biogeography and the Conservation of Endangered Island Birds in the Indian Ocean. *Biological Conservation,* 20(2):147-151. June.
13. Olson, Storrs. 1978. A Paleontological Perspective of West Indian Birds and Mammals. *Zoogeography of the Caribbean.* Academy of Natural Sciences of Philadelphia, Special Publication No. 13.
14. Allen, Glover P. 1972. *Extinct and Vanishing Mammals of the Western Hemisphere.* Cooper Square Publ. Originally published 1942.
15. International Union for the Conservation of Nature. 1978. *Red Data Book. Vol. 1: Mammalia.* Morges, Switzerland.
16. Honegger, Rene E. 1981. List of amphibians and reptiles either known or thought to have become extinct since 1600. *Biological Conservation,* Vol. 19(2):141-158.
17. International Union for the Conservation of Nature. 1979. *Red Data Book, Vol. 3: Amphibia and Reptilia.* Morges. Switzerland.
18. Laycock, George. 1966. *The Alien Animals. The Story of Imported Wildlife.* Natural History Press, N.Y.

Unlearned Lessons from the Past Abuse of the Land, pages 25 to 41

1. Jolly, Alison, 1980. *A World Like Our Own. Man and Nature in Madagascar.* Yale University Press, New Haven.
2. Amos, William H. 1980. *Wildlife of the Islands.* Harry N. Abrams, Publishers, N.Y.
3. Curry-Lindahl, Kai. 1972. *Let Them Live.* Morrow Paperback Edition, N.Y. & "Man and Nature in Madagascar", *Defenders,* April, 1975. (Wash. DC).
4. Marden, Luis. 1967. Madagascar—Island at the End of the Earth. *National Geographic.* Oct.
5. H.R.H. Prince Philip, and James Fisher. 1970. *Wildlife Crisis.* Cowles Book Co., Inc. N.Y.
6. Wetmore, Alexander. 1967. Re-creating Madagascar's Giant Extinct Bird. *National Geographic.* Oct. pp 488-493. (This article includes a photograph of the x-rayed egg, and a painting of its possible appearance. The Malagasy described the bird as white, but Dr. Wetmore decided it probably resembled the ostrich. I believe the Malagasy legends to be valid since so much of their other wildlife lore has been authenticated).
7. McNulty, Faith. 1975. "Madagascar's Endangered Wildlife." *Defenders,* Vol. 50 April. (This issue of *Defenders* magazine was entirely devoted to Madagascar, with articles on birds, mammals, reptiles, plants & a variety of excellent photos).
8. Petter, Jean Jacques. 1965. The Lemurs of Madagascar. In Primate Behavior.

Field Studies of Monkeys and Apes. ed. by Irven DeVore. Holt, Rinehart & Winston, N.Y.

9. Davis, Raymond. 1975. "Madagascar's Birds." *Defenders.* April. 50:174-179.

10. *Red Data Books.* International Council for Bird Preservation (*Aves*) & International Union for the Conservation of Nature (*Mammalia, Reptilia* and *Plants*).

11. Brown, Leslie. 1976. *Birds of Prey, their Biology and Ecology.* The Hamlyn Publishing Co., Ltd., Reprinted in 1979 by A&W Publishers, N.Y.

12. Hancock, James, and Hugh Elliott. 1978. *The Herons of the World,* Harper and Row, N.Y.

13. Todd, Frank S. 1979. *Ducks, Geese and Swans of the World.* Sea World Press Publ., Harcourt, Brace, Jovanovich, N.Y.

14. Juvik, J.O., A.J. Andrianorivo, and C.P. Blanc. 1981. The ecology and status of *Geochelone yniphora,* a critically endangered tortoise in northwestern Madagascar. *Biological Conservation,* 19(4):297-316. April.

15. Juvik, J.O. 1975. The Radiated Tortoise of Madagascar. *Oryx.* Oct. Vol. 13(2):145-147.

16. Sussman, Robert W., and Peter H. Raven. 1978. Pollination by lemurs and marsupials: an archaic coevolutionary system. *Science,* Vol. 200:731-736.

17. IUCN. 1980. *World Conservation Strategy.* Living Resource Conservation for sustainable development. (with UNEP and WWF). Gland, Switzerland.

18. Allen, Robert. 1980. *How to Save the World.* Strategy for World Conservation. IUCN, UNEP & WWF, Kogan Page.

19. Council on Environmental Quality. 1980. *The Global 2000 Report to the President.* Volumes 1-3. U.S. Government Printing Office, Wash. DC.

20. Mitchell, Richard. 1980. Report to the U.S. Fish and Wildlife Service on Nepal Trip, June 15-30, 1980. Unpublished.

21. IUCN. 1978. Sourcebook for A World Conservation Strategy. Threatened Vertebrates. Prepared by Robert Allen and Christine Prescott-Allen. 2nd Draft. General Assembly Paper GA.78/10 Add. 6, 17 pp. Gland, Switzerland.

22. Gore, Rick. 1979. The Desert: An Age-old Challenge Grows. *National Geographic,* Nov. Vol. 156(5):594-639.

23. Odum, Eugene P. 1971. *Fundamentals of Ecology.* 3rd Revised edition. W.B. Saunders, Philadelphia, 574 pp.

24. *IUCN Bulletin.* 1978. Vol. 9(9):55. Sept.

25. *IUCN Bulletin.* 1980. Vol. 11(12):98-100. Nov./Dec.

26. Ehrlich, P. and A. 1980. *Extinction.* quoting, Brad Kennedy, "Protecting wildlife." *New York Times,* Jan. 13, 1980.

27. Davis, George M. 1977. Rare and endangered species: a dilemma. *Frontiers,* Vol. 41(4):12-14.

28. *Endangered Species Technical Bulletin,* June, 1979. Vol. 4(6):6, 12.

29. Rees, W.A. 1978. Do the dams spell disaster for the Kafue Lechwe? *Oryx,* June. 14(3):231-235.

Trade in Wild Animals
The Great Whales, pages 42 to 51

Drawing by T. W. Wood

Hornbill *and young.*

1. Sagan, Carl. 1980. *Cosmos.* Random House, N.Y.

2. Allen, G.M. 1972. *Extinct and Vanishing Mammals of the Western Hemisphere.* Reprinted from the 1942 edition. Cooper Square Press, N.Y.

3. Garrett, Tom. 1981. Whaling. *Collier's Encyclopedia.* pp 444-448.

4. Reeves, Randall R. 1979. Right Whale: Protected but Still in Trouble. *National Parks and Conservation Magazine,* Feb. 53(2):10-15.

5. Scheffer, Victor B. 1974. The Largest Whale. *Defenders.* August, pp 272-274.

6. Marine Mammal Commission. 1975. Annual Report. *Federal Register.* July 22, 1975.

7. Australia, Government of. 1979. *Whales and Whaling.* Vols. I & II. Australian Government Printing Office.

8. Van Note, Craig. 1979. *Outlaw Whalers. An Expose of Unregulated Whaling around the World.* The Whale Protection Fund, Washington, DC 28 pp.

9. Lean, Geoffrey. 1981. Whales Give Up Their Lives to Save A Friend. *The Observer.* Nov. 8.

10. Garrett, Tom. 1981. Statement to the Subcommittee on Human Rights and International Organizations, Committee on Foreign Affairs, House of Representatives. *Review of the 33rd International Whaling Commission Meeting.* Sept. 22, 1981. U.S. Government Printing Office.

11. Grunberg, Carol, 1981. *Report on the 33rd Annual Meeting of the International Whaling Commission.* U.S. House of Representatives Hearing, Sept. 22, 1981.

12. Japan Whaling Association. 1980. *Living With Whales.* (booklet).

13. Van Note, Craig. 1981. Statement before the U.S. House of Representatives Hearing on the 33rd International Whaling Commission Meeting, Sept. 22, 1981. U.S. Government Printing Office.

Fur, pages 51 to 59

1. Poland, Henry. 1892. *Fur-bearing Animals in Nature and in Commerce.* Gurney and Jackson, London.
2. Curry-Lindahl, Kai. 1972. *Let Them Live. A Worldwide Survey of Animals Threatened With Extinction.* William Morrow & Co., Inc., New York.
3. Allen, Glover. 1972. *Extinct and Vanishing Mammals of the Western Hemisphere.* Cooper Square Publishers, Inc., New York.
4. Rohter, Larry. 1979. "Peru Kills Vicunas, Irks Conservationists" *Washington Post,* July 15.
5. Correspondence. 1980. Dr. Antonio Brack Egg. Ministry of Agriculture and Food, Republic of Peru, to ISPA.
6. U.S. Department of Commerce, import statistics.
7. Inskipp, Tim, and Sue Wells. 1979. *International Trade in Wildlife.* Earthscan Publications, London.
8. CITES. 1979. "Review of the Implementation of the Convention 1978 Annual Report of the Secretariat-Annex 2, The International Trade in Felidae 1977." 2nd Meeting of the Conference of the Parties to the Convention on International Trade in Endangered Species of Wild Fauna and Flora, Costa Rica.
9. *Fur Age Weekly.* 1978. p. 1, September 11.
10. Curry-Lindahl, Kai. 1972. *op. cit.*
11. *IUCN Bulletin.* 1979. pp. 20-21, March.
12. Australian National Parks and Wildlife Services. 1978. *Management of Kangaroo Harvesting in Australia.* Occasional Paper No. 2, Canberra.
13. Anon. 1975. "New Threats to Kangaroos." *Animalia,* World Federation for Protection of Animals (WFPA), October-December.
14. Endangered Species Scientific Authority (ESSA). 1978. Proposed Exports of Appendix II Species, Federal Register, Vol. 43(131):29476, July 7.
15. Curry-Lindahl, Kai. 1965. "The Plight of Scandinavia's Large Carnivores", *Animals,* Vol. 7(4):92-97.
16. Brand, Christopher J., and Lloyd B. Keith. 1979. "Lynx Demography during a Snowshoe Hare decline in Alberta." *Journ. Wildlife Management,* 43(4):827-849.
17. Anon. 1979. "Save that Tiger." *IUCN Bulletin,* Vol. 10(5):36-37, May.
18. Conway, William G. 1971. *"The Impact of the Trade in Wild Animal Skins upon Wildlife",* unpubl. testimony for legislation.
19. Bailey, Vernon. 1936. The *mammals and life zones of Oregon.* North American Fauna, No. 55, U.S. Government Printing Office.
20. Talbot, Lee M. 1974. "Our Ecosystem is an Unraveling Web", pp. 24-28. *Endangered Species,* National Wildlife Federation.
21. Vernon, Sue. 1975. "I Can Get It For You Wholesale", *Defenders of Wildlife,* February.
22. Anon. 1979. "Big-time smugglers love small fines," p. 18, "The Man behind the Clean-up", *IUCN Bulletin.* Vol. 10(3), March.
23. Anon. 1979. *IUCN/SSC TRAFFIC Bulletin.* January-February.
24. CITES. 1979. Review of the Implementation of the Convention, 1978 Annual Report of the Secretariat, Second Meeting of the Conference of the Parties, Costa Rica, March. p. 21.
25. Conway, William. 1968. "The consumption of wildlife by man." *Animal Kingdom,* pp. 2-7, June.

The Reptile Product Trade, pages 60 to 64

1. Mack, D., N. Duplaix, and S. Wells. 1979. *The Sea Turtle: An Animal of Divisible Parts.* TRAFFIC (USA) Special Report 1, World Wildlife Fund, Wash. DC.
2. Anon. 1980. *Minutes.* Survival Service Commission Meeting. IUCN, Gland, Switzerland.
3. Carr, Archie. 1973. *So Excellent a Fishe.* Anchor Books.
4. Milliken, Tom. 1981. Wildlife Shopping in Tokyo—1981. *IUCN TRAFFIC Bull.* Wildlife Trade Monitoring Unit. Vol. 3(3/4):43-46. May/Aug.
5. Anon. 1981. More Wildlife Exports from Colombia. *IUCN TRAFFIC Bull.* Wildlife Trade Monitoring Unit, Vol. 3(3/4):39. May/Aug.
6. Anon. 1980. CITES Uncovers Fur Trade Scandal. *IUCN Bull.* Vol. 11(12):108. Nov./Dec.

Wild Pets, pages 64 to 69

1. Forshaw, Joseph M. 1978. *Parrots of the World.* 2nd Edition. Lansdowne Press, Melbourne, Australia.
2. Beste, Hans. 1974. The parrot with a price on its head. *Animals,* Jan. pp. 29-30. London.
3. O'Brien, James. 1980. Spix Macaw puzzle for customs men at Heathrow. *The Daily Telegraph,* Jan. 29, 1980. p. 15.
4. Dale, John. 1979. Wildlife racket uncovered. *London Observer,* Jan. 14, 1979.
5. IUCN. 1979. *Red Data Book. Aves.* Vol. II, Part II. Gland, Switzerland.

6. Ridgely, Robert. 1981. The Current Distribution and Status of Mainland Neotropical Parrots. pp 233-384. *In Conservation of New World Parrots*. Int. Council for Bird Preservation, Tech. Publ. 1, Smithsonian Institution Press.

7. *Scope*. 1980 "Cargo of Cruelty." January 25, 1980. pp. 23-31. Cape Town, South Africa.

8. Nilsson, Greta, and David Mack. 1980. *Macaws—Traded to Extinction?* World Wildlife Fund—TRAFFIC/USA, Report No. 2. Washington, DC.

9. Fish and Wildlife Service *News Release*, September 30, 1981.

10. RSPCA. 1980. *The Tortoise Trade*. Horsham, England.

11. Behme, Bob. 1982. *Pet Business*. January, p. 14.

12. Anon. 1982. Pet Trade III. An examination of the wildlife trade. Pet Industry Joint Advisory Council and other trade groups.

Overhunting and Persecution, pages 74 to 88

1. Ziswiler, Vinzenz. 1967. *Extinct and Vanishing Animals. A Biology of extinction and survival*. Springer-Verlag, N.Y., Inc.

2. McClung Robert. 1976. *Lost Wild Worlds. The Story of Extinct and Vanishing Wildlife of the Eastern Hemisphere*. William Morrow and Co., N.Y.

3. IUCN. 1978. *Red Data Book. Mammalia*. Gland, Switzerland.

4. Anon. 1979. Save that Tiger. *IUCN Bulletin*, Vol. 10(5):36-37. May.

5. Anon. 1977. La Vie Sportive en Chad. *Oryx*. Vol. XIV(1):18.

6. Edroma, Eric L. 1980. Road to Extermination in Uganda. *Oryx*, Vol. XV(5):451-452.

7. U.S. Fish and Wildlife Service. 1982. *News Release*, Leopard in southern Africa reclassified to "threatened" species. Jan. 29, 1982.

8. Anon. 1981. Mexico Jungle Hunt—Trip of a Lifetime. *Sports Afield*, Jan.

9. Anon. 1981. Hunting in Mongolia. *IUCN TRAFFIC Bulletin*, Wildlife Trade Monitoring Unit, Cambridge, England. Vol. 3(3/4):40-41. May/Aug.

10. Anon. 1977. What Kills Young Peregrines? *The Peregrine Fund Newsletter*, No. 6, p. 10.

11. Anon. 1981. Lammergeiers & Taxidermy. *IUCN TRAFFIC Bulletin*, Wildlife Trade Monitoring Unit, Vol. 3(3/4):41. May/Aug.

12. ICBP. 1981. *Red Data Book. Endangered Birds of the World*. Smithsonian Institution Press.

13. Arbib, Robert. 1981. The Changing Seasons. *American Birds*, Vol. 35(5):789-793. September.

14. Murie, Adolph. 1944. *The Wolves of Mount McKinley*. Fauna of the National Parks of the United States, Fauna Series 3, U.S. Gov. Printing Office.

15. U.S Fish and Wildlife Service. 1982. *News Release*, New Executive Order issued to permit effective predator control under statutory environmental safeguards. Jan. 29.

16. Nowak, Ronald M. 1972. The Mysterious Wolf of the South, *Natural History*, Jan.; and Nowak, R.M. 1979. *North American Quaternary Canis*. Museum of Natural History, University of Kansas, Monograph No. 6, 154 pp.

17. Carley, Curtis J. 1975. *Activities and Findings of the Red Wolf Field Recovery Program from late 1973 to 1 July, 1975*; McCarley, Howard, and Curtis Carley. 1979. *Recent Changes in Distribution and Status of Wild Red Wolves*; Carley, Curtis J. 1979. *Status Summary: The Red Wolf*. All the above reports published by the U.S. Fish and Wildlife Service, Albuquerque, New Mexico.

18. Chambers, Glenn. 1978. Little fox on the prairie. *Audubon*, July. Vol. 80(4):62-71.

19. Henderson, F. Robert, Paul F. Springer, and Richard Adrian. 1969. *The Black-footed Ferret in South Dakota*. South Dakota Dept. of Game, Fish, and Parks, Technical Bulletin No. 1.

20. McNulty, Faith. 1971. *Must They Die? The Strange Case of the Prairie Dog and the Black-footed Ferret*. Doubleday & Co., N.Y.

21. Linder, Raymond, and Conrad N. Hillman (eds.) 1973. *Proceedings of the Black-footed Ferret & Prairie Dog Workshop*. South Dakota State University. 208 pp.

22. Clark, Tim W. 1982. *Status of the Rare and Endangered Black-footed Ferret in Wyoming*. National Geographic Society Research Reports, Vol. 14:95-105.

23. U.S. Fish and Wildlife Service. 1980. *Fisheries and Wildlife Research 1979*. USDI, Denver.

24. U.S. Fish and Wildlife Service. 1981. *News Release*, "Rare Black-footed Ferret Found in Wyoming." Nov. 6, 1981: "Ferret Finders" New York Times, Feb. 28, 1982.

25. Haitch, Richard. 1981. Rare Tiger Quest. *The New York Times*, March 29, 1981.

26. U.S. Fish and Wildlife Service. 1980. Death of California Condor Under Investigation. *Endangered Species Technical Bulletin*, Vol. 5(7):3. July.

Drawing by T.W. Wood

This old engraving of Greater Birds of Paradise being shot at by natives of Aru Island, Indonesia has contemporary parallels. In late 1977 large piles of this species of Bird of Paradise as well as King Birds of Paradise were being sold in the Aru Islands in spite of laws protecting them. Indonesia is now party to CITES and may shut off this market. In Papua New Guinea and Australia, Birds of Paradise receive strict protection.

27. Ogden, John C. 1981. Failure of the California Condor Nest in Santa Barbara County; Barbour, Bruce. Report from the Field. both in *Condor Field Notes*. Calif. Condor Research Center, Vol. 1(5):1-2, & 3-4. July 23, 1981.

28. U.S. Fish and Wildlife Service. 1981. *News Release* Trapping of California Condors to Begin in September. August 10, 1981.

29. Phillips, David, and Hugh Nash. (eds.) 1981. *The Condor Question, Captive or Forever Free?* Friends of the Earth, San Francisco, 304 pp.

30. Jones, Robert A. 1982. Risky, Disputed Condor Rescue Project Set to Begin. *Los Angeles Times,* Jan. 22.

31. Daggett, Frank S. 1901. Capture of a California Condor near Pomona, California. *The Condor,* Vol. 3(2):48.

Unintended Victims, pages 89 to 104

1. Carson, Rachel. 1962. *Silent Spring.* Houghton Mifflin Co., Boston, and in paperback, 1970, Fawcett World Library.

2. Graham, Frank Jr. 1966. *Disaster by Default.* M. Evans. N.Y.

3. Ehrlich, Paul, and Anne Ehrlich. 1981. *Extinction.* Random House, N.Y.

4. Herbert, Richard A., and Kathleen G.S. Herbert. 1965. Behavior of Peregrine Falcons in the New York City area. *The Auk,* 82(1):62-94. Jan.

5. Ratcliffe, D.A. 1963. The status of the Peregrine Falcon in Great Britain. *Bird Study,* 10:56-90.

6. Stickel, Lucille. 1968. *Organochlorine pesticides in the environment.* U.S. Department of the Interior. Fish and Wildlife Service, Special Scientific Report—Wildlife No. 119.

7. Bollengier, Rene M., Jr., et al. 1979. *Eastern Peregrine Falcon Recovery Plan.* U.S. Fish and Wildlife Service, 147 pp.

8. ICBP. 1981. *Endangered Birds of the World. The ICBP Red Data Book.* Smithsonian Institution Press.

9. The Peregrine Fund. 1978. Pair Formation in New Jersey. *Newsletter* No. 6, Fall, p. 7.

10. *Ibid.* 1979. First Nestings by our Released Falcons; Captive Breeding—the 1979 Season. *Newsletter* No. 7, Fall.

11. *Ibid.* 1980. Peregrines Nest and Raise Young in New Jersey; Scarlett Meets Rhett. *Newsletter* No. 8, Fall.

12. *Ibid.* 1981. Urban Peregrines. *Newsletter* No. 9, Fall.

13. Laycock, George. 1974. Hang on, pelican! *Audubon,* Nov. pp 2-17.

14. Anon. 1975. Pesticides decimate transplanted pelicans. *Audubon.* July, pp 127-128.

15. U.S. Fish and Wildlife Service. 1982. *News Release* Ten Years Later: Bird Populations Rise as DDT Declines in the Environment. March 8.

16. Luckens, M.M., and W.H. Davis. 1964. *Science,* 146:948.

17. Cockrum, E.L. 1970. Insecticides and Guano Bats. *Ecology,* 51(5):761-762.

18. Clark, Donald R., Jr., Richard K. LaVal, and Douglas M. Swineford. 1978. Dieldrin-induced mortality in an endangered species, the Gray Bat (*Myotis grisescens*). *Science,* 199:1357-1359.

19. Brewer, Jo. 1972. How to kill a butterfly. *Audubon,* March, 74(2):76-88.

20. Abbott, Warren. 1982. Butterfly population declines due to insecticides. *Christian Science Monitor,* Jan. 20. p. 16.

21. Environmental Protection Agency. 1977. *Suspended and Cancelled Pesticides.* (Booklet), 16 pp.

22. Council on Environmental Quality. 1980. *The Global 2000 Report to the President.* The Technical Report, Vol. II, 766 pp.

23. Cowell, Alan. 1981. Pesticides are endangering wildlife in an African valley. *The New York Times,* Oct. 22.

24. Hendry, George R. 1981. Acid Rain and Gray Snow. *Natural History,* 90(2):58-65. Feb.

25. Anon. 1982. "Acid Rain Linked to Tree Deaths." *Washington Post,* March 3: Bufe, C.G., F.W. Lester, K.M. Lahr, V.C. Lahr, L.C. Seekins, and T.C. Hanks. 1976. Acid precipitation and embryonic mortality of Spotted Salamanders, *Ambystoma maculatum. Science,* Vol. 192:68-74.

26. Carr, Archie, Larry Ogren, and Charles McVea. 1980. Apparent hibernation by the Atlantic Loggerhead Turtle *Caretta caretta* off Cape Canaveral, Florida. *Biological Conservation,* 19:7-14. Nov.

27. Radwell, Steven. 1981. Whale Collisions with Boats, Gear Increase. *Wildlife Involvement News,* (Sierra Club) 5(3):4.

28. Perrin, William F. 1970. *The Problem of Porpoise Mortality in the U.S. Tropical Tuna Fishery.* Proceedings, 6th Annual Conference on Biological Sonar and Diving Mammals. Stanford Research Institute.

29. International Council for Bird Preservation. 1981. Correspondence to NMFS.

30. Ainley, David G., A.R. De Gange, L.L. Jones, R.J. Beach. 1981. Mortality of Seabirds in High Seas Salmon Gill Nets. *Fishery Bulletin.*

31. Sharp, Eric. 1981. Man and powerboats vs. endangered manatee is no contest. *Miami Herald,* Dec. 1.

32. Byers, Anne M. 1982. Of Manatees and Mermaids. *Americas.* 34(2):20-25. March-April.

33. Spolar, Chris. 1982. Manatee seminar marred when boat hits mammal. *Miami Herald,* Jan. 17.

34. Matera, Dary. 1982. Save the Manatees. Company installs radar to protect sea cows. *Miami Herald,* Jan. 26.

35. Fish and Wildlife Service 1971. *News Release,* Death is a Highway. Department of Interior, December 19.

36. Fish and Wildlife Service. 1980. Key Deer Recovery Plan Approved. *Endangered Species Technical Bulletin,* July, 5(7):9.

37. Fish and Wildlife Service. 1981. *Endangered Species Technical Bulletin,* May, 6(5):2.

Legislation and
Citizen Action

Mikhail Baryshnikov *broadcasts for whales.*

Published in Whales vs. Whalers, A Continuing Commentary, Animal Welfare Institute

International Legislation

How can a Peregrine Falcon that breeds in North America, but migrates to Latin America to winter, be protected throughout its travels? A sea turtle that swims thousands of miles in open sea needs protection from killing and from the sale of its meat and shell in other parts of the world. Animals do not recognize political boundaries. The protection of a species in its breeding area is of limited value if it is unprotected in migration and in its wintering area. The international trade in both endangered animals and plants has burgeoned over the past few decades. As open space dwindles, the need for international agreements to establish national parks and reserves grows. Toxic chemicals spread in one country can enter the oceans and air, circumnavigating the globe contaminating food chains and causing direct mortality. These issues have been the subject of legislation, treaties, agreements and conventions between countries of the world.

Trade in Endangered Species

Lacey and Tariff Acts

In the United States, the devastating wildlife slaughters of the 19th century that brought about the extinctions of the Passenger Pigeon and the Carolina Parakeet caused widespread shock and dismay among the American public. To respond to the continued unregulated killing of wildlife, such as the shooting of thousands of plumed birds for their feathers at the turn of the century, the Lacey Act was enacted in 1900. It prohibited the interstate transport of wildlife killed in violation of a state law. The Lacey Act also allowed a state to prohibit import of an animal even if killed lawfully. Thus, for example, egret plumes taken in a state where the birds were protected could not be shipped to other states. A state could outlaw their entry even if the exporting state did not protect them. In 1908, the Act was first applied to wildlife imported from another country which had taken it illegally, thus expanding its scope to cover laws of other countries.

The Lacey Act was a major step toward elimination of the meat markets where the last Labrador Ducks were sold, and the plume trade which nearly spelled extinction for the Snowy and Common Egrets, Roseate Spoonbill, and other waterbirds.

The international trade in wildlife was further restricted by the passage of the Tariff Act of 1930. It provided that if the laws of any foreign country restricted the taking or exportation of any wild mammal or bird, a certification from the U.S. Consul at the place of export needed to be acquired. The wildlife taken in contravention to the Tariff Act could be seized and forfeited. The Lacey Act was amended in 1969 to apply to unlawfully acquired foreign amphibians, reptiles, mollusks and crustaceans. In 1981 major strengthening of the Lacey Act increased fines up to a maximum of $20,000 for felony charges and jail sentences of up to five years per offense. Conviction of a misdemeanor can now bring a $10,000 fine. The Lacey Act was also combined with the Black Bass Act of 1926 at this time, to extend coverage to fish, and fish roe; coral and certain plants were added to the list of species covered by the Act. The Lacey and Tariff Acts have been of great value in enforcing the laws of foreign countries. There is a growing trend in the world to restrict trade in wildlife. Many countries have passed legislation banning all commercial export of wildlife and wildlife products—Brazil, Costa Rica, Colombia, Venezuela, Panama, Nicaragua and other Latin American countries for example. Australia has had a ban on commercial export as well as importation of wildlife for some years, and Papua New Guinea has strict export regulations. Other countries have imposed export quotas on certain species, to protect their wildlife.

CITES

The most important legislative step that has been taken to regulate trade in declining species is the Convention on International Trade in Endangered Species of Wild Fauna and Flora. Drafted in 1973, it came into effect on July 1, 1975, when the tenth country ratified. CITES was the result of almost ten years of effort by the International Union for the Conservation of Nature and Natural Resources (IUCN) to enact a worldwide treaty to regulate trade in endangered, rare and protected species of wildlife and plants. CITES establishes rules for trade (importation, exportation, and re-exportation) whether or not for commercial purposes. The wildlife that is regulated by CITES is listed in three appendices. Appendix I contains the names of species or other taxa (such as families) that are threatened with extinction, and trade in these species is authorized only in exceptional circumstances. Appendix II includes species or other taxa which, although not necessarily presently threatened with extinction, may become so unless their trade is subject to strict regulation. Appendix III contains species identified by each country party to CITES as being subject to conservation regulations within its jurisdiction, and requiring the cooperation of other parties to make such regulation effective. Trade in Appendix I species (such as Tiger, Leopard, and Vicuna) is allowed only with both an export permit from the country of origin, and an import permit from the country of destination; permits are issued only after recommendations by a Management Authority and a Scientific Authority in each country. The Management Authority issues a permit after the Scientific Authority evaluates whether trade or shipment of the species would be detrimental to its survival. For trade in Appendix II species, an export permit must be issued in the country of origin, then a certificate of re-export must be issued by the Management Authority. The same rules apply to Appendix III species. CITES provides that parties should accept similar documentation to that required by CITES for trade with countries that are not parties. At present, 77 countries have ratified the Convention.

CITES has a compliance loophole allowing a country to take a "reservation" on a species thereby notifying other members that it does not plan to comply with the trade restrictions on that species. Japan, for example, has taken reservations on the Fin Whale, Himalayan Musk Deer, Green Turtle, Hawksbill Turtle, Olive Ridley Turtle, Yellow Monitor, Bengal and Desert Monitors, and the Saltwater Crocodile.

U.S. Endangered Species Act

The Endangered Species Act of 1973 passed by the U.S. Congress includes both endangered and threatened categories and, in general, prohibits commercial trade in endangered species except under permit granted for scientific or breeding purposes only, while allowing trade in some species of the threatened category, should their status allow such trade without detriment. Trade includes importation, exportation or interstate commerce.

For further information on the U.S. Endangered Species Act see the following chapter.

Migratory Species and Nature Reserves

The Migratory Bird Treaty Act, first signed into United States law in 1918, was an agreement with Great Britain on behalf of Canada to protect most species of migratory birds from hunting, taking, capture or killing except under permit or during declared hunting seasons. Authority for enforcing the Act was first delegated to the Secretary of Agriculture and later to the Secretary of Interior. This Act allowed many bird species heavily depleted or even endangered by year-round hunting to recover their numbers. In 1936 a Convention was signed with Mexico limiting the hunting season for migratory birds to a maximum of four months under permit from "respective authorities." This Convention also prohibited the hunting of migratory birds from aircraft, and called for refuge zones where hunting would be prohibited. Exceptions to both treaties were made for scientific and propagating purposes and under certain conditions where birds became injurious to agriculture. The United States signed a similar Convention with Japan in 1972 protecting birds which migrate between the two countries and their island territories. The Japanese Convention did not specify dates or lengths for hunting seasons, but required that they not coincide with nesting seasons and "maintain their populations in optimum numbers."

For the first time, the issue of enhancing and protecting birds' environment was introduced in the Japanese Convention. Oceanic pollution and introduction of injurious exotic species were among the conditions to be prevented under the Convention.

A migratory bird treaty with the Soviet Union, signed in 1976, was ratified in 1978. It provided that special attention be paid to species of birds threatened with extinction. This treaty extended jurisdiction to some species of birds not protected by existing agreements. There are over 200 bird species of mutual interest to both countries. Oil spills, exotic species introduction and other environmental problems were addressed as mutual concerns, and the establishment of refuges for birds was part of the treaty.

The Convention on Wetlands of International Importance especially as Waterfowl Habitat was originated at Ramsar in Iran. It is concerned with wetland ecosystems. Some 28 countries have ratified the convention, designating over 216 wetlands as protected sites, covering a total of over 25,000 square miles. The IUCN has published a directory of Western Palearctic wetlands. The Convention now lacks force in that member nations are required to select only one wetland for conservation, and no guidelines for selection or safeguards against delisting are part of the Convention. The IUCN is now working to increase membership among African and Asian countries.

The Marine Mammal Protection Act of 1972 was enacted by the U.S. Congress to protect marine mammals—all cetaceans, Polar Bears, Sea Otters, seals and Walrus—from harassment, hunting, capture or killing. United States citizens must apply for a permit to capture marine mammals in all waters worldwide for public display or scientific research. Foreign vessels fishing in U.S. waters must get permits if their operations result in incidental kills. Permits may be issued only if wild populations are not depleted. Importation or exportation of marine mammals is regulated by the same principles. Marine mammals captured for public display must be taken humanely.

Convention on Nature Protection and Wildlife Preservation in the Western Hemisphere

This 1940 Convention is administered by the Organization of American States (OAS). To date, 17 countries have ratified. It is more far-reaching than the Migratory Bird Treaties, extending jurisdiction to all animals and plants. It mandates the setting up of national parks, reserves, nature monuments and strict wilderness areas. Laws to protect wildlife and plants outside reserves are to be adopted and a list of species needing strict protection is included in the Annex to the Convention. To date, the Convention has not been fully implemented by the United States, a signatory, or by most other parties. The need is great to implement this Convention as well as for the United States to negotiate migratory bird treaties with Latin American countries. The destruction of forests, heavy pesticide use and other factors reducing migratory species, primarily birds, requires strong remedial actions.

The following comments on this Convention were made by Michael Bean of the Environmental Defense Fund at Congressional Hearings, 1982: "The World Wildlife Fund-U.S. has for several years been investigating migratory birds in the New World tropics, in part as a contractor for the U.S. Fish and Wildlife Service. One-half of U.S. birds (322 species) winter in the neotropics and spend at least half their lives there. Some scientists believe that U.S. breeding populations of these migrants are declining and that in several cases the decline is probably caused by destruction of wintering habitat. Some number of these species is shared with every country south of the United States, including all parties to the Convention. The United States should cooperate with these countries to determine the conservation needs of shared migratory bird species and the desirability of more formal joint commitments to the conservation of these species. Unless we address this problem now, under the rubric of the Western Hemisphere Convention, we may later have to address it under other provisions of the Endangered Species Act. We must accept the biological reality that 'our' migratory birds constitute an internationally shared resource that can only be protected through international cooperation in policy formulation, research and management.

"We believe this Committee should take several immediate steps to improve implementation of the Western Hemisphere Convention. First, the Secretary of the Interior and the Secretary of State should be directed to submit to the Congress a report describing the status of U.S. actions to implement the Convention and identifying additional actions to comply more fully with our obligations, including those concerning the conservation of migratory birds as discussed previously. These proposals should also address the recommendations of the five technical meetings and should include specific budgetary commitments."

Convention on the Conservation of Migratory Species of Wild Animals

This new treaty, signed in 1979, would have jurisdiction over all migratory species of animals—birds, mammals, fish, reptiles, and other animals which migrate over national borders. Modeled to a degree after CITES, the Convention has appendices with species listed receiving degrees of protection. Endangered species would be listed in Appendix I. Unfortunately, of 29 signatory countries in late 1981, only three countries have ratified: The Netherlands, Portugal, and Niger, an insufficient number to allow the treaty to come into force. In the United States, some state Fish and Game Departments have expressed opposition to the Convention on the grounds that it would interfere with their traditional responsibility over resident wildlife. This attitude does not further the important work of this Convention which would be based on cooperation between foreign countries, federal and state governments. One of the major reasons it is needed is the annual slaughter of millions of migratory song birds in Mediterranean countries, mainly in Italy and Malta. These birds are netted on their way back to more northern countries for breeding each spring and sold in meat markets or exported. The cries of protest have increased yearly from the United Kingdom, West Germany, and other countries that saw the declines in the number of birds returning each spring, as well as individual species endangerment. Efforts to curb the hunting in Italy have been strongly protested by Italian hunters who marched to Rome 20,000 strong after a directive was proposed limiting the kill. Very recently, Italy announced that it will sign the convention thus making a major step toward cessation of these slaughters.

International Convention for the Regulation of Whaling

In 1946, 14 nations formulated this Convention which appointed a standing commission, the International Whaling Commission (IWC) to set annual quotas for the number of whales to be killed. It did not have a means to enforce the quotas, however, and also allowed any member nation that did not accept an IWC decision to file an "objection" to escape any obligation to comply. The IWC proved to be incapable of resisting the demands of the whaling industry over the next decades, and whale populations continued to decline. Not until the 1970's did major changes take place in the IWC. A New Management Procedure (NMP) to adopt quotas was adopted in 1975, but more meaningfully, many non-whaling countries began to join the IWC, and they voted for the conservation of whales. There are now 35 countries in the IWC, of which 17 have joined since 1978, and only 10 countries belonging to the Commission still whale commercially. Other international sanctions have been enacted to limit the trade in whale products such as the addition of all large whales to CITES, and curbs on fishing rights and importation of whale products by the European Economic Community and the United States. For further information, see the section on whales.

Questions and Answers About the Endangered Species Act

prepared by Michael Bean, Attorney, Chairman Wildlife Program, Environmental Defense Fund

Tigers receive protection under the U.S. Endangered Species Act, preventing unregulated trade in these animals or their pelts.

Photo by Lion Country Safari

Q. What is the Endangered Species Act?

A. The Endangered Species Act is a federal law passed by Congress in 1973. Its purpose is to provide a means of assuring the preservation of plant and animal species that are currently in danger of extinction ("endangered" species) or that may become so in the foreseeable future ("threatened" species).

Q. Why do we need a law to preserve endangered species?

A. The rate of species loss has accelerated dramatically in recent decades and is probably greater today than at virtually any other time in the earth's history. Most of the extinctions caused today are attributable to human activity and many could be avoided. The avoidance of unnecessary loss of species serves the interest of human welfare. The many material benefits of species preservation include opportunities for improved crop production through crossbreeding with related wild species, the production of new medicines and industrial chemicals from substances found naturally only in wild plants or animals, and the generation of energy from various biological sources. Non-material benefits include the opportunity for photographing, or simply observing wild creatures that many millions of people enjoy.

Q. What species are eligible for protection under the Endangered Species Act?

A. Any species of animal or plant is potentially eligible for protection. This includes not only birds and mammals familiar to most people but also invertebrates like mollusks, crustaceans, and others. Many of these less familiar animals, as well as plants, have contributed to major discoveries of value to medicine, industry, and agriculture. The Endangered Species Act also makes it possible to protect local populations of some species even though the species as a whole may not be endangered. This flexibility in the Act facilitates taking action to protect certain members of a species before the species as a whole is threatened.

Q. How are species designated for protection?

A. The United States Fish and Wildlife Service in the Department of Interior and the National Marine Fisheries Service in the Department of Commerce are responsible for designating species as threatened or endangered. The designation procedure requires public notice of a proposed species designation and considerable opportunity for public participation in determining the actual biological status of the species. The determining factor, however, is whether the best

The beautiful **Lange's Metalmark Butter-fly** *lives on a few acres of the Antioch dunes in California. If not for the U.S. Endangered Species Act, it would probably be extinct, since it has not received state protection.*

Photo by U.S. Fish and Wildlife Service

available scientific evidence indicates that the species is in danger of extinction throughout a significant portion of its range or is likely to become so in the foreseeable future.

Q. What protections apply to endangered or threatened species?

A. The answer to this question depends in part upon the type of species involved and whether it is endangered or threatened. Subject to certain limited exceptions, endangered species may not be purchased or sold in interstate or foreign commerce. Endangered animal species may not be "killed, hunted, collected, harassed, harmed, pursued, shot, trapped, wounded or captured" (actions described as "taking"). The restrictions applicable to threatened species can vary from species to species, depending upon the conservation needs of the species. Threatened species protections can be as restrictive as those applicable to endangered species. In addition, Section 7 of the Endangered Species Act requires that all federal agencies insure that actions authorized, funded, or carried out by them not jeopardize the continued existence of any endangered or threatened species or destroy the critical habitat of any such species.

Q. What is the function of "critical habitat"?

A. The designation of "critical habitat" is a means of alerting federal agencies, landowners, and others to the presence of endangered species in a particular area and the importance of that area to the conservation of the species. Areas designated as critical habitat are of special significance to the conservation needs of the species and may require special protection. The designation of an area as critical habitat does not, of itself, restrict the rights of a property owner or prevent any particular type of use or development of the area. Federal agencies are required, however, by Section 7 of the Endangered Species Act to insure that their actions do not impair the value of a critical habitat area to the survival of an endangered or threatened species.

Q. Does the listing of a species as endangered or threatened or the designation of its critical habitat impede economic development?

A. No. Section 7 of the Endangered Species Act requires federal agencies to insure that actions authorized, funded, or carried out by them neither jeopardize the continued existence of any endangered or threatened species nor destroy the critical habitat of any such species. This requirement is implemented through a formal process of interagency consultation which is intended to identify reasonable development alternatives that do not conflict with species conservation needs. Where there are no reasonable alternatives and the proposed federal action is economically sound, the Act provides a means of exempting the action from the requirements of Section 7.

Q. What role do the states play in endangered species preservation?

A. The states play an important role. Most states have adopted endangered species laws that complement the federal Act. The Act provides authority for federal funding to the states for the more effec-

Photo by Russell Mittermeier

*An illegal shipment of two **Red Uakari Monkeys** was seized in Miami, the first seizure of foreign wildlife under the U.S. Endangered Species Conservation Act.*

tive implementation of their laws. In the current fiscal year, however, the Administration has eliminated all funding for state endangered species programs.

Q. What role do private citizens have under the Endangered Species Act?

A. Private citizens have a number of important roles. They can participate in the administrative processes that lead to the designation of endangered or threatened species and their critical habitats. They can even initiate these processes by petitioning the Secretaries of Interior or Commerce. Perhaps the most important role, however, is the opportunity for citizens to assist in the enforcement of the Endangered Species Act by consulting an attorney and filing citizen lawsuits against violators of the Act.

Q. Does the Endangered Species Act protect species in other countries?

A. Yes. The principal way in which the Act does this is by implementing a treaty among more than 80 nations that have agreed to restrict international trade in endangered and threatened species. The Act also authorizes the use of excess foreign currencies and granting of technical assistance to aid endangered species conservation efforts in foreign nations.

Q. What is the future outlook for the Endangered Species Act?

A. The future outlook is mixed. The current Administration has cut funding for the Act, virtually eliminated the listing of additional species, and delayed key measures necessary for the effective preservation of endangered species. On the other hand, Congress has recently reauthorized the appropriation of funds to implement the Act through 1985, despite strong pressures from powerful commercial and industrial interests to weaken it. Congress' recent action in reaffirming the value of the Act was largely a response to strong citizen support for continued protection of endangered species.

State Endangered Species Programs

Twelve years ago, only a few states had begun programs to aid rare and endangered species. Today, over 40 states have enacted legislation and sponsored programs for endangered species preservation. The Bald Eagle has been successfully reintroduced and is breeding again in New York State, the Kirtland's Warbler has a stable population in its Michigan breeding grounds, and habitats for rare Indiana and Gray Bats have been acquired—all as a result of state and/or combined state and federal programs under the Endangered Species Act of 1973. Countless species are better off today than they were a decade ago, having benefitted from state endangered species programs.

The growth of these state programs has been an exciting phenomenon fueled to a large extent by growing public interest and concern. Support has grown for protecting all types of plants and animals, from the well-known endangered species such as the Whooping Crane and Bald Eagle to lesser known animals and plants. Bats, salamanders, butterflies, tiny fish and endangered cacti have new champions among the public today.

State Legislation and The Endangered Species Act of 1973

The federal Endangered Species Act of 1973 encouraged state participation in the preservation of endangered species both through grants and a mandated consultation process with states when federal projects affected endangered species. Section 6 of the Act authorized grants of ⅔ funding of state programs on behalf of federally listed species, and ¾ funding from the federal government on projects in which two or more states cooperated on a specific endangered species project. The response has been very strong—36 states now participate in the federal cooperative agreements through which funds are allocated to state programs. Cooperative agreements require that states meet certain criteria:

1. That authority resides in the state wildlife agency to conserve resident wildlife determined by the agency to be endangered or threatened.

2. That the state has established acceptable conservation programs consistent with the purposes and policies of this Act for all federally listed species, and furnished details on its programs to the Secretary of Interior.

3. That the state agency has authority to conduct investigations to determine the status and requirements for survival of resident wildlife.

4. That the state agency is authorized to establish programs including land or aquatic habitat, or interests (such as leases) for endangered species conservation.

5. That provision is made for public participation in designating resident species of wildlife as endangered or threatened.

Under the 1973 Act, Congress placed a ceiling of $10 million to be appropriated for state programs through June 30, 1977. In fact, no cooperative agreement was signed for almost three years and federal expenditure by the end of fiscal 1977 amounted to only $1,568,400 for all state programs. The first state to sign a cooperative agreement was Arkansas, in April, 1976, and 16 more states followed suit before the end of the year. These agreements were all for fish and wildlife conservation rather than for plants; agreements for the latter were not authorized until Congress amended the Act in 1978. So far, 11 states have cooperative agreements for plant conservation. In 1977, four more states signed wildlife agreements bringing the total number of states involved in cooperative agreements to 21, with one more signing in 1978.

Congress passed amendments to the Endangered Species Act in 1978 which loosened some of the criteria which states would have to meet in order to sign agreements. Prior to 1978, many states did not qualify for the agreements because their acts did not conform to the criteria. For example, some acts passed by the states did not include invertebrates. Other states objected to some federal listings of species which they did not agree were endangered or which for some reason they did not wish to protect. The 1978 amendment allowed the states a new option: limited agreements could be signed for both plants and wildlife, which allowed states to decide whether to recognize federally listed species. Therefore, these states might not have authority to list some species, or they could choose to list only some of the species listed by the federal government.

Six states have signed limited cooperative agreements: three of these are limited plant agreements with states which had already signed full fish and wildlife agreements, and three signed limited fish and wildlife agreements. These latter states had not previously had any agreement. Guam and the Virgin Islands signed limited fish and wildlife agreements in 1979 and 1980. All agreements must be reviewed by the Fish and Wildlife Service annually, and to date, no program has warranted cancellation.

Programs

The state endangered species programs are still fairly new and working out the "kinks." Some have achieved superb successes in a few short years, most notably Missouri, California, Michigan, Wisconsin, and South Carolina. Others have excelled in various ways as well, and the descriptions which follow highlight some of these activities. Approaches, such as the ecosystem protection concept, the invertebrate and plant protection by several states which far surpasses the federal list, the public education programs, and the public involvement achieved by some states, are highly commendable. The concept of ecosystem protection is inherent in the Natural Heritage programs now carried out in 28 states. Under these, inventories are being made of unique, rare and endangered species, and threatened ecosystems. These data are entered into computers and aid in programs to preserve species and habitats. The Nature Conservancy, an organization based in Arlington, VA, coordinates these very significant state programs. The federal Nongame Act enacted in 1980 could also be linked into both natural heritage and endangered species programs, but Congress has so far failed to appropriate any money to set it into action. The traditional funding for most state wildlife agencies has been from hunting, fishing and trapping license sales. The state agency approach to wildlife has been influenced by these income sources. On the whole, their biologists are oriented toward increasing game and fish populations rather than toward preserving ecosystem diversity and endangered species. Integration of nongame and endangered species programs into this entrenched system, which has long catered only to consumptive wildlife users, has been rocky in some states, yet surprisingly smooth in others. A few state wildlife agencies have been forced to include endangered species in their programs to accommodate the wishes of the public, and still have only reluctant commitment to endangered species protection. Also, just as the activities of some federal agencies, bureaus and departments conflict with endangered species protection, game and fish management programs of some states are sometimes in direct conflict with endangered species conservation for some species. Fish stocking, for example, has often involved the introduction of non-native species of fish into many areas, out-competing native species and

Photo by W.F. Kubichek, U.S. Fish and Wildlife Service

*The **White Pelican** has declined in many states. Colorado has listed it as threatened, and Washington state as endangered (see page 124).*

within their borders, and some states, notably California and Florida, have a strict permit system, the former having rigid regulations on the importation and transport of wildlife within the state.

Lists

A number of states have endangered species laws, or authority under state game laws to protect endangered species, but have so far chosen to protect only those species listed by the U.S. Endangered Species Act. Most of these lists are not an accurate reflection of the states' endangered species since the federal list is basically quite limited insofar as native species are concerned. Most states have provisions in their laws which mandate citizen participation in list formulation, and well-documented suggestions can be made for additions to their lists. Alaska, Arkansas, Connecticut, Delaware, Kentucky, Louisiana, Maine, Massachusetts, Montana, Nevada, North Carolina, Oklahoma, Pennsylvania, Rhode Island, Utah, Virginia and Wyoming—almost half of the states having passed endangered species legislation—fall into this category of honoring the federal list only. In a few states, notably Arkansas and North Carolina, extensive research has been done by outside organizations or other state departments on the state's endangered species. Recommendations were made in published reports to enlarge the state lists. In the case of Arkansas, the Department of Planning of the state government published an excellent report in 1974, *Arkansas Natural Area Plan,* which listed fully 258 species in the state in need of protection, or status research. This list did not encompass invertebrates, which will be added to the revised list to be published in 1982 by the Natural and Cultural Heritage Department. The Arkansas Game and Fish Commission recognizes only the 13 animals on the federal list which occur in the state, and so far has not conducted research to authenticate the *Natural Area Plan*'s recommendations.

On the positive side, many states have extensive lists and programs to aid these species. Missouri (see page 121) has one of the country's most comprehensive lists: 136 animals and 365 plants, only six of which are federally listed species. Other states with long lists of endangered and threatened species are California (63 animals), Florida (99 animals), Michigan (66 animals, 209 plants), New Jersey (52 animals), New Mexico (109 animals), Ohio (78 animals, 417 plants), Tennessee (57 animals), Texas (124 animals), and Wisconsin (46 animals, 56 plants). The accompanying chart shows in detail these state lists.

Invertebrates and plants are among the least "popular" endangered species, with even less appeal than reptiles for most of the public. The federal list, after a series of withdrawn proposals and changes in the listing process, has had very few invertebrates and plants added. Many states have shown amazing initiative by their expanded lists. Besides Missouri, which has listed 57 invertebrates, Indiana, Ohio and Tennessee have listed about 17 invertebrates each. Ohio has the most inclusive list of plants—417 species, Michigan has listed 209, and Georgia 58 plant species.

One advantage to these lists is that they can identify species endangered or threatened throughout their ranges which have not been identified as such by Federal authorities. Both the Piping Plover, and the Snowy Plover, diminutive shore birds, seem to be in trouble based on the state lists. Most states where they occur have listed them as threatened or endangered because of disturbance and destruction of the sand beaches they require for nesting. The Gopher Tortoise, also, is listed in most southern states where it occurs. It was the subject of a short film by the state of Georgia (see films section) that described its precipitous decline caused by development of its habitat in sandy pine woods, the gassing of its burrows by snake hunters, and capture for the pet trade.

Funding

A key to the success of state programs is the level of funding. Between 1977, when the first funds were allocated to state programs, and 1981, a cumulative total of $23,615,400 has been distributed to states and commonwealths. Since 1978, about $5 million per year was spent. In all, 37 states and two commonwealths now participate in the program, indicating a major commitment from almost 75% of the states.

reducing the latter to endangered status. The Rainbow Trout, for example, has been widely introduced in the West, endangering the native Cutthroat Trout. In addition, heavy fur trapping is pushing a few species into threatened status. The indiscriminate steel-jaw leghold trap kills many endangered species such as the Bald Eagle each year, and yet it continues to be defended by most state game departments.

The experience of each state can be helpful in aiding programs of other states, and communication between states—comparing notes, and hopefully sharing endangered species programs, will be important to the future of all state programs. The Colorado Division of Wildlife has begun publication of a Nongame Newsletter to fill a related need, and such a newsletter for state programs on endangered species would be very useful.

Many state programs are extending protection to species which are in need of help, but which are not receiving federal protection. The Southern Gopher Tortoise, for example, is in great decline, and some states protect it. This is one of the unique contributions to wildlife conservation that can be made on a state basis.

On the whole, state laws protecting endangered species are less restrictive in terms of penalties for violations than the federal law, and do not embody such legal concepts as prohibiting agencies from engaging in activities which would destroy critical habitat of endangered species. There are exceptions to this general rule. For example, Michigan's endangered species law prohibits killing or uprooting of all endangered animals and plants except under permit, even those on private property. Laws of most states extend legal control over all species of native wildlife. Plant protection is not always part of the state game law framework. The states regulate "taking" of wildlife and plants

Several other states, including Indiana, Louisiana, Mississippi and Texas, have their own endangered species laws, but have not sought federal aid.

Federal funding for state endangered species programs has been miniscule when compared to other federal aid programs for wildlife. Funds from excise taxes on guns and ammunition, archery equipment, and fishing equipment, for example, which are distributed to states, amounted to $107 million in 1981, four times the amount allocated to all state endangered species programs for the five-year period 1977-81, and over 20 times the annual average amount for state endangered species programs.

It is obvious that federal funding, even when allocated in Fish and Wildlife Service budgets, is insufficient to meet the needs of the states, especially those that have extensive programs. The fact that an administration can delete the funds, as it did in 1982 and 1983, and thereby negate the funding appropriation, further underscores the need for an outside or at least a permanent source of funds. The Congress can over-rule recommendations from budgets proposed by the President, but it did not choose to do so in the 1981 session. The states have been the innovators as far as sources of funding and some of their methods may be applicable to future federal funding.

Missouri's sales tax may be the most successful fund-raiser in the country. All items sold in the state are taxed at the rate of 1/8 of 1% for the state's nature conservation programs. This might seem an insignificant percentage, but the funds accrued have been as much as $32 million per year. These funds are not spent exclusively on endangered

State Endangered Species Programs
Numbers in ( ) = species not *federally listed*

	State Law	Coop. Agreements w. USF&W	Natural Heritage Programs	Federal E.S. list only	Total # Animals	Sp. listed # Plants	# Birds	# Mammals	# Reptiles	# Amphibians	# Fish	# Invertebrates
Alabama												
Alaska	X	FW		X								
Arizona			X									
Arkansas	X	FW	X	X								
California	X	FW P	X		63	174	15 (7)	15 (11)	7 (4)	8 (6)	15 (9)	3 (3)
Colorado	X	FW L-P	X		25		8 (5)	6 (3)			11 (8)	
Connecticut	X	FW,P		X								
Delaware	X	FW		X								
Florida	X	FW	X		99		32 (22)	25 (15)	22 (13)	2 (1)	15 (13)	3 (0)
Georgia	X	FW P			23	58 (58)	7 (0)	8 (2)	6 (2)		2 (1)	
Hawaii	X				53	5 (0)	36 (5)	5 (0)	3 (0)			9 (0)
Idaho	X	FW		X								
Illinois	X	FW			70		40 (36)	8 (6)	6 (6)	3 (3)	13 (12)	
Indiana	X		X		70		3 (0)	14 (11)	8 (8)	5 (5)	21 (21)	19 (19)
Iowa	X	L-FW	X		110		28 (25)	25 (22)	18 (18)	5 (5)	34 (34)	
Kansas	X	FW			24		6 (2)	2 (0)	1 (1)	5 (5)	6 (6)	4 (4)
Kentucky	X		X	X								
Louisiana	X			X								
Maine	X	FW		X								
Maryland	X	FW	X		33		4 (0)	13 (4)	9 (4)	5 (5)	2 (0)	
Massachusetts	X	FW	X	X								
Michigan	X	FW P	X		66	208 (208)	14 (3)	5 (3)	5 (5)	3 (3)	18 (17)	21 (21)

Key: FW = full cooperative agreement on fish and wildlife
P = full cooperative agreement on plants
L-FW = limited cooperative agreement on fish and wildlife
L-P = limited cooperative agreement on plants

	State Law	Coop. Agreements w. USF&W	Natural Heritage Programs	Federal E.S. list only	Total # Animals	Sp. listed # Plants	# Birds	# Mammals	# Reptiles	# Amphibians	# Fish	# Invertebrates
Minnesota	X	L-FW	X	X								
Mississippi	X		X		31		8 (1)	4 (1)	11 (5)	2 (2)	6 (6)	
Missouri	X	FW	X		136	365 (365)	18 (17)	14 (10)	12 (12)	3 (3)	32 (32)	57 (55)
Montana	X	FW		X								
Nebraska	X	FW			14		5 (2)	3 (1)			6 (6)	
Nevada	X	FW		X								
New Hampshire	X	FW			19		14 (12)	3 (2)			2 (1)	
New Jersey	X	FW			42*		24 (22)	1 (0)	5 (5)	7 (6)	5 (4)	
New Mexico	X	FW	X		94		30 (27)	15 (14)	18 (17)	6 (6)	24 (20)	1 (1)
New York	X	FW			13		4 (0)	3 (0)	1 (1)		3 (0)	2 (0)
North Carolina	X	FW L-P	X	X								
North Dakota			X									
Ohio	X	P	X		77	417 (417)	7 (4)	4 (3)	3 (3)	5 (5)	40 (38)	18 (16)
Oklahoma	X		X	X								
Oregon	X		X		11		6 (3)	4 (3)		1 (1)		
Pennsylvania	X	FW	X	X								
Rhode Island	X	FW P	X	X								
South Carolina	X	FW L-P	X		28	1 (0)	8 (0)	10 (0)	7 (1)	2 (1)	1 (0)	
South Dakota	X	FW	X		30		7 (3)	5 (1)	7 (7)		11 (11)	
Tennessee	X	FW	X		57		14 (11)	4 (3)	2 (2)	1 (7)	19 (18)	17 (17)
Texas	X				124	10 (0)	23 (14)	30 (10)	30 (24)	16 (13)	25 (22)	
Utah	X	FW		X								
Vermont												
Virginia	X	FW		X								
Washington	X	FW P	X		27		10 (6)	13 (3)	3 (1)			1 (1)
West Virginia			X									
Wisconsin	X	FW P			46	56 (56)	13 (11)	3 (2)	8 (8)	4 (4)	17 (17)	1 (1)
Wyoming	X	L-FW	X	X								

Key: FW = full cooperative agreement on fish and wildlife
P = full cooperative agreement on plants
L-FW = limited cooperative agreement on fish and wildlife
L-P = limited cooperative agreement on plants

*Endangered and Threatened Species only—declining, peripheral, Special Case & undetermined status categories were omitted.

species, but on combined game-nongame-endangered species conservation. This concept of combining the latter programs is sound biologically, as it may prevent additions to the endangered species lists by protecting species when they are still fairly common and play an important role in ecosystems.

Funding from general tax revenues is used in some states, and when not pruned heavily by state legislatures, can be a stable source of income. Many states—18 at last count—have passed legislation for nongame programs which allows state tax rebates or portions thereof to be signed over to nongame or endangered species programs by tax rebate recipients. This has been very successful as a funding source, since even small amounts signed over to the programs can, when contributed by large numbers of people, amount to significant sums. Most state wildlife agencies consider this the most promising funding source. Personalized license plate sales provide California's and Washington's funding, and this has proved to be fairly, but not spectacularly, successful. The concept of wildlife stamps, modeled after the duck stamps which waterfowl hunters are required to buy, has been tried by at least one state with minimal success. The stamps were offered for sale on a voluntary basis and unfortunately were not purchased in large numbers. Other suggestions have been proposed, such as taxes on birdseed, binoculars and camping equipment, and other products bought by "nonconsumptive" wildlife users. These may be taxed on a state-by-state basis, but the concept does not have strong support as federal legislation. Few have raised the possibility of private business and corporate responsibility in contributing to endangered species programs. A tax on toxic chemical producers has already been enacted for cleanup of toxic wastes, and it might be proposed that some of this money be used to aid species such as the Bald Eagle and the Peregrine Falcon which have suffered from toxic chemicals. The Nongame Act authorized $4 million to be spent on studying potential sources of revenue for that program which might have been applicable to endangered species funding, but the studies were not funded by Congressional appropriation. There may not be a single answer to the funding question. Each state may have to work out solutions best suited to it. The need to provide substantial funding is crucial, however, and many species' survival will surely depend on its successful resolution. The public support is there; it is only a matter of tapping it.

Conservation Organizations and State Programs

The citizen role can make an enormous difference in both state and federal programs, and its influence can decide whether species get listed, habitat protected, and above all, whether the general public is convinced of the need to preserve endangered species.

Individual participation can be very effective, but often conservation organizations can have an even stronger voice in the way state endangered species programs are run, which species get listed, which habitat acquired, and other critical issues. Chapters of the National Audubon Society have been active in state endangered species programs in many states. The Nature Conservancy's Natural Heritage Program is doing an exceptional job in field surveys for its inventory system. With the cutoff of federal funding for state programs, the role of Nature Conservancy's biological surveys will become even more vital. Unfortunately, as a result of the Department of Interior's policy in regard to the Land and Water Conservation Fund, monies will no longer aid in the Natural Heritage Programs. The Land and Water Conservation Fund derives its revenues from oil and gas leasing on Department of Interior land and offshore waters, and the Interior Department had traditionally diverted some of these funds to state Heritage programs. This and many other sources of funding for state programs have abruptly ceased, forcing states to locate other sources of funding. These programs will still be supported by The Nature Conservancy, however.

A few grassroots organizations have also been active in state programs. The Michigan Nature Association of Avoca, Michigan, has set a goal to acquire habitat for every one of the state's endangered plants. The California Native Plant Society has been especially active in participating in the state's inventory of endangered plants. It has aided in getting several of these federally listed. The State of California has been

active in rare plant protection.

For information on state organizations and national groups involved in state programs, see Organizations aiding endangered species in this book.

Three State Endangered Species Programs

Focus: Alabama

The State of Alabama has not enacted an endangered species law. In 1972, the Department of Conservation and Natural Resources (DCNR) published a report—"Rare and Endangered Vertebrates of Alabama"—with the input of scientists from various colleges and universities in Alabama and Florida. It noted that public interest was increasing in endangered species, and the Department received an increasing number of requests for state lists of endangered and threatened species. The report separated species into endangered, rare-1 (species not presently threatened with extinction, but existing in small numbers) and rare-2 (species of restricted habitats, though sometimes of locally abundant numbers) and status undetermined. In the endangered category, the report recognized five mammals, 10 birds, nine reptiles and amphibians, and 10 fishes.[*] Many were not federally protected.

In 1976, an even more detailed report, which included invertebrates and plants along with vertebrates, was published by the Alabama Museum of Natural History, endorsed by the DCNR. It found 106 full species of plants and 55 species of mollusks to be endangered with continued concern expressed for an expanded list of endangered and declining vertebrates.[**] This report is the proceedings of a symposium sponsored by the Game and Fish Division of the DCNR and the Alabama Museum of Natural History.

There were attempts in the early 1970's to introduce endangered species legislation in the state legislature, but all such bills failed. There is apparently a strong opposition to such a bill among many landowners, who believe that it would interfere with their use of the land, erroneously thinking that condemnation of land and/or severe restrictions on its use would result. Also, there are fears that construction projects would be stopped. The Division of Game and Fish has endorsed both proposed lists mentioned earlier, and supports an endangered species list. There has not been active citizen participation in the process of educating the state legislature and the public that such a program need not have the negative consequences feared by its opponents. The Division of Game and Fish has decided to place its major support behind a nongame bill, to be reintroduced in 1982, which would finance research from tax refund checkoffs. This type of bill has been introduced in the past few years, but has always gotten bogged down in committee and never reached the voting stage.

There is much interest among Alabama scientists and citizens in endangered species protection, and the two reports issued were the result of a great deal of specialized information and concern on the subject.

Needed now for Alabama: a strong effort by citizens and the state DCNR to convince the public and state legislature of the need for an active conservation program for the state's threatened and endangered fauna and flora.

Focus: Missouri

Missouri's endangered species program is unique in its integration of all wildlife programs into one and its active programs for invertebrates and plants as well as the more "popular" endangered species. The Missouri state legislature passed a law in 1977 which designated 1/8 of one percent sales tax to a "Design for Conservation" program. The funds accrued have been substantial—over $30 million yearly are designated by law for "nature conservation" of which endangered

---

[*]Rare and Endangered Vertebrates of Alabama. Alabama Department of Conservation and Natural Resources, Division of Game and Fish. 1972. 92 pp.
[**]Endangered and Threatened Plants and Animals of Alabama. Bulletin No. 2, Alabama Museum of Natural History, University of Alabama, University, AL 35486. 1976, 92 pp ($5)

Photo by Luther C. Goldman, U.S. Fish and Wildlife Service

The **Greater Prairie Chicken,** *once abundant on the Great Plains, is now a rare species, listed by six states' endangered species acts. Only the* **Attwater's** *subspecies of Texas, pictured here, receives federal protection.*

These are high goals and might represent hollow rhetoric if the state had not backed them up with substantial programs. The 1977 list of rare and endangered species includes 14 mammals, 18 birds, 12 reptiles, 3 amphibians, 32 fishes, 57 invertebrates and 365 plant species. The extensive listing of invertebrates and plants shows the emphasis being placed on ecological system stability, of which these life forms constitute the base. The list is under revision. It was compiled by scientists, the public and official agencies.

The Natural History Section, which administers the program, coordinates research through a staff of 30 biologists who work on endangered species along with other wildlife projects. The Research Unit is housed in a building adjacent to the University of Missouri, and there is active communication between state biologists and those at the University.

Federal funds under the Endangered Species Act grant-in-aid program have helped finance studies on the Indiana, Ozark Big-eared, and Gray Bats, Bobcat, Pallid, Lake and Shovelnose Sturgeons, Blue-stripe Darter and Curtis Pearly Mussel—about $384,000 received between 1977 and 1981. In 1978, $58,000 of federal money was used to purchase Great Scot Cave and 275 acres of adjacent land for the Indiana Bat. The major funding, however, has come from the state itself, which is fortunate since federal funds have been cut for all state endangered species programs in 1982 and 1983.

Some of the projects the Department has carried out include the following:

- the only known habitat in the state of a very rare plant, the Pondberry Shrub, a 200-acre tract of sandy soil, swale and ravine, was purchased recently.

- 23 prairie tracts, endangered ecosystems in the state, have been acquired, home to a rich variety of prairie flowers and wildlife, including the Prairie Chicken, listed as rare by the state.

- River Otters, exterminated in all but the southeastern portion of the state, are to be reintroduced in the central region by release of 20 otters from other states.

- a long term status survey of the Indiana Bat by biologists Richard and Margaret LaVal has revealed much about the status, winter and summer abundance, food habits, habitats, and other facets of its life history which will aid in the species' survival throughout its range. One cave where 100,000 of these bats hibernate has been purchased by the state and protected with a gate which will keep intruders and vandals from disturbing or killing them.

A possible drawback to the state's program is the lack of priorities defined in terms of expenditure of funds. Since the major source of income for the Design for Conservation program is the sales tax which is marked for "nature conservation," the percentage applied to endangered species protection is not defined. There is no doubt about the state's commitment to endangered species preservation, and the key will be encouraging it to devote a substantial amount for this purpose.

Publication available from the state: *Rare and Endangered Species of Missouri.* 1977. by Gary R. Nordstrom, William L. Pflieger, Kenneth C. Sadler, and Walter H. Lewis. 130 pp. Missouri Department of Conservation and USDA Soil Conservation Service. This publication has a paragraph on each animal species accompanied by range maps. The plant section has briefer descriptions. An excellent reference.

Articles about the program:

"The Dwindling of the Species" by Peter Hernon. *Globe-Democrat,* St. Louis. March 14, 1981

"Missouri's 'Design for Conservation' Plan is Broadening ES Protection; More Habitat is Being Acquired." *Endangered Species Technical Bulletin* (US Fish and Wildlife Service), April, 1978. Vol. 3(4):4-6.

Focus: Washington

The State of Washington has an active and growing program for both nongame and endangered species, which came about after years of persistent citizen lobbying. Requests to the state legislature for funding for nongame research and management beginning in 1971 were unsuccessful. When citizen groups succeeded in persuading the state

species preservation is a major program. These tax revenues make up about 60% of all funds on which the Department of Conservation functions, with about 30-40% coming from the traditional hunting, fishing, and trapping licenses, and other minor sources of income such as the sale of timber on state lands. The state's endangered species act had been passed five years earlier in 1972, and it directed the Department of Conservation to establish a list of animal and plant species as rare and endangered, and it provided statutory protection for them. The program did not get into full swing, however, until the sales tax law passed, providing a substantial financial base for endangered species protection.

Of the revenue accrued from the sales tax, about one half million dollars a year are spent on buying and managing land that supports rare and endangered wildlife. Land purchase is a major component of the "Design for Conservation" program with 80% of all funds earmarked for this purpose. For all wildlife, over 20,000 acres of habitat have been acquired since the program began, much of this land benefitting endangered species. Each year the state spends some $29 million on land purchases.

The program as a whole has as a goal involvement of the public, private organizations and governmental agencies to deter extirpation of rare and endangered species and deterioration of their habitats. The published list of endangered, rare, status undetermined and possibly extirpated species was intended, in the words of the Department of Conservation, to "encourage programs of research, preservation and management—e.g. acquire, preserve and/or restore needed habitats, effect necessary regulations and legislation, and carry out information and education programs to create a public awareness and concern for the plight of these species and their importance to the overall environment." *

---

*Rare and Endangered Species of Missouri. 1977. Missouri Department of Conservation.

legislature to enact a bill in 1973, funded by the sale of personalized license plates, it was vetoed by the Governor. At this point, the citizen groups turned the issue over to the people through a referendum. The state's voters approved the funding program by a two to one majority in November, 1973.

This program, enacted into law which benefits both nongame and endangered species, now produces an income of $400,000-$500,000 yearly from the sale of "vanity" license plates. In addition, Washington was one of the first eleven states to sign a cooperative agreement with the Fish and Wildlife Service for endangered species funding. In June, 1976, it qualified for two-thirds funding of a number of endangered species programs. Since 1977, the state has received $669,000 in federal aid from this cooperative agreement.

Washington is one of the few states with a citizen's nongame advisory board established by the Game Department which plays a major role in reviewing the program, suggesting priorities, and serving as a pipeline of communication between the Department of Game and the public. It would be even more effective if this Council were established by legislative mandate, since it may be abolished by the Department of Game at any time as it is outside a legal framework.

Major programs of the Nongame Program have been concentrated on federally listed species such as the Columbian White-tailed Deer, Peregrine Falcon, and Bald Eagle, but increasing attention is being paid to a number of species endangered state-wide. The Department of Game updated a list of endangered species in October, 1981; it includes federally listed species mentioned above, although the Bald Eagle is listed as a "sensitive species", while it is federally listed as threatened, and the Grizzly Bear and Sea Otter are endangered, while "threatened" under the Federal Act. This is actually a reflection of the status of these species in the state, however. The Woodland Caribou, which numbers only about 25 individual animals in Washington, is listed as "sensitive", not a true reflection of its status. It will be reconsidered for endangered status.

The Bald Eagle Counts—A Cooperative Effort

Washington harbors more wintering Bald Eagles than any other state—some 1,600 of the 12,000 + which winter in the lower 48 states. The Bald Eagle counts which the Nongame Program has co-sponsored with the National Wildlife Federation since 1979 are therefore of great importance in monitoring the wintering eagles. Counts are held between January second and 16th, with a wider public participation each year. In 1981, 895 people took part representing a wide cross-section of Washington's citizens and agencies: six federal and state agencies, one city, three Indian nations, one university, two consulting firms, one private utility, one commercial rafting company, two timber companies, various Audubon chapters, one private bird club, one sportsmen's club and numerous private citizens. So far, each of the yearly counts has been published in report format.

To protect some of the Bald Eagles' wintering habitat, the Department of Game bought or leased land adding to a Nature Conservancy preserve, dedicated in 1976 as the Skagit River Bald Eagle Natural Area. There are several hundred Bald Eagles that winter in this area in northern Washington. The Nature Conservancy had acquired 850 acres since 1971 along the Skagit River and retains title to 300 of the preserve's 1,800 acres, as well as providing the preserve's only full-time steward.

Data is now being compiled by radio tracking and marking eagles to determine the movements and the source of the state's wintering population. Preliminary results show that sub-adults, at least, appear to be coming from British Columbia and southern Alaska, with a few from the San Juan Islands in the state where a small breeding population exists.

In 1980, for the first time, Bald Eagle nest trees in Washington were climbed, and 13 young eagles were banded. Prey studies and blood and cloacal swabs were taken to test for PCBs, heavy metals, pesticides and viral and bacterial presence. Also in 1980 a symposium on the Bald Eagle in Washington was held, with many papers given on eagle numbers and ecology. The Department has produced four public service announcements to educate the public on the Bald Eagle in the state, has conducted talks on eagles and contacted owners of nesting habitat.

Peregrine Falcon

Washington appears to be a meeting ground for three subspecies of Peregrine Falcon—the American (*Falco peregrinus anatum*), Arctic (*F.p. tundrius*), and Peale's (*F.p. pealei*). There is only one study published to date on the peregrine in the state, conducted by Clifford M. Anderson and Paul DeBruyn under contract to the state from 1978-1980. It radio-monitored Peregrine movements in the Puget Sound area and traced one wintering Peregrine to its nesting area in south-central British Columbia, indicating that it was probably of the *anatum* subspecies. The Peale's Peregrine, whose main population centers in coastal British Columbia, southeastern Alaska and the Aleutian Islands, may also occur in Washington but in very low numbers. In 1978, the Department, with aid from the Fish and Wildlife Service, began a search of the literature for historic eyrie and sighting records of the Peregrine Falcon in the state. Since then, historic sites were visited and none were found to be active. Three nests have been located elsewhere, however; two of these produced young in 1980 and all three were productive in 1981. There is a relatively large number of wintering falcons in the state, primarily in coastal areas near Grays' Harbor, Samish Bay and Willapa Bay. The next step in Washington's Peregrine Falcon program includes continuing searches for potential habitat, the possibility of future releases of captive-bred falcons, and study of their winter habitats.

Mammals

The Columbian White-tailed Deer (*Odocoileus virginianus leucurus*) once occupied the lowland brush and marshy river bottoms of west-central Washington and bordering areas of Oregon. Its decline began in the 19th century with settlement of both states. Agricultural and industrial development in its woodland habitat have reduced its population to only about 280 deer inhabiting the lower portion of the Columbia River area; the Columbian White-tailed Deer National Wildlife Refuge was created in 1972 to protect 200 of these deer and another 80 survive on other lower Columbia River islands. Studies of habitat preference and availability sponsored by the Nongame Program have identified suitable areas for reintroduction.

The Grizzly Bear and Gray Wolf, both federally and state listed, occur in very small numbers—probably less than 10 individuals of each species in the state. Wolves are occasionally sighted, and are thought to be wanderers from British Columbia, the species having been exterminated by settlers. The state has no plans for conservation efforts to establish a permanent breeding population. Grizzly Bears, in two or three small family groups, occur in the Selkirk Mountains in the northeast, and in the northern Cascade Mountains, The latter population occurs within the North Cascade National Park and adjoining Forest Service lands. The Selkirk population is found on Forest Service lands.

The Sea Otter is considered endangered by the state. It was totally eliminated by the fur trade in the 1900's from its coastal range, and of 59 otters transplanted in 1969-1970 from Alaska, many did not survive; a small population of about 50 otters inhabits the coastline at present, and its future is not secure because of heavy industrial development along the coast, and the constant traffic of oil tankers and commercial fishing boats. An oil spill could eliminate the entire population.

The Mountain Caribou (*Rangifer tarandus montanus*) numbers only about 26-30 animals in the Selkirk Mountains of the northeast. It has been proposed for federal listing, and at present it is clearly endangered from a shrinking habitat and heavy losses each year from illegal shootings and roadkills.

Species Threatened or Endangered Statewide

Both the Upland Sandpiper and the Sandhill Crane have declined drastically from conversion of prairie and water diversion in the east and central part of the state. The Upland Sandpiper seems to number only about three breeding pairs in the state, in one small area, while the

Sandhill Cranes have bred in only one year, 1975, since 1941, and in that year only one pair raised young. The White Pelican once bred in the state's eastern lakes until the 1930's when it was eliminated by land reclamation, irrigation projects, destruction of breeding colonies and killing during migration. About 300 spend the summer in one reservoir east of the Cascades and no breeding occurs. The Snowy Plover is coastal in distribution, nesting only on sand dunes, and was never abundant in the state. At present only two known breeding localities remain and habitat loss continues as the coastline is developed with homes, recreational facilities, roads and parking lots. All four birds species above are listed as endangered by Washington.

"Sensitive" species, or those that could become endangered within Washington in the foreseeable future without active management or removal of threats, include, besides the Mountain Caribou and Bald Eagle, the Pygmy Rabbit (*Sylvilagus idahoensis*), the Ferruginous Hawk (*Buteo regalis*) Peale's Peregrine Falcon, Spotted Owl (*Strix occidentalis*), Western Pond Turtle (*Clemmys marmorata*), Green Sea Turtle (*Chelonia mydas*) and Oregon Silverspot Butterfly (*Speyeria zerene hippolyta*).

Additional projects have been funded to study the feasibility of restoring breeding populations of White Pelicans and Sandhill Cranes. The status of the Cascade Red Fox (*Vulpes vulpes cascadensis*), a rare carnivore of the Cascade Mountains, has been studied as well as the Larch Mountain Salamander (*Plethodon larsellii*), known only from a narrow strip bordering 30 miles of the Columbia River, and the Ferruginous Hawk (*Buteo regalis*), a majestic bird of prey which has become rare in many parts of the west. A study of the state's endangered plants, begun in 1978 as a cooperative effort of the Washington Natural Heritage Program and the Native Plant Society, has produced a list of endangered, threatened and sensitive plants.

The Nongame Program: Methods and Goals

In July, 1981, the Nongame Wildlife program published a plan for its future goals and activities.* It details expansion of its computer data inventory of wildlife data along with extensive manual, slide, and library files gathered through a network of inhouse and outside sources. Studies of reptiles, amphibians, fish and invertebrates are projected, along with the birds and mammals which have heretofore dominated the program. Management activities will entail habitat protection, acquisition, restoration of populations, and damaged habitats, and cooperative agreements with agencies or landowners. Revision of the game code to give more emphasis to nongame wildlife is recommended by the plan. If carried through, this would be a significant step forward.

The present funding mechanism through the sale of personalized license plates was characterized as an inadequate and uncertain source of income. It was suggested that additional sources such as a state tax on recreational equipment, bird seed, general fund or earmarked taxes, be investigated with the goal that "the amount of fiscal support of nongame wildlife should reflect the proportion of nonconsumptive wildlife users within the state."

Input from the nongame section on other department activities regulating hunting, fishing, trapping and wildlife control activities would be provided according to the plan. A broad program of education on endangered and nongame species is also planned.

If implemented, this plan would result in many innovative improvements and programs.

Publications

Over the past few years, a spate of publications has appeared on state endangered species and their programs. The most informative and thorough tend to be the result of studies, symposia, and conferences on the endangered species problem in that particular state. Some of these studies were sponsored by state wildlife agencies. Divided into major sections for each taxon, e.g. mammals, birds, fish, plants, each section

*Nongame Wildlife Program Plan. 1981. Washington Department of Game. 69 pp

is usually written by an authority in that field. Most are fascinating reading, and some are wide in scope, discussing the major ecological problems in the state and endangered ecosystems. Species distribution maps and color photos illustrate many of these reports.

The publications vary in quality as well as in the amount of information on individual species. For many animals and plants, little is known of their status in the wild, but these reports often call attention to those of limited distribution, of unusual and threatened habitat, or those considered threatened, even though field research has not been conducted. The status of bird species is usually better known than other vertebrates because of the army of birdwatchers who report and publish sightings. In all cases, these reports are a prime source of information to be augmented by further field research.

For those states in which no conferences or symposia have taken place, or reports compiled, encouragement from the public might be successful in initiating them.

Several bibliographies have been compiled on state lists, programs and publications.

Endangered Species. Concepts, Principles and Programs: A Bibliography. by Don A. Wood. Florida Game and Fresh Water Fish Commission, May 1981. This is a major source of information with 3,135 references on endangered species worldwide; most of the state reports are included. It has an index listing publications pertaining to each state's endangered species.

Eastern States Endangered Wildlife. U.S. Department of the Interior. Bureau of Land Management, Eastern States Office, Alexandria, Virginia. May 1979, reprinted 1980. Free. This report is a compilation of eastern state (states east of the Mississippi River) endangered species lists as of May 1979. It does not always make clear whether a list is official or the result of a report recommendation, and some lists are out-of-date, but it is a handy reference. The state lists may also be obtained from the individual wildlife agencies.

Directory of State Protected Species: A Reference to Species Controlled by Nongame Regulations. Association of Systematics Collections, Museum of Natural History, University of Kansas, Lawrence, Kansas 66045, 1980, $50 to nonmembers, $25 to members. This publication lists all official state endangered, threatened and other categories of species in state acts, along with species which are protected. It is updated annually, and its only drawback is its high price.

Mammalian Status Manual. A state by state survey of the endangered and threatened mammals of the United States. Compiled and edited by John Morgan. Linton Publishing Co., N. Eastham, MA 1980. $18.95. This publication compiles data from state lists and reports by species, and then state-by-state. The text does not make clear whether the species are officially protected or merely suggested for such status in reports. Such information is valuable if the above distinctions are made but of marginal value when not, and data is quickly outdated.

Endangered and Threatened Amphibians and Reptiles in the United States. Compiled by Ray E. Ashton, Jr., Edited by Stephen R. Edwards and George R. Pisani. The Society for the Study of Amphibians and Reptiles, Liaison Committee to Regional Societies. 1976. $3. (Order from Dr. Douglas Taylor, Dept. of Zoology, Miami Univ., Oxford, Ohio 45056.) This is an assessment by contributors of this society on status of reptiles and amphibians, state-by-state, intended as recommendations to state wildlife agencies. Current problems, or cause of status, current protection if any, and recommendations are arranged for each species by code. It should be valuable as a source of species needing to be added to state lists.

Selected state reports are discussed below.

Arkansas Natural Area Plan. Arkansas Department of Planning. 1974. (Available free from the Arkansas Natural and Cultural Heritage Dept., Continental Building, Main and Markham, Little Rock, AK 72201.) This ambitious report was written as a result of a 1971 law providing for establishment of a system for the preservation of natural areas, an inventory of these and recommendations for acquisition of major natural areas. It gives an excellent picture of the major ecosystems, unusual and endemic wildlife as well as suggestions with species descriptions of rare and endangered wildlife and plant species. 248 pages. It has many color photos, maps and illustrations.

The Arkansas Natural Heritage Inventory Program. Arkansas Natural Heritage Inventory Program. 1980. (Continental Building, Main and Markham, Little Rock, AK 72201). This 16-page booklet was published with the cooperation of The Nature Conservancy which helped set up this state Natural Heritage Program. It gives an excellent picture of the program, how it works, and how it benefits endangered species, mainly by habitat acquisition.

At The Crossroads 1980. A Report on the Status of California's Endangered and Rare Fish and Wildlife. State of California Resources Agency, Fish and Game Commission and Department of Fish and Game. 1980. 147 pages. California has one of the most active programs in the country for vertebrates. The program publishes reports every few years with updates on species' status, a page for each species and distribution map. The summaries note what recovery efforts have been accomplished and make recommendations for future action.

Essential Habitat for Threatened and Endangered Wildlife in Colorado. Wildlife Management Section, Division of Wildlife, State of Colorado. 1978. 84 pages. Similar to the California report, this gives descriptions of species in one or more pages, with range maps. Emphasis is placed on habitat requirements and limiting factors, recommendations for habitat acquisition and gives historic as well as present range. The state also publishes a small booklet, *Wildlife in Danger,* 31 pages, with more general information and suggestions for public participation.

Rare and Endangered Species of Connecticut and Their Habitats. by Joseph J. Dowhan and Robert J. Craig. State Geological and Natural History Survey of Connecticut. The Natural Resources Center, Dept. of Environmental Protection. Report of Investigations No. 6, 1976. 137 pages. $1. Most of this report assesses the status of the state's endangered plants, and vertebrates are also treated with short descriptions of status which are somewhat vague. It is not the state's official list, and to date, the state has not included any non-federally listed species into their act.

The Rare Vertebrates of Connecticut. by Robert J. Craig, U.S. Department of Agriculture, Soil Conservation Service, 1979, 169 pages. This report examines the status of the same vertebrate species described in the report above. The major difference is the amount of information given—it is far more detailed, giving specifics on status, location of breeding areas, historical information on range and present range. It is a well-researched and thorough reference.

Delaware Conservationist. Endangered Species Issue. Vol. XXV, No. 2, 1982. 30 pages. This special issue of the Department of Natural Resources and Environmental Control's magazine features 10 articles on the endangered species of Delaware. The Bald Eagle, Shortnose Sturgeon, sea turtles, Peregrine Falcon, and endangered plants are among those discussed in depth.

Rare and Endangered Biota of Florida Series ed. Peter C.H. Pritchard. 1978. Florida Audubon Society and Florida Defenders of the Environment. Pub. for Fla. Game & Fresh Water Fish Comm.
Mammals. Vol. I. ed. by James N. Layne, 52 pages. $5
Birds. Vol. II ed. by Herbert W. Kale II. 121 pages. $7
Amphibians & Reptiles. Vol. II. ed. by Roy W. McDiarmid, 74 pages. $5.50
Fishes. Vol. IV. ed. by Carter R. Gilbert, 58 pages. $5
Plants. Vol. V. ed. by Daniel B. Ward, 175 pages. $10.50
It is fortunate that a state as biologically rich and diverse as Florida has been researched in such depth. These reports, though somewhat expensive in the aggregate, are unique in the country. A blue ribbon panel of zoologists and botanists contributed to these reports, and they provide an excellent picture of the state's endangered species—status, distribution, life history and ecology, unique characteristics, recommendations and description. Range maps and

many color photos are included. Each species is given about one page of text, and descriptions including plants were prepared by individuals credited at the end of each listing. These reports are invaluable to the state's natural heritage preservation, and it is hoped the Florida Game and Fresh Water Fish Commission will take action on their recommendations. A sixth report on invertebrates is in progress.

Florida's Vanishing Wildlife by Laurel Comella Hendry, Thomas M. Goodwin and Ronald F. Labisky. Florida Cooperative Extension Service, and the School of Forest Resources and Conservation, Univ. of Florida, and the U.S. Fish and Wildlife Service. 1980. 69 pages. This booklet discusses vertebrates only, and is much less detailed than the series described above, though useful in its assessments. It gives the state of Florida's endangered species list at the end of the report.

Georgia's Protected Wildlife and Georgia's Protected Plants. Georgia Department of Natural Resources, Game and Fish Division, 1977. 50 and 64 pages, respectively. These reports are done in looseleaf mimeo style with separate pages on each species. They describe the state's official list of endangered species, status, distribution (with maps), actions taken for them, and proposed management plan. They are well done and the information contained includes much specific data. The state has done many related projects in the form of pamphlets on individual species, has sponsored endangered species conferences, and prepared a series of films on the state's endangered species. A list of publications and films will be sent on request.

Proceedings, Rare and Endangered Wildlife Symposium. ed. by R. Odum and L. Landers, Georgia Department of Natural Resources, Division of Wildlife Technical Bulletin WL 4. 1979.

Proceedings of the Conference on Endangered Species of Georgia, ed. by J. McCollum. Georgia Department of Natural Resources, 1974, 66 pages. The state-sponsored symposia are another valuable reference and the 1981 symposium will soon be available. They include reports on wildlife and plants by scientists in Georgia and from neighboring states, discussions of endangered species programs and other relevant subjects.

Endangered and Threatened Species of Illinois: Status and Distribution. Illinois Department of Conservation. 1981. 189 pages plus appendices. This is a comprehensive scientific guide to endangered species of Illinois. (Available on limited distribution from Endangered Species Program Coordinator, Division of Wildlife Resources, Dept. of Conservation, 605 Stratton Bldg., 600 N. Grand Avenue, West Springfield, Illinois 62702).

The Proceedings of The Iowa Academy of Science—Perspectives on Iowa's Declining Flora and Fauna, A Symposium. 1981. 47 pages. $3 (University of Northern Iowa, Cedar Falls, Iowa 50613). This symposium contains fascinating articles on the forests, prairie and wetlands along with assessments of fish, amphibian and reptile, bird and mammal status in the state. The endangered species discussions are not species-by-species accounts, but general information on trends of the wildlife in the state. Declining species are listed with status in tables. The general discussions have background material on environmental changes, legislation, pollution and other factors that have affected wildlife in Iowa.

Endangered Iowa Vertebrates compiled by Dean M. Roosa. State Preserves Advisory Board and Iowa Conservation Commission. 1977, 25 pages. The official Iowa list of threatened species, this publication gives short species-by-species accounts of listed vertebrates.

Kansas Nongame, Endangered and Threatened Wildlife. Kansas Fish and Game Commission. 1981. 28 pages. This is an annual report of the activities of the Fish and Game Commission on behalf of nongame and endangered species, some reports with results and others are job descriptions of research to be undertaken. The Commission also publishes a list of its endangered species and separate reports on investigations, including exhaustive searches for the Black-footed Ferret.

Rare and Endangered Species of Missouri. Missouri Department of Conservation and U.S. Department of Agriculture, Soil Conservation Service. 1977, 130 pages. See Focus: Missouri for a description of this publication.

Nebraska's Endangered and Threatened Wildlife. Nebraska Game and Parks Commission, Wildlife Division, 1977, 35 pages. A booklet on the state's 14 endangered and threatened species of birds, mammals, and fish, this publication has photos, range maps, and summaries of each species' status.

Handbook of Species Endangered in New Mexico. New Mexico Department of Game and Fish. 1978. $5. This publication gives specific information on the state's 94 listed species. This state has been far more active in endangered species conservation than neighboring Arizona, with which it shares many of the unusual and rare wildlife found only in this part of the southwest—Gray Hawks, Jaguarundi, Ocelot, Gila Monsters, and others of the border area.

Fish and Wildlife Program Plan 1977-78. New York State Department of Environmental Conservation. 1977, 46 pages. This is not specifically a report on endangered species, but on the state's wildlife programs including some information on endangered species projects, the major two being Bald Eagle reintroduction and Bog Turtle habitat acquisition. The state has published numerous press releases and short summaries of endangered species in the state which are available from the Department of Environmental Conservation.

Endangered, Threatened, and Peripheral Wildlife of North Dakota. ed. by Michael G. McKenna and Robert W. Seabloom. Institute for Ecological Studies, University of North Dakota, Research Report No. 28, 1979, 62 pages. Similar in format to Nebraska's report, vertebrate animals are discussed in some detail. Range maps are for distribution in North America, and species discussions are fairly short. The state has not enacted an endangered species act, and this report should give it a framework for action.

Proceedings of the First South Carolina Endangered Species Symposium. South Carolina Wildlife and Marine Resources Department and the Citadel. 1979, 201 pages, $7. This symposium took place in 1976 and gives a very thorough look at the state's endangered species problems. Much attention is paid to invertebrates and plants, along with vertebrate species. Following synopses of the endangered species is a series of articles on specific species or groups of species such as leeches, coleoptera, insects, mussels, and various bird, mammal and reptile and amphibian species. One article for example gives the status of the Pine Barrens Treefrog in South Carolina, another a seven-page discussion of the Swallow-tailed Kite in the state, and two articles discuss the searches for one of the rarest birds in America, the Bachman's Warbler, in South Carolina, which may be its last refuge. Altogether this is an excellent publication.

Tennessee Rare Wildlife. Vol. I. The Vertebrates. Eager, D.C., and R.M. Hatcher (eds.) Tennessee Wildlife Resources Agency, and Tenn. Natural Heritage Program, 1980. This is one of the best state-sponsored endangered species reports. It is a lengthy and detailed account of the status of the state's declining vertebrates based on the combined resources of the Wildlife Agency and the inventory of the Natural Heritage Program. *Volume II* on *Invertebrates* is in press. The Natural Heritage Program has jurisdiction over endangered plants in the state and has proposed a list for the state, which has not been finalized. It is available from the Program.

Endangered and Threatened Plants and Animals of Virginia. ed. by Donald W. Linzey. Center for Environmental Studies, Virginia Polytechnic Institute and State University, Blacksburg, VA. 1979, 665 pages, $12. The proceedings of a symposium held in 1978, this mammoth publication gives an even more detailed account of Virginia's endangered species than the South Carolina symposium of its declining flora and fauna. Besides plants, 190 pages are devoted to invertebrates, with a long discussion of endangered insects by a scientist from the Office of Endangered Species, and both freshwater and marine fishes are treated. Leading scientists have edited each section. Dr. Charles O. Handley, Jr., Curator of Mammals of the Smithsonian Institution's Museum of Natural History, edited the mammal section. At the end of this publication, Geographic Areas of Special Concern are highlighted by type and region. Highly recommended.

Nongame Wildlife Program Plan. A Guide to the Management of Washington's Nongame Wildlife Resources. Washington Dept. of Game, 1981, 70 pages. This plan is discussed in Focus: Washington. Besides this report, the state nongame department has published several reports on their yearly Bald Eagle counts.

The Washington Natural Heritage Program and *Endangered, Threatened, and Sensitive Vascular Plants of Washington.* State of Washington and the Nature Conservancy. Washington has a very active Natural Heritage Program which has published the reports above. It coordinates its data processing system of threatened species and ecosystems with the Nongame Program of the Washington Department of Game, located at The Evergreen State College, Olympia, WA 98505.

The Vanishing Wild. Department of Natural Resources, Wisconsin, 1979. This 36-page booklet gives status reports on Wisconsin's threatened species by habitat. It is illustrated with color photos and divides the state into four habitat types: forest, prairie/open field, water/wetland and dune, beach, and cliff. This interesting presentation makes people aware of the vital links between species and their habitats, and includes an informative discussion of the status of these habitat types. In addition Wisconsin encloses with the report two Life Tracks publications on the state's endangered species, the Wisconsin state law, a bibliography of the publications on its natural history and those publications available through the Wisconsin DNR. Educationally, these publications are among the best of the states, but unfortunately ignore invertebrates.

All states respond to inquiries on endangered species, and most have pamphlets or booklets or lists that will be sent on request. The publications above which do not have prices listed are usually free, but donations will aid the endangered species programs and help to cover publication costs.

People Who Make a Difference

The prospects for endangered species have discouraged some who say, "What can I, one person, do to make a real difference?" In this section that question is answered resoundingly by the examples—and these are only a few—of great progress that individuals have made for one or a number of threatened or endangered creatures, and through them for their species as a whole. Everyone who reads this book can take action—different kinds of action, to be sure. Letter-writing is one of the most important and most readily available. When the State of Massachusetts put the leopard on its foreign endangered species list, legislators pointed to the many letters they had received from young Kenyans writing from Africa to urge them to do so as well as those from Massachusetts students and citizens.

The Society for Animal Protective Legislation will regularly send you circular letters telling you about pending legislation affecting animals, often endangered species, if you agree to write letters to help animals. If you are willing to do this, there is no charge for sending the interesting information.

Providing needed food for wildlife in distress is another contribution that some can make.

The first of the following outstanding examples of people who have made a vital personal contribution to preventing extinction of a species tells of a young girl, Trudy Edwards, who trudged miles every day through ice and snow to bring necessary food to a small flock of starving Trumpeter Swans.

The Edwards' Who Helped to Save the Trumpeter Swan

"Occasionally on a cold moonlit night when the timber is cracking and the ice booms, all the adults in the flock get together and stage a concert. It is the most thrilling thing I have ever heard, aside from a pack of wolves in chorus. The wolves are spine-tingling while the trumpeter music is majestic and harmonious. . ." So Trudy Edwards Turner describes the song of the Trumpeter Swans she and her family helped to save.

The wilderness of British Columbia, dotted with pristine lakes surrounded by virgin evergreen forest was the chosen homesite of Trudy's father, Ralph Edwards, some 60 years ago. He settled near a lake he named "Lonesome Lake" and found it "alive with . . . geese, ducks, ravens, eagles and crows" and some 35 Swans. Ralph and his wife had great sympathy for the wild animals of their region, and instilled this respect and admiration in their three children. He had no way of knowing that the magnificent Swans which arrived each fall to winter on Lonesome Lake were among the last of their species, driven from their haunts in almost all the rest of their once vast realm.

Largest of all waterfowl, the snow white Trumpeter Swans can have a wingspread of eight feet, and once they flew proudly in huge flocks over western North America, wintering as far east as the Carolinas. They call to one another in voices the Kootenai Indians described as "Ko-Hoh", a resonant trumpet-like sound. Afraid of no animal, they fiercely protect their life-long mates and downy cygnets.

Photo from Fogswamp by Trudy Turner & Ruth M. McVeigh. Hancock House

Trudy Turner *feeding the magnificent* **Trumpeter Swans** *of Lonesome Lake.*

Photo by Winston Banko, U.S. Fish and Wildlife Service

***Trumpeter Swans** are now recovering from near extinction, helped by the Edwards family.*

The near demise of the Swans came very quickly in the 19th century when a market was created for their feathers. The slaughter was all the more appalling because it was for so frivolous a cause—swan feathers and down were used to make powder puffs and writing quills, and to decorate ladies' hats. The Swans made a large target for market hunters, and fell by the thousands—18,000 skins were traded by the Hudson's Bay Company from 1853 to 1877, and thousands more had been sold in prior years. By the turn of the century, the stately Trumpeters were gone entirely from all but a few remote areas in the United States and Canada, and may have numbered less than 100 birds. The Swans of Lonesome Lake made up about a third of all known Trumpeter Swans in the early years of the 20th century.

To the Edwards, the Lonesome Lake Swans were very special wild creatures, and when Ralph saw them starving and ice bound in severe winters in the 1920's, he chopped open the ice and even used some of his scanty supply of chicken feed to help them survive the winter. The feeding and care of this remnant flock continued year after year, and if not for this extraordinary family, these Swans would have dwindled and perhaps even been eliminated by a particularly harsh winter.

Then, a wilderness traveler, John P. Holman, happened upon Lonesome Lake in 1926 and learned of this virtually unknown wintering area of the rare Trumpeter Swans. He called the Canadian government, and as a result Ralph Edwards was appointed a bird warden, and supplied with grain to feed this flock. He and his wife have kept a log of the number of Swans which return each year for the Canadian Wildlife Service, a number which increases yearly.

When their daughter Trudy was only twelve years old, she was given the responsibility of feeding the Swans. Each day she struggled through the heavy snow drifts, carrying grain for the hungry birds. Over the years the Swans, which were originally very shy and fearful of people, having been shot at by hunters wherever they flew, gradually became tame. After some years, the Swans began to learn Trudy's schedule and now they circle the farm at 11 sharp each morning, calling out until someone emerges from the feed shed with a grain sack. Trudy, now married with her own daughter, settled a few miles from the family homestead, and each day makes the two and a half mile trek through the snow to feed the birds and keep the ice open. So trusting have the Swans become that they will eat from her hand. The Swans have reflected the long commitment of this family to their survival—400 Trumpeter Swans now spend each winter on Lonesome Lake. Although their numbers have slowly increased, they are still a rare species. Alaska harbors the largest population, counted at 8,000 in 1980, and in all the rest of North America there are only a few thousand. The Swans still receive legal protection from hunting.

Today, with thanks to the Edwards' the description by Silvia Bruce

Note: The Edwards' story is the subject of a film and two books. The Canadian Wildlife Service sponsored the film, "Footnote to Genesis" (see Films) and the books are recent publications: *Fogswamp. Living with Swans in the Wilderness* by Trudy Turner and Ruth M. McVeigh, Hancock House, 1977, and *Ralph Edwards of Lonesome Lake* by Ed Gould, Hancock House, 1979. For more on Trumpeter Swans, Silvia Bruce Wilmore's book, *Swans of the World,* published in 1974 by Taplinger Publishing Co. is good, and their recent status was reported in *Audubon,* January, 1982, and *American Birds,* September, 1981.

Wilmore in her book on Swans is still a reality, "There is no more beautiful and stirring a sight in the whole waterfowl kingdom than a flight of Trumpeters cleaving through the air against a setting of rugged rocky mountains and dark conifers."

Fighting for Africa's Wildlife

In a continent famous for its wildlife spectacles, Kidepo Valley National Park was outstanding for its huge herds of elephant and antelope which grazed in the shadow of beautiful mountain peaks. Paul Ssali knew every inch of the park, and his dedication to protecting its wildlife has become legend. He was promoted to the post of Senior Warden of this magnificent park in the north of Uganda in 1972 when his predecessor, Alfred Labongo, was nearly assassinated by President Idi Amin's men. Labongo was able to escape into Tanzania, and Ssali assumed the responsibility of defending the park's abundant wildlife against the onslaughts of ever-increasing hordes of poachers, many of them government officials.

Ssali trained his 70 rangers like soldiers, and military skills were needed. Kidepo's location in the far north of Uganda adjoining Sudan and Kenya made it highly vulnerable to incursions by Sudanese rebels who have long believed part of the park belongs to the Sudan. These rebels were not traditional native poachers killing with poison darts, wire snares and traps. Armed with weapons that would impress James Bond, Ssali and his men saw elephants, hippopotamuses, rhinoceroses, and antelope gunned down with mortar, rocket-propelled grenades, and automatic rifles. The wardens' lives were in constant danger since the Sudanese did not hesitate to open fire on them. Ssali used diplomacy in the form of free beer on one occasion, and managed to forestall a poaching raid. He pretended to be armed when he wasn't on another, by aiming his jeep's starter handle directly at the rebels, so that it looked like a weapon.

His job was made all the more difficult by the ever-present threat of Idi Amin's officers and troops. "During Amin's time, any warden could be a target anytime. It depends on how you dodge. Unless I did so, all my animals would have been finished. Majors, colonels, state research personnel—all of them were involved in poaching. You had to make sure that if your rangers killed one or two of them in the bush, not a word of it would be said. If you were not quiet, your whole ranger force would be wiped out."

His most terrifying moment came when Amin himself visited the park and issued orders that his rifle be brought to him so that he could shoot a nearby waterbuck. Ssali was masterful in his reaction. It would cause bad publicity, he said, because international treaties would be contravened and Amin would be condemned by foreign conservationists. He offered to show Amin better hunting outside the park. Amin's aide backed up Ssali and the incident was over.

Under the circumstances, it is indeed impressive that Ssali survived at all, but that he was able to supervise both Kidepo Valley and later Kabalega Falls' National Park, successfully guarding them from poaching, is truly astonishing. During these dark days most other national parks in Uganda lost thousands of elephants, rhino and other animals to the Sudanese or more frequently to the guns of Amin's own men. Bernhard Grzimek, President of the Frankfurt Zoological Society and a world renowned conservationist, rates Ssali very highly. "When Paul Ssali took over Kabalega Falls, it was seriously endangered by poaching. By the use of strict measures, he stopped poaching in a few months. Of course, in doing so, he acquired a lot

Photo by F. Vollmar, World Wildlife Fund

Paul Ssali worked to save Uganda's **rhinoceroses** *from poachers.*

of enemies among both the surrounding tribes and members of his own staff whom he had fired because of their corruption and inefficiency."

His enemies succeeded in convincing Amin to order his execution in 1979. Paul Ssali managed to escape to Kampala using the quick wits that had served him so well in the past, disguised as a bus driver. Paul Ssali's greatest fear was torture, if captured. "The one torture I most dreaded was when they drag you behind their Land Rovers at 40 miles an hour until you watch your skin falling away from you. I wasn't that worried about death. I was lucky to be dying for the cause of game rather than for no cause at all. I was lucky because I had been able to educate most of my children. What I didn't like was to think about that slow death . . ."

Finally after more attempts on his life, he was forced to leave the country and enter Kenya. Today, he is again in Uganda, but as the pilot of the National Park Directors. He refuses to leave the country because he identifies so closely with the land and animals. After his escape the slaughter in Kidepo Valley and Kabalega Falls became totally unregulated. Of the 1,200 elephants that once roamed Kidepo Valley, only 450 remain today, and of Kabalega Falls' 10,000 elephants, 172 survive, and all the rhinos were slaughtered. With Amin's departure, there is some hope that the wildlife populations may rebuild, but the fact that Ssali has not been reappointed does not bode well for the country's dedication to its wildlife.

Among the many brave wardens in Africa, Paul Ssali's work is of the first rank. He received the African Wildlife Leadership Foundation's highest honor for outstanding service to African wildlife. He serves as the Uganda representative of the East African Wildlife Society. Someday, if he does not reassume his old post, which he wants above all else, he may found a ranger training school, "Parks need men who are trained like soldiers and can fight for the game."

Note: Most of this information was contained in a recent article in the *New York Times Magazine*, by John Heminway. "A Warrior for Wildlife." Jan. 10, 1982.

Protectors of Primates

Janis Carter teaches *chimpanzees* to return to the wild.

The little chimps find their first encounter with freedom frightening, and cling to one another or their new found friend Janis Carter. When they were captured at an early age by the destructive traders in chimpanzees for pets, laboratories or zoos, their world was shattered. Usually the mother is killed and the infant is stuffed into a dark burlap bag to begin a long and often fatal journey away from its African home. In the wild, dependence on their mothers would have lasted at least eight years, filled with constant reassurance, affection and interaction with others of the troop. The bonds between mother and young are so strong that the newly captured chimps, usually still of nursing age, can die of stress. Eight to 10 wild-caught chimpanzees die for every one that survives to reach its destination.

A few African countries have banned chimpanzee capture, sale and export, The Gambia in West Africa being one of the strongest conservationist countries. Moreover, chimpanzees are listed on the Convention on International Trade in Endangered Species (CITES) and the U.S. Endangered Species Act, both of which ban commercial trade in endangered species. However, the trade flourishes through unscrupulous dealers and countries which are not party to CITES. Fortunately, some chimpanzees being illegally traded are confiscated, and through rehabilitation programs, such as that run by Janis Carter in The Gambia, they are being returned to the wild.

The beautiful **Yellow-tailed Woolly Monkey** was rediscovered by Russell Mittermeier and fellow scientists in the Peruvian Andes.

Photo by Russell A. Mittermeier

Janis has patiently and painstakingly taught nine chimpanzees to be wild again. She has spent over five years in an isolated part of The Gambia reintroducing, or in a few cases, introducing for the first time, these chimpanzees to their wild heritage. Each day she takes them on walks through the forest instructing them on finding food by giving imitations of chimp food barks when she sees edible fruit or leaves; for the slow learners she has chewed and swallowed leaves; her reluctant pupil would open her mouth to look inside and be sure she had really eaten them. Ant hunting with tools fashioned from twigs was taught to Janis by a chimp captured at age four who must have seen wild chimpanzees in the act. She found it wasn't as easy as it looked, after many painful ant bites.

Chimp rehabilitation projects are also being carried out by Stella Brewer, daughter of the Chief of Wildlife Conservation of The Gambia, Eddie Brewer, who helped sponsor Janis' project. In Ghana, Meredith Rucks has begun such a project. Time is proving that doubters, who believe chimpanzee rehabilitation to the wild is impossible, are very wrong.

In the neighboring country of Sierra Leone, Dr. Geza Teleki has accomplished major victories for primates. After long and delicate negotiations, he convinced the government of Sierra Leone to set aside its first protected area, to be called Outamba-Kilimi National Park. This region of 1,000 km² harbors ten species of primates, including several hundred chimpanzees, and is considered the best surviving wildlife habitat in the country. Until recently a major exporter of primates, Sierra Leone has now made a commitment to conservation by banning all exports of primates. This presidential decision, influenced in major part by Geza Teleki, will surely save the lives of thousands of monkeys, chimpanzees and baboons which might otherwise have supplied the market for exotic pets, zoos and medical research.

Another primate scientist, Dr. Russell Mittermeier, is chairman of the IUCN Primate Specialist Group, which now has 79 members in 25 countries and publishes a fascinating newsletter of its activities. He recently made a major rediscovery of a South American primate. Russell organized a search for the Yellow-tailed Woolly Monkey (*Lagothrix flavicauda*), a very rare Peruvian monkey that had never been seen alive by a scientist and no specimen had been seen since 1926. Russell Mittermeier located, with fellow researchers Hernando Ruiz and Anthony Luscombe, a young monkey of the species (see photo) kept as a pet in a remote Andean village. This beautiful monkey is now known to inhabit only a very restricted area in the Peruvian Andes, and is under grave danger of extinction from hunting. At the time of its rediscovery, a local school teacher in the area wrote a letter to Lima's biggest newspaper, *La Prensa*, expressing great concern for its survival, ". . . it is being eliminated without compassion by the workers constructing the . . . road . . . It is very easy to hunt since it travels in 'herds' and does not try to escape when it sees hunters. When one of the members of a group is injured, the others reunite around it, which facilitates the slaughter of the entire group. . . . If protection is not provided very soon, the species . . . will have been wiped out by the time the . . . road is completed."*

*quoted in Mittermeier, Russell A., Hernando de Macedo-Ruiz, B. Anthony Luscombe and John Cassidy. 1977. Rediscovery and Conservation of the Peruvian Yellow-tailed Woolly Monkey (*Lagothrix flavicauda*). *Primate Conservation*, p. 95-115. Academic Press, N.Y.

Drawing by Narca Moore-Craig

Arun Rangsi *is a young gibbon rescued by Shirley McGreal after he had been used in cancer research experiments.*

The Yellow-tailed Woolly Monkey is now listed on the U.S. Endangered Species list, the CITES and IUCN Red Data Book, affording it some protection from international trade, and the country of Peru has afforded it legal protection.

Another project of the IUCN Primate Specialist Group is the preservation of primates in southeastern Brazil, notably the Muriqui or Woolly Spider Monkey. The few remaining forests of the region harbor Golden Lion Marmosets as well, and World Wildlife Fund is raising money for their protection and a primate research and breeding center.

Another primate conservationist, Dr. Shirley McGreal, founder and chairwoman of the International Primate Protection League (IPPL), has been active and effective in this role. She and her field representatives uncover information on illegal and inhumane trafficking in primates for the research, zoo and pet markets.

Recently, she adopted a young gibbon (all gibbons are on the U.S. Endangered Species list) that had been mistreated in a medical laboratory and was being "disposed of". Little Arun Rangsi arrived terrified of people and grossly underweight. The number 98 had been tattooed on his body by the University of California's Comparative Oncology Laboratory where he was born, and where he was kept for cancer experiments. For weeks he cowered or flailed his arms in terror when approached. He banged his head constantly against the wire of his cage. The skin color of his face was pink unlike the black faces of normal gibbons and only after a few weeks in daylight did it turn black. For the entire two years of his life, Arun had probably never been outside his tiny cage except for injections and other manipulations used in the experiments. He could not even walk more than a few steps without collapsing.

In the spacious new cage at IPPL's headquarters in South Carolina, Arun showed amazing improvement in only three months. "When he arrived, Arun Rangsi seemed to think every object, even a green bean or a grooming brush, was a hypodermic needle!" Shirley observes. "He would attack them furiously! People's approaches

Photo by W.Y. Brockelman, World Wildlife Fund

These baby **macaques** *were seized as they were smuggled from Bangkok to Brussels. The International Primate Protection League played a role in convincing Thailand to ban export of all primates.*

were associated with about-to-be-experienced pain. It is only recently that Arun Rangsi has started reaching out his hand to hold the hand of a human. If released, he took hold again. He now likes being held closely in the evenings." He has doubled in weight and is beginning to exhibit signs of the acrobatic skills for which gibbons are famous.

Operating on a shoestring budget, Shirley and her volunteer staff have had a number of other successes. When IPPL exposed the fact that the Rhesus Monkeys shipped from India were being used in radiation experiments by a military laboratory, in violation of India's export conditions, the country stopped all export of these monkeys. Later, IPPL played a role in convincing Bangladesh and Thailand to do likewise. Strong pressure is now being exerted by a U.S. firm on the government of Bangladesh to export 71,500 Rhesus Monkeys for sale to laboratories, but scientific assessment shows the population would be decimated.

IPPL uncovered a large market for baby chimpanzees in Spain, where beach photographers approach tourists to pose with the chimps for a fee. Over 200 chimpanzees were being used by beach photographers in 1980 in the Canary Islands and the Spanish coast. To maintain the supply of infant chimps, which are replaced regularly, constant smuggling fuels the market. Adult family members are frequently killed during capture of the young, many of whom die in transport. IPPL estimates that 1,000 or more West African chimpanzees die each year to supply this senseless trade and nine or ten die for each young that survivies.

Note: Janis Carter's story is told at length in "A Journey to Freedom", an article which she authored in the April, 1981 issue of *Smithsonian* magazine. Shirley McGreal's rescue of Arun Rangsi was described in IPPL's January, 1982 newsletter. Membership information available from IPPL, P.O. Drawer X, Summerville, SC 29483. The activities of Dr. Geza Teleki and Dr. Russell Mittermeier are described in the August, 1982 IUCN/SSC Primate Specialist Group Newsletter. He recounted the rediscovery of the Yellow-tailed Woolly Monkey in *Animal Kingdom,* June, 1975.

"To Save The Cranes of the World"

George Archibald, co-founder of the International Crane Foundation, has one goal in life: "To save the cranes of the world." In the few short years since he and fellow Cornell alumnus, Ron Sauer, founded the organization, the outlook for several crane species has markedly improved as a result of their efforts. George achieved national press and TV coverage in 1978, when he was filmed as part of an "odd couple." He and Tex, a captive female Whooping Crane who was "imprinted" on people, performed a mating dance at the Foundation's headquarters. She was thoroughly convinced that he was another Whooping Crane, having been raised by people, and he responded to her dance with raised arms, uplifted head and dancing, to encourage a breeding state preparatory to allowing artificial insemination. The man who dances with cranes received his doctorate at Cornell, appropriately enough, in crane mating behavior. The International Crane Foundation (ICF) has achieved unusual successes in captive breeding. Fourteen of the 15 crane species in the world reside at the headquarters, a renovated Arabian horse farm in Baraboo, Wisconsin. The Foundation has a professional staff, including a veterinarian. In 1981, 25 young cranes were captive-bred including several endangered species—Red-crowned or Japanese, White-naped, and the most exciting of all, Dushenka, the first Siberian Crane ever hatched and fledged in captivity. Siberian Cranes have dwindled to about 150 birds in the wild, only slightly

Photo by Norris Klessman, International Crane Foundation

Dr. George Archibald *takes a walk with* *Tex, a female* **Whooping Crane.**

more numerous than the Whooping Crane. Marsh drainage and shooting, as they migrate through Afghanistan and other Himalayan countries to India, have played a role in reducing their numbers, and Siberian Cranes are decreasing nearly every year.

George considers his most significant achievement to be his role in getting the Han River estuary in Korea protected. His field research led him to discover that the region of the Demilitarized Zone (DMZ) separating South and North Korea had become a wildlife paradise in the 20 years it has been uninhabited since the Korean War ended. Rare White-naped Cranes were recently discovered congregating in the Han River estuary just south of the DMZ; it turned out that they were discovered in the nick of time since their feeding marshes were about to be diked for rice production. George, with the aid of Korean ornithologist Kim Hon Kyu convinced the South Korean government to set this 40-square-kilometer marsh aside after publicizing the threat to the cranes. It became National Monument #250, and the estuary also protects White-tailed Eagles and shorebirds and waterfowl by the thousands. The 35 Japanese Cranes that feed in the DMZ were aided by the ICF plan to get a feeding station set up with both North and South Korea cooperating. ICF has also conducted delicate and successful negotiations with the Iranians, Chinese and Soviets to obtain Siberian Crane eggs, conduct censuses of wild cranes, and begin, through introduction, a new population of Siberian Cranes in Iran.

Each year students come to ICF to study crane behavior and help the staff with the care of cranes, as the Foundation encourages young people to take an interest in crane preservation.

Note: Issues of *The Brolga Bugle*, ICF's newsletter, were a major source of information, and additional facts were derived from David Zimmerman's 1981 article "A fragile victory for beauty on an old Asian battleground" in the October *Smithsonian* magazine. ICF membership information: International Crane Foundation, City View Road, Baraboo, Wisconsin 53913.

Other successful wildlife protectors

• Tracking Giant Pandas through the bamboo groves of China's Sichuan Province, Dr. George Schaller has had some glimpses of this very rare, spectacular and lovable animal. One Panda whose tracks he was following had evidently used a snow slope for a pleasure slide, even returning to the top of the hill to slide down again. Only about 1,000 Giant Pandas remain in the world, reduced by starvation when their major food, bamboo dies out cyclically, by poaching and by illegal capture. Dr. Schaller's project to learn more about wild Giant Pandas is sponsored mainly by the World Wildlife Fund. He has done pioneering field research on African Lions, Jaguars, Tigers and Himalayan wild goats and sheep. His books are acclaimed for their eloquent and exciting observations of these species (see Books Section of this book). He has been instrumental in getting several national parks set aside in Nepal.

• Since childhood, Dr. David Wingate has devoted himself to protecting the highly endangered Cahow, or Bermuda Petrel, a sea bird which would probably be extinct if it were not for his efforts. The Petrel was killed off for food on the main island of Bermuda by early colonists and for 290 years was presumed extinct. In 1951 it was rediscovered on a tiny islet where it was on the brink of extinction. David Wingate received a degree in ornithology and devoted himself to protecting this remnant population. The tropicbirds which nested on the islet preyed on the Cahows, entering their burrow nests and killing the young to take over the nesting site. David devised a special baffle for placement at the mouth of burrows which permitted the Cahows to enter, but prevented entry by the larger tropicbirds. Predatory rats on the islet have been reduced, and floodlights of the nearby U.S. military bases, that attracted the birds at night, causing them to fly to their deaths colliding with the structures, have been modified. The Cahow population still numbers less than 30 pairs, but, under David Wingate's constant supervision, is slowly increasing.

• Not too many years ago, the Sea Otters which once flourished along the California coast were considered extinct, eliminated by the ruthless hunting of the fur industry in the early part of the century. Margaret Owings, wildlife protector and resident of the magnificent Big Sur coast area, was informed of a tiny population discovered along the coast nearby. For years, the few people who knew of these Otters kept them a secret, for fear that they would be killed for their fur. Margaret Owings organized the Friends of the Sea Otter group to help protect them. The Otters' presence was finally announced when it was certain that they would receive strict protection. Their slow comeback to about 1,000 animals has been under constant threats posed by abalone fishermen, oil spills and proposed oil drilling. The fishermen, who have accused them of depleting shellfish, are alleged to be responsible for illegally killing a number of Sea Otters. Friends of the Sea Otter has employed lobbyists to fight for the legal rights of the Sea Otters, and biologists who ascertained scientifically that it was the shell fishermen themselves who were depleting abalone and clam beds by overfishing. Abalone fishermen have even accused Otters of taking abalone in areas where the otters did not exist! Friends of the Sea Otter has won battles with fishermen who persuaded the California Fish and Game Department to endorse several projects that would have been very detrimental to the Sea Otters. The Southern Sea Otter was listed as threatened under the U.S. Endangered Species Act due largely to the organization's efforts. Their latest battle involves the proposed oil drilling off the California coast. An oil spill would cause very high mortality to Sea Otters who are able to survive in the cold Pacific waters only by maintaining their fur in immaculate condition which insulates and keeps it buoyant through a layer of air under the top hairs. Friends of the Sea Otter publishes a handsome and informative newsletter available to members at a modest fee—see Organizations list in this book.

Individual contributions can be significant. One can take a job protecting animals, found an organization for preservation of endangered species, contribute to such an organization, participate in bird counts, write legislators and decision-makers, aid injured wildlife, report for a newspaper or magazine on assaults against wildlife, create paintings, music, theatrical performances or lectures on protection of wildlife, or run for public office in order to improve laws to help them. The opportunities to aid endangered species are limited only by one's imagination.

This **Sea Otter** was drawn by Margaret Owings, founder of Friends of the Sea Otter.

Projects
For the Classroom, Science Fairs or Independent Study

Photo by Erich Hartmann, courtesy Rachel Carson Council

Rachel Carson, *author of* Silent Spring, *believed that students must observe the lives of creatures in natural conditions to develop reverence and awareness of the wholeness of life.*

This section of The Endangered Species Handbook is a sequel to the Animal Welfare Institute's manual, *Humane Biology Projects,* first published in 1969 and revised in 1975. Single copies have been provided free on request to teachers for the past 22 years at a rate of approximately 5,000 a year. When the last printing was exhausted, the Institute decided to expand the projects and to provide basic information on endangered species, often requested by teachers and students.

When *Humane Biology Projects* was first published Rachel Carson, author of *Silent Spring,* and an active and greatly valued member of AWI's Scientific Advisory Committee, wrote these words as a foreword:

"I like to define biology as the history of the earth and all its life—past, present, and future. To understand biology is to understand that all life is linked to the earth from which it came; it is to understand the stream of life, flowing out of the dim past into the uncertain future, is in reality a unified force, though composed of an infinite number and variety of separate lives. The essence of life is lived in freedom. Any concept of biology is not only sterile and profitless, it is distorted and untrue if it puts its primary focus on unnatural conditions rather than on those vast forces not of man's making, that shape and channel the nature and direction of life.

"To the extent that it is ever necessary to put certain questions to nature by placing unnatural restraints upon living creatures or by subjecting them to unnatural conditions or to changes in their bodily structure, this is a task for the mature scientist. It is essential that the beginning student should first become acquainted with the true meaning of his subject through observing the lives of creatures in their true relation to each other and to their environment. To begin by asking him to observe artificial conditions is to create in his mind distorted conceptions and to thwart the development of his natural emotional response to the mysteries of the life stream of which he is a part. Only as a child's awareness and reverence for the wholeness of life are developed can his humanity to his own kind reach its full development."

It is now generally agreed that any study or experiment below university level should never cause harm or any sort of distress to an animal. The guidelines adopted by the National Science Teachers Association (NSTA), the National Association for Biology Teachers (NABT) and the American Institute for Biological Studies (AIBS) in 1980-81 are exceedingly useful in bringing home this point. A pioneer in the preparation of detailed guidelines is Harry Rowsell D.V.M., D.V.PH, PhD, who worked with the Youth Science Foundation in Canada in developing guidelines which evolved over a period of years and culminated in the following excellent statement:

Guidelines for Regulation of Animal Experimentation in Science Fairs

"Biological experimentation is essential for an understanding of living processes. Such studies should lead to a respect for all living things. Capable students anxious to pursue a career in biological sciences must receive the necessary encouragement and direction. It is important that all aspects of the project be within the comprehension, and capabilities of the student undertaking the study.

"If experiments are to be conducted on living subjects for Science Fair projects then only lower orders of life may be used. Lower orders such as bacteria, fungi, protozoa and insects can reveal much basic biological information.

"Vertebrate animals are not to be used in experiments for projects for Science Fairs, with the following exceptions:
a) Observations of normal living patterns of wild animals, in the free living state, or in zoological parks, gardens or aquaria.
b) Observations of normal living patterns of pets, fish or domestic animals.

"No living vertebrate animal shall be displayed in exhibits in Science Fairs.

"Cells such as blood cells, other tissue cells, plasma or serum or anatomical specimens such as organs, tissues or skeletons purchased or acquired from biological supply houses or research facilities may be used in Science Fair projects. Observational type studies, on only chicken egg embryos, may be used in Science Fair projects. If normal egg embryos are to be hatched, satisfactory humane consideration must be made for disposal of chicks. If such arrangements cannot be made then the chicken embryos must be destroyed on the 19th day of incubation. No eggs capable of hatching may be exhibited in Science Fairs.

"Experiments involving the human animal shall conform with these regulations as they apply to other animals. Normal physiological and behavioral studies may be carried out. Projects must be carefully selected so that neither physiological nor psychological harm can result from the study.

"All experiments shall be carried out under the supervision of a competent science teacher. It shall be the responsibility of the qualified science teacher to ensure the student has the necessary comprehension for the study to be undertaken. Whenever possible, specifically qualified experts in the field should be consulted."

The Animal Welfare Institute recommends that these guidelines be followed by every student who plans to enter a science fair.

Photo by Bedford Photography

Dr. Harry Rowsell *developed guidelines for humane biology study.*

Using These Projects

The following projects are arranged by category rather than being divided between those suggested by teachers for classroom use and those which a student might choose for a science fair project, or for a take-off point in designing a related project.

We are grateful for the projects designed by scientists and classroom teachers, some especially for this book, and for the additional ideas suggested by interested friends.

Categories include both arts and sciences. The Table of Contents lists each project.

Animal Behavior

Collecting Data on Animal Play Behavior

Photo by Michael W. Fox

Dogs *play tug of war with a stick and will naturally enjoy this dog game with you.*

A pioneering book, *Animal Play Behavior,* by Robert Fagen (Oxford University Press, New York, 1981) gives scientific references to play in about 500 different species of mammals and birds. Dr. Fagen states (p. 485) "Increased efforts to obtain visual records of play would benefit science, conservation, dance, and the general public." Student observations can contribute to such records.

You can choose one or more species based on your ability to observe them. Young animals are more likely to play than are adults, but pairs of dogs and cats may play throughout their lifetimes, and if you own playful adult pets, recording your observations with a camera and with written notes will be easy. If you have access to a home video system or movie camera, such records are especially valuable.

You can observe the play of kittens and puppies at your local animal shelter where unwanted litters are often brought. Toys for the young animals to play with can be brought to encourage their play. Be sure the toys are safe and do not have metallic pieces or string which infant animals might swallow. Check with the director of the shelter as to what toys will be approved. Offer to help care for the animals if the shelter needs volunteer workers, or help find good homes for animals and encourage owners of female cats and dogs to have their pets spayed to reduce the number of kittens and puppies for whom there are no good homes.

Other places to observe play behavior are at a zoo, an oceanarium, or a wildlife rehabilitation center. Some such centers encourage volunteers to assist with the care of the animals. Watching and photographing young birds and mammals playing could be combined with such volunteer activity if you happen to live nearby (see page 245 for a listing).

Library research should accompany your direct observations. Following are a few quotations from publications by authoritative observers and some books and films that include references to play in different species.

On natural diversity, Dr. Fagen writes (p. 485) "In view of current threats to animals and their environment, a case could be made for the proposal that the most crucial future need in play research will be for systematic observations and film records of play in animals in undisturbed environments under naturalistic conditions. . .preservation of natural diversity is the only tactic that will ensure that we will be able to try to answer questions not yet formulated."

Wolves

"Running play, including chasing and ambushing, is frequent both in captive and in free-living wolves. Another common form of play in wolves is biting play or muzzle-wrestling. Wolf play also includes zigzag jumps, head tossing, and side-to-side shoulder swaying as well as the relaxed, open-mouth play-face; all of these movements may initiate play. Wolves compete playfully for objects, play with objects by themselves, and play together for extended periods. Erik Zimen once watched five young wild wolves at a lake in British Columbia, Canada, play almost without interruption for five hours. The wolves chased back and forth across the beach, jaw-wrestled, played "King of the Castle" on a large stone in the water, and took occasional breaks to play-bite each other or play with objects." (p. 140)

Elephants

Among the Elephants (Viking, New York, 1975) by Iain and Oria Douglas-Hamilton, is a major field study of African elephants.

Play-fighting has a very significant role in the social development of elephants and continues in importance throughout the life of the bulls in particular. Often baby elephants will climb atop sleeping relatives. Tight family bonds seem to be forged by play.

Play-fighting allows young calves to learn of their own strength in comparison to others who inhabit the area. Skill increases with encounters, which are almost always gentle but on occasion become serious and lose their harmless nature.

Bulls continue to play-fight throughout their lifetime, behavior which Douglas-Hamilton describes as being a "social mechanism for them continually to check their position in the adult hierarchy."

Bobcats and Skunks

"The play of young spotted skunks (*Spilogale putorius*) at a campsite in the Nantahala Mountains of North Carolina interested a bobcat who sat for ten minutes on a fallen log and watched them and then sauntered off." (*Animal Play Behavior* referring to an article by W.H. Gates in *Journal of Mammalogy* 18:240, 1937)

Monkeys

The play of young monkeys of many species has been reported in the scientific literature. A 16mm color film of rhesus monkeys playing on land and in water is available for rental from the University of California Extension Media Center, Berkeley, California. It was filmed by J.M. Bishop and D. Symons in 1978 and is titled, "Aggressive Play in Rhesus Monkeys."

After viewing the film, observations at a zoo of rhesus or other species of monkeys could be made and compared with the activities recorded in the film. Comparisons might include age and number of monkeys, space available to them, variety of natural objects available to them in which or with which to play, attitude of the monkeys to observers, (some animals stop playing when they know they are being watched, others play just as readily when observed), their apparent state of health and nutrition. What conclusions did you reach about the degree of playfulness of the monkeys? What do monkeys need in order to play?

This pet baby **Woolly Monkey** *looks impish waiting for the next game to begin.*

Photo by R.A. Mittermeier

Chimpanzees *are among the most intelligent and playful of all mammals.*

Photo by Tony Pfeiffer

Chimpanzees

A film of wild chimpanzees playing is available from Rockefeller University Film Service, New York, New York. Entitled "Vocalizations of Wild Chimpanzees," it was produced by P. Marler and Jane van Lawick-Goodall in 1971.

Comparisons with chimpanzees, gorillas or orangutans at a local zoo may be made as suggested above with regard to monkeys.

Dogs

Konrad Lorenz, who received the Nobel Prize in 1973 with Niko Tinbergen and Karl von Frisch, gives a remarkable portrait of human-canine relationships in *Man Meets Dog* (Methuen, London, 1955), and *King Solomon's Ring* (Thomas Y. Crowell, New York, 1952) includes fascinating observations of other animals, especially geese and jackdaws. These books provide good background for observation of play behavior in your own animal friends.

Interspecific Play

Do individuals of different species play with one another? Of course pet animals and people often play together, but what other species do? David Mech describes play between ravens and wolves (*The Wolf: the Ecology and Behavior of an Endangered Species*, Natural History Press, Garden City, New York, 1970). Have you observed play between a domestic cat and dog that were raised together?

Lucy, a chimpanzee who learned sign language and lived with a human family, had a cat as a pet. Lucy was once observed trying to teach the cat the sign for "book."

Migration

The powerful urge which leads migratory species to follow their ancestral travel paths has long been studied by scientists but the mystery remains.

Select one or more migratory species—Monarch Butterflies, Chinook Salmon, warblers, and Gray Whales are among the diverse species that regularly travel thousands of miles—and find out all you can about them. Describe the dangers each member of each species is likely to encounter, the hardships it must endure, and how they are overcome.

If you live near a coast, you may be able to go on a whale-watching trip. These are increasing in number as interest in whales and the observation of nature increase. Descriptions and photographs of the whales you observe could be combined with information you obtain by library research and correspondence with organizations listed at the end of this Handbook.

If you live near a migratory route used by salmon you may be able to visit and observe a fish ladder such as the one at Seattle where Chinook, Coho and Sockeye Salmon and Steelhead and Cutthroat Trout fight their way from step to watery step in order to return to the stream where they were born. The determination and energy displayed by the fish as individuals are enormously impressive and worthy of careful observation and description.

Migratory birds of some species are almost sure to fly past the area where you live. Consult your library and organizations that have particular interest in birds to find which migratory routes you are located near. For example, great warbler migrations go through "The Ramble," a part of New York City's Central Park, each spring on their ancestral flyway. Thirty years ago, "The Ramble" was almost paved over for television viewing, but citizen protests headed off destruction of this important warblers' resting roost on their intercontinental journey.

You can become alert to such threats to migratory birds in your own area and ask assistance of organizations listed in this Handbook in protecting the places of particular importance to the sometimes exhausted small travelers.

Prepare an exhibit to show the different areas through which the species you have selected pass and the national boundaries they cross.

Why are international treaties necessary to protect migratory species? What treaties exist?

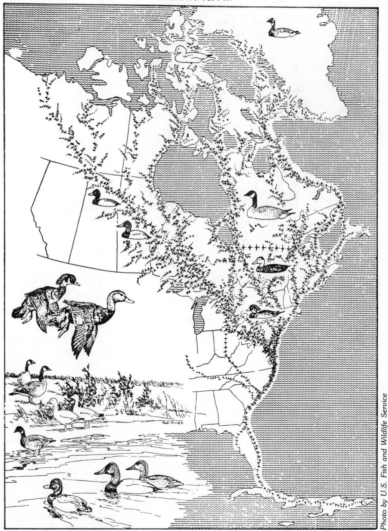

ATLANTIC FLYWAY

Photo by U.S. Fish and Wildlife Service

Waterfowl migrate in ancestral flyways each fall. How does the Migratory Bird Treaty protect them?

Conversing with a Threatened Species: Washoe, the First Chimpanzee to Acquire a Human Language

by Roger S. Fouts, Ph.D.
Department of Psychology
Central Washington University

Washoe and **Loulis**, *her adopted son.*

Photo by Dr. Roger Fouts

The first successful attempt to see if a nonhuman primate could acquire a human language was begun in 1966. Drs. R. Allen Gardner and Beatrice T. Gardner began Project Washoe by obtaining a six month old infant chimpanzee from the U.S. Air Force. The infant chimpanzee, Washoe, was wild collected by the Air Force at a time when chimpanzees were still being imported from Africa for the purposes of space and medical research.

The purpose of Project Washoe was to determine whether or not a chimpanzee could acquire a human language. Since chimpanzees use gestures to communicate in the wild, the Gardners chose American Sign Language for the Deaf (ASL) as the human language because it is a gestural, rather than vocal, language. Chimpanzees also use vocal calls, but these are mainly involuntary emotional sounds.

The Gardners assumed that if a young chimpanzee is going to learn a human sign language, it has to be one that s/he is capable of understanding as well as producing. ASL meets that requirement. They also reasoned that because language is a social behavior, and if Washoe were going to acquire it, she would have to have interesting companions to talk to and interesting things to talk about. They also realized that human children are not taught their language but, instead, actively acquire their language themselves by being immersed in a social world where it is used in a meaningful fashion around them. Children are not taught language by their parents as if they were passive beings—trained seals in circuses or rats being forced to press a bar in order to get food.

Because of the above assumptions about the nature of chimpanzees as well as language, the Gardners decided to raise Washoe as much as they could like a deaf human child. She also had to have good friends to talk to, which were at that time graduate students, of which I was one. So, as a result, we raised Washoe in an enriched environment where *only* ASL was used in her presence to converse with her as well as with other humans. A human companion was with Washoe every waking moment of the day. We signed to her while playing games with her; while making her breakfast, lunch, tea and dinner; while playing in the sand box, jungle gym or in the trees; while getting her dressed for car rides and while on outings to the countryside. Of course, we mainly signed to her as you would to a friend or relative.

Because of the assumptions the Gardners made and the resulting manner in which we raised Washoe, she was indeed a very fortunate chimpanzee. It meant that she was respected as a living, feeling being that had important communications to share with us in our social interactions and conversations. She was fortunate because it also meant that she would be raised in the caring and loving environment of a human family which is, sadly, quite different from the prisons in which most captive chimpanzees are raised when they are used, for example, in medical research.

Because we respected Washoe as a nonhuman *being,* the project was a great success. Washoe made use of ASL just as do children. She initiated conversations about games, her wants, or to comment on things going on around her and so on. She lied in ASL, expressed her love or anger, and even commented when something was funny. One time she accidentally (I think) had a potty accident while riding on my back. When I felt the warmth running down my back, she started signing *funny, funny.* At the time, I didn't share the point of her humor. She has even used derogatory signs in ASL, such as *dirty,* to insult people and animals she wasn't happy with. Like most children, she also used ASL to talk to herself while playing alone or while naming the pictures in a magazine when sitting alone in the top of a tree thirty feet off the ground.

Washoe had indeed acquired language. She was the first nonhuman to acquire a language, to invent signs, and use her signs in short grammatical phrases. But the research did not stop with Washoe. Several other chimpanzees have successfully acquired ASL when they were treated properly. Moja, Peli, Dor, Tatu, Aly, Lucy, Booee, and Bruno also learned ASL. So Washoe was not an unusual chimpanzee by any means.

I am now doing research to see if Washoe, at seventeen years old, will pass her language abilities on to her adopted infant—Loulis. Loulis has been with Washoe now for three years. To date he has acquired 33 signs from Washoe and he uses these signs to talk to both humans and chimpanzees in phrases of up to four signs in length. Loulis, as a result, is the first chimpanzee to learn a human language from another chimpanzee! To make sure that Loulis learned these signs from Washoe, the humans around Loulis used vocal English to communicate with Washoe and limited their signs to only seven: *who, what, want, where, which, sign* and *name.*

Moja *drawing.*

Photo by Dr. Roger Fouts

Washoe's accomplishments have also helped humans. I have been able to use some of the things we've learned from Washoe to teach noncommunicating human children to talk. For example, I was able to teach a nine year old, noncommunicating, autistic, with ASL. He not only began to communicate and relate to people using ASL, but he also began to acquire vocal English. Since that study in 1971, several other researchers have used ASL to help autistic children. New therapies for the treatment of cerebral palsied and other noncommunicating children have also been inspired by Washoe's scientific accomplishments. So, by treating Washoe and other chimpanzees with love and respect, we have been able to learn a great deal and help our own species in the process as well.

Perhaps the most unusual aspect of this project, as compared to the typical research done with primates, is that this project is mutually beneficial to both chimpanzees and humans. For example, the research done with Washoe and her friends has had a profound effect upon scientific thought in regard to what scientists used to think made humans unique from other animals. Most scientists tended to view animals as being nothing more than machines that do not feel, think or suffer. But because Washoe can talk about what she thinks, how she feels and when she's feeling sick or hurt, it means that this assumption that animals are machines is incorrect. As a result, most animal research has no moral justification. Unfortunately, with most laboratory animal research, the animals are exploited by the scientists. Also, many of the findings from this unfeeling, "objective" research has questionable value to human welfare—and certainly nothing for animal welfare. The research animals are almost always killed or "sacrificed" after the experiments are completed.

When chimpanzees and other animals are used in physiological or medical research, grave moral questions should be raised. The chimpanzees are a threatened species and should not be abused or exploited. I've yet to meet chimpanzees who applied for immigration status to this country in order to participate in medical research. What we have found, thanks to Washoe, is that chimpanzees are not different in kind from ourselves. They can talk and express their thoughts and feelings. Washoe has clearly shown that we, as humans, are not separate from nature—but, indeed, we do share a

Friends of Washoe symbolizes the friendship and communication between chimpanzee and human, the dawn of a new era in our relations with animals.

common origin with all life. Thus, Washoe and her friends have demonstrated that humans are not separate from nature but are as much a part of it as every living thing. The implications of this have profound moral implications for human/animal relationships.

The archaic notion that we are superior to every other living thing is incorrect. Some people trace the beginning of this notion to the Bible. For example, in the book of Genesis it states that we have dominion over all life. Some people who don't know the Bible may well use this to justify the abuse and exploitation of other life on this planet. If they would read it a little further, they'd realize that in the third chapter of Ecclesiastes, Solomon states that "man hath no preeminence over the beasts." When this is taken together with our dominion in Genesis, it certainly does not mean exploitation—but instead it means that we have a responsibility to care for, protect and respect other life.

The implications of the above conclusion are that we, as a people, have a moral responsibility to improve the conditions of animals under our care and with whom we share this planet. My personal dream is to find the resources to develop a place where mature chimpanzees can be protected while being treated with the respect and love due them. My dream is to find a warm place of a thousand acres or more where the captive chimpanzees could live. It would be modeled after their natural habitat and enriched with many interesting things to do, as well as fruits and vegetables to forage for and eat. We could then study the chimpanzees—their language and behavior—in an environment that was suited to their needs and welfare. In this place the human scientists observing the chimpanzees would be in cages and the chimpanzees would be free to roam the area. The refuge would also serve as a lifeboat for a threatened species because their natural habitat in Africa is rapidly being destroyed. After all that the chimpanzee has done for our species, we certainly owe them this.

If you wish to find out more about this dream, to assist in its quest, and/or subscribe to the *Friends of Washoe Newsletter,* please write to: The Friends of Washoe Foundation, 1003 Craig Avenue, Ellensburg, WA 98926.

A Class Project

Many students may be curious as to how Washoe felt being signed to in a gestural language by humans. Your teacher might wish to divide your class into two groups—human companions and chimpanzees. The human companions would learn ASL from dictionaries available at a library. They might learn signs that would be used during a meal, during play, or at bedtime. The human signers would then use these signs in one of these social situations to talk with the students playing the part of chimpanzees who did not know ASL. The purpose of this would be to see how many signs used by the human companions in the social situation could be learned and understood by the young "chimpanzee" students.

For the "chimpanzee" students, the teacher might show them a film by Jane Goodall, put out by National Geographic, so that they would know how to pretend to be a chimpanzee.

After the students have completed the project, the teacher should show them a film entitled *"The First Signs of Washoe,"* distributed by Time/Life, so that the "chimpanzee" students can see how well they did compared to Washoe.

Observations on Tree Squirrel Behavior

**by Professor Vagn Flyger
University of Maryland**

Squirrel behavior can make a fascinating study project.

Various species of tree squirrels are present in wooded portions of most of North America. Each species has its own characteristic patterns of behavior which can readily be observed under proper conditions. Squirrels are diurnal and pay relatively little attention to movements inside of a glass window. Thus by placing a feeding station a foot or two from a convenient window, they can be watched closely enough to observe details of expressions.

A convenient feeding station can be made by inserting two ice picks (handles removed, points up) into a 12″ long log. An ear of dry corn is impaled on each ice pick. Once squirrels have discovered the corn they will eat it one kernel at a time while sitting on the log. Only the germ is consumed; the rest is dropped and consumed by birds. As the corn is consumed new ears should be placed on the ice picks once or twice a day.

After a number of squirrels have become regular visitors to the feeding station observations can be started. First it will be necessary to learn to recognize individuals and give them names. Look for differences in body color, length and fullness of tail, torn ears, facial scars, sex and other characteristics. It is necessary to look closely. Keep a record for each animal and record when the squirrel feeds and its reactions toward other squirrels. Try to determine the following:

1. Who dominates whom. Observe who chases whom. Can you make a table ranking individuals from the most dominant to the most submissive? Is rank related to sex and age? What is the advantage of social hierarchy or territoriality? What seems to determine the rank of an individual? Does relative rank change with age?

2. If you have two squirrel species present how does their behavior differ?

3. At what time of day are squirrels most active? If you have a school weather station you can compare weather and activity. How does this vary with weather and seasons?

4. How do squirrels communicate? What sounds do they utter? What are their threat gestures? Watch them lash out with their claws at each other. What signals or expressions can you determine from the tail, ears and face?

5. What senses are used in social interactions? How?

6. What happens when a can of peanuts (in the shell) is placed on the feeder? Do they eat them or bury them? Where are peanuts buried, all in one place or scattered about? Try to find a buried nut. How do the squirrels find the nuts when they need them?

7. How do squirrels interact with birds? How do they respond to danger—approaching dog, cat or *man?*

Reference Book

The World of the Gray Squirrel, Frederick S. Barkalow, Jr. and Monica Shorten, J.B. Lippincott Co., Philadelphia, Pa., 1973.

Animal Senses

It is well known that the power of different senses is more fully developed in some species than in others; however, very little is known about many of these, and it is a field in which keen observers can make significant observations.

A pet dog can demonstrate his ability to hear sounds and to smell odors which are imperceptible to human beings. For example, using a high frequency dog whistle whose high-pitched sound cannot be heard by members of the class, observe the dog cock his head and

Photo by Martha Swope

Sandy, *in his solo scene in the musical "Annie," learned to come alone to center stage by sniffing a piece of bologna.*

listen. A dog who comes to such a whistle may be shown to the class.

The simplest demonstration of a dog's highly developed sense of smell is a walk in the country with a dog, watching him follow scents of animals whose identity cannot always be guessed but which will sometimes be seen when the dog causes a rabbit to run into view or a pheasant to fly up out of the grass. In the classroom, the dog's sense of smell might be demonstrated by dragging a sausage or some other tidbit over the floor to a desk and placing it in the drawer of the desk. The dog, if he is not nervous owing to strange surroundings, will be able to trace the tidbit and stand sniffing where it is hidden. A dog visiting a classroom should be given time to make himself acquainted and feel at home before he is asked to show any of his abilities.

Although the dog's sense of hearing and sense of smell are more highly developed than the corresponding senses in human beings, his sense of vision is less acute.

A student project might give evidence of the relative sensory powers of the dog collected by direct observation on the part of the student. A correlative project might be presentation of information gathered from the literature on sensory powers highly developed in other animals, for example: vision in hawks and other birds of prey; the sense of touch in nocturnal or burrowing animals whose whiskers transmit very delicate touches; the so-called "radar" of bats in which high-pitched sounds, above the range which the human ear can perceive, are emitted and the distance from objects judged by the bat on the rebound of his cries, the ability of dolphins to distinguish between metals under water by similar means.

Color perception by different species of animals might be tested. The general assumption that most birds and many insects but few mammals can distinguish between colors may be tested. Is there a correlation between the coloring of the animal itself, the coloring of its food, and species sensitivity to color?

A Project in the Observation of the Roosting Habits of Birds

Students of bird behavior have recently discovered that during the nesting season the female robin spends the night alone on the nest: although during the day the male bird defends the nesting territory, at night he goes to roost with all the other males of the vicinity. Roosting habits vary from species to species, and little is known of the habits of many species, so that the observations of students in this field could be both interesting and valuable.

Choose some readily observable species of bird which is resident in your vicinity. House sparrows or starlings are suitable if other species are difficult to find. Observe the social behavior of the chosen species. Does it live in a closely-knit flock, staying together and feeding together for the greater part of the day, and roosting together at night? Does the whole flock fly away from an area at once, on a given signal? Or is a flock formed only for certain purposes, for roosting together, at nesting time, as a colony, or when feeding? Is the flock seasonal? Does it exist during the winter only? For purposes of migration only? Does the flock roost in the same place each night, or does it move from place to place to roost? If the chosen species does not roost as a flock, what are its habits?

Students may make detailed reports of their findings in this field; they may find it interesting to read some of the extant studies of bird behavior, which will give them an orientation to the subject (see also the bibliography on Page 199).

Insect Behavior

**by Dr. Dewey M. Caron
Professor of Entomology
and Applied Ecology,
University of Delaware**

Insects are the most abundant animals on earth. The student who studies living insects will find them fascinating. A wide variety of insects can be studied in their natural habitat, and it is also very easy to keep several insects in captivity to study at closer range.

The Social Insects

A project designed to introduce students to a study of animal behavior, through the observation of the behavior of bees, ants, or termites, living as a colony.

The social instinct in bees, ants, and termites, and the intricate structure of their social life, are readily observable phenomena which will attract students on a number of levels. Students whose interests are oriented away from science towards history or literature should be encouraged to study this project. Insect society shows the extent to which social organization can be developed and integrated on a physiological instinctive basis, so comparisons between insect society and human government can be interesting, if pursued in a scientific manner. Also, on the subject of the social insects, there are a number of very readable books which, though recognized as factually accurate, have literary value as well; some students may enjoy reading Maeterlinck or Fabre on the subject. There are also many other scientific studies in the field, some of which are listed in the bibliography of this project.

Laboratory Work: Establish a colony of bees, ants or termites for observation in the classroom.

Bees, ants and termites and specially constructed observation hives or nests may be obtained from biological supply houses.

Ant Colony

Establishing an ant colony is not difficult. Find a natural ants' nest by watching ants on a warm day and following their tracks back to their colony. Ants may be collected into a jam jar with a screw-top lid.

Excavate the natural nest cautiously with a trowel, and collect ants, with earth, on a teaspoon, taking care not to maim them. You will need:

About 100 worker ants, which are small and wingless.

Some of the earth from the nest.

Some pupae, about 50.

At least one wingless queen. (Without a queen the colony will not perpetuate itself, but still will last for awhile and be of interest.)

If the ants are to be carried far, the queens should travel in a separate bottle. Small winged males may be included but they are not essential.

The ants should be put into the artificial nest as soon as possible. To make an observation nest, take:

3 glass plates, 6″ × 8″ or larger
2 pieces of cardboard 6″ × 8″ or larger
4 pieces of 1/4″ × 1/8″ balsa wood
balsa cement
gummed paper
4 slices of cork 1/2″ thick
a piece of wood 1″ thick and 1″ wider and longer than the nest
a baking pan larger than the piece of wood

Diagram of half-section of observation ants' nest

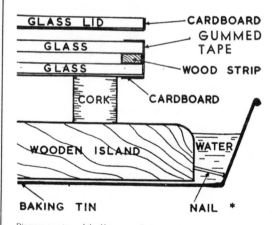

Diagram courtesy of the Universities Federation for Animal Welfare,
Animals in Schools, *by P. Volrath*

The wooden stage rests in the baking pan, held in place by four nails, driven at an angle into the corners, and projecting as far as the walls of the baking pan. Attach the cork legs with glue to the stage, and to the floor of the nest. (This floor is made of a glass plate attached with gummed tape to a sheet of cardboard. The cardboard side must be on the outside of the nest, facing down.) Affix the walls of balsa wood, in which there should be an entrance gap of 1/2″, with balsa cement to the floor and to the glass plate which is the ceiling.

Bind the whole nest box around the edges with gummed tape. Prepare the third sheet of glass in the same way as the floor; it rests on top of the lid to keep out light when the colony is not under observation. Into the space between the floor and ceiling pour moist sand, almost filling the compartment. Fill the moat with water. Ants will feed on honey, which may be spread on the wooden stage. If the sand in the nest becomes dry, introduce a few drops of water through the entrance hole with a pipette, taking care not to moisten the larvae.

Ants may be released at the end of the school year near their original nest.

Students may observe the different classes in the colony, the life cycle of each class, its function, and the daily routine of activity, and record the expansion of the nest and the activities of the ants.

Bee Hive

It is not difficult to establish an observation bee hive, but, if this is your first experience with honey bees, it is advisable to ask a bee-keeper to help you. Hobbyist bee-keepers are usually willing to share their knowledge.

Observation bee hives are available commercially or you can construct one from wood and glass. If you want to order a bee hive write: Entomology Extension, 1735 Neil Avenue, Columbus, Ohio 43210.

You can install your observation hive in the spring as soon as daytime temperatures go above 60°F. The earlier the installation, the more important it is to provide supplemental food. Bees can be fed a dilute sugar solution (one part sugar to one part water).

Bees and a queen can be purchased. The bees are sold by the pound and are shipped through the United States mail. You will want a two-pound package with queen. The bees are shaken from the package, and the queen added in her separate cage so the bees can release her after another day or two. A bee-keeper should help in installation.

It is better to establish your observation bee hive from a frame taken from an established bee colony. Select a frame that has a developing bee brood, honey, and pollen. Shake in extra worker bees. It is not necessary to add a queen if you have a young brood on the frame since the bees will raise a new queen.

The frame and bees should be established directly from the bee-keeper's colony without transportation delay. As soon as the bees are inside, close all entrances and move the hive to your prepared location. Modify a window to allow the bees to fly outside while the observation unit rests on a sturdy platform inside. If the observation hive needs any modification or service, take it outside (after plugging all entrances) and do the necessary work. When handling bees always wear a bee veil to protect the face from stings and use a smoker to disrupt guard bees and make them gentle. Gloves should

Drawing by Sarah Landry, The Insect Societies, Wilson, 1971.

Bees *have complicated and fascinating behavior which you can learn about by observing a bee hive.*

be worn if you fear being stung. IF YOU HAVE AN ALLERGY TO BEE STINGS, DO NOT ATTEMPT TO DO ANY OF THE WORK WITH THE HIVE. You may still observe once they are safely established since they cannot get out into the room.

An alternative to establishing an observation bee hive yourself would be to use an existing one. Many parks, nature centers, and some museums maintain them.

Things to Do

Time the queen in her egg laying activities.

Observe worker bees and drones and record their activities.

Observe and record the process of storing ripening nectar into honey.

Make records of returning foragers with bright balls of pollen on their hind legs.

Measure the progress of wax comb construction and determine the percentage of bees involved in this.

Determine the pattern of foraging by counting the number of bees leaving and returning at time intervals over daylight hours. Repeat on cloudy and partly cloudy days and compare the figures.

Your observation bee hive will have openings for ventilation and feeding. Introduce pieces of grass or wood and record the behavior of bees cleaning their hive.

Find a dead bee and mark it with a tiny dot of airplane paint and drop it in the top so you can watch the bees remove it.

If, through accident, bees escape into the room, turn off the lights and the bees will be attracted to a window; open it to let them escape.

Keeping and Studying Living Insects

Little equipment is necessary to keep live insects in captivity for short time periods. Insects can be placed in glass jars, cardboard boxes, screen or gauze cages. Sometimes, it is best to leave the insects in their natural habitat and construct a cage or cages around the insects.

When insects are taken from their habitat, food and water must be kept available. Plant feeding insects need fresh and healthy plant parts. Flower feeding insects can be given sugar water or a diluted honey solution. Small amounts should be put in containers that will not permit the insect to fall in and drown. Predaceous insects are much more difficult to feed but many do not eat frequently, so they can usually be caged for a brief time, examined and then released without the need for feeding. If feeding is necessary, the food should be the same as in their habitat and should be presented as naturally as possible.

Studying Insect Life History

There are two basic types of life histories among the larger insects. Beetles, flies, butterflies and bees are a few of the insects that have complete metamorphosis: they have four life history stages—egg, larva, pupa, and adult. Cockroaches, bugs, and many aquatic insects exhibit only three life history stages—egg, nymph, and adult. Nymphs are basically wingless, smaller forms of the adult, while a larva or pupa usually is completely different from the adult form.

Insects may be raised from any stage and may be selected from a natural environment or at one of the biological supply firms that offer eggs, larvae, pupae or nymphs of several species together with complete instructions, containers, and food.

The booklet, "First Aid and Care of Small Animals" by Ernest P. Walker, an Animal Welfare Institute publication distributed free on request to science teachers, describes a method of starting and maintaining a house fly culture. Two books listed in the reference, "An Introduction to the Study of Insects" and "A Manual of Entomological Techniques," also describe the methods for maintaining insect cultures. The April, 1976 issue of "The American Biology Teacher," devoted entirely to insects, has a section on their rearing.

Another insect you might want to rear is the cockroach. Cockroaches are omnivores and easy to maintain. Wax moths and dry food beetles are interesting and easy to keep. Aquatic insects can be raised. Wood boring insects are easily brought to adulthood, but observing can be difficult. Caterpillars are interesting to watch as they grow, pupate, and emerge as moths or butterflies. Fresh food must be kept available and the waste must be removed.

When rearing insects, you should make detailed observations, measure the food and water consumed, observe and categorize each life stage. You can do population studies with some of the insects such as the dry food beetles, crickets, or flies. The behavior of singing insects is a separate study.

Field Trip to a Flower

Virtually any natural environment can be used to observe and perform experiments on insects. An excellent place is a patch of wildflowers. Start your studies before the plants bloom, or when you first notice some of the flowers. Make a record of the way insects behave in your patch.

Observe at different times of the day from early growth to full flower to the end of the growing season. Do not disturb the patch in a way that could alter the environment.

Things to Do

Note what insects visit the flowers to collect pollen and nectar. Which is the most common? How much time does the bee spend on the flower? From that, estimate how many flowers can be visited in a day. What insects prey on the flower visitor? How do they hunt and capture their prey? What insects are present feeding on other parts of the plant, and what species are feeding on them? Make fresh bouquets of the same type of flower from other locations to see if they attract more flower visitors and more predators. Cover a portion of your flowers and determine how that affects your flower visiting population of bees. Add droplets of sugar water to parts of the flower or plant that do not have sugar and see if the flower visitors alter their normal behavior to take advantage of the sugar water.

Camouflage and Defense Coloration in Moths

Let the student attract a collection of moths with a strong light by night in the spring months and observe and sketch a number of typical wing patterns. Or let the student consult a textbook on entomology for the same purpose. How are the many patterns and colors of moths adapted to blend with their environment? Let the student read the chapter "Defence by Color" in "Curious Naturalists" by Niko Tinbergen. Tinbergen's studies show that the eye-like patterns on the wings of certain moths discourage predatory birds by frightening them. Do any of the other moths observed have such wing patterns?

Acer dasycarpum. April 6.

Drawing by May Lees

Watercolor of Acer Dasycarpum, *April 6.*

Animal Pairs

Ken Runyon, Camp Director, Duck Creek Youth Conservation Corps Camp. Adapted from "Exploring Your Environment."

Purpose:

To view the environment through the eyes of another organism.

Working with another person, evaluate a specific area as you think a pair of animals would by answering the following questions. "We are a pair of _____(Animal)_____."

1. How would you rate this area for your needs?
   a. General habitat:
   b. Winter and summer food supply:
   c. Evidence of predators:
   d. Other factors:
2. What evidence can you find that others of your kind live here? How will they feel about you two moving in?
3. Which of the habitat types will you choose? Where will you locate your home nest, burrow or den?
4. What evidence can you find that shows that man has changed this area?
5. How do you animals feel about the changes that have been made here?
6. Why are you important to this environment?
7. Considering all things that we have investigated here, we _____ remain here. (will, will not)
8. Are things usually considered from an animal's viewpoint? Are decisions made with animals in mind? Do they ever get to vote? How can you help to protect their interests?

Animal Clues Scavenger Hunt

Adapted from a project by Margaret Campbell.

Goal:

To increase awareness of ecological principles that govern the environment.

Purpose:

To be able to recognize evidence of the existence in an area of different animal species.

Task:

Locate and identify as many clues as you can to animals' presence. This means anything left behind: last year's bird nests that are obviously not going to be reused, snake skin, pellets (a bird of prey's way of dealing with undigestible parts), skulls, bones, bear scratchings.

Here are additional clues that you might look for:
a) evidence that the vegetation has been used, as food-twigs browsed by deer, shrubs nibbled by rabbits, and husks of acorns discarded by squirrels;
b) the presence of scats (fecal material) which give, through their size, distribution, and composition, an indication of the size of the animals, the time spent in the area, the number of animals, and the nature of their feeding habits (herbivorous or carnivorous);
c) tracks, which are as good as fingerprints in determining the identity of the animal. Tracks made in mud, sand or snow can be followed to trace some of the animal's activities. For example,

Raccoon tracks.
*Animal tracks can tell
a great deal—the species
of animal that made them,
its weight and size, and the
pace at which it was traveling.*

they may indicate feeding or bedding sites. Obvious trails are usually better indicators than a single set of tracks. Interspecific and intraspecific interactions can be investigated by observing the relationships between the trails of different animals using the same area. Territorial boundaries can often be estimated using tracks. Of course, you must be able to identify the tracks. Carry with you a copy of *A Field Guide to Animal Tracks* by O. Murie, Houghton Mifflin, 1954 or *Animal Tracks of the Pacific Northwest* by Karen Pandell and Chris Stall, The Mountaineers, Seattle, 98101, 1981. List on a chart giving such information as:

1. Evidence Observed
2. Distinguishing trait
3. Date
4. Location
5. Observed by
6. Miscellaneous Observations

Discussion:

1. What types of evidence were most frequently found?
2. What was affected by time and weather, most, least?
3. Does the area you selected to study have as wide a diversity of species as it contained ten years ago? 20 years ago? 50 years ago? 100 years ago? If you can find out whether any species disappeared or became rare, try to explain why this happened.

Environment and Ecology

The Wisdom of the Earthworms—An Acid Rain Study

Adapted from "Wormturns: Raindrops Keep (pH)alling On My Head" by Mac Adam City High School, ACID PRECIPITATION AWARENESS PROGRAM.

As a result of the combustion of tremendous quantities of fossil fuels, such as coal and oil, the United States discharges approximately 50 million metric tons of sulfur and nitrogen oxides into the atmosphere annually. Through a series of complex chemical reactions these pollutants are sometimes converted into acids, which may return to earth as components of either rain or snow. This acid precipitation, commonly known as acid rain, may have severe ecological impacts on widespread areas of the environment. And, in fact, it may cause the extinction of threatened or endangered animals.

Hundreds of lakes in North America and Scandinavia have become so acidic that they can no longer support fish life. More than 250 lakes in the Adirondack mountains in New York State are fishless because acidic conditions have inhibited reproduction. Recent data indicate that other areas of the United States, such as northern Minnesota and northern Wisconsin, may be vulnerable to similar adverse impacts.

Vertebrates and invertebrates can die in aquatic ecosystems from the effects of acid rain, but the problem is seldom discussed as an animal welfare and animal rights issue. Such discussions tend to focus, if at all, on the economic loss of a sport or recreational fishery, such as the significances of the loss of trout in Adirondack lakes, or marring of paint on automobiles. What do you think?

pH

The pH, a numerical value used to describe the strength of an acid, is determined by a mathematical formula based on a solution's concentration of hydrogen ions (H^+). The pH scale ranges from a numerical value of 0-14. A value of pH 1 is very acidic (battery acid), pH7 is neutral, and pH 13 is very alkaline (lye). Because of the logarithmic nature of the scale, pH 4 is 10 times more acidic than pH 5, and 100 times more acidic than pH 6, and so on. Precipitation is defined as being acidic if the pH is less than 5.6, the pH of normal, unpolluted rain. The slight natural acidity of normal rain is due to the presence of carbonic acid (H_2CO_3), which is formed by the reaction of atmospheric carbon dioxide (CO_2) with water.

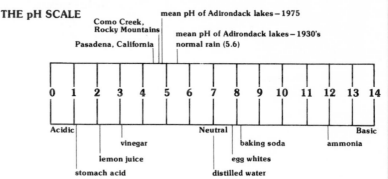

THE pH SCALE

Experiment

Agricultural practices change the natural vegetation, affect soil structure and therefore have important effects on its inhabitants and soil fertility. Soil fertility is closely related to the amount of organic matter incorporated into the soil, and much of the natural mixing of organic and mineral components is done by earthworms. They ingest soil and eject the ingested material in the form of castings which have a fine crumb structure. Some species of earthworms deposit these on the surface and others below ground.

Through earthworm surface castings the soil is slowly overturned; the rate depends on the numbers, size and species present in the soil. Estimates on the amount of castings vary (castings within the soil are difficult to assess). Studies in England suggest an average turnover of 11 tons per year per acre. This amounts to 2 cm of soil every 10 years. The worm burrows enhance drainage, root penetration, soil aeration, and the overall effect of the earthworms helps create habitats for smaller soil animals.

Are earthworms tolerant of acid soils or acid rain? In this activity students investigate some of the responses of one group of soil-living animals, earthworms, to acid rain. Be careful that the earthworms are always permitted to choose where to go during the experiment.

Housing and Food

Earthworms: Wooden containers are best (cigar box or greenhouse flat size). The soil should be damp, rich in humus or peat moss (2-6″) and with a layer of leaves covering the top. The box can be covered with cardboard. It should be kept in a temperature range of 45° to 65° F. A large variety of foods may be used: small amounts of corn meal can be scattered over the top of the soil; twice a week bury small pieces of bread soaked in milk and lettuce leaves. It is important not to add too much food at a time and to remove any that becomes moldy. If the soil is rich in humus, feeding is almost unnecessary. The environment should be kept damp.

You will need: Shallow pans (paper shirt/blouse boxes lined with plastic), paper toweling, pH paper: range 1–7, labels/masking tape, 10% H_2SO_4, acidic solutions, pH 2–6, spring water, stirring rods, medicine droppers/dropper bottles.

Acidic Solutions

The number of drops suggested in the chart below are *estimates*. As *drops* are added be sure that the solutions are stirred thoroughly because the pH must be stabilized before you use the solutions.

Solutions	Scale
a. 500 ml of spring water	pH 6
b. 500 ml of spring water + 5 drops 10% H_2SO_4	pH 5
c. 500 ml of spring water + 15 drops 10% H_2SO_4	pH 4
d. 500 ml of spring water + 25 drops 10% H_2SO_4	pH 3
e. 500 ml of spring water + 30 drops 10% H_2SO_4	pH 2

That organisms respond to environmental change is one of the basic characteristics of life. The repertoire of responses that characterizes an organism is called its behavior and the diversity of behaviors exhibited by organisms is remarkable.

Observation of Natural Behavior of Earthworms

It is important to become familiar with the behavior of the earthworm before doing the acid rain investigation. The suggested acid rain activity relies on careful observations, and the experimental design students choose will rely, to a great extent, on familiarity with the behavior of the earthworm.

You will need a tray, metric ruler, hand lens (optional), watch with second hand (optional), and an assortment of "papers": plastic sheets, plastic wrap, waxed paper, paper toweling, notebook paper, aluminum foil. Gently place an earthworm in a tray and answer these questions:

a. Draw a sketch and label it, using biological names. How does the front end differ from the rear end? How many segments does it have?

b. How long is your worm? What is its character?

c. Use a hand lens to answer these questions.
—Does it have eyes? A mouth? Blood vessels? Is it smooth? Does it have an odor?

d. Can you see the heart and locate it on your drawing? Can you see any evidence of a heartbeat? Is it fast or slow?
—What does the earthworm do if you lift the tray (place a book under one end)?
—"Experiment" with a *few* tray surface materials: plastic, dry paper, wet paper, smooth paper, rough paper, wet tray surface, plastic wrap, aluminum foil, *etc*. Which surface is best for crawling? Is there any surface the worm can't crawl on?
—Is there any evidence of choice, i.e., in general, do worms prefer dry or wet surfaces? What is the evidence you are using?
—Does your earthworm respond positively or negatively to light? How are you sure? Why?

The plough is one of the most ancient and most valuable of man's inventions; but long before he existed the land was in fact regularly ploughed, and still continues to be thus ploughed by earth-worms. It may be doubted whether there are many other animals which have played so important a part in the history of the world, as have these lowly organized creatures.

From *The Living Thoughts of Darwin* presented by Julian Huxley. Longmans, Green and Co., N.Y., 1939.

e. Watch your earthworm and record your observations, e.g.
   —How does it move around?
   —Can it move backwards as well as forward?
   —How fast does it move?
   —What does it do when it meets an obstacle? Be sure your earthworm is returned to its damp earth box before it has time to become dry in the air.

f. (Optional) If you have time, make some comparisons between a "short" worm and a "long" worm. Are there any observable differences in the way they move, the rate at which they move, the amount of time they move, etc?

Asking Questions of Earthworms

What would happen if you placed an earthworm in a container in such a way that it was presented with a *choice* of moist paper toweling, *each* of a different acidity, to crawl over or to crawl to?

You will need a pan or box lined with plastic, acidic solutions pH 2-pH 6, and paper toweling or paper sheets.

Experimental Design

Experiments have been described as one way that humans have of asking questions of nature.

The assignment is to conduct an experiment that will provide meaningful results.

A Question:
   Will an earthworm (or earthworms) show a preference for habitat (think of the acid paper as habitat) of a specific pH?
Habitat preference is the variable.

The earthworm will avoid the moist paper of a certain pH; the worm will go on the moist paper of a certain pH and stay there; the worm will go on the moist paper of a certain pH and stay there for ____ second(s). Record the response of the earthworms on a chart.

If several populations have been studied, you may want to pool the data and construct a histogram with frequency (n) on the ordinate (y-axis) and pH on the abscissa (x-axis).

Food Chain Stories

Telling stories can be a good way for students to express their ideas and make the learning of ecological concepts more fun. They can be done individually or as a small group effort. Discuss the stories after they have been told.

The following food chain stories are true. Read them and then see if you can write your own food chain story.

I. In deep caves with underground streams in San Marcos, Texas, lives a tiny blind salamander. Having evolved in darkness, it lost eyes, and its skin became a pale ivory-colored. A long fish-like body and thin weak legs propel it about in its subterranean streams. It senses invertebrate prey with a long, flattened snout. In the 1960's, it was known to inhabit only one area, Ezell's Cave, in San Marcos. The owner of the cave feared lawsuits from people who might be injured exploring the cave, many of whom were biologists looking for the salamander, and he sealed up the entrance.

This would have seemed to be the perfect protection for the Texas Blind Salamander, but when The Nature Conservancy bought the

Geckoes eat large amounts of insects, but pesticides can be fatal to them.

Photo by U.S. Fish and Wildlife Service

cave in 1967 to protect the species, they discovered that its food chain had been destroyed and the species was almost extinct. Sealing up the cave had destroyed the bat colony, which in turn had led to the disappearance of the invertebrates—tiny snails, copepods, amphipods and shrimp—that had fed upon the bat guano. The invertebrates had provided food for the Texas Blind Salamander. The cave was unsealed, but bats still have not returned to Ezell's Cave. Fortunately, the species has been located in several other caves in the area, or it might have become extinct.

II. Strange things happened in Borneo when the government sprayed large amounts of the pesticide DDT all over the countryside to get rid of mosquitoes. The mosquitoes died but so did the predatory wasps. These wasps eat large numbers of a certain kind of caterpillar. The caterpillars were not harmed by the DDT. As a matter of fact, they began to increase in numbers. All of these caterpillars needed more and more food. They were so hungry that they began to munch on the thatched roofs of the native people's houses. The caterpillars literally ate the people out of house and home!

But the story does not stop there.

Soon the government began to spray DDT *indoors* to kill houseflies. Normally, these flies were eaten by geckos—lizards with tiny "suction cups" on their feet. They can walk on the ceilings and catch flies. The geckos began to die from eating the poisoned flies. The house cats that ate the poisoned geckos also died. Since there were so few cats left, the rats began to invade the people's houses. Many of the rats in Borneo carry a deadly disease. The people became very afraid of dying from this disease. So, the government had to parachute in a new supply of cats to kill the rats.

References

Bury, R. Bruce, C. Kenneth Dodd, Jr. and Gary M. Fellers. 1980. Conservation of The Amphibia of the United States: A Review. U.S. Department of Interior, Fish and Wildlife Service, Resource Publication 134.

Biological Services Program. 1980. The Texas Blind Salamander. U.S. Fish and Wildlife Service, 4 pp.

Ecology: Science of Survival, by Laurence Pringle, MacMillan Press, N.Y., 1971.

International Problems in Animal Ecology

International problems in animal ecology, while not susceptible to classroom demonstrations, could be made the subjects of interesting displays or talks. International conservation organizations to which interested students can write for first-hand information and literature are listed below.

Suggested Topics:

I. The Importation of Foreign Species of Animals and its Ecological Impact.

In some cases, notably the rabbit in Australia, the House Sparrow in America, and the mongoose in Jamaica, imported species have taken hold and multiplied beyond all expectation. In other cases, as for instance the importation of domestic cattle in Africa, non-native species survive with difficulty.

Exotic species introduction has been a major cause of animal extinctions over the past 300 years. It is still a major threat endangering species. Choose two of the species endangered by such introductions and write an account of how the exotic species was introduced, how and when it proliferated, and the ways it threatens the species in question. Which exotics have been the most harmful? How? Is there legislation in your state regulating the release of exotic species? What are the Federal regulations? (Another aspect of this subject is the accidental importation of animal disease and insect pests from other countries and the precautions taken by the U.S. Customs and Agriculture authorities to prevent this.)

II. The Protection of Migratory Birds.

With the draining of marshes and the rapid expansion of urban areas, the provision of feeding and nesting areas for migratory birds poses a growing problem in this hemisphere and in Europe. Chart both the major flyways of migratory birds and the sanctuaries afforded them. What species are particularly endangered by urban growth? What steps are being taken on an international level for their protection?

III. The Pollution of the Sea.

Oil pollution of the sea, by ships dumping excess oil and petroleum waste, is a major international problem because of its disastrous effect on sea-birds. Birds that become contaminated by petroleum waste are unable to fly because their feathers are weighed down and stuck together, and they ingest poisons from the water. Large numbers die of exposure and starvation. In many parts of the world, where such birds are washed up on the beaches, citizens often band together in voluntary bird-washing programs to clean the birds, feather by feather. What should one do if one finds an oiled bird? Proper treatment can now save the lives of these oiled birds. Write the Humane Society of The United States for its publication on the subject. If you live near a coast, find out which organizations help oiled birds and how rescue work is coordinated in an oil spill.

Photo by U.S Fish and Wildlife Service

*Sea birds are vulnerable to **oil spills**. In order to save their lives, it is critical to follow procedure outlined in manuals or notify rescue centers.*

Domestic Problems in Animal Ecology

For a project paralleling that of "International Problems in Animal Ecology," in the domestic field, students should write to Members of Congress asking for information on conservation legislation pending in the U.S. Senate or House of Representatives, as for instance, legislation affecting parks and wilderness areas, endangered species, marine mammals, or restrictions on steel traps. The student may examine the purpose of the legislation, the need for it, and the conflict of interests which it involves.

Alternatively, what conservation legislation is now in force? What benefits accrue from it? Is it adequate to prevent the extinction of many species of plants and animals?

A Project in the Observation of the Effects on Birds of Spraying Insecticides

The use of insecticides is especially hazardous to an endangered or threatened bird. Because many species are migratory, it is impossible to control what is ingested during a long ranging flight. Therefore, the study of the effects of insecticides on birds is particularly relevant to endangered species if we are to prevent them from becoming extinct.

Because, by definition, endangered species are not abundant, a bird population common to your particular area may be selected for study. After conducting the following field project, your results can be extrapolated to a threatened or endangered bird species. However, the endangered birds must be closely matched to the bird population under observation. For example, special care must be

taken to select species with similar dietary habits, migratory patterns, and other characteristics.

If insecticides are used on a large scale in your community, there are a number of observations which may be made in the field. Field counts in areas which have been heavily sprayed are relevant to a study of ecology, since they indicate a breakdown in the balance of nature brought about by human interference.

I. Make repeated field trips to count the number of birds, and species of birds, to be found in a given area before the area has been sprayed with insecticides, while the spraying is going on, immediately afterwards, a few days afterwards, a week afterwards, a month afterwards. Do not forget to allow for seasonal migrations. If there is a similar area which has not been sprayed with insecticides within reach, make similar counts there. If not, try to get in touch with bird watchers who have taken counts in the area before the spraying program was initiated. The Audubon Society, 950 Third Avenue, New York, N.Y. might be helpful in this respect.

Besides making a count of the living birds, search the ground for dead birds and make a count of these. What kind of pesticide was used? Call the nearest office of the U.S. Fish and Wildlife Service to report the bird kill. In some cases, such spraying may be illegal. Learn about the toxicity of the pesticide by contacting the Environmental Protection Agency. Note whether the species are resident or migratory in your area. Comparing the count of living birds, the count of dead birds, and any information about normal conditions in such an area, attempt to determine which species have the greatest resistance to insecticides. What is the relation of mortality to diet? Also consider the relation of the poisoning of songbirds to the welfare of the larger predators, and to the ecology of the area as a whole.

II. It has been suggested that the use of insecticides on a large scale in the very early spring, before migrations or nesting, results in a lower mortality rate, especially in the northern states, since most of the resident winter birds there are seed-eating, and so are susceptible to poisoning only by direct contact or by contamination of their drinking supply. (However, since the young of many seed-eaters are insectivorous, seed eaters will suffer during the nesting season.) The federal government, state governments, and local governments, as well as private individuals who may use insecticides on a large scale on their own property, may have different policies on poison distribution. They may spray different areas at different times of the year, with different concentrations of insecticides. Make counts before the first spraying in all the areas, and continue to count weekly in every area under consideration until several weeks after the last area to be sprayed has been sprayed. What conclusions do you reach? How can these conclusions be applied to endangered birds? Remember to consider the effects of the insecticides not only on the existing population but also on the unborn birds, mating possibilities, and the food chain.

Similar studies may be carried out on fish, in rivers polluted by insecticides or industrial wastes.

Other measures adopted in some areas to kill unwanted mammals and birds also affect endangered species. Examination of the results of these activities can form a valuable project for a student or class. Examples include spraying by air of PA-14 over woodlands favored by blackbirds as winter roosting areas. PA-14 dissolves oils in the feathers and causes sprayed birds to die of exposure if the weather is cold. The intent is to kill flocks of redwing blackbirds, cowbirds, grackles and starlings, considered pests by some farmers although the birds consume huge quantities of insects. It has been reported that the starling, a species introduced from Europe in the last century, is the most resistant to PA-14 spraying, thus further increasing the preponderance of this non-native bird over native species. Robins, cardinals, woodpeckers of different kinds and other non-target birds are also killed in the sprayings. If this type of "blackbird control" is carried out in your area, make bird counts by species before and after, as outlined in the previous section on spraying of insecticides.

Do you think this spraying should be conducted? Give reasons for your views. Discuss with other members of your class. If you have collected convincing information demonstrating harm to birds, present it to local authorities who make decisions on spraying.

Medicinal Plants

Digitalis floribus purpuris. 6

Trace the use of medicinal plants as far back as possible in time and in different civilizations. How did medieval herb gardens compare with early American herb gardens? What herbal medicines are used today? Were they used continuously or rediscovered (for example, reserpine used in India centuries ago, reintroduced as a tranquilizer in recent years). What is the earliest use you can find of digitalis, whose source is the fox glove? What modern medicines incorporate or synthesize digitalis? What medicines come from members of the primrose family? What is the most recent discovery? (see page 32) Forty percent of current prescriptions are written for medicines derived from plants. List the most frequently prescribed drugs and trace their discovery and development. How would you describe the stake which the medical profession, pharmaceutical companies, and the general public have in the preservation of the broad diversity of plant species which have developed over millions of years? What do you think our country should do to protect species worldwide and prevent extinctions?

Statistics in Biological Studies

by Marjorie Anchel, Ph.D.

The use of statistics is well illustrated in ecological studies, and for the mathematically inclined, it would be instructive to consult the references on statistics given here, or other elementary treatments of the subject (perhaps the best to begin with is Warren Weaver's "Lady Luck"). The methods might then be applied in evaluating the results of the observations made.

A biologist should understand the concepts of chance, significance and probability in the statistical sense. The use of statistics enables the biologist to evaluate his results, so as to determine, for example, the probability that an apparent difference between two groups is real, or alternatively, that it is due only to chance. It also enables him to design experiments so that he can extract the maximum information from the minimum number of subjects. The importance of such design is very well expressed by C.W. Hume, in "Man and Beast": In talking about unplanned or poorly planned experiments, he says: "So long as the worst that happens is that large quantities of expensive chemicals are poured down the drain, nobody need worry except the man who pays for the chemicals; . . . in experiments on animals ethical requirements demand even more strongly than does scientific virtuosity, that an experimenter should not be content with pedestrian empiricism but should plan his experiments in the light of a great deal of preliminary hard thinking." One requirement is that he should "consult a statistician if he is not sure of his design being maximally efficient." This advice applies to all scientists, and is a principle that should become part of their thinking at the very beginning of their scientific training. Because very few can be specialists in more than one field, it is important to know when to collaborate with those in other fields.

References:

Abramovitz, A.M., 1970. *Probability Theory*. C.V. Mosby, Co., St. Louis.

Croxton, I.E., 1959. *Elementary Statistics*. Dover Publications, N.Y.

Hume, C.W. *Man and Beast*. Second Edition, 1982. Universities Federation for Animal Welfare, 8 Hamilton Close, South Mimms, Potters Bar, Hertfordshire.

Lotka, A.D., 1956. *Elements of Mathematical Biology*. Dover Publications, N.Y.

Mather, K., 1964. *Statistical Analysis in Biology*. Methuen & Co., Ltd., London.

Pearce, S.C., 1965. *Biological Statistics*. An Introduction. McGraw-Hill, N.Y.

Schwartz, R.T., 1972. *Elementary Statistics for the Biologist*. Addison-Wesley, N.Y.

Stegun, L., 1974. *Statistics: A programmed guide*. MacMillan Co., N.Y.

Thomas, G.E., 1974. *Data Manipulation*. McGraw-Hill, N.Y.

Weaver, Warren, 1963. *Lady Luck. The Theory of Probability*. Doubleday, Inc., N.Y.

An Interdisciplinary Series of Discussion Papers

by Andrew Orlans

Franz Hals

René Descartes' *philosophy influenced many generations to believe that animals were merely machines.*

Purpose

To trace the history of man's relationship with a specific wild animal. The topic may be approached from one or more of the following perspectives:

A. Biological

Trace the history of the animal's evolution, emphasizing the biological and behavioral adaptations which have been affected by man.

Examples: The wolf, *Canis lupus*, has a healthy fear of man. This behavioral trait is the single most important factor insuring the wolf's continued survival in the face of unrelenting human persecution.

The Virginia white-tail deer is far more plentiful today than it was in the 18th century. The dramatic increase in deer populations may be traced to interdependent natural and human factors affecting the species. When the European settlers began displacing the native American population in the 18th century they cleared the forests for agricultural land. As the Eastern forests dwindled the deer population thrived, as deer need open land for grazing. The carrying capacity of deer in climax forests is less than on cleared land or sub-climax forests as the plants which deer feed on are not as plentiful in the densely shaded climax forests as they are in recently cleared or sub-climax forests. In recent years wildlife management policies, prompted by a high demand for deer by hunters, have helped to maintain deer population levels at an unnaturally high level in order to provide a "surplus" which may be culled by hunters.

B. Philosophical

Examine from a historical perspective the philosophical and theological questions concerning man's relation to animals. How has the mechanistic philosophy of the French 17th century philosopher, René Descartes, led us to see animals as machines without feelings?

C. Literary

How have animals been portrayed in literature? Or, more specifically, what can a study of the way in which animals are depicted in mythology, folklore and fairy tales tell us of the psychological relations between animals and men? Barry Lopez has done such a study in *Of Wolves and Men*.

Suggested References
General

Cleveland Amory, *Man Kind? Our Incredible War on Wildlife*, (New York: Harper & Row, 1974). This book is worth reading for its account of what humans have done to wild animals.

Roger Caras, *Dangerous to Man*, (New York: Holt, Rinehart & Winston, 1975). Myths about wildlife; separates fact from hearsay and superstition about animal nature and behavior.

Gerald Carson, *Men, Beasts and Gods: A History of Cruelty and Kindness to Animals*, (New York: Charles Scribner's Sons, 1972). A thoughtful review of our treatment of animals.

Michael W. Fox, *Between Animal and Man*, (New York: Coward, McCann & Geoghegan, 1976). On the similarities between human and animal behavior.

Bettyann Keules, *Watching the Wild Apes*, (New York: E.P. Dutton & Co., 1976). The natural behavior of chimpanzees, gorillas and orangutans.

Barry Lopez, *Of Wolves and Men*, (New York: Charles Scribner's Sons, 1978). Man's fascination with wolves and our persecution of them.

Philosophical

Stephen Clark, *The Moral Status of Animals*, (Oxford: Clarendon Press, 1977). A radical reappraisal of man's relationship with the animal kingdom.

C.W. Hume, *The Status of Animals in the Christian Religion*, (London: The Universities Federation for Animal Welfare, 1957). A historical perspective of the status of animals in Christianity.

C.W. Hume, *Man and Beast*, (Potters Bar: The Universities Federation for Animal Welfare, 1982 edition). First published in 1962, it was ahead of its time in analyzing rights of animals.

Bernard E. Rollin, *Animal Rights and Human Morality*, (Buffalo: Prometheus Books, 1981). A philosophical book accessible to non-philosophers which asks the question, "Do animals have moral and legal rights?"

Peter Singer, *Animal Liberation: A New Ethics for our Treatment of Animals*, (New York: The New York Review, 1975). Makes a compelling case for the equality of all creatures; see particularly chapters 5 and 6 for a discussion of speciesism.

Tom Regan and Peter Singer, eds., *Animal Rights and Human Obligations*, (Englewood Cliffs: Prentice-Hall, Inc., 1976). A collection of writings on man's relation with non-human animals.

Richard Knowles Morris and Michael W. Fox, eds., *On the Fifth Day: Animal Rights and Human Ethics*, (Washington, D.C.: Acropolis Books, 1978). An anthology of essays by philosophers, theologians and animal behaviorists on man's relation to animals.

Drawing by Fougasse from Man and Beast

Ecology in the High School
by Lee R. Dice

(Reprinted with modifications from "Opportunity for Investigation in Natural History by High-School Teachers," University of Michigan Press, Ann Arbor.)

The best introduction to biology is through natural history and the essence of natural history is ecology. Every young person is interested in living plants and mammals, and wishes to know not only their names but also their habits. Part of the past failure in teaching biology in the high schools, is the teacher's attempt to present the same materials which he or she studied in college courses.

The teaching of natural history is more difficult than the teaching of anatomy or physiology. To teach natural history properly, the teacher must first be able to identify the common plants and animals of the locality. Little information about habits and habitats can be given unless the names of the plants and animals are known. To rely upon textbooks describing the natural history of other regions will be a disappointment; it is more important that the student become acquainted with the ecology of the local flora and fauna.

After the student has learned to identify the common plants and animals of the region, the next step is to learn about their habits and ecological relationships (to distinguish between green plants and parasites—between herbivores and carnivores). A view of the complex interrelationships within a biotic community leads to a consideration of the human being's place within this community and a regard for the interdependence of all living organisms.

The habits and ecology of plants and animals are less known than their names. It is difficult to find any valuable information concerning the behavior of a local species of animals and then surprising to realize that some of one's discoveries about local natural history cannot be found in any published work. Information about the ecological interrelationships of plants and animals is lacking for most regions. We know very little about the number of plants or animals of one species which can live satisfactorily on a given acre of land. We know little about the habitat limitations of either plants or animals. We know very little about the cycles of abundance which many animals exhibit, such as the presumed ten-year cycle of the snowshoe hare. When one kind of animal becomes abundant, it comes into competition for food and space with numerous other species; when it becomes rare, the carnivores which fed upon it may starve to death.

More facts about all of these ecological relationships are greatly needed. Here is a field in which high school students of biology can serve science as well as themselves. Many high schools are in regions in which the natural history is still little known. For no region is the natural history completely worked out. Almost anyone could observe for a week the behavior of any common animal and discover a new important fact! Some of the things which the teacher uncovers while preparing for class or teaching will be new to science and should be reported to the proper scientific society.

The teacher who knows the natural history of his or her locality is certain to be a better biology teacher. The students will secure an understanding of the interrelationships between living plants and animals which will help them to be responsible participants. Learning should be enhanced by focusing on the immediate environment—that which can be experienced sensorially day in and day out. What could be more interesting or relevant than what is just out of doors? Those who continue to study biology in college will have a better foundation for advanced courses.

References

Bailey, Robert G. 1976. *Ecoregions of the United States.* U.S. Dept. of Agriculture, Forest Service, Ogden, Utah

National Audubon Society series of field guides to trees, wild flowers, ferns, mushrooms, mammals, reptiles and amphibians, butterflies and insects.

Plant Ecology Studies

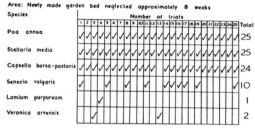

Figure 1

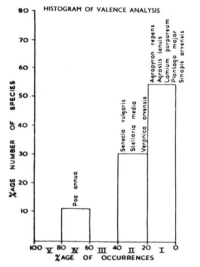

**Fig. 2. Cabbage Patch
Neglected Nov. - April**

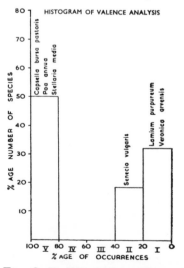

**Fig. 3. Building Site Cleared
Feb. and Left Until April**

In "Botanical Fieldwork in a Suburb", B.E. Bayliss writes, "Field ecology provides an excellent opportunity for training in methods of scientific investigation and preparation of the observed results for presentation and, since each field project carried out is indeed a piece of original research, a class is perhaps more satisfactorily imbued with the spirit of scientific discovery by a field project than by some routine experiment in the laboratory."

School playing fields, weedy garden beds, nearby building sites, and public parks are among the suggested places to carry out these studies.

1) Transects. Record the plants occurring along a line and within a fixed distance along the line. Draw simple pictures of the plants occurring on the line. Where several similar species (e.g., grasses) occur in the transect, colors may be used to show the different species in the drawing.

Example: Six students might take a transect starting under trees and running into the open for 100 or 150 feet. Plants occurring every four inches along the line might be identified and recorded. Light intensity might be recorded with a photo-electric exposure meter at intervals to find the connection between variations in plant growth and light intensity. Soil along the transect might be measured for acidity and amount of water present. Diagrams of the transect may be made, the vertical scale about four times greater than the horizontal scale. Each pair of students may be made responsible for one part of the transect and for the pictorial representation and the three sheets joined together for exhibit at the end.

Similar transects can be made in any area offering differences in vegetation, for example: grass which is mown regularly, and edges near a fence which grow taller and are not reached by the mower; spots which have good and bad soil drainage, variation in soil depth, unequal applications of fertilizer, weed killer or other application, or unequal wear by walking.

2) Belt transects. Belt transects a foot or more wide may be laid down between two trees and a count made of seeds or fruits which have fallen. Such results may be shown pictorially or may be analyzed statistically.

3) Statistical analysis. To make a valence analysis of vegetation in a reasonably uniform area, such as a lawn, 25 random samples in a square foot will provide adequate sampling. Attach a string 6½ inches long to two pegs or meat skewers. Push one peg into the ground at a point in the area under study, chosen at random. Rotate the other, giving the name of each species as it occurs. Fill the notebook pages as shown in Fig. 1. Choose another area at random and continue. Total the occurrences of each species in the 25 samples and multiply by four to obtain the percentage occurrence of a hundred trial areas. Arrange the species in five groups according to frequency of occurrence as follows:

Group I	0 - 20 per cent
Group II	21 - 40 per cent
Group III	41 - 60 per cent
Group IV	61 - 80 per cent
Group V	81 - 100 per cent

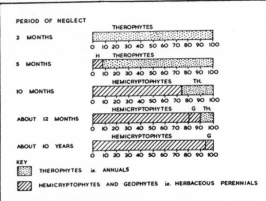

Fig. 4. Biological Spectra for Plots of Cultivated Land Neglected for Varying Periods (April 1958)

Watercolor of Linaria Canadensis, *May 27.*

Adaptation to Environment

Draw a histogram as shown in Figures 2 and 3:

4) Biological Spectrum. To analyze plant communities the classification made by the Danish botanist Raunkiaer may be used as follows:

1. Phanerophytes
   Woody plants with surviving buds more than 25 cm. above soil level, e.g. Oak.

2. Chamaephytes
   Woody or herbaceous plants with surviving buds above soil level but below 25 cm., e.g. Carnation.

3. Hermicryptophytes
   Herbs (very rarely woody plants) with buds at soil level (i.e. on the soil surface), e.g. Dandelion

4. Cryptophytes
   Herbs with surviving buds below the soil level or under water (include geophytes, helophytes and hydrophytes), e.g. Bluebell.

5. Therophytes
   Plants which pass the unfavorable season as seeds, (i.e. annual plants), e.g. Groundsel.

The percentage occurrence obtained by valence analysis is used as a basis as follows:

Species	Total Occurrence in 25 trials	Per cent. Occurrence	Group
Poa annua .. (Annual meadow grass)	25	100	V
Stellaria media .. (Chickweed)	25	100	V
Capsella bursa-pastoris (Shepherd's purse)	24	96	V
Senecio vulgaris .. (Groundsel)	10	40	II
Lamium purpureum .. (Red dead nettle)	1	4	I
Veronica arvensis .. (Wall speedwell)	2	8	I

Out of a total of six species:
   3 are classed in Group V, i.e. 50 per cent.
   1 is classed in Group II, i.e. 16 per cent.
   2 are classed in Group I, i.e. 33 per cent.

How do different forms of life adapt to their environment? This is a vast question which offers many possible projects in providing partial answers to it.

For example, what are the adaptations to pond life, to a fast flowing stream, to the seashore, as demonstrated in plants and animals ranging from simple unicellular forms through different types of worms, mollusks, crustaceans and other arthropods, fishes, amphibians, birds and mammals?

Ecological studies showing the interdependence and relationship between the different forms in each environmental situation would be of very great interest.

For example, which wading birds are found near ponds in your part of the country? Near streams? Why do sandy beaches support flocks of sandpipers and plovers while herons and bitterns prefer still waters? Which species of fish are adapted to life in both salt and fresh water? Why can't most forms of water-living animals and plants shift from salt to fresh water?

A good Science Fair project would be the study, by careful observation, of the habits of the different living things in one selected area. Such an area could be a clearing in a wood, a piece of uncultivated ground, a patch of weeds, a wood pile, the edge of a lake or pond, a corner of the school yard or a park. The requirements of each species might be shown; in the case of plants, the conditions of soil, water, and light; in the case of animals, the food, resting or hiding place, activities at different times of day or of season. The relationship between the plants and the animals insofar as it can be discovered should be described. Unanswered questions might also be noted in such a project, to show the extent to which knowledge in this area is lacking.

For more advanced studies in comparative care of the young, observations in nature are of great interest. A reading of Tinbergen, Lorenz, Eckstein and others (see Pages 199-200) will give ideas for observations of birds and insects in natural surroundings.

Life History Projects

The detailed life history of a chosen animal or plant can provide an almost unlimited field for original scientific work whose length in time is determined by the life cycle of the form of life studied. Opportunities abound for original observations and records in the form of accurate description, statistical data, photographs or drawings of the subject under different conditions. Observations should be made on structure, habitat, adaptations and way of life.

In city schools, plants which will grow indoors or insects which can be maintained in an environment sufficiently similar to natural conditions are the most advantageous forms of life to study. The metamorphosis of caterpillar to butterfly is a classic example.

In suburban and rural schools, interesting studies can be made of insects, amphibians, reptiles, birds and mammals in nature. The fascinating observations of wasps by Dr. Niko Tinbergen described in "Curious Naturalists" (Garden City, N.J.: Natural History Library, 1968) offer ideas for ways to observe individual insects in their natural surroundings.

For example, after watching each wasp returning to her nest without hesitation or difficulty in locating the small hole in the sand that was its entrance, Dr. Tinbergen changed the location of sticks, leaves, stones or other small landmarks near the hole to see if this would confuse the wasp. He tried this with a number of different individuals. In each case the wasp showed confusion when she arrived near her nest, hovering and hunting for the entrance, taking as long as twenty-five minutes to reach the hole that she had always found so easily before. When she found it, she went in, and when she emerged ready for another hunting trip, she hovered over the area for about two minutes, circling repeatedly to learn the new appearance. The next time she returned, she found the entrance to the burrow again almost without hesitation. Theories of insect learning may be tested by simple experiments, and supplemented with reading of books listed in the Resources section.

The life history of a chosen plant may be portrayed for a Science Fair in the form of preserved specimens of the plant at different stages in its development showing it 1) as a seed, 2) as a seedling, 3) as the leaves unfold, 4) as buds form, 5) in full flower, 6) with petals dropping and seeds forming, 7) in its dormant form, if a perennial, or at the end of its life, if an annual. Variations on the life history of individual plants in different environments could be shown for a more complicated set of observations. The effect of different degrees of light and shade, of composition of soil, of amounts of water and of fertilizers, both natural and artificial, may be shown. The number of insect visits per hour to a flowering plant may be recorded.

For animals and plants which live for many years, seasonal studies are more appropriate. The seasonal study of a chosen tree provides an interesting project. The famous photographer, Steichen, observed a small shad blow tree near his home for several years and made a fascinating photographic record of it under many different seasonal and weather conditions. Young scientists with an interest in photography may follow his lead.

In a city park, squirrels may be the object of observation throughout the different seasons of the year, differences in coat and in degree of plumpness may be estimated by observation, and the squirrels' interest in food and bedding materials of different types at different seasons of the year recorded. Date of emergence of young squirrels from the nest, as well as the degree of activity during the winter and how it relates to temperature variations, may be recorded. Population studies might also be made of squirrels. Recording by means of camera, together with charts on temperature and activity, might be used to supplement a written report.

Observation of How Birds Help Destroy Insects

Locate the nest of a catbird, swallow, flycatcher or other insect-eating bird. Then find a spot where you can watch it without disturbing the birds. After eggs are hatched, watch the nest for an hour at the same time each day and count the number of trips the parent birds make to the nest. Do this for several days and average the number of trips they make in an hour. You can be fairly sure that on each trip they make the birds are carrying at least one insect of some kind and maybe several. After you have made the count for several days and have averaged the number of trips they make per hour, multiply this figure by the number of hours of daylight. This will give you an estimate of the total number of insects this pair of birds destroys in a day.

Interpretation: Most forms of wildlife help farmers and ranchers produce more and better crops by checking insects, weeds and other pests. Wildlife is equally helpful to the orchardist, gardener and city dweller. The number of beneficial forms of wildlife a well-managed farm supports is surprising. For example, on a 100-acre farm in the Eastern United States we might find more than 40 kinds of beneficial birds, and more than a thousand beneficial small mammals and several million beneficial insects such as ladybeetles, aphis lions, and syrphus flies which feed on plant lice; chalcid and tachinid flies which feed on many kinds of insects; and assassin bugs, robber flies, and nabids, which capture and feed on other insects. The food habits of birds make them especially valuable to agriculture. Because birds have higher body temperatures, more rapid digestion, and greater energy than most other animals, they require more food. Nestling

Photo by Amyas Ames in
Private Lives of Our Natural Neighbors

*These baby **swallows** are begging for insects, which their parents catch in large quantities.*

166

birds usually consume as much or more than their own weight in soft-bodied insects every day. One young robin, weighing 3 ounces, consumed 165 cutworms weighing 5½ ounces in 1 day. If a 10-pound baby ate at the same rate he would eat 18⅓ pounds of food in a day.

Some Factors in the Optimum Environment for Crop-Destroying Insects

Dr. William A. Albrecht of the Department of Soils at the University of Missouri, College of Agriculture, demonstrated experimentally a correlation between soil fertility and the resistance of crop plants to insect pests. One of his tests would be suitable for demonstration if students have access to gardening facilities.

Dr. Albrecht divided his experimental plot into two parts: soil rich in compost and natural nutrients, and exhausted soil on which too many crops had been grown and harvested, leaving no organic matter to return to the soil during the winter months. He planted spinach equally on the two parts of the plot. He found that spinach grown on fertile soil was less subject to attacks by insect pests than spinach grown on infertile soil. He concluded that by correcting soil deficiencies, plants may be protected against insects; in other words, exhausted soil is a favorable environmental condition for some insect pests.

Vanishing Species

The Great White Bird

Photo by U.S. Fish and Wildlife Service

Whooping Cranes have increased from their near extinction, but still number only about 100 birds. What are the reasons for their decline and what is being done to help them?

The Whooping Crane (*Grus americana*) is perhaps the best known endangered species of the United States and Canada.

To increase the knowledge and awareness of what is being done to enhance the survival of this highly endangered species, the following discussion topics can be used as the basis for a project by a single student or for the whole class, which may be divided into three groups each of which is assigned a single topic.

1) Whooping Cranes were formerly widely distributed across North America. Describe past and present distribution, and principal causes for the species' decline.

2) Because many avian species have declined as a result of pesticide use, many people believe that Whooping Cranes have been adversely affected by pesticides. Is there any evidence that Whooping Cranes have been affected by pesticides?

3) The U.S. and Canadian governments are currently attempting to establish a new, separate population of Whooping Cranes. How are they trying to do this? What problems have been encountered?

In addition to using the local library as a source of information, you may also write to one of the leading centers involved in Whooping Crane research: Patuxent Wildlife Research Center, U.S. Fish and Wildlife Service, Laurel, MD 20811, and also to the National Audubon Society.

Helping Migratory Song Birds

More than half of the 650 species of birds that we regard as U.S. birds spend half to two-thirds of their lives in Latin American countries. Recently, it has been observed that some species of warblers, vireos and flycatchers are becoming far less numerous. Scientists working with The World Wildlife Fund and the U.S. Fish and Wildlife

Service point to the fact that the neotropical forests, where so many of our song birds winter, are being cut down at such a pace that more than half will be gone by the year 2000! Even if we protect their nesting areas, prevent pesticide spraying and direct killing in the United States, our native song birds are threatened severely by loss of the forests in which they have wintered for millions of years.

What you can do:

1) Write to the World Wildlife Fund for the latest information on this urgent problem.

2) Write to a student in a Latin American country asking him about deforestation in his or neighboring countries. (See Pen Pal project)

3) Find out what happens to tropical rain forests when they are felled. Can the diverse trees and plants regenerate? How long would it take those that are capable of regenerating? Which bird species disappear when old forests are cut? Which species can adjust to second growth forests?

4) Ask your teacher to arrange for showing of films about the rain forest and about our native song birds.

5) Prepare an exhibit showing what is known of migratory routes of one or more species of birds between the United States and another country. Find out where they winter and whether there is forest destruction there. Show pictures of the birds so that those who see the exhibit will be able to identify them. You can copy a picture from a bird guide, painting the colors correctly, or take a photograph yourself. Tell about the birds' habits, their favorite foods, and their preferred nesting places.

6) Write to your U.S. Senators and Representative to ask their help in international negotiations to protect the birds' winter habitat from destruction.

Bibliography on Migratory Birds and Tropical Forest Destruction

Aldrich, John W., and Chandler S. Robbins. 1970. Changing Abundance of Migratory Birds in North America. pp 17-24. In: The Avifauna of Northern Latin America, ed. by H. and J.H. Buechner. Smithsonian Institution Press.

Council on Environmental Quality. 1980. The Global 2000 Report. Vol. I-III. U.S. Government Printing Office, Washington, D.C.

Foster, Robin B. 1980. Heterogeneity and disturbance in tropical vegetation. pp 75-92. In: Conservation Biology, ed. by M.E. Soule, and Bruce A. Wilcox. Sinauer Associates, Sunderland, Massachusetts.

International Union for the Conservation of Nature. 1980. World Conservation Strategy. Gland, Switzerland.

Janzen, Daniel H. 1974. The Deflowering of Central America. *Natural History*, April, pp 49-53.

Keast, Allen, and Eugene S. Morton (editors). 1980. Migrant Birds in the Neotropics: Ecology, Behavior, Distribution and Conservation. Smithsonian Institution Press, paper, 576 pp.

Meggers, Betty J., Edward S. Ayensu, and W. Donald Duckworth (editors) 1973. Tropical Forest Ecosystems in Africa and South America: A comparative review. Smithsonian Institution Press, 350 pp.

Myers, Norman. 1979. The Sinking Ark. Pergamon Press, N.Y.

Pasquier, Roger F. and Eugene S. Morton. 1982. For avian migrants a tropical vacation is not a bed of roses. *Smithsonian*, Oct. Vol. 13(7):169-188.

Russell, W.M.S. 1968. The Slash-and-Burn Technique. *Natural History*. March, pp. 58-65.

Photo by Russell Mittermeier

This is the sight greeting an increasing number of North American birds in their wintering grounds. Many of "our" beautiful warblers, vireos, flycatchers and tanagers are declining as a result of tropical forest destruction.

Helping Song Birds at Home

Dimensions shown are for boards ¾ " thick.

Use 1¾ " galvanized siding nails or aluminum nails.

Pivot nails must be located exactly opposite each other as shown for proper opening of side board.

Cut top edges of front and back boards at slight angle to fit flush with top board.

Cut ⅜" off each corner of bottom board as shown.

Insert bottom board so that the grain of the wood runs from front to rear of box.

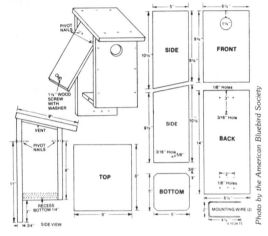

Photo by the American Bluebird Society

*Building a **nest box** can help bluebirds and other declining bird species.*

Bird Housing. Although forests in the United States are not being destroyed in the massive way noted above, nevertheless, there is a substantial loss, in parts of our country, of old trees with holes that hole-nesting birds and other wildlife can use for homes. Many birds will welcome nest boxes so that they can lay their eggs and raise their broods in safety.

For information on how to construct nest boxes for different species of birds you can write to:

North American Bluebird Society
Box 6295
Silver Spring, MD 20906

Audubon Naturalist Society
8940 Jones Mill Road
Chevy Chase, MD 20815

KIND Magazine
c/o The Humane Society of the United States
2100 L Street, N.W.
Washington, D.C. 20037

Bird Feeding. You can help those native species of birds that "stay home" all winter by providing extra food through the cold months. Winter kills many birds because they need extra food to maintain their body temperature when the thermometer drops.

Insectivorous birds welcome a piece of suet tied to a tree. You may observe woodpeckers eating the suet, then working over the tree trunk and branches for insects under the bark. Chickadees, nuthatches, Blue Jays and crows may visit.

For seed-eaters, various types of bird seed are available. You can make a bird feeder yourself. Designs for bird feeders are available from the organizations noted above.

Purple Finches, Goldfinches, and various sparrow species appreciate the small black seeds of thistles, so fine and light that they must be poured into a narrow net "stocking" and hung on a tree. As many as six of these small birds may be seen clinging to the stocking at once.

A listing of the seeds most favored by a sampling of 30 bird species is available from Duncraft:

Duncraft
Wild Bird Specialists
Penacook, N.H. 03303

A listing of foods suitable for young birds of 19 species is given in "First Aid and Care of Small Animals." Your teacher may request a free copy from the Animal Welfare Institute for classroom use.

Red-cockaded Woodpecker

The Red-cockaded Woodpecker, once described by Audubon in the early 1800's as being "abundant," has dwindled to a population of less than 10,000—the major cause of this decrease in population being habitat destruction.

The Red-cockaded Woodpecker, being a cavity nester, has very specific habitat requirements. It resides in the Southern pine forests, particularly those of the Southern National Forests, and chooses only old and diseased trees in which to nest. Unfortunately, these are the trees that the forest industry selects to cut down first, when surveying an area for any type of clearing. These old, diseased trees have no use in the eyes of the forestry industry, but looking at the situation from a wildlife biologist's point of view, they are vital for the enhance-

Drawing courtesy of Texas Parks and Wildlife Department

Red-cockaded Woodpeckers *have become endangered. Discovering the causes and evaluating the efforts to help them make a challenging project.*

ment of a delicate population such as the Red-cockaded Woodpecker and other cavity nesters. Find out what programs are being enlisted at the state and federal level to help these birds. What other cavity nesting species are under this same type of pressure from habitat destruction? Are there programs to help them also?

Trees selected by these birds in which to nest and roost are almost always infected with a disease called "red heart." The woodpeckers drill holes around the nest to allow the sap to form around the entrance. This flow of sap is characteristic of all nests and is thought to ward off predators. What is red heart disease, and what effect does it have on southern pines to make it advantageous for these birds to nest and roost in trees affected by it?

Red-cockaded Woodpeckers usually occur in small groups anywhere from two to ten birds, which can consist of a pair, several other adults and several young. They apparently pair for long periods of time and perhaps even for life. Read the references on the Red-cockaded Woodpecker listed in the bibliography at the end of this project.

The birds which are not involved in breeding in the clan serve as "helpers at the nest," an occupation similar to babysitting. Animal behaviorists who have studied this phenomenon have usually found these birds to be older siblings that have returned to help raise the new generation of nestlings. Sixty species of birds have been observed to have this type of parental care assistance. One well known study is that of the Florida Scrub Jay by G.E. Woolfenden, who found that although the helpers did not participate in nest construction or incubation, they took part in every other activity, including territory and nest defense from other jays, attacks on predators, and feeding of the young. He also found that the presence of helpers at the nest increases the survival rate of offspring. Find out through a literature search other species that have helpers at the nest, and various benefits that have arisen because of this activity. For example, the Superb Blue Wren (Rowley, 1965), Mexican Jays (Brown, 1972, 1974), and others.

The Red-cockaded Woodpeckers nest in colonies, with each tree in the colony having from one to nine cavities, but usually two. Depending on the clan size and tree holes available, some birds may have their own cavity in which to nest and roost throughout the whole year. A bird may occupy the same cavity for several years and a single cavity may be used for at least 20 years.

Some Red-cockaded Woodpeckers are an asset to farmers. Those that live near cornfields feed heavily upon earworms, which do much damage to corn crops. When corn is in the tassel and ear state, a period of about four to six weeks, adults and recently fledged young may feed almost entirely on earworms. Find out other foods that comprise the diet of the Red-cockaded Woodpecker, and also why they like to feed on lightning-struck and other dying pines.

Bibliography

To obtain a nine-page status report entitled "The Red-cockaded Woodpecker," 1980, write to the U.S. Fish and Wildlife Service, Biological Service Program, c/o The National Fish and Wildlife Laboratory, 412 N.E. 16th Avenue, Gainesville, FL 32601. Also, a 188-page report from the 1971 symposium on the Red-cockaded Woodpecker entitled "The Ecology and Management of the Red-cockaded Woodpecker" published by the U.S. Department of Interior in 1972, is available from the U.S. Government Printing Office, Washington, D.C. Ask for report #741-140/8526, Region four.

Brown, J.L. 1972. "Communal feeding of nestlings in the Mexican jay: interflock comparisons." *Animal Behavior*, 20(2): 395-403.

Brown, J.L. 1974. "Alternate routes to sociality in jays—with a theory for the evolution of altruism and communal breeding." *American Zoologist*, 14(1): 63-80.

Rowley, I. 1965. "The life history of the superb blue wren." *Emu*, 64(4): 251-297.

Chamberlain, E. Brunham. 1974. *Rare and Endangered Birds of the Southern National Forests*. U.S. Department of Agriculture Forest Service, Southern Region.

Terres, John K. 1980. Audubon Society Encyclopedia of North American Birds. Alfred A. Knopf, N.Y.

Wilson, E.O. 1975. *Sociobiology: The New Synthesis*. The Belknap Press of Harvard University Press, Cambridge, MA.

Bird Count Field Day

At the peak of the spring migration thousands of ornithologists and amateur "birders" make field trips to see how many species of birds they can identify in one day. This sort of expedition is fully discussed in Roger Tory Peterson's "Birds over America" (New York: Dodd Mead and Co., 1948). It is customary to chart the route in advance so that each habitat will be visited at the time when the most birds are visible there. A field trip may start before dawn, when different species of nightbirds can be identified by their song. The group or individual may then move to a pond or marsh at daybreak, then to a wooded area, and during the day, to a coastal area, if possible. In May in Massachusetts, up to 161 species have been counted on such expeditions.

Participate in the annual Christmas Bird Count conducted by the National Audubon Society. For dates and places write: The National Audubon Society, 950 Third Avenue, New York, N.Y. 10002. Field guides include Roger Tory Peterson's "A Field Guide to the Birds: A Completely New Guide to all the Birds of Eastern and Central North America," (Boston: Houghton, Mifflin Co., 1980). For those living west of the Rockies, "Field Guide to the Western Birds" by the same author (Boston: Houghton, Mifflin Co., 1961). And yet another source, "A Guide to Field Identification: Birds of North America" by Chandler S. Robbins, Bertel Bruun, and Herbert S. Zim (Golden Press, Western Publishing Co., Inc., 1966).

Birds of Prey Injured by Traps and Poison

Photo by Don Reese

Each year hundreds of birds of prey are caught in steel jaw leghold traps. This eagle was later freed, but injuries usually require amputation of the leg.

Traps

In some areas, steel jaw leghold traps are baited with a dead rabbit or a piece of meat in order to capture mammalian predators, especially coyotes. These traps are not selective, and many of the animals caught are non-target species. Eagles, owls, hawks and other raptors are caught in these traps. Even if the injuries to the trapped foot may not appear to be severe, the University of Minnesota Raptor Research and Rehabilitation Program reports that the bird usually will have to have its foot amputated. "There is only limited potential for mitigating the effects of trapping injuries to raptors because of the irreversible soft tissue damage usually associated with such injuries, which results in the loss of the extremity," notes Katherine Durham, who works with the Minnesota Raptor Program, in an article in the *International Journal for the Study of Animal Problems* (November-December 1981); "The extent of soft tissue damage usually cannot be determined at the time the bird is found, as the signs of necrosis require several days to develop....Of the raptors received for leg injuries involving only soft tissue damage and

Dr. Pat Redig *of the Raptor Research and Rehabilitation Center holds a* **Bald Eagle** *being treated for injuries received when it was caught in a leghold trap. The majority of such injuries result in the bird's death. 19 Bald Eagles caught in traps were brought into the Center in 1981. Often the eagles were attracted to open bait sets.*

Compound 1080
REGISTERED TRADE MARK
Technical
SODIUM FLUOROACETATE

FATAL POISON

ANTIDOTE
Internal—Speed is essential. Immediately give a tablespoon of salt in a glass of warm water and repeat until vomit fluid is clear. Then give two tablespoonfuls of Epsom Salts in water. Have victim lie down and keep warm and quiet. Call A Physician Immediately!

**Manufactured by Tull Chemical Co., Inc.
Oxford, Alabama, U.S.A.**

which survived long enough for assessment of the severity of the injury, 85% had irreparable damage that would result in loss of the foot. Unfortunately, persons who are unfamiliar with the serious nature of this kind of injury would probably assume that they could release these birds from the trap 'without serious injury'," she continued.

The Raptor Research and Rehabilitation Program has treated many raptors that have been caught in traps, although most die before they receive treatment. In 1980, 33 eagles were treated at the center, 10 of which had been caught in leghold traps, and only one could be returned to the wild. (See "St. Paul's Haven for Broken Birds" by Don L. Johnson in *Defenders*, December, 1981.)

List the raptors protected by state or federal law as endangered or threatened species. All raptors were accorded protection by the Migratory Bird Treaty.

Check your state law on trapping. Are baits permitted? How often does the law require the trapper to visit his traps? Who checks to see whether each trapper visits each trap as required by law? How much manpower is assigned to enforcement of the law in this regard? How many violations have been observed in the past three years by the state Fish and Game Department? How many were successfully prosecuted? How many cases involved protected birds? How many involved the failure to inspect traps as frequently as the law required? Requirements on state trapping laws and information on trapping is contained in the Animal Welfare Institute's book, *Facts About Furs*. A free copy will be sent on request to any public or school library.

Is there an injured wildlife care center near you? What animals have they treated for leghold trap injury? How many were recovered enough to be released to the wild?

Poison

Toxicants intended to kill predators or rodents are another source of destruction for endangered birds. As those who feed birds in the winter know, insectivorous birds are fond of suet and meat scraps. Raptors and corvids such as ravens, crows and magpies are also attracted to meat baits. Find out whether any predator poisons are used in your area. Who puts them out? How are they supervised? What federal and state laws govern their use? Trace the status of predator poisons since 1973 when strychnine, 1080, thallium and cyanide were banned by Presidential Executive Order on federal lands, to 1982 when the Order was lifted. Write to wildlife conservation organizations, the Environmental Protection Agency, and Patuxent Wildlife Research Center for more information. The Environmental Protection Agency did studies on the effects of predator poisons on non-target wildlife and found that the highly toxic and painful poison, strychnine, was highly lethal to birds. Ask them for information on their studies.

Endangered Reptiles and Amphibians
**Dr. George Middendorf,
Department of Zoology, Howard
University, Washington, D.C.**

Most people, when asked to name an endangered species, would probably mention one of the well-known, highly publicized species, like the Snail Darter or the Whooping Crane, little realizing that many other plants and animals are also endangered or threatened. Many people do not know why they are endangered, why they should be protected, and how they can be saved. The probable causes of extinction should be examined and publicized.

Twenty-four species of native amphibians and reptiles are currently listed by the United States Endangered Species Act of 1973 (see table below); 17 of these are reptiles and seven are amphibians. Choose one of the species and, using the resources available in your school and community library and references listed at the end, write a brief description of its status and biology. You should include information on:

range — where the species is found. Is its present range diminished from its former range?

habitat — environment in which it lives, plants and vegetational needs, climate, and environment needed for feeding, breeding, etc.

description — what it looks like, size, male-female differences (sexual dimorphism).

ecology — other species with which it is interdependent (this is particularly interesting in relation to the Texas Blind Salamander — see page 155).

life history and reproductive biology — how old at sexual maturity, mode of reproduction, i.e. egg-laying or live-bearing, number of offspring per clutch, how many clutches per year, behavior towards young, life span, how many young could it produce in a lifetime under ideal circumstances?

feeding biology — where and what does it eat, how does it capture food?

movements — seasonal migration patterns.

behavior — types of interactions between individuals, reproductive behaviors involved in courtship, territorial behaviors, defense mechanisms.

major threats — habitat destruction, direct killing, etc. (see below) Much of this information may be found in the field guides listed in the bibliography. Additional information can be obtained from other sources.

Using the information you have gathered, decide why this species was placed on the endangered list. Obviously, the survival of the species is in doubt, but your task is to identify the factors which led to the present situation. Possibilities include habitat destruction, commercial exploitation, or absence of a large, stable population. If habitat destruction appears to be a causal factor, you should investigate the reason(s) for this. For instance, agricultural development, livestock degrading the habitat, urbanization (housing development, road construction), manipulation of aquatic habitat (damming, channelization), lumbering, mining, pollution, and pesticide usage are all possible causes of habitat destruction. You should consider whether the causal factor(s) is (are) natural or due to man's manipulation of the environment. Finally, you should discuss how these causal factors interact with the life history characteristic of the species to bring about its being placed on the endangered list. Discuss what is being done to increase members of this species. Is habitat being acquired? Are legal restrictions preventing killing or capture adequate and enforced? What are the long-term prospects for its survival? Do you have any suggestions for aiding this species? Does the state(s) in which it resides protect it? Are there state, organizational or private efforts to aid it?

Species of reptiles and amphibians within the United States protected by the Endangered Species Act:

Status: T—Threatened, E—Endangered

The **American Crocodile** is endangered in the United States, numbering less than 100 animals in the wild in Florida.

Photo by World Wildlife Fund

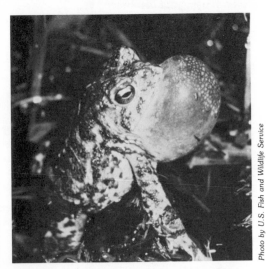

Almost all of the habitat of the **Houston Toad** *has been paved over or built on. It survives only in two tiny areas of eastern Texas which have been declared critical habitat by the Fish and Wildlife Service.*

Photo by U.S. Fish and Wildlife Service

Status	Amphibians
E	*Ambystoma macrodactylum croceum* — Santa Cruz Long-toed Salamander
E	*Batrachoseps aridus* — Desert Slender Salamander
E	*Bufo houstonensis* — Houston Toad
T	*Eurycea nana* — San Marcos Salamander
E	*Hyla andersonii* (Florida) — Pine Barrens Treefrog
T	*Phaeognathus hubrichti* — Red Hills Salamander
E	*Typhlomolge rathbuni* — Texas Blind Salamander

Status	Reptiles
*T&E	*Alligator mississippiensis* — American Alligator
T	*Caretta caretta* — Loggerhead Sea Turtle
**T&E	*Chelonia mydas* — Green Sea Turtle
E	*Chrysemys rubriventris bangsi* — Plymouth Red-bellied Turtle
E	*Crocodylus acutus,* American Crocodile
T	*Crotalus willardi obscurus* — New Mexican Ridge-nosed Rattlesnake
E	*Dermochelys coriacea* — Leatherback Sea Turtle
T	*Drymarchon corais couperi* — Eastern Indigo Snake
E	*Eretmochelys imbricata* — Hawksbill Sea Turtle
E	*Gambelia silus* — Blunt-nosed Leopard Lizard
T	*Gopherus agassizii* (Beaver Slope Dam, Utah) — Desert Tortoise
E	*Lepidochelys kempii* — Atlantic Ridley Sea Turtle
T	*Lepidochelys olivacea* — Olive Ridley Sea Turtle
T	*Nerodia fasciata taeniata* — Atlantic Salt Marsh Water Snake
E	*Thamnophis sirtalis tetrataenia* — San Francisco Garter Snake
T	*Uma inornata* — Coachella Valley Fringe-toed Lizard
T	*Xantusia riversiana* — Island Night Lizard

* American Alligator — E in all states except Florida, Georgia, Louisiana, South Carolina, Texas where T, unlisted in parts of Louisiana.

** Green Sea Turtle — E in Florida, T elsewhere.

Bibliography

Ashton, R.E., Jr. 1976. Endangered and threatened amphibians and reptiles in the United States. Soc. Study Amphib. and Rept., Herp. Circular No. 5, 65 pp.

Behler, J.L. and F.W. King. 1979. The Audubon Society field guide to North American reptiles and amphibians. Knopf, New York, 719 pp.

Bury, R. Bruce, C. Kenneth Dodd, Jr., Gary M. Fellers. 1980. Conservation of the Amphibia of the United States: A Review. United States Department of the Interior Fish and Wildlife Service Resource Publication #134, 34 pp.

Conant, R. 1975. A field guide to reptiles and amphibians of eastern and central North America. Houghton Mifflin, Boston, 429 pp.

Dodd, C.K., Jr. 1979. A bibliography of endangered and threatened amphibians and reptiles in the United States and its territories. Smithsonian Herpetological Information Service No. 46, 35 pp.

Dodd, C.K., Jr. 1981. A bibliography of endangered and threatened amphibians and reptiles in the United States and its territories: supplement. Smithsonian Herpetological Information Service No. 49, 16 pp.

The Fur Business

Photo © Dick Randall, Defenders of Wildlife

Badger *in leghold trap.*

To check on uses of fur bearing animals in your community, find out whether local hardware stores sell steel jaw, leghold traps. If they do, ask them to stop selling these indiscriminate devices that can catch any creature that unwarily sets off the jaws. Endangered species (for example, Bald Eagles) are often caught and lethally injured in their struggles to be free. Dogs and cats frequently have to have their paws amputated because the trap has cut off circulation and gangrene has set in. Show the hardware store owner what this trap does and why he should not provide means for further maiming of animals, whether domestic or wild.

Write to the Animal Welfare Institute for the most current information on this subject. AWI's book *Facts About Furs* will be sent free to any library on request. To learn how to carry out a project similar to that of high school student Richard Kramer, who has terminated steel trap sales through purchase and persuasion, write him at the International Ecology Society, 1471 Barclay St., St. Paul, MN 55106.

What kind of furs are most frequently advertised in your local newspaper? Are these furs raised on fur farms or trapped in the wild? The steel jaw, leghold trap is used to capture nearly all wild animals whose fur is sold in the United States and Canada, although 48 nations have banned the use of this cruel trap. How many animals does it take to make one coat? A survey conducted under the auspices of the U.S. Fish and Wildlife Service and Yale University shows that more than three-quarters of the American public wants the steel trap banned, but trappers and furriers do not want to switch to less painful capture methods.

Make an informational display on fur and trapping incorporating the facts you have learned.

Bats: Useful Insectivores and Pollinators

Many of the world's 950 species of bats are becoming endangered. Most bats are healthy and beneficial but misinformation and superstitious fear have led to their relentless persecution. Systematic programs of extermination have killed millions of bats in the name of public health. Only one-half of 1% of bats contract rabies. In the past 30 years, only ten people in the U.S. and Canada have died from the disease. Most problems involve people carelessly picking up obviously sick bats found out in the open or on the ground in the daytime. These should always be avoided, according to Dr. Merlin D. Tuttle, Curator of Mammals of the Milwaukee Public Museum, President and Co-Director of a new organization, Bat Conservation International (c/o Milwaukee Public Museum, Milwaukee, Wisconsin 53233). Dr. Tuttle and Stephen J. Kern discussed the disease problem in a paper, "Bats and Public Health" published by the Milwaukee Public Museum in 1981. It points out the rarity of bats transmitting disease to man and the serious consequences of many bat control programs, and comments, "Poisons used in bat control may seriously threaten humans as well, and cause sickened bats to scatter and fall to the ground, where they die slowly and may be picked up by inquisitive children or pets. Recently a single application of a toxicant resulted in a 700% increase in human contact with bats." Those who do the most to keep the public afraid of bats are usually those who profit from their destruction. Killing bats is lucrative in generating repeat business for the pest control industry, because in the absence of physical exclusion, dead bats eventually are replaced. Additional deleterious effects of pesticide use against bats involve environmental contamination and needless destruction of bats, whose value to medicine, research and insect control has long been acknowledged.

Nectar-feeding bats and some fruit bats pollinate over 130 genera (plural of genus) of plants. The co-evolution of many bats and plants, the latter evolving prominent, odiferous large flowers blooming at night with copious nectar and pollen and the former specialized tongues and muzzles for flower-feeding, and acute senses of sight and smell, is a fascinating study in itself.* Among plants that bats pollinate are valuable fruits, nuts and spices: plantain, bananas, breadfruit, mangos, guavas, avocados, almonds, cashews, cloves, vanillin, carob and figs. Many of these bats are disappearing however, as their caves are destroyed or they are killed. In Southeast Asia, one species, the Cave-dwelling Nectar-feeding Bat, pollinates the Durian tree, which produces fruit marketed for almost $90 million a year. This bat is being killed for food, and its caves quarried for limestone. Few people in the region, however, are aware that it is threatened with extinction. The Durian tree is believed to be pollinated exclusively by bats.

Find out which species of bats live in your area. Use reference books such as *Bats in America* by Roger W. Barber and Wayne H. Davis (University Press of Kentucky, 1969, also in paperback) and the chapter on bats by Dr. Merlin Tuttle in *Wild Animals of North America* National Geographic Society, 1979). Glover M. Allen's

*An excellent article on this subject, "Plant-loving Bats, Bat-loving Plants," was published in *Natural History* magazine in February, 1976, authored by Donna J. Howell.

Photos by Merlin Tuttle, Bat Conservation International

*How bats pollinate plants. The **Lesser Long-tongued Bat** (left) feeds on nectar while brushing against pollen. The **Greater Short-nosed Fruit Bat** (right) has pollen on its nose from a wild banana plant. When the bats fly off, some of the pollen grains are consumed in flight; others are transferred to the next flower the bat visits, thereby pollinating the plant.*

Fruit bats *in flight.*

Photo by Merlin Tuttle, Bat Conservation International

classic book, *Bats,* is available in a Dover paperback edition (1962) and provides much natural history information on bats.

Different species of bats can occupy the same general area, yet have different diets and habitats, or feed in differing environments. How do the bats in your area differ in these ways? What do they eat? Most bats consume large quantities of insects, making them among the most useful of all animals. One single Gray Bat, for example, can eat up to 3,000 insects nightly according to Bat Conservation International. A colony of 20 million Free-tailed Bats can eat a quarter of a million pounds of insects per night. Pesticides and poisons have killed off bats in many areas. Has there been bat control in your area? What do you calculate are the effects on the insect populations?

There are several endangered bat species in the United States. The United States Endangered Species Act list includes the following species:

Gray Bat, *Myotis grisescens*
Indiana Bat, *Myotis sodalis*
Ozark Big-eared Bat, *Plecotus townsendii ingens*
Virginia Big-eared Bat, *Plecotus townsendii virginianus*

All are listed as endangered. See the Appendix for the states that protect these and other bats and those listed on CITES and in the *Red Data Book*. The Indiana Bat's entire population winters in only a few caves in the U.S. Approximately 95% of the entire known Gray Bat population hibernates in only nine caves with more than half in a single cave in northern Alabama. The Fish and Wildlife Service and The Nature Conservancy have been intrumental in purchasing numerous caves to protect these species.

Using the criteria in the project on Endangered Reptiles and Amphibians, select one of the species of bats listed as endangered or threatened and do a study of its status, life history, and what is being done for it. For additional information, contact the Office of Endangered Species, U.S. Fish and Wildlife Service, Washington, DC 20240 or Bat Conservation International. The Biological Services Program of the U.S. Fish and Wildlife Service published short reports on the Gray Bat and the Indiana Bat in 1980, and the Fish and Wildlife Service produced a bibliography on the Indiana Bat in 1976 (Special Scientific Report—Wildlife No. 196). Other sources of information on endangered bats are the reports written on individual states' endangered species. (See the section on State Endangered Species Programs for a bibliography.)

Habitat

Using a copy of *The Red Data Book* prepared by the International Union for the Conservation of Nature and Natural Resources (1196 Gland, Switzerland), prepare maps showing the habitat of a threatened or endangered species or of several species with overlapping habitats.

Wildlife Rescue Centers

Find out whether there is a wildlife rescue center in your area. (See page 245 for a listing of some established centers.) Volunteer to help care for injured animals being rehabilitated. Help the center to raise funds necessary for food and medical supplies.

If there is no center specially for wildlife in trouble, ask your local humane society about its rescue work for wild and domestic animals. Does the society have an educational program involving wildlife? Offer to assist the organization in animal care and public information. All humane societies may obtain a free copy of each AWI book or manual including *First Aid and Care of Small Animals, Facts About Furs*, and *The Bird Business*. (See list of AWI publications, page 190.)

Endangered Species Game
by Denise Tindall

Objective:

This project is designed to introduce the topic of endangered species to 10th and 11th grade science students to develop their awareness of the need to study endangered species.

One week for lecture and discussion divided as follows:

Monday — lecture 45-minute period.
  a. What are endangered species? (definition)
  b. What animals are endangered? Name some.
  c. Why are plants and animals endangered, threatened or extinct? (an overview of ecology and the community).

Tuesday — lecture 45-minute period.
  a. The Endangered Species Act — the law itself and test cases.
  b. The Marine Mammal Protection Act.

Wednesday — lecture 45-minute period. Case studies of several species.

Thursday — lecture 30 minutes.

What can you do to help? Organizations, projects, education.

Last 15 minutes go over rules for JEOPARDY.

To find out what the students learned, I developed an educational game, JEOPARDY.

JEOPARDY is played in the same manner as the once-popular daytime game show. The player choses a category then selects a card for the Master of Ceremonies (teacher) to read aloud that will contain an ANSWER to a question. The object of the game is for the player to supply a QUESTION that will fit that answer. For example, the player chooses the category of marine mammals. After picking a card, the Master of Ceremonies reads: "A marine mammal found in Florida whose decline in numbers is rapidly increasing due to motor boats traveling too fast in inhabited waters and causing severe injuries and death with their propeller blades." The player should then correctly respond with, "What is a manatee?"

Equipment:

Prior to the actual playing of the game, I obtained one large sheet of mat board, upon which I glued 20 plastic carrying cases. The JEOPARDY board had these headings in magic marker:

  a. Birds and Fishes
  b. Reptiles and Amphibians
  c. Mammals
  d. Law and the Land

On 3 × 5 cards I wrote five questions per category. I also graded the difficulty of the questions and wrote cards out that had increasing monetary value ($10, 20, 30, 40, 50).

Procedure:

1. Set up three teams by dividing the class and selecting one captain per team.

2. The teacher will act as narrator, scorer and judge.

3. The game begins with a face-off question worth no monetary value, moderator reads the answer. Team with the answer must inform captain who will signal (ring bell). If the captain gives the correct answer, they may continue.

4. If the captain gives an incorrect answer (question) other teams may attempt to give the correct one.

5. Continue playing until the board is cleaned, tally up the monetary values and announce the winning team.

Exotic Pets

Over the past few years, wild pets have become very popular. Almost all wild animals sold in pet shops were captured in the wild. The consequences for wildlife have been disastrous. Species have often become rare or endangered from over-collecting, and mortality is very high from capture to pet shop. The Animal Welfare Institute's book, *The Bird Business* is a study of the commercial cage bird trade, pointing out that four wild birds die for each one that reaches the pet shop alive, and mortality continues to be high after the animals are sold. A free copy of the report on the cage bird trade will be sent to your school library at the librarian's request. Turtles, snakes and lizards have also become popular, and this trade has had similar consequences. In addition, turtles have been shown to transmit salmonella to people, and the Public Health Service banned the sale of one species some years ago. Sometimes wild mammals such as Raccoons are sold and these also were usually taken from the wild.

In many cases, wild animals fail to adjust to people's homes and die or become sick, or the owner finds that the beautiful parrot screams loudly at dawn and bites people, and the Raccoon grows up to be unruly and unmanageable.

Visit pet stores in your area and make lists of the wild animals being sold. Find out if there are captive-raised birds. Budgerigars, the little parakeets sold in most stores, are captive-bred, as are Cockatiels and Zebra Finches. These are not wild birds, but most parrots and macaws sold were captured in the wild. Look at the appendix in this book to see if any of the animals being sold are listed. One alert customer in New York City recently found a Thick-billed Parrot in a pet store. Since this Mexican parrot is an endangered species, and the store's owner did not have a permit, it was confiscated by the Fish and Wildlife Service. If you find an endangered bird, reptile or other animal, immediately contact the nearest office of the U.S. Fish and Wildlife Service.

Photo by U.S. Customs Service

*These baby **Yellow-naped Parrots** were seized as they were being smuggled into California. Their beaks were taped to keep them quiet. Up to 50,000 birds per year may enter the U.S. illegally and a large percentage die in the process from asphyxiation, shock or stress-induced illness.*

Check the pet store also for cleanliness and see whether you think the animals are healthy. Find out from the state Attorney General if there are state laws pertaining to pet store sale of wild animals. If so, get copies and see if the stores are cooperating. Some states such as Connecticut ban the sale of Monk Parakeets. Florida and California have many restrictions on the sale of wild animals. Urge your local pet store to sell only captive-raised and domestic animals.

If the animals are being kept in dirty cages and seem unhealthy, write or call your local humane society, and the Animal and Plant Health Inspection Service, U.S. Department of Agriculture, Washington, DC 20782. The Animal Welfare Institute is interested in hearing about your research.

Evaluating Your Local Zoo
by Peter Batten

Photo by R. Scott Chilcote

The **Atlas** or **Barbary Lion,** *Panthera leo leo, became extinct in its native North Africa in 1922. Lions which are nearly identical genetically to the Atlas Lion survive in zoos.*

The following series of questions were prepared by Peter Batten, author of Living Trophies *(Thomas Y. Crowell Company, N.Y. 1976).*

On your next visit to a zoo, look beyond the public relations brochures and "endangered species" signs, and check the following:

Are pens and cages of adequate size; can the animals walk at least four times their own length?

Does the animal have free access to sanctuary from visitors; is there a "den" in the cage? (Or are inside shelter doors closed; no box or den provided?)

Do "daytime" animals have adequate light and/or sun? (Or are they in dark interior cages with no access to outside runs or ultraviolet light?)

Is food eaten promptly at feeding time? (Or is there leftover food on floors and dishes?)

Are cages clean and sanitary? (Or are stools and urine on the floor; are stools loose?)

Is there clean drinking water, free of algae and debris, in all cages?

Are nocturnal animals able to avoid direct or bright light?

Are young animals with parents? (Or labeled "rejected" in a glass-fronted nursery?)

Do hoofed animals walk easily? (Or do they look as if they're wearing snowshoes?)

Are great apes active? Do they have company and things to do? (Or are they in small pens, alone, with nothing to do but sleep and eat?)

Are keepers close to animal exhibits, supervising visitors? Are they working? On what?

Do elephants and other large animals have rubbing posts or mounds in their pens?

Are bars or other restraint methods safe? (Or are there sharp spikes or other fixtures which might harm the animals?)

If exhibits are water-moated, are there visible means of escape for animals should they fall in?

Do dry-moated exhibits have a heavy layer of soft material (hay, straw, etc.) to protect animals if they fall?

Do birds have at least two separate perches or roosts? (Or can they fly only into walls, fences, or floor if frightened?)

Are the animals at the front of the cage, and do they appear alert and relaxed? (Or are they curled up near the back of the exhibit, or pacing nervously?)

Are birds in open areas able to fly? (Or are their wings pinioned?—look for short wings when they stretch)

Do birds in aviaries have ample flight space and height? (Or are perches difficult to reach except by helicopter?)

Do cages or dens have artificial heat or cooling installed; on a warm day do animals breathe normally?

Which endangered species are bred in zoos?

Do all animals have free access to a choice of heat, shade, light?

Are marine mammals kept in salt water; are the pools large, round or oval, and with adequate haul-out space, and a suitable color? (Or does the color of the pool reflect sunlight?) Is the water absolutely clear and clean? (Or is fish debris floating on top and bottom?)

Are sea lions active and alert? (Discount visitor-fed seals begging.) Are they fed by hand, individually? (Or are fish thrown to them in the pool?) Are their eyes a dark, lustrous brown? (Or are they closed, slightly closed, or opaque bluish-white?) Do they appear to be in generally good condition? (They should look rubbery with no visible vertebrae or ribs.)

Do animals that naturally dig in the earth have a floor which permits this activity? (Or are they on concrete, bricks, tile, or other synthetic material?)

The first part of each question should be answered YES. If this is not so, ask to see the zoo director or his assistant—not the public relations person or "educational curator"—and ask WHY.

It should be mentioned here that captive animals need continual attention and living quarters that approximate their own environment.

Students should be made aware of the thoughtless exploitations that are imposed on non-domesticated animals and that they can help by staying alert in observing the way the inhabitants are treated in zoos and animal parks.

Cruel treatment or unhealthy conditions can be reported to the Animal Welfare Institute, P.O. Box 3650, Washington, D.C. 20007.

Learning Centers

Drawing by Marcus Redditt

The **American Bison** has been brought back from the edge of extinction. How did this happen?

Establishing learning centers in the classroom has proven to be a valuable aid in education. Some good suggestions for categories are "Animal Communities," "Predation" and "Extinct is Forever" centers. Place activity cards in each learning center. Suggested activities are listed below:

1) Name some animals which have become extinct in the U.S. since 1800. What were some of the reasons the animal became extinct?
2) List the animals in your state that are on the state and/or federal endangered species list. Choose one of these animals and write a report on the forces pushing your species towards extinction. What is being done to protect your species?
3) Establish a vocabulary list including such terms as: adaptive radiation, adaptation, endangered, extinct, reproductive rate, threatened.
4) Distinguish between threatened and endangered. What do the different classifications mean in terms of federal legislation?
5) What federal and state laws protect threatened or endangered animals?
6) At one time, some species were nearly extinct, but have now been "brought back" to some extent. Select one of these species and explain the methods used to help the species. (Examples: Whooping Crane, Tule Elk, Bison).
7) Select an endangered species and describe its habitat.
8) How does the reproductive rate of a species affect its population?
9) Write a letter to a national conservation group and ask about its goals and objectives.

10) Write a letter to a knowledgeable individual or organization and request information on an endangered species that you have selected for study. Share your information with the class.
11) Explain the difference between habitat and niche—give examples.
12) What animals used to live where your school now stands? What factors have caused the animals to move, adapt, or die?

Broadening Horizons

Following is a list of project ideas which can be developed by students or teachers in cooperation with other classes such as Art, Music, Dance, History, and English.

Dance

Earthworks: A Ballet-in-Residence Project

A project conducted by the New York City Public Schools in 1982 could be adapted for use by other schools through consultation with Martita Goshen, the ballerina/choreographer who has created dances centered on endangered whales, sea turtles and wolves. The goals of the program are to develop awareness of these and other endangered creatures, a sense of responsibility for the environment, and the interrelationships of these species and mankind within the physical environment.

The auditorium presentation begins with the 12-minute National Geographic Society film, "A Portrait of a Whale." Next, Martita dances, with commentary. Volunteers from the audience execute quick runs and are asked to stop in mid run; the shapes that ensue are called forward lunges (breaches in whales) and skids (as in wolf lopes)—depending on the placement of the hips and shoulders where students come to a halt. The smallest movement can be used and developed—from a stretched palm to a fist—as in each of the listed species, a discussion of dynamics follows: percussive and sustained walks, jumps such as a whale and wolf would execute. The silence and beauty of these endangered species is described. Humans forget the alacrity and precision needed to survive in the wilderness so often invaded by predators. An artist/teacher conference follows to help integrate the materials offered with in-school academics.

On the second day, Martita works with two classes doing whale-pod patterns and wolf travel patterns—movement patterns are done in lines, circles, in canon and syncopated. Other interested teachers join the sessions at which Martita explains the science of movement in three forms of dance as related to wolves, whales, seals and sea turtles; Modern (fall and recovery) represent whale dynamics; Jazz (isolation) for wolves; and Ballet (spine/pelvis) for sea turtles and seals. The movement workshops focus on major characteristics of each species.

Whales: Using soft runs, suspended movements, runs are done in arcs and entwining ribbon floor patterns, small jetés, sissones, deep, bending jumps in which the arms follow the shape of the back. To feel suspension—students raise arms, with shoulders in place and

Martita Goshen *teaching a whale ballet.*

Photo by Mary Bloom

down, and slowly melt them down; heels are raised and lowered very slowly—a basketball pivot is discussed and done in slow motion.

Wolves: Jazz isolations with shoulders, isolated scratches, different gaited runs, use of face, especially the eyes. Bent over positions, circle patterns with students running into center of circle to execute a position.

Seals: Emphasis on spine—everyone lies on floor, stomach down, and tries to lift arms and legs in arch; walks down on arms, lifting backs and dragging feet—use of ankles, legs on side while lying on one hip.

Sea Turtles: Use of pressure and weight—emphasis of arms, hands, pairing students to show leverage of weight in water; two students press against each other's backs and when balance of weight is equal, the students will press against each other, into a standing position.

Finally, the two participating classes share what they have learned with the school as a whole by performing a 3-minute "movement choir." There is a culminating phrase that is taught (see film) to be done to Paul Winter's "Lullabye" or "Songs of the Humpback Whale." It is like a movement choir, done standing or in chairs.

The program can be adapted for all age levels. Workshops preceded the school residencies and included a talk by a teacher in the Science Unit entitled "Integrating the Arts and Science—Endangered Species."

A *video cassette* showing Martita's work with the New York City Schools is available on loan from the Animal Welfare Institute. Teachers may also write to Martita in care of AWI.

Martita Goshen leading a celebration of Earth Day, May, 1982, for an enthusiastic audience of New York Public School students and teachers.

Photo by Mary Bloom

Music

Compose a song to help endangered species, a tribute to a particular species or a general category of wild creatures—songbirds or sea mammals, for example, both of whom are well represented with recordings of their songs or sounds.

For example, a song recently composed by a student at Florida State University and often sung by a popular student quartet celebrates the music of song birds. A group of singers at your school might develop a repertoire focusing on wildlife.

The famous quintet by Franz Schubert, entitled "The Trout," has been transposed as a song with piano accompaniment. A symphonic piece that incorporates segments of recorded songs of the Humpback Whale was composed by Hovaness and could be adapted for human voices, too. A record narrated by Robert Redford has remarkable wolf voices with musical howls readily repeatable by a good mimic. Paul Winter has accompanied a wolf on the saxophone, and his recording, "Common Ground," is one which a vocal group could join in and transpose.

Organize a concert, including songs you and other students of music compose about endangered species or other wild creatures, and music by established composers which relate to animals, for example, Tchaikovsky's music for the ballet "Swan Lake." Include bird and mammal voices from records. Some are very surprising, for example, the walrus, recorded under water, sounds like a gong. The variety of calls of the loon sometimes resemble a human voice. Include human imitations of animal voices such as whales and wolves. These will be most impressive if a number of people join in a chorus. Such a concert could also feature songs about or with animals, for example, Crosby and Nash's "To the Last Whale" or Paul Horn's recording with Haida, the orca who responds to the flute solo.

Records

Antarctica. Edwin J. Mickleburgh, 1971. Saydisc Specialized Recordings Ltd., The Barton, Inglestone Common, Badminton, Glos, GL9 1BX, ENGLAND.

Bird Songs in Literature. From the Sound of Nature Series. Joseph Wood Krutch and the Cornell Laboratory of Ornithology, 1967. For additional information on other wildlife recordings from the Sound of Nature Series write: Laboratory of Ornithology, Cornell University, Ithaca, N.Y. 14850. Houghton Mifflin Co.

Callings. Paul Winter, 1980. A & M Records, Inc., P.O. Box 782, Beverly Hills, CA 90213.

Common Ground. Paul Winter, 1978. A & M Records, Inc.

The Edge of the Meadow. James Baird, 1969. Droll Yankees Inc., Providence, RI 02906.

The Gibbons. Joe and Elsie Marshall. John William and Carol K. Hardy, ARA Records, 1615 N.W. 14th Avenue, Gainesville, FL 32605.

Haida and Paul Horn. Paul Horn. Sealand of the Pacific.

Paul Horn: Inside II. Paul Horn, 1972. Epia Records.

Hovaness And God Created Great Whales. Andre Kostelanetz. Columbia Masterworks.

The Language and Music of the Wolves. Narrated by Robert Redford, 1971. Natural History Magazine, Central Park West at 79th Street, New York, N.Y. 10024.

EXISTENCE

Words & Music by:
ED LIVINGSTON JR.

A long time a-go when this world be-gan. God made a mam-mal, the big-gest in the land. This mam-mal lived in water, It breathed like you and me, It mat-ed and had ch-il-dren, Its home the vast blue sea, Its home the vast blue sea, Its home the vast blue sea. Then came man's pol-lu-tion, plastic, oil, and waste. The o-ceans slow-ly choked and died, man had changed their face. Not con-tent with his des-truc-tion, man chased the mam-mals too, so-nar, har-poon, whal-ing ship, a plane in which he flew, a plane in which he flew, a plane in which he flew. At first, a day brings only one, then it's three or four, a whal-er knows no lim-it. He sear-ches on for more. No one's there to stop him, noth-ing does he fear. Not an ounce of ca-ring, he sheds not one small tear, he sheds not one small tear, he sheds not one small tear. So, now we li-ve, in fear of death and pain. For the lone-ly wha-le there's noth-ing left to gain. God a-lone can save him, from man's gree-dy need, Will we learn our les-son? Hu-man-i-ty take heed, Hu-man-i-ty take heed, Hu-man-i-ty take heed.

Night of the Four Moons; Voice of the Whale. George Crumb, 1974. Columbia Records.

Songs of the Forest. Peter Kilham and Alfred Hawkes, 1964. Droll Yankees Inc., Providence, RI 02906.

Songs of the Humpback Whale. Roger Payne, 1970. Capitol Records.

Songs of Insects. From the Sound of Nature Series. Peter Paul Kellogg and Arthur A. Allen, for the Laboratory of Ornithology, Cornell University. 1956. Houghton Mifflin Co.

Sounds of Nature: A Day at Flores Moradas, W.W. H. Gunn, 1968. Houghton Mifflin Co., Boston, MA.

Sounds and the Ultra-Sounds of the Bottle-nose Dolphin. Dr. John C. Lilly, 1973. Folkway Records, 43 W. 61st Street, New York.

Voices of the Loon. William Barklow, 1980. North American Loon Fund, Meredith, N.H. 03253. Also available from National Audubon Society.

Wind on the Water. "To the Last Whale." David Crosby and Graham Nash, 1975. ABC Records.

Art

Make drawings of the animals and plants that are threatened, endangered or now extinct in your state. Consult David Day's "Doomsday Book of Extinct Animals," 1981, your state wildlife agency, and departments of ecology and botany in your state universities. Present a show of the drawings or bind them into a book for your school library.

Making Drawings of Endangered Species in Different Styles

Look at the drawings in this Handbook by different artists. *Alice in Wonderland,* by Lewis Carroll, was first illustrated by Sir John Tenniel, a leading nineteenth century artist. A sketch he made of the Dodo, before making the final drawing of Alice and the Dodo, is reproduced on page 10. Try making a copy. Use a hard pencil, sharpened to a fine point. Try to master his technique so you can use it to draw another bird.

The brush and ink drawing of a Duck-billed Platypus on page 187 was made by a contemporary Australian artist, Brett Whitely. It is three feet in height and hangs in the Australian Embassy in Washington, D.C. The Ambassador kindly gave permission for the Animal Welfare Institute to reproduce it in the Handbook. Using a large sheet of paper, a watercolor brush and black ink, try making a freehand copy. Look at an animal or a photograph of an animal and try using this technique to draw it in the style of Brett Whitely.

The drawing of a mouse lemur on page 25 was done by a young American artist, Marcus Redditt. The delicacy of his pen and ink description of the lemur and its habitat is worth trying to imitate. Try your hand at it, using a fine-point pen, black India ink, and smooth, white paper. Try another drawing in this style, either from life or from a photograph. Use pen and ink to copy the rhinoceros by Albrecht Dürer, page 203. Try a painting based on the tiger by Eugene Delacroix, page 74, or the cranes by Korin on page 201.

If you would like to paint some endangered species in color ask your librarian to help you find colored photographs of endangered birds, mammals, reptiles or amphibians.

Mount your drawings and join with other interested students in presenting an art show of endangered species.

Drawing by Brett Whiteley

"Pen-Pal"

Write to a student in another country about an endangered species in that country. Write your letter in the language of the country. Tell your correspondent about a U.S. endangered species and about the need for protection of such species. Ask him or her to write to you about a native species that is threatened or endangered.

Simon Muchiru of the Wildlife Clubs of Kenya writes:

Discover Endangered Wildlife Through a "Pen-Pal"

The African wildlife is nature's gift to mankind, part of the world's heritage. Some of the wildlife is now endangered or threatened with extinction. The young people of Africa are committed to saving it. They would like to share the information on these animals with you.

There are wildlife clubs in several English and French speaking countries in Africa in primary schools through university colleges. If you would like to share information on endangered species of Africa, you can get a pen-pal through the wildlife clubs. I can help you get in touch with these clubs in Africa. If you wish to do so, please write to me and I will help you wherever I can. They would also love to know about your wildlife.

My address is: Simon Muchiru
Environmental Liaison Center
P.O. Box 72461
Nairobi, KENYA

A few names and addresses of others to whom you can write to find a correspondent who shares your interest in the protection of endangered species are given below.

Sra. Anna Chaves Quiroz
Programa de Education Ambiental
Universidad Estatal a Distancia
Apdo. 2, Plaza Gonzalez Viquez
San José
COSTA RICA, Central America

Sr. Julio Jaen
Asociación Estudiantil para la Conservación Ambiental (AECA)
c/o Smithsonian Tropical Research Institute
APO
Miami, FL 34002

Erika Sela
Julian Hernandez 8
Madrid 33
SPAIN

Beauty Without Cruelty
c/o Mrs. Jean Meade
112 Aberdeen Place
Whangamata
NEW ZEALAND

Frédéric Henry
Animaux Informations Jeunes
B.P. 74 35403
Saint-Malo Cedex
FRANCE

Photo by S. Price

Simon Muchiru *has begun a worldwide network of young people who want to help wildlife.*

Literature   Write a poem or prose tribute to a threatened or endangered species. Write an accompanying essay on human obligations to other species. Discuss speciesism as defined by philosophers such as Peter Singer and Tom Regan. How does it relate to extinction of species? Make a collection of poems that refer to rare or endangered creatures, for example, William Blake's "Tiger, tiger burning bright," Samuel Taylor Coleridge's "Rime of the Ancient Mariner" (who killed an albatross), Edgar Allan Poe's "Raven." Make a booklet of them, or, with members of a drama group, present a reading of the poems.

The following poem by David Day, author of *The Doomsday Book of Animals,* is a personal reflection on the extinction of the Elephant Bird of Madagascar.

Silhouettes by Esta Belcher

The Roc's Egg by David Day
Elephant Bird—Extinct 1700

i.
This was the Roc
that Sinbad knew and Aladdin
For its size we called it
Elephant Bird
Towering ten feet out of the earth
Daggers for talons and a half-ton bulk
Its dark shape crossed the dunes in great strides
blocking out the Malagasy sun

The tiny whirling forms
of scavenging men fleeing
Each clutched a huge egg
to his narrow breast

ii.
The egg was the talisman
Three foot round, shell thick as a gold coin
Alive within—one vast living cell
It was its own world

Like seers we held it
heavily in two hands
One egg to feed a village or a ship's crew
We drained it of life

iii.
This was not a phoenix
None would arise from the flame
of its destruction
But the bird of the Apocalypse

The egg itself was the revelation:

White world, barren desert of chalk
or empty sunbleached skull

Vision of our world to come

Resources

Teachers' Aids

Source Guidelines

Regan, Alison. 1982. *Directory of Marine Education Resources.* Center for Environmental Education, Washington, D.C., 90 pages.

Smith, J.M. 1978. *Endangered Species: An Educator's Handbook.* Wilderness Graphics, Tallahassee, Florida, 50 pages.

Magazines & Newsletters

The American Biology Teacher published by the National Association of Biology Teachers, 1420 N St. NW, Washington, DC 20005

The Instructor published by The Instructor Publications, Inc., Dansville, NY 14437. Distributes endangered species posters with reading lists and teacher references

NAEE Newsletter published by the National Association for Environmental Education, P.O. Box 1295, Miami, Florida 33143

National Geographic School Bulletin published by the National Geographic Society (see Organizations)

Scholastic News Explorer, 50 West 44th Street, N.Y. NY 10036

Materials

Endangered Species Issue Pac. Folder with 3 lesson plans, poster & endangered species puzzle. U.S. Dept. of the Interior, Fish and Wildlife Service, Office of Extension Education, Washington, DC 20240

Florida's Manatee, An Educator's Guide. Bound 64-page publication which discusses the status, causes of decline, what is being done, suggested reading, films, classroom and field activities; questionnaire, illustrated. Florida Audubon Society in cooperation with the Office of Education and Information, Florida Dept. of Natural Resources. 1980.

Issue Pacs: *Whales, Seals* and *Sea Turtles.* Folders with general information pages, and individual sheets on ten or more species. All include suggested activities and are illustrated. Center for Environmental Education, 1925 K St. N.W., Suite 206, Washington, DC 20006

Endangered Species Publications

Endangered Species Packet #1—16 pages
The Sperm Whale—54 pages
Legions of the Night (bats)—20 pages
The Northern Bottlenose Whale
Teaching About Endangered Species, 18 pages
The Bald Eagle, 12 pages
The Polar Bear, 11 pages
Biological Diversity, 50 pages
The Need for Comprehensive Wildlife Programs in the United States: A Summary by John H. Fitch, 23 pages
The "Economizing" of Ecology: Why Big Rare Whales Still Die—130 pages

The above publications from Center for Action on Endangered Species, 175 West Main Street, Ayer, MA 01432, priced at $5 or less, many with posters and illustrated.

Exhibits

The Audubon Ark is a traveling educational exhibit on endangered species. Contact the National Audubon Society for its itinerary.

Publications available from The Animal Welfare Institute

Whales vs. Whalers: A Continuing Commentary—Articles published from 1971 to 1981 in the *AWI Information Report* $3

Outlaw Whalers by Greenpeace International, 1980, 32 pages; 1981, 24 pages, $5 each

How to Liven Up Your Classroom with a Pod of Whales, for teachers, 2 pages, free

A Whale of a Friend, article reprint from *Toronto Star,* free

Humpbacks, The Gentle Whales, Jan. 1979 issue of *The National Geographic* with a special sound sheet recording, "Songs of the Humpback Whale" with commentary by Roger Payne, Ph.D., $1.50

Campaign Materials—Save the Whales, write for list

International Trade in Wildlife by Tim Inskipp and Sue Wells. Published by Earthscan, London, 1979, 104 pages, $3

Rare and Endangered Birds, 108 pages, free to teachers

Endangered, Threatened and Unique Mammals of the Southern National Forests, U.S. Forest Service, 121 pages, free to teachers

Mexico: The Turtles are Gathering for Their Nesting Season Massacre, reprint from the *IUCN Bulletin,* free

The Shame of Escobilla by Tim Cahill, reprinted from *Outside,* an eyewitness account of the mass killing of sea turtles in Mexico, free

Help for Hooked Birds, by Ralph Heath, Jr., Pete Van Allen and Dr. Harold Albers, pamphlet on care of birds snared by fish hooks and lines, free

Facts About Furs by Greta Nilsson, Christine Stevens and John Gleiber. AWI publication, 1980, 257 pages, free to humane societies and libraries, to others $4

Let Us Live, leaflet on trapping in color, free

Animals and Their Legal Rights by Emily Leavitt and other authors. Summary of laws affecting welfare of animals in the U.S., third ed. 1978, AWI publication, 215 pages, free to libraries and humane societies on request, others $4

Attitudes Towards Animals, by Christine Stevens, reprint from the American Biology Teacher, 3 pages, free

Regulations for Animal Experimentation in Science Fairs, new humane rules for Canadian Science Fairs, 1975, free

Live Organisms in High School Biology, by Barbara F. Orlans, Ph.D., reprint from the American Biology Teacher, 3 pages, Nov. 1970, free

Statement on Animals in Secondary Schools by Dr. W.W. Armistead, Institute for Agriculture, Univ. Tennessee, 1 page, free

First Aid and Care of Small Animals by Ernest P. Walker, designed for use by teachers in primary and secondary schools. Free to teachers, librarians, humane societies and scout leaders. To others $3

The Bird Business. A Study of the Commercial Cage Bird Trade by Greta Nilsson, with a Foreword by S. Dillon Ripley and a chapter by Tim Inskipp. AWI publication, 1981, 121 pages, illus. Free to teachers and librarians. To others, $5

Films

An amazing variety of films on wildlife and the environment has been produced since 1970. Prior to 1970, which marked the first Earth Day, dramatic wildlife films were a rarity.

The educational value of good wildlife films is significant, because the audience reached may be far greater than for the written word. Films can spark interest in wildlife and teach a remarkable number of lessons on habitat, status, behavior and ecology with a minimum of words.

Undoubtedly some valuable films have been omitted from our list, but every attempt was made to seek out and preview all pertinent films. All are in color unless otherwise noted. The title is listed first, and length of film, followed by the producer and the distributor.

Endangered Species — General

At the Crossroads, 26 minutes; Stouffer Productions; Penn State University, 1975.

This film has appeared on television and is an excellent introduction into the problems of North America's endangered species. It shows drawings of extinct species as well, illustrating how easily species' extinctions can occur. It is well-produced and written and has excellent, dramatic photography.

The Business of Extinction, 50 minutes; WGBH; King Features Entertainment.

A film in the NOVA educational TV series, "The Business of Extinction" is a very hard-hitting documentary about wildlife trade. The emphasis is on both the rampant smuggling and illegal trade in such species as tiger, leopard, reptile skins and live birds. The film makers actually went undercover to obtain footage of animal smugglers in Asian forests. The trade in wild pets, the negative effects of collecting for zoos, and the value of the Convention on International Trade in Endangered Species (CITES) are all discussed in depth. This documentary shows the extreme greed and shocking insensitivity to animal mortality occurring in so many parts of the world. Scenes include shots of cockatoos seized from a Los Angeles importer when illegally brought into the U.S. from Indonesia to satisfy the new "cockatoo craze" brought about by the TV program "Baretta"; a shop in Singapore with 15 stuffed tigers; piles of python skins ready to be shipped to the Netherlands which has not yet signed the CITES; and interviews with animal dealers, smugglers and conservationists. Since this film was made, many more countries have signed the Convention, but wildlife traffic has not substantially decreased, and it remains an excellent exposé of the wildlife trade.

Last Chance, 27½ minutes; National Zoological Park; Bullfrog Films, Inc., 1979.

The 3000-acre breeding compound of the National Zoo at Front Royal, Virginia, is the scene of most of the productive breeding programs of the zoo's many endangered species. It allows the rare Père David's Deer enough habitat to establish territories and fight over harems, for example. This species exists only in zoos and it is fortunate that at least one zoo is able to provide it with an environment not unlike its original home in China. Other endangered animals kept at Front Royal are Persian Wild Asses, Scimitar-horned Oryx, Golden-lion Marmosets, South American Bushdogs, and several species of rare birds. The dialogue and photography tend to be somewhat dry and the sequences are not well-organized to give a coherent message, but the film has much educational value.

Memories from Eden, 57 minutes; WGBH; Time-Life Films, 1977.

This NOVA film, produced for educational TV, examines zoos and their role as educators and conservers of wildlife. It is a balanced view with both critics and proponents speaking out. Various zoos are toured and innovative approaches to animal exhibition and captive breeding of endangered species are explored.

The Predators, 50 minutes; Stouffer Productions, 1977.

This film presents a sympathetic view of such victims of predator control and prejudice as the wolf, Bobcat, and Grizzly Bear, species that play major ecological roles. These and other predators (alligators, Bald Eagles and otters) are shown in their beneficial roles, which have not been recognized by many ranchers, hunters, trappers or even game managers. This film gives an uncompromising educational view of predators and a plea for their conservation.

Say Goodbye, 52 minutes; Wolper; Films Inc., 1970. Penn State.

When "Say Goodbye" appeared on television in 1970, the sensational response from the public surprised its sponsor, the Quaker Oats Company. Its approach to the disappearance of endangered species is direct. Sequences of rare and endangered species of the U.S. concentrate on birds and mammals with dramatic dialogue and songs. One shot of a female Polar Bear with two cubs was greatly criticized when it later developed that it showed biologists temporarily immobilizing the bear rather than trophy hunters killing it; there is now an explanatory note included in the film to make this clear. On the whole its impact is very strong in motivating desire to protect endangered species, and it is therefore highly recommended.

A Time for Choice: The Story of Georgia's Endangered Wildlife, 27 minutes; Georgia Department of Natural Resources, 1978.

This is a good film on endangered species in Georgia. Its dialogue on general causes pushing wildlife to near extinction is somewhat vague, but on specific species, the explanations are clear and well-presented. This is one of the few films which does not ignore the "unlovable ones" — salamanders, fish, bats and snakes for example. It would also be useful for other states since many of the animals are found elsewhere (whales, sea turtles, Peregrine Falcons, Brown Pelicans, alligators), and it gives specific information on what states can do for endangered species.

The Vanishing Breed, 20 minutes, Man Builds, Man Destroys Series; Great Plains Instructional TV Library.

Our Vanishing Wildlife, 11 minutes; A.J. Milton Salzburg; Macmillan Films.

Endangered Animals: Will They Survive? 22 minutes, Encyclopedia Britannica Corp., 1977

There are very few films on the problem of endangered species as a whole. These three films are all mediocre, but have good moments here and there. One of the problems in making such a film is that it quickly becomes dated. "The Vanishing Breed" has whaling photos that are effective in showing the cruelty, but gives harvest figures long outdated. There are rare photos of snared animals in this film, such as an elephant with its trunk nearly bisected by a wire snare, slowly wandering as it starves to death. "The Vanishing Breed" suggests game ranching, or heavy cropping of Africa's ungulates for food, as a possible solution to saving the habitat, and this concept is still being hotly debated. "Our Vanishing Wildlife" is a short and overly dramatic film on the value of a swamp, and the wildlife that is dependent on it. "Endangered Animals: Will They Survive?" is a disconnected film — scenes shift suddenly from Cheetahs being raised in captivity which they describe very naively as for reintroduction, now thought difficult to impossible, to a raging fire in the Everglades described in vague and confusing terms. There are some excellent shots in this film of Black-footed Ferrets courting, and it makes the point that wildlife as a whole is being crowded out by man's activities. The causes of endangered species are not explored very coherently, however.

Zoos of the World, 52 minutes; National Geographic Society, 1970.

A world-wide tour of zoos, this film is less objective than "Memories of Eden", the NOVA special, but is interesting nonetheless. It shows the insectarium at Tokyo's Tama Zoo, white tigers in the New Delhi Zoo, pandas and other endangered species in the world's zoos.

Endangered Environments—World

Animals of the Living Reef, 15 minutes; Educational Media Corp; Centron Films.

This film is aimed at junior high and and high school levels. The Great Barrier Reef off Australia is filmed and the ecology of the coral reef is explained. This film has beautiful photography, solid information and is fast-moving. It does not have a conservation message, however, and is included because coral reefs are among the most diverse and threatened of all ecosystems. Knowledge about them is important for everyone to acquire and few films are available explaining these marvelous areas.

An Ecosystem: Struggle for Survival, 22 minutes; National Geographic Society, 1975.

This film focuses on one of the most threatened ecosystems in the world, the Gir Forest of India. The Gir is the home of Asia's last lions and other endangered species, and it is the last of the entire region's forests. The effects on the ecosystem of livestock are seen with clarity and objectivity. This may be a sampling of tomorrow's conflicts in other parts of the world as the human population approaches five billion.

The Galapagos: Darwin's World Within Itself, 20 minutes; Encyclopedia Britannica Educational Corp., 1971.

This film explores the islands' unique environment and wildlife, and quotes Darwin's observations which led to his theory of evolution. It shows man's harmful influence on delicate ecosystems, islands being a prime example. See also Reptiles and Amphibians: "The Galapagos Tortoise."

Voyage to the Enchanted Isles, 54 minutes; CBS; BFA, 1969.

A longer film than that done by Encyclopedia Britannica, this CBS documentary gives an in-depth look at the Galapagos Islands, Darwin's theory of evolution and the need to preserve endangered species there.

Island of the Moon: Madagascar, 60 minutes; Canadian Broadcasting Corp., 1979.

The environmental destruction on Madagascar was described in Chapter 1. This film shows many of the island's unique wildlife species (lemurs, birds, reptiles and endemic plants) and shows forest burning, an activity which has destroyed so many species. It was voted best film of the 1981 International Wildlife Film Festival.

Kôrup—An African Rain Forest, 50 minutes; Partridge Films, 1981.

Five years in the making, this remarkable film records many of the creatures and plants that inhabit the Kôrup rain forest in the Cameroon. Botanists and zoologists erected scaffolds hundreds of feet high to take some unusual and beautiful shots of tree-top wildlife. Nectar-covered flowers hanging from a high tree attract bats and other night creatures which pollinate them. Other mammals and birds are seen feeding on them during their short flowering period. The fragility and beauty of the forest, which World Wildlife Fund is raising funds to acquire, are described in a sensitive, interesting narrative.

Life in a Tropical Forest, 30 minutes; Time-Life Films.

The teeming richness of tropical forests is a delicate ecosystem being decimated by agricultural development. The interrelationships among tropical forest species are very complex with no waste of energy. This film explains the basics of how tropical forests function, concentrating on Barro Colorado Island in Panama, site of a Smithsonian Institution tropical research station. The conservation message is not a major element, but like the coral reef film, it can teach about the myriad diversity and beauty of the ecosystem.

Endangered Habitats—North America

Atchafalaya, 26 minutes; C.C. Lockwood; Marty Stouffer, Stouffer Productions, 1975.

This region of Louisiana covers 1½ million acres and is the largest bottomland swamp in the U.S. Its wildlife, the seasonal changes in water table and their effect on wildlife, as well as on the Cajun fishermen who depend on its bounty are the subjects of this film which stresses the importance of preserving it. The fate of the Atchafalaya has been hotly debated for many years. In 1982, decisions on acquiring a large percentage of the swamp for conservation were made.

The Big Thicket, A Vanishing Wilderness, 21 minutes; Jim East Associates. Coronet Instructional Films, 1970.

A relaxed and fascinating tour of the Big Thicket of east Texas, a wilderness that once covered 3½ million acres. Less than 300,000 acres remain, and even now 50 acres a day are disappearing to the chainsaw which drones ominously in the background of the opening of this film. The steps of a naturalist are followed as he encounters the unique flora and fauna and describes it to his companions. The viewer has a sense of being there, of discovering carnivorous pitcher plants and sundews trapping ants on their sticky leaves, gawky heron chicks in huge stick nests, and huge old trees. The photography of wild flowers is particularly brilliant as is the old footage of timber cutting which slowly destroyed these vast piney woods. Bogs and streams intersperse the Big Thicket, and the naturalist paddles about in a canoe expressing his quiet appreciation of the natural wonders in a slow Southern drawl. Unmentioned are the past presence of two endangered species, the Ivory-billed Woodpecker and the Red Wolf, the former a casualty of the forest cutting, and the latter of predator control which has eliminated almost all native predators of the Thicket including the Black Bear. This is an eloquent plea for the preservation of the last of this wilderness area. (Two books provide further information—*The Natural World of the Big Thicket,* photographs by Blair Pittman, Texas A&M University, 1978, and *The Big Thicket, a Challenge for Conservation,* by Dr. Pete Gunter, Jenkins Publishing Co., 1971).

The Everglades Region: An Ecological Study, 24 minutes; U.S. Department of Interior, National Park Service and the University of Miami; Penn State University, 1972.

The Everglades comprise the largest continuous wetlands in the U.S. They have been greatly reduced by draining but the Everglades National Park protects a large portion. This film discusses the complex water table which controls the entire ecosystem, and shows how the bountiful wildlife occupies individual ecological niches, each species in its own food habitat role, not conflicting with related species.

Inside the Golden Gate, 59 minutes; WGBH; Time-Life Films, 1976.

A NOVA film shown on educational TV, it describes the environmental degradation of San Francisco Bay. It is a thorough investigation of an estuary which has been filled, dumped in, and polluted like so many estuaries. Cities have often been built on these complicated and productive ecosystems because they make good harbors for shipping access to inland areas. The estuaries of Boston, New York and Philadelphia, which once supported extensive marshlands where fish, shrimp, and birds reproduced, have all been filled. San Francisco Bay still has enough marsh and natural area left to serve as a lesson for the folly of such destruction, and efforts have been successful to preserve parts of it, including habitat for several endangered species such as the Salt Marsh Harvest Mouse and the San Francisco Garter Snake.

The Salt Marsh: A Question of Values, 22 minutes; Encyclopedia Britannica Educational Media Co., 1975.

The productivity and ecology of salt marshes and the rich habitat they provide for wildlife are presented. The effects of losing these ecosystems and the need to conserve them are a part of this film's educational message.

Prairie Killers, 30 minutes; NET Indiana University, 1970.

The Great Plains destruction—first the 19th century slaughter of the Bison and Plains Indians and later its conversion to farmland—is the subject of this National Educational Television documentary. Ranchers and farmers continue to destroy the remnant wildlife—Coyotes and prairie dogs—and the important role of these animals in the Plains ecology makes clear our misuse of the prairie.

Vanishing Prairie: Buffalo—Majestic Symbol of American Plains, 12 minutes; *Large Animals That Once Roamed the Plains,* 12 minutes; *Small Animals of the Plains,* 15 minutes; Disney, 1963.

These are old films but made in the best Disney nature film tradition. The photography is superb. They concentrate on the individual animals of the Great Plains rather than the general picture. There is even a shot of Black-footed Ferrets. These ferrets were live-trapped for the film and later released in Yellowstone National Park.

Where Did the Colorado Go? 59 minutes; WGBH; Time-Life Films, 1976.

A NOVA series film, it is the story of the damming and diversion of this once-mighty river and resultant negative effects on the river's ecosystem. It would be very useful as background for studying the endangered species of the river—the Colorado River Squawfish, Humpback Chub, Yuma Clapper Rail and others—although the film does not actually discuss these species.

Ecology

Baobab: Portrait of a Tree, 53 minutes; Alan and Joan Root; McGraw-Hill, 1973. (Also available from Penn State University.)

The husband and wife team of Joan and Alan Root has produced many excellent films and this award-winner on the African Baobab tree is one of their best, a superlatively interesting and beautiful film. The creatures that live in the tree both day and night present an active drama of interplay with one another and the surrounding environment. Hornbills nest in the tree, and the female is literally sealed in the nest hole by the male who feeds her and the young during the long nesting season. Bright-eyed galagos, nocturnal primates, leap about the tree at night, weaver birds build their complicated apartment nests, insects and reptiles of many types are all seen in their dependencies on each other and the Baobab tree, a microcosm of nature.

A Desert Place, 30 minutes; WGBH; Time-Life Films, 1976.

One of the excellent NOVA series which appear regularly on educational TV, this film is an instruction in desert ecosystems, focussing on the Sonoran Desert of the southwestern United States. The varieties of plants and animals and their adaptations to extremes of heat and aridity are well presented. The seasonal rains and the plants' and animals' ability to exist year-round on the water which falls during a short period are highlighted.

The Year of the Wildebeest, 55 minutes; Alan Root; Penn State University, 1976.

This film traces the 2000-mile migration of one million East African wildebeest throughout one year. The predators which rely on their annual migration—lions and leopards—and other African wildlife—antelope, giraffe and elephants—are all part of this species' ecology. This is perhaps the largest remaining herd of hoofed mammals on earth, and its long journey may soon be over as Africa develops agriculturally and its expanding human population forces the wildebeest into smaller migrations. This may be also instructive to show what the huge Bison and Caribou herds of North America were once like.

Note: Other films on ecology and ecosystems are available and listed in distributors' catalogs. The films listed here are exceptional in one way or another, or deal with subjects relating to endangered species.

Birds

Fight for Survival, 11 minutes; Georgia Department of Natural Resources.

Georgia has begun a program of reintroducing the Bald Eagle to the state where it has not bred since 1970, and this film shows the first release of captive-raised birds from a tower on the coast. It is a lively, interesting film with good photography.

Last Stronghold of the Eagle, 30 minutes, National Audubon Society; Learning Corp. of America, 1981.

This National Audubon film gives a remarkably beautiful view of the wintering Bald Eagles of Chilkat Valley in southeastern Alaska—their ecology and the threats to their environment. Few films give such a complete picture of eagles—their vocalizations, relations with each other, habitat, feeding and flight. This valley attracts eagles from British Columbia and other parts of Alaska since it is one of the few areas not frozen over in the winter that also has late salmon spawning; in May, 1982 the Alaska legislature passed a bill creating the Alaska Chilkat Bald Eagle Preserve, thus protecting the valley for these magnificent birds.

To Free an Eagle, 47 minutes; F.R.E.E. Ltd., 1980.

The search for the endangered Philippine Eagle, one of the most dramatic of all eagles, and the subsequent filming of its nesting and hunting make an interesting tale. The forest destruction threatening it is depicted. This is the first film about one of the rarest birds in the world. It won a Merit Award for the presentation of research on an Endangered Species at the 1981 International Wildlife Film Festival.

Osprey, 34 minutes; Royal Society for the Protection of Birds; Beacon Films, 1980.

This exceptional film is an ultra-close-up view of the Osprey in Scotland. For many years no Ospreys nested in Scotland. This majestic bird of prey had been persecuted by fishermen and suffered reproductive failure from pesticide contamination. Then one year a male was seen in an ancestral breeding area, and he was later joined by a female. Their fishing, nesting and general behavior are exciting and beautiful. Day to day events of their life are shown, such as one Osprey's unsuccessful struggle to dislodge a large dead branch for its nest. This is a superbly photographed film and an intimate glimpse of a species that has suffered declines in many parts of the world. In 1981, the film was voted Best Professional Film in the International Wildlife Film Festival.

Footnote to Genesis, 25 minutes; Canadian Broadcasting Corp.; Carousel Films, 1971.

Relates the story of Ralph Edwards, who settled with his family on Lonesome Lake, British Columbia and played a major role in researching the Trumpeter Swan when it had been hunted nearly to extinction. (See the chapter, "People Who Make a Difference.")

A Great White Bird, 51 minutes; National Film Board of Canada and U.S. Fish and Wildlife Service; National Audio Visual Center, GSA, 1977.

This is the story of the Whooping Crane's slow recovery from near extinction. Its wintering habitat in Aransas National Wildlife Refuge, Texas, and long migration to its breeding area in Wood Buffalo Park, Northwest Territories, Canada are shown. Some very unusual footage not seen elsewhere was included—Whooping Crane chicks taking their first spindly steps in the Canadian wet bogs, feeding on clams in Texas, and beautiful shots of these stately birds in flight. A very thorough, if not completely up-to-date, picture of the crane's biology and life history is presented. The scientists most active in its preservation, from Robert Porter Allen's early crusade in the 1930's to those removing eggs from nests for transfer to Sandhill Crane nests where a second population is being established, are shown.

Kirtland's Warbler: Bird of Fire, 10 minutes; Walter and Myrna Berlet; Berlet Films, 1972.

This short film gives the life history of this endangered bird which breeds only in a portion of Michigan's jackpine forest.

The Parrots of Luquillo, 20 minutes; U.S. Forest Service & U.S. Fish and Wildlife Service; U.S. Department of Interior, Office of Audio Visual Service, 1978.

This beautiful film about the endangered Puerto Rican Parrot was written and produced by Dr. Noel Snyder, a Fish and Wildlife Service biologist who worked to conserve this parrot for many years. It has marvelous shots of baby parrots emerging from their nest holes and describes the many tribulations that beset them.

Woodpeckers: Birds in Trouble, 9 minutes; Georgia Department of Natural Resources, 1980.

The two species this film focusses on are the Ivory-billed and the Red-cockaded Woodpeckers. The only sound motion pictures ever taken of the Ivory-billed Woodpeckers are included in this film which makes it worth seeing for these alone. The only cause of its endangered status discussed is habitat loss; although this is the major cause of its decline it is not the only one—over 400 specimens of this bird, which was always rare, lie dead in museums, 150 in one museum alone. The Red-cockaded Woodpecker of the southeast is a rare inhabitant of Georgia and its habitat requirements are so unusual that foresters will have to protect the diseased pine stands they inhabit. The dialogue is a little vague and dull.

Wild Wing, 35 minutes, British Transport Films; International Film Bureau, 1967.

An award-winning British film about the Wildfowl Trust at Slimbridge, England, created by Sir Peter Scott. This world-famous organization specializes in breeding endangered birds, primarily waterfowl. The film concentrates on the study of birds—migrations, life history, behavior and relationships with one another.

Mammals — General

The Big Cats: The Endangered Predators, 22 minutes; Alan P. Sloan; Encyclopedia Britannica, 1979.

Each big cat species is focussed on briefly and its range shown on a map. Almost all the big cats except the Lion are on the endangered species list and this film shows the causes: the fur trade, habitat loss, hunting, and predator control. The film is marred by a long discussion on training big cats for circus acts; there was no real justification for this, and the filmmakers did not seem to see the magnificent cats in such circumstances as pathetic and undignified.

Wolves and the Wolf Men, 52 minutes; MGM Films, Inc.; Penn State University, 1969.

One of the first films to show the fascinating wolves—their close ties with fellow members of the pack, hierarchy within their complicated social unit, and their ecology. The focus is on work of Dr. L. David Mech and Dr. Durwood Allen, who have studied wolves in Minnesota and on northern Michigan's Isle Royale for over a decade. This film was originally seen on commercial TV and made a major contribution to a true understanding of this remarkable animal. Since 1969 when the film was made, further research has revealed that the relationships between the wolf and its prey species—deer and moose—are more complicated than the film would lead one to believe, but the information as a whole is of high quality.

Wolf Pack, 20 minutes; National Film Board of Canada; Penn State University, 1977.

A wolf pack in Northern Canada is followed from winter through its breeding season. Adapted from "Death of a Legend" this is an intimate glimpse of a wolf pack's interrelationships—the devotion of the leader to his lifelong mate, the mutually helpful nature of the pack which revolves around raising the pups and their struggle for survival.

Bighorn, 10 minutes; National Film Board of Canada; McGraw-Hill, 1971.

A short film without narration on the Rocky Mountain Bighorn Sheep in Canada's Banff and Jasper National Parks, landscapes untouched by man.

Bighorn!, 26 minutes; Stouffer Productions, 1974.

A herd of Rocky Mountain Bighorn Sheep is followed during one year in which the old male leader of the herd dies. The ewe he bred the fall before survives to carry on the line with the lamb born in the spring. Their magnificent habitat is shown in all seasons.

The Rhinoceros, 22 minutes; Ivan Tors; Macmillan Films, Inc., 1974.

One of "The Last of the Wild" Series narrated by Lorne Greene, this film originally was seen on television. The rhinoceroses have survived almost unchanged from prehistoric times, yet the 20th century may see their extinction. Their heavy-skinned armor and sharp horns are no protection against the guns of today's poachers. They are killed for their horns which are used for folk medicine in Asia and dagger handles dear to Yemenites. The latter is the major threat to the species now. This film, however, was made prior to the most recent slaughters, and concentrates mainly on describing the biology, habitat and status of the five rhino species of Asia and Africa, now all on the verge of extinction. This is a well-written, fast-moving and valuable film for learning about these survivors from past ages, and it encourages conservation efforts.

Last Stand in Eden, 59 minutes; National Geographic Society, 1979.

This long film reveals the plight of Africa's elephants in conflict with agriculture and development in East Africa and active efforts to save them. Winner of two awards, including an Emmy, it is an especially poignant look at the crowding out of Africa's elephants from one area after another, and their slaughter for ivory. The photography is splendid.

The First Signs of Washoe, 59 minutes; Time-Life Films; Penn State University, 1974.

This remarkable NOVA film reviews the various projects and evidence for teaching language to Chimpanzees. The five-year project by Allen Gardner teaching Washoe American Sign Language; D. Rumbaugh and E. von Glaserfeld's work at Yerkes Institute with the Chimpanzee Lana using computers and a special structured language; and finally, Roger Fouts' project teaching several Chimpanzees to communicate among themselves in sign language.

Miss Goodall and the Wild Chimpanzees, 52 minutes; National Geographic Society, 1966.

One of the earliest animal behavior films, this and other National Geographic films about Jane Goodall's pioneering research with wild chimpanzees are very important conservation milestones. The individuality, intelligence and sociability of chimpanzees never cease to amaze one, and her trusting relationship with them built up over years of patiently following them in their African forest home is a lesson in animal behavior research.

Other National Geographic Society films on Chimpanzees:

Introduction to Chimpanzee Behavior, 23 minutes, 1977.

Infant Development, 23 minutes, 1977.

Hierarchy and the Alpha Male, 23 minutes, 1977.

Feeding and Food Sharing, 23 minutes, 1976.

Gorilla, 59 minutes; National Geographic Society, 1981.

This new film spends much of its footage on captive gorillas—in zoos and in a sign language program. Much progress has been made in captive breeding and keeping these animals in groups rather than isolating them in dark cages. The last quarter hour is devoted to wild gorillas. We learn that Digit, the first gorilla to make friends with researcher Dian Fossey, was killed in 1977, beheaded by poachers who sold his head and hands for $20. The gorillas are under even greater pressure today than when Fossey's research began in 1967 because of increased killing of the gorillas while agriculture and development are destroying their habitat.

Search for the Great Apes, 52 minutes; National Geographic Society, 1975.

This documentary shows the fruits of the long-term research of Dian Fossey on the Mountain Gorilla and Birute Galdikas on the Orangutan. Their findings are revealed in the film almost as they actually occurred, showing how they slowly gained the confidence of these shy apes. The life histories and ecology of both species emerging through their observations make this film lively and interesting.

Mammals—Marine

The Great Whales, 59 minutes; National Geographic Society; Karol Media, 1978.

This beautifully photographed and well-documented film discusses the many facets of whales and whaling. It includes the history of whaling, protection that has evolved, and the remarkable filming of a killer whale giving birth while in captivity. Also discussed is research on behavior and migration. 1978 Emmy Winner of the Best Documentary.

The Right Whales: An Endangered Species, 23 minutes; National Geographic Series, 1976.

This award-winning film depicts zoologist Roger Payne's research on the Right Whale in the waters off Patagonia, Argentina. The whales' play, communication, and their precarious status are woven into an absorbing tale.

In Search of the Bowhead Whale, 49 minutes; National Film Board of Canada; Penn State University, 1974.

This lively and colorful movie allows us to follow an expedition to find and photograph the Bowhead whale, a seriously endangered species which lives in the Arctic Ocean off the northern coast of Alaska. Documentation includes habitat, behavior and plight of this great species.

The Singing Whales, 52 minutes; Jacques Cousteau; Churchill Films, 1975.

Jacques Cousteau and his crew filmed the Humpback Whales as they swam and cavorted. Their beautiful songs are included in this long film. It explores the history of whaling that nearly caused the extinction of this great whale, called Humpback because of the high arch it makes when it leaps to dive. Cousteau points out that each bump on the Humpback's snout contains one hair, a relic from its ancient roots as a land animal. The meanings of the songs remain a mystery and Cousteau researched the connections with their behavior. The narration and photography are exceptional.

The Whales That Wouldn't Die, 28 minutes; KPBS-TV; San Diego State University; McGraw-Hill, 1981.

This close-up look at the Gray Whale tells the story of its slow recovery from near extinction by commercial whaling. The Gray Whales' 10,000-mile migration, the longest of any mammal, takes them from the Siberian coast to the waters of Baja California where they breed and bear their young.

Research on this species has been extensive, and many of the whales are even known as individuals to scientists and the public. Beautiful photography shows these whales breaching, frolicking about and encountering film crews. One protective mother with her calf butted the boat in mild remonstrance. Of all whales, the Gray is the one most familiar to the public, as whale watching has become a real enthusiasm. Some consider it a disturbance and possible threat to the whales. However, a closer acquaintance with this friendly cetacean may lead to a better understanding of all whales, and a sympathy for their plight. More and more people all over the world see them as fascinating and intelligent creatures rather than potential dog food and lipstick. This excellent film is accompanied by an instructor's leaflet with background information on the Gray Whale.

Whales, Dolphins and Man, 52 minutes; BBC; Time-Life Films, 1973.

The intelligence of dolphins and whales and traits we share with them are shown by researchers. Whaling and its brutality are documented, making the loss of these remarkable animals all the more vivid. This is another film in the NOVA series.

Last Days of the Dolphins?, 27 minutes; Environmental Defense Fund, 1976.

Dick Cavett narrates this film containing footage obtained after a court fight with tuna interests showing the tragic killing of dolphins in tuna purse seines.

Silent Sirens: Manatees in Peril, 20 minutes; Florida Audubon Society, 1980.

The Florida Manatee once ranged along both coasts of Florida and the Gulf coast of Mississippi, Alabama and Louisiana in fairly large numbers. Their population now is less than 1,000, and this film shows the many threats that endanger these gentle marine mammals. The major peril is motorboat propellers wounding or killing them. Research is now revealing much of their life history and movements and suggesting conservation programs to aid them. This film covers all the major points of behavior, research and even their evolutionary ties to the elephant as shown by similar nails on their forelimbs. It has a strong conservation message and fine underwater photography.

Saga of the Sea Otter, 26 minutes; Survival Anglia; Penn State University, 1976.

The photography and narration of this film make it the best of numerous films on the fascinating Sea Otter. Sea Otters off California, decimated by the fur trade, number only about a thousand even after years of protection. Their ecology, behavior, including their use of stones to open mollusks, and other facets of their life in the kelp beds are explored in this beautiful and interesting film.

Reptiles and Fish

Creatures of the Night: Georgia's Giant Sea Turtles, 9 minutes; Georgia Department of Natural Resources, 1980.

This short film is another in the film series sponsored by Georgia's nongame and endangered species program. The narration is somewhat stilted, which detracts from the impact, but little known facts about the turtles' nesting make this film interesting. It documents their refusal to nest where there is any light showing on the beach—even a lighted match can cause them to turn back to the sea. Their death by drowning in shrimp nets is emphasized.

Sea Turtles, 13 minutes; Wild, Wild World of Animals; Time-Life Films, 1976.

This award-winning film was originally shown on the TV series "Wild, Wild World of Animals" which was probably the best of many TV animal programs that came and went in the 1970's. The drama of a sea turtle laying eggs, their hatching, the hoards of predators that kill them in their dangerous first walk to the sea, is the core of this film. Dialogue and photography are excellent.

The Galapagos Tortoise, 23 minutes; Galapagos: Laboratory for Evolution Series; Penn State University, 1973.

The historical decline of these enormous land tortoises from over-exploitation by ship crews seeking food has been arrested by protection, but new problems keep the species from recovering rapidly. Rats and dogs left on the islands by ships prey on the eggs and young tortoises. The story of the tortoises and the recovery program of the Charles Darwin Foundation in hatching eggs in captivity for release when the turtles are large enough to care for themselves is told in this interesting film. Since 1973 when the film was made, some progress has been made, and tortoises have been released on one island which has been declared rat-free. Unfortunately another subspecies may be doomed (several are already extinct) as it has been reduced to one elderly male. This is a film which shows graphically the effects of introduced species on fragile island species.

Sand Hill Survivors, 11 minutes; Georgia Department of Natural Resources Information Office, 1980.

The Gopher Tortoise of Georgia inhabits the sandy open pine forest region. It has declined to endangered status because its habitat is being bulldozed for agricultural development. It is an important animal in this ecosystem because its burrows provide shelter from the sweltering summer heat for a wide variety of wildlife. The endangered Indigo Snake which is killed by snake hunters and captured for the pet trade is one of the species dependent on this tortoise. Tortoises are among the most fascinating and yet helpless creatures. They are killed in large numbers as they slowly lumber across roads, by snake hunters gassing burrows, and for food. This is one of the few films on reptiles and it does a good job in showing the threats to this rare tortoise which is also endangered elsewhere in the South.

The Crocodiles, 20 minutes; Ivan Tors; Macmillan Films, 1974.

Crocodiles, feared and worshipped for eons, are now seen as amazing creatures, unchanged for millions of years because of their unique survival abilities. Their anatomy, mating habits and ecology are shown with focus on the Nile Crocodile. Also shown briefly are the Mugger, Gavial, and Saltwater Crocodiles of Asia and the Pacific. New World crocodiles are not mentioned. The skin trade has eliminated most large, old crocodiles and caused many species to become endangered.

Rulers of the Swamp, 10 minutes; Georgia Department of Natural Resources, 198x.

The alligator's status has improved in the past five years in most places including Georgia where it now ranges across 90 counties. This ancient species is a key element in ecosystems, creating 'gator holes other species use in times of drought, and this is shown in graphic cross-section drawings. The hide-hunting is shown from a historical viewpoint with declines beginning as early as 1800 when skins sold for $1 a foot. Alligators have now become common enough to become pests in some areas, but the film does not propose simple solutions such as regulated markets in their hides, nor does it suggest that civilization and alligators will be totally compatible. The species must be guaranteed a place in the ecosystem in which it has survived and to which it has contributed for 60 million years.

Pupfish of the Desert, 18 minutes; Stanton Films, 1975.

The unique little pupfish of the desert springs are survivors of earlier eras when much of the west was covered by an inland sea. Their survival, often in water saltier than seawater, is remarkable in itself. They are currently under siege from the over-pumping of ground water and other alterations in their habitat. This film provides a view of their plight and its causes.

At press time several new award-winning films became available:

Flight of the Condor — Parts 1-3. Wildlife of South America. Part 3 won best film of the 1982 International Wildlife Film Festival. 55 minutes. Producer and Distributor: British Broadcasting Co.

Temple of the Elephant The fauna of Sri Lanka. Best commercial Film — 1982. 57 minutes. Producer and Distributor: Canadian Broadcasting Corporation.

Autumn with Grizzlies Ecology and behavior of Grizzly Bears living in the Canadian Rockies. Best Cinematographic Treatment of a species in its habitat. 15 minutes. Producer and Distributor: Karvonen Films Ltd.

Birds of the Indian Monsoon A year at the Keoladeo Ghana Bird Sanctuary in Bharatpur, north India, showing many rare species including the Siberian Crane. Merit Award for the treatment of an ecosystem. 50 minutes. Produced by Stanley & Belinda Breeden. Distributed by Survival Anglia.

America's Wetlands The value, ecology and conservation of the nation's precious swamps, marshes and prairie potholes. 28 minutes. Distributed by the U.S. Fish and Wildlife Service and E.P.A.

Film Distributors and Addresses

Animal Welfare Institute
P.O. Box 3650
Washington, D.C. 20007

Beacon Films*
1250 Washington Street
Norwood, MA 02062

Berlet Films
1646 W. Kimmel Road
Jackson, MI 49201

BFA Educational Media
2211 Michigan Avenue
Santa Monica, CA 90404

British Broadcasting Co.
Villiers House
The Broadway
Ealing, London, U.K.

Bullfrog Films, Inc.
Oley, PA 19547

Canadian Broadcasting Corp.
Export Sales
354 Jarvis Street
Toronto M5W 1E6
CANADA

Carousel Films, Inc.
1501 Broadway
New York, N.Y. 10036

Centron Films
1621 West 9th
Lawrence, KS 66044

Churchill Films
662 N. Robertson Blvd.
Los Angeles, CA 90069

Coronet Instructional Films
65 E. South Water Street
Chicago, IL 60601

Encyclopedia Britannica
Educational Corp.
425 N. Michigan Avenue
Chicago, IL 60611

Environmental Defense Fund
1525 18th Street, N.W.
Washington, D.C. 20036

Films Incorporated
733 Green Bay Road
Wilmette, IL 60091

Florida Audubon Society
921 South Lake Sybelia Drive
Maitland, FL 32751

F.R.E.E. Ltd.
201 N. Wells
Chicago, IL 60606

Georgia Dept. of Natural Resources
Information Office
270 Washington Street, S.W.
Atlanta, GA 30334

Great Plains Instructional
TV Library
University of Nebraska
P.O. Box 80669
Lincoln, NB 68501

Indiana University
Audio-Visual Center
Bloomington, IN 47401

*Write for list including the Royal Society for the Protection of Birds' films.

International Film Bureau
322 S. Michigan Avenue
Chicago, IL 60604

Karol Media
625 Foam Road
Paramus, N.J. 07652

Karvonen Films Ltd.
Box 8, Site 11, R.R.#2
Sherwood Park
Alberta, Canada

King Features Entertainment
235 East 45th Street
New York, NY 10017

Learning Corp. of America
1350 Avenue of the Americas
New York, N.Y. 10019

Macmillan Films, Inc.
34 Mac Questen Parkway S.
Mt. Vernon, N.Y. 10050

McGraw-Hill Films
110 15th Street
Del Mar, CA 90214

National Audio Visual Center
General Services Administration
Washington, D.C. 20409

National Geographic Society
17th and M Streets, N.W.
Washington, D.C. 20036

Partridge Films Ltd.
12 Millfield Lane
London N66JD
ENGLAND

Penn State University
Audio Visual Services
Special Services Building
University Park, PA 16802

Stanton Films
2417 Artesia Blvd
Redondo Beach, CA 90278

Stouffer Productions
300 Spring Street
Aspen, CO 81611

Survival Anglia
c/o Picture Film Distributing Corp.
1118th Avenue
New York, NY 10011

Time Life Films, Inc.
54 E. 16th Street
New York, N.Y. 10011

U.S. Department of the Interior
Fish and Wildlife Service
Office of Audio Visual Services
Room 8070
Washington, D.C. 20240

Walt Disney Productions
Educational Film Division
500 S. Buena Vista Avenue
Burbank, CA 91503

WGBH
125 Western Avenue
Boston, MA 02134

Wildlife Preservation Trust*
    International
34th Street & Girard Avenue
Philadelphia, PA 19104

*Write for list of films available at cost of return postage and insurance.

Books and Publications

To The Reader:

This is a broad-based list to give you an idea of the rich variety of books available. Some of the titles listed here are available in hardcover, some in paperback and some, unfortunately, are out of print and will have to be sought in libraries. It may be your bookshop will have to special order a title for you, for most of the older books are no longer kept on hand. When you use your library and find they do not have the book you want, be certain to ask them if they can obtain it through the inter-library loan plan. And remember, this list is just a beginning, a jumping off place from which to search out interesting books on your own.

Endangered Species of the World— General Books

Burton, Maurice, and Robert Burton. 1978. *The World's Disappearing Wildlife*. Marshall Cavendish, London & N.Y. 192 pages.
Caras, Roger A. 1966. *Last Chance on Earth. A Requiem for Wildlife*. Chilton, Philadelphia, 207 pages.

Colinvaux, P. 1979. *Why Big Fierce Animals Are Rare: An Ecologist's Perspective*. Princeton University Press.
Cox, James A. 1975. *The Endangered Ones*. Crown Publishing Co., N.Y.
Curry-Lindahl, Kai. 1972. *Let Them Live; A Worldwide Survey of Animals Threatened with Extinction*. Morrow, N.Y. 394 pages.
Day, David. 1980. *The Doomsday Book of Animals*. Viking Press, N.Y.
Eckholm, Erik. 1978. *Disappearing Species: The Social Challenge*. Worldwatch Paper 22, 38 pages.
Ehrenfeld, D.W. 1972. *Conserving Life on Earth*. Oxford University Press, N.Y.
Ehrlich, Paul, and Anne Ehrlich. 1980. *Extinction; The Causes and Consequences of the Disappearance of Species*. Random House, N.Y. 305 pages.
Farrell, Adrienne. (editor). 1981. *World Wildlife Fund Yearbook 1980-81*. World Wildlife Fund, Switzerland, 511 pages.
Fisher, James, Noel Simon, and Jack Vincent. 1969. *Wildlife in Danger*. Viking Press, N.Y. 368 pages.
Holloway, C.W. 1970. *Threatened Vertebrates in Northern Circumpolar Regions*. IUCN Publication New Series 16:175-192.
Holloway, C. (ed.) 1970. *Problems of Threatened Species*. IUCN 11th Technical Meeting, IUCN Publication New Series 18.
Martin, R.D. (ed.) 1975. *Breeding Endangered Species in Captivity*. Academic Press, N.Y. 420 pages.
McClung, Robert M. 1976. *Lost Wild Worlds: The Story of Extinct and Vanishing Wildlife of the Eastern Hemisphere*. Morrow, N.Y. 288 pages.
Milne, Lorus, and Margery Milne. 1971. *The Cougar Doesn't Live Here Anymore*. Prentice-Hall, Englewood Cliffs, N.J.
Myers, Norman. 1979. *The Sinking Ark; A New Look at the Problem of Disappearing Species*. Pergamon Press, N.Y. 307 pages.
Regenstein, Lewis. 1975. *The Politics of Extinction. The Shocking Story of the World's Endangered Wildlife*. Macmillan, N.Y. 280 pages.
Scheffer, Victor B. 1974. *A Voice for Wildlife*. Scribners, N.Y. 245 pages.
Simon, N.M. and P. Geroudet. 1970. *Last Survivors: The Natural History of Animals in Danger of Extinction*. World, N.Y., 275 pages.
Soulé, M.E., and B.A. Wilcox (eds.) 1980. *Conservation Biology: An Evolutionary-Ecological Perspective*. Sinauer, Sunderland, MA, 395 pages.
Stuart Gene S. 1980. *Wildlife Alert! The Struggle to Survive*. National Geographic Society, 104 pages. (secondary level).
Time-Life. 1976. *Vanishing Species*. Time-Life Books, N.Y., 264 pages.
Wilson, Ron. 1979. *Vanishing Species*. Chartwell Books, Inc., Secaucus, N.J., 93 pages.
Wood, Don A. 1981. *Endangered Species. Concepts, Principles, and Programs. A Bibliography*. Florida Game and Fresh Water Fish Commission. 228 pages. (3,135 references)
Ziswiler, Vincenz. 1967. *Extinct and Vanishing Animals*. Springer-Verlag, N.Y., 133 pages.

Endangered Species and Habitats of North America

Allen, Thomas B. 1974. *Vanishing Wildlife of North America*. National Geographic Society, 208 pages.
Bean, Michael J. 1977. *The Evolution of Wildlife Law*. Council on Environmental Quality, U.S. Government Printing Office, 485 pages.
Beard, Daniel B. 1942. *Fading Trails: The Story of Endangered American Wildlife*. Macmillan, N.Y. 279 pages.
Brokaw, H. (ed.) *Wildlife and America*. Council on Environmental Quality. U.S. Government Printing Office, 532 pages.
Christman, S.P. and W.S. Lippincott, Jr. 1978. *Rare and Endangered Vertebrates of the Southeastern United States Coastal Plain—A Summary of Public Concern for Sensitive Wildlife*. U.S. Dept. of

Interior, Fish & Wildlife Service, Office of Biological Services, Publication FWS/OBS-71/31, 46 pages.

Hornaday, William T. 1913. *Our Vanishing Wildlife; Its Extermination and Preservation*. Scribner's, N.Y. 411 pages.

LaBastille, Anne. 1973. *Rare, Endangered and Threatened Vertebrate Species of the Atlantic Coastal Plain and Maine Coast*. Smithsonian Institution Office of Environmental Science, 148 pages.

Laycock, George. 1969. *America's Endangered Wildlife*. Norton & Sons, N.Y., 226 pages.

Leen, N. 1973. *And Then There Were None: America's Vanishing Wildlife*. Holt, Rinehart & Winston, N.Y., 128 pages.

Lockwood, R. (ed.) 1979. *Proceedings of the Second Symposium on Endangered North American Wildlife and Habitat*—June 1-6, 1977. Wild Canid Survival and Research Center, St. Louis, MO.

Matthiessen, Peter. 1959. *Wildlife in America*. Viking, N.Y. 304 pages.

McClung, Robert M. 1969. *Lost Wild America: The Story of Our Extinct and Vanishing Wildlife*. Morrow, N.Y., 240 pages.

Meredith, D.P. 1979. *Eastern States Endangered Wildlife*. U.S. Dept. Interior, Bureau of Land Management, 155 pages.

Mosquin, T., and C. Suchal. (eds.) 1977. *Canada's Threatened Species and Habitats*. Canadian Nature Federation and the World Wildlife Fund, 185 pages.

Nelson, B.B., and S.E. Taylor. 1980. *Endangered and Threatened Species and Related Habitats in Five Southeastern States*. U.S. Dept. Interior, Bureau of Land Management, Eastern States Off., 104 pages.

Nowak, Ronald M. 1976. Our American Wildlife: 1776-1976. *National Parks & Conservation Magazine*, 50(11):14-18.

Olsen, Jack. 1971. *Slaughter the Animals, Poison the Earth*. Simon & Schuster, Inc. and Manor Books Inc. in paperback, 288 pages.

Opler, Paul A. 1976. The Parade of Passing Species: A Survey of Extinctions in the U.S. *Science Teacher*, 43:30-34.

Parker, W., and L. Dixon. 1980. *Endangered and Threatened Wildlife of Kentucky, North Carolina, South Carolina and Tennessee*. U.S. Dept. Interior, Fish and Wildlife Service, & North Carolina Agriculture Extension Service, 116 pages.

Stewart, D. 1974. *Canadian Endangered Species*. Gage, Toronto, 172 pages.

Thomas, Bill. 1976. *The Swamp*. W.W. Norton & Co., N.Y. 223 pages.

U.S. Department of Interior, Fish and Wildlife Service.
1973 *Threatened Wildlife of the United States*. Resource Publication 114, 289 pages.
1976. *Endangered Species. Program Progress Report*. 54 pages.
1981. *Endangered Means There's Still Time*. 32 pages.

Wood, Stephen L. (ed.) 1979. *The Endangered Species: A Symposium*. Great Basin Naturalist Memoirs No. 3, Brigham Young University, 171 pages.

Rare and Endangered Birds

Chancellor, R.D. (ed.) 1977. *Proceedings of the World Conference on Birds of Prey, Vienna, 1975*. ICBP, London, 442 pages.

Greenway, James C., Jr. 1967. *Extinct and Vanishing Birds of the World*. 2nd rev. edition, Dover, N.Y., 520 pages.

Halliday, Tim. 1978. *Vanishing Birds: Their Natural History and Conservation*. Sidgwich & Jackson, London, & Holt, Rinehart & Winston, N.Y., 296 pages.

King, W.B. (ed.) 1980. *ICBP Red Data Book of Endangered Birds of the World*. Smithsonian Institution Press, Washington, DC.

Lack, David. 1976. *Island Birds*. University of California Press.

Littlewood, C. 1972. *The World's Vanishing Birds*. Arco, N.Y., 63 pages.

Mackenzie, J.P.S. 1977. *Birds in Peril*. Houghton Mifflin, Boston, 191 pages.

McClung, Robert. 1979. *America's Endangered Birds. Programs and People Working to Save Them*. Wm. Morrow & Co., N.Y., 160 pages.

Temple, Stanley A. (ed.) 1977. *Endangered Birds: Management*

Techniques for the Preservation of Threatened Species. Univ. of Wisconsin Press.

Whitlock, Ralph. 1981. *Birds at Risk. A Comprehensive World-Survey of Threatened Species*. Moonraker Press, Wiltshire, England, 159 pages.

Zimmerman, David R. 1975. *To Save a Bird in Peril*. Coward, McCann & Geoghegan, N.Y., 286 pages.

Rare and Endangered Mammals

Allen, Glover M. 1942. *Extinct and Vanishing Mammals of the Western Hemisphere* with the Marine Species of All Oceans. American Committee for International Wildlife Protection, Special Publ. 11, 620 pages.

Bertram, G.C.L. and C.K.R. Bertram. 1973. The Modern Sirenia: Their Distribution and Status. *J. Linnaean Society*, 5(4):297-338.

Harper, Francis. 1945. *Extinct and Vanishing Mammals of the Old World*. American Committee for International Wildlife Protection, Spec. Publication 12, 850 pages.

IUCN. (eds.) 1973. *Proceedings of the Working Meeting on Threatened and Depleted Seals of the World*. IUCN Suppl. Paper 39, 176 pages.

1978. *Threatened Deer: Proceedings of a Working Meeting of the Deer Specialist Group of the Survival Service Commission*, IUCN, Gland, Switzerland, 434 pages.

Jorgenson, S.E., and L.D. Mech. (eds.) 1971. *Proceedings of the Symposium of Native Cats of North America*. U.S. Dept. Interior, Fish & Wildlife Service.

Littlewood, C. 1970. *The World's Vanishing Animals: Mammals*. Arco, N.Y. 63 pages.

Lowmann, G.E. 1975. *Endangered, Threatened and Unique Mammals of the Southern National Forests*. U.S. Dept. Agriculture, Forest Service, Southern Region, 121 pages.

Paradiso, John L. 1972. *Status Report on Cats (Felidae) of the World, 1971*. U.S. Dept. Interior, Fish & Wildlife Service, Spec. Scientific Report—Wildlife 157, 43 pages.

Prince Rainier III, and G.H. Bourne (eds.) 1977. *Primate Conservation*. Academic Press, N.Y., 658 pages.

Thornback, Jane (ed.) 1978 and 1982. *IUCN Red Data Book. Vol. 1: Mammalia*. IUCN, Gland, Switzerland.

Rare and Endangered Reptiles and Amphibians

Ashton, R.E., Jr. 1976. *Endangered and Threatened Amphibians and Reptiles of the United States*. Society for the Study of Amphibians and Reptiles, Herpetol. Circular 5, 65 pages.

Bury, R.B., C.K. Dodd, Jr., and G.M. Fellers. 1980. *Conservation of the Amphibia of the United States: a Review*. U.S. Dept. Interior, Fish & Wildlife Service, Resource Publ. 134, 34 pages.

Carr, A.F. 1972. Great Reptiles, Great Enigmas. *Audubon*, 74(2): 24-35.

Cook, F.R. 1970. Rare or Endangered Canadian Amphibians and Reptiles. *Canadian Field-Naturalist*, 84(1):9-16.

Dodd, C.K., Jr. 1979. *A Bibliography of Endangered and Threatened Amphibians and Reptiles in the United States and its Territories*. Smithsonian Herp. Info. Service No. 46, 35 pages.; Supplement, No. 49, 16 pages, 1981.

Guggisberg, C.A.W. 1972. *Crocodiles*. Stackpole, Harrisburg, PA, 195 pages.

Honegger, Rene E. (ed.) 1979. *IUCN Red Data Book. Vol. 3: Amphibia and Reptilia*. IUCN, Gland, Switzerland.

IUCN. (eds.) 1971 & 1973. *Proceedings of the First and Second Working Meeting of Crocodile Specialists*. IUCN Suppl. Papers 32 and 41, Gland, Switzerland.

Neill, W.T. 1971. *The Last of the Ruling Crocodiles: Alligators, Crocodiles, and Their Kin*. Columbia Univ. Press, 486 pages.

Perrero, L. 1975. *Alligators and Crocodiles: The Disappearing Dragons*. Windward, Miami, 64 pages.

Pritchard, Peter. 1977. *Marine Turtles of Micronesia.* Chelonia Press, San Francisco, 83 pages.

Riedman, S.R., and R. Witham. 1974. *Turtles, Extinction or Survival?* Abelard-Schuman, N.Y., 156 pages.

Rare and Endangered Fish and Invertebrates

Deacon, J.E., G. Kobetich, J.D. Williams and S. Contreras. 1979. Fishes of North America, Endangered, Threatened or of Special Concern: 1979. *Fisheries,* 4(2):29–44.

Heard, W.H. 1975. *Determination of the Endangered Status of Freshwater Clams of the Gulf and Southeastern States.* USDI, Fish & Wildlife Service, Office of Endangered Species Rept. & Florida State University, 31 pages.

Jorgenson, S.E., and R.W. Sharp (eds.) 1971. *Proceedings of the Symposium on Rare and Endangered Mollusks (Naiads) of the United States.* U.S. Dept. Interior, Fish and Wildlife Service, Region 3, 79 pages.

Miller, R.R. (ed.) 1977. *IUCN Red Data Book. Vol. 4: Pisces.* IUCN, Gland, Switzerland.

Pister, E.P. (ed.) 1980. *Desert Fishes Council: a Summary of the Proceedings of the Tenth Annual Symposium.* Desert Fishes Council and Univ. of Nevada, Las Vegas, 80 pages.

Pyle, Robert M. 1976. Conservation of Lepidoptera in the United States. *Biological Conservation,* 9(1):55–75.

Reiger, George. 1977. Native Fish in Troubled Waters. *Audubon,* 79(1):18–41.

Rare and Endangered Plants

Ayensu, E.S., and R.A. DeFilipps. 1978. *Endangered and Threatened Plants of the United States.* Smithsonian Institution Press & World Wildlife Fund, 403 pages.

Everard, B. 1974. *Vanishing Flowers of the World.* Bartholomew World Pictorial Map Ser., Bartholomew & Son, Edinburgh.

Hogner, D.C. 1977. *Endangered Plants.* Crowell, N.Y., 79 pages.

Kartesz, J.T., and R. Kartesz. 1977. *The Biota of North America. Part I: Vascular Plants, Volume I: Rare Plants.* Biota of North America Committee, 361 pages.

Little, E.L., Jr. 1975. *Rare and Local Conifers in the United States.* U.S. Dept. Agriculture, Forest Service Research Report 19, 25 pages.

1977. *Rare and Local Trees in the National Forests.* U.S. Dept. Agriculture, Forest Service Research Report 21, 14 pages.

Lucas, G.L., and A.H.M. Synge. (eds.) 1978. *The IUCN Plant Red Data Book.* IUCN, Gland, Switzerland.

Miasek, M.A., & C.R. Long. 1978. *Endangered Plant Species of the World and Their Endangered Habitats: A Compilation of the Literature.* New York Botanical Garden, 46 pages.

Prance, G.T., and T.S. Elias. (eds.) 1977. *Extinction is Forever: The Status of Threatened and Endangered Plants of the Americas.* New York Botanical Garden, 437 pages.

Ricciuti, Edward R. 1979. *Plants in Danger.* Harper & Row, N.Y. 86 pages.

Simmons, J.B., R.I. Beyer, P.E. Brandham, G.L. Lucas and V.T.H. Parry (eds.) 1976. *Conservation of Endangered Plants.* NATO Conf. Series I: Ecology, Vol. 1, Plenum Press, N.Y., 336 pages.

Wiley, L. 1968. *Rare Wild Flowers of North America.* MacGibbon & Key, Portland, Oregon, 501 pages.

Behavior, Survival and Humane Treatment of Wild Animals

Adamson, Joy. 1974. *Born Free.* Random House, N.Y.

Amory, Cleveland. 1974. *Mankind?* Harper & Row, N.Y.

Bates, Marston, 1960. *The Forest and the Sea. A Look at the Economy of Nature and the Ecology of Man.* Random House, N.Y.

Borror, D.J., and D.M. DeLong. 1970. *An Introduction to the Study of Insects.* Holt, Rinehart & Winston, N.Y.

Brues, Charles T. 1972. *Insects, Food and Ecology,* Dover, N.Y.

Burkhardt, Dietrich, Wolfgang Schliedt, and Helmut Altner. 1967. *Signals in the Animal World.* McGraw-Hill, N.Y.

Carlquist, Sherwin. 1974. *Island Biology.* Columbia Univ. Press, N.Y.

Carrighar, Sally. 1975. *The Twilight Seas. A Blue Whale's Journey.* Weybright & Talley, N.Y.

Carson, Rachel. 1954. *The Sea Around Us.* Natural History Press, N.Y.

1962. *Silent Spring.* Houghton Mifflin, Boston.

Cousteau, Jacques-Yves. 1981. *The Cousteau Almanac. An Inventory of Life on Our Water Planet.* Doubleday & Co., Garden City, N.Y.

Craighead, John J., and Frank C. Craighead, Jr. 1969. *Hawks, Owls and Wildlife.* Dover, N.Y.

Crisler, Lois. 1973. *Arctic Wild.* Ballantine Press, Westminister, MD.

Douglas-Hamilton, Iain, and Oria Douglas-Hamilton. 1975. *Among the Elephants.* Viking Press, N.Y.

Eckstein, Gustav. 1965. *Everyday Miracle.* Harper & Row, N.Y.

Emmel, Thomas C. 1975. *Butterflies.* Borzoi Book, Alfred A. Knopf, Inc.

Goodall, Jane. 1967. *My Friends the Wild Chimpanzees.* National Geographic Society, Washington, DC.

1971. *In the Shadow of Man.* Houghton Mifflin Co., Boston.

Grzimek, Bernhard. (ed.) *Animal Life Encyclopedia.* 13 Volumes, Van Nostrand Reinhold Co., N.Y.

Hammond, Kenneth A., George Macinko, and William B. Fairchild (eds.) 1978. *Sourcebook on the Environment. A Guide to the Literature.* University of Chicago Press.

Hancocks, David. 1973. *Master Builders of the Animal World.* Harper & Row, N.Y.

Hanley, Wayne. 1977. *Natural History in America. From Mark Catesby to Rachel Carson.* Quadrangle/New York Times, N.Y.

Kieran, John. 1971. *A Natural History of New York City.* Natural History Press, Garden City, N.Y.

Krutch, Joseph Wood. 1971. *Grand Canyon.* Morrow & Co., N.Y.

1963. *The Desert Year.* Viking Press, N.Y.

1957. *The Great Chain of Life.* Houghton Mifflin Co., Boston.

Linden, Eugene. 1974. *Apes, Men and Language.* Saturday Review Press/E.P. Dutton & Co., Inc.

1981. *The Education of Koko.* Holt, Rinehart, and Winston, N.Y.

Lorenz, Konrad. 1952. *King Solomon's Ring.* New American Library, N.Y.

McGiffin, Heather, and Nancie Brownley (eds.). 1980. *Animals in Education, The Use of Animals in High School Biology Classes and Science Fairs.* Institute for the Study of Animal Problems, 160 pages.

Milne, Lorus, and Margery Milne. 1960. *The Balance of Nature,* Knopf, N.Y.

McNulty, Faith. 1975. *Whales: Their Life in the Sea.* Harper & Row, N.Y.

1974. *The Great Whales.* Doubleday & Co., N.Y.

1971. *Must They Die? The Strange Story of the Prairie Dog and the Black-footed Ferret.* Doubleday & Co., N.Y.

Mech, L. David. 1970. *The Wolf: The Ecology and Behavior of an Endangered Species.* Natural History Press, Garden City, N.Y.

Mowat, Farley. 1972. *A Whale for the Killing.* Little, Brown & Co., Boston.

Portmann, Adolf. 1959. *Animal Camouflage.* University of Michigan Press, Ann Arbor, Michigan.

Ryden, Hope. 1975. *God's Dog.* Coward, McCann and Geoghegan, N.Y.

1978. *Little Deer of the Florida Keys.* Putnam, N.Y.

1981. *Bobcat Year.* Viking, N.Y.

Schaller, George B. 1964. *The Year of the Gorilla.* University of Chicago Press.

1967. *The Deer and the Tiger. A Study of Wildlife in India.* University of Chicago Press.

1977. *Wild Sheep and Goats of the Himalaya.* University of Chicago Press.

Scheffer, Victor B. 1969. *The Year of the Whale*. Scribner & Sons, N.Y.

Small, George. 1971. *The Blue Whale*. Columbia University Press, N.Y.

Tinbergen, Niko. 1973. *The Animal in its World*. Harvard University Press, Cambridge, MA.

1966. *Social Behavior in Animals*. Halstead Press, N.Y.

1958. *Curious Naturalists*. Basic Books, N.Y.

von Frisch, Karl. 1955. *The Dancing Bees*. Harcourt, Brace & Co., N.Y.

Warner, William W. 1975. *Beautiful Swimmers. Watermen, Crabs and the Chesapeake Bay*. Little, Brown & Co., N.Y.

Welty, Joel Carl. 1975. *The Life of Birds*. W.B. Saunders, Co. Philadelphia.

Wood, Frances E. and Ralph T. Heath, Jr. 1981. The Suncoast Seabird Sanctuary, Hazlett Publishing Inc. 93 pages.

Zeleny, Lawrence. 1976. *The Bluebird, How You Can Help Its Fight for Survival*. Indiana University Press, Bloomington, IN.

Organizations and Their Publications

African Wildlife Leadership Foundation, Inc., 1717 Massachusetts Ave., N.W. Washington, DC 20036; *African Wildlife News*

American Association for the Advancement of Science (AAAS), 1515 Massachusetts Ave. N.W., Washington, DC 20005; *Science* (weekly)

American Association of Zoological Parks and Aquariums, Oglebay Park, Wheeling, WV 26003; *Newsletter* (monthly)

American Cetacean Society, 4725 Lincoln Blvd., Marina del Rey, CA 90291; *The Whalewatcher* (monthly)

American Fisheries Society, 1319 18th St., N.W., Washington, DC 20036; *Transactions* (quarterly); *Newsletter* (bimonthly)

American Humane Association, Box 1266, Denver, CO 80201; *National Animal Protection Newsletter*

American Museum of Natural History, Central Park West at 79th St., N.Y., N.Y. 10024; subscription: Box 4300, Bergenfield, NJ 07621; *Natural History* (monthly)

American Ornithologists' Union, c/o National Museum of Natural History, Smithsonian Institution, Washington, DC 20560; *The Auk* (quarterly)

American Society of Mammalogists, Sec.-Treasurer, Duane A. Schlitter, Section of Mammals, Carnegie Museum of Natural History, 4400 Forbes Ave., Pittsburgh, PA 15213; *Journal of Mammalogy* (quarterly)

Animal Protection Institute, P.O. Box 22505, Sacramento, CA 95822; *Mainstream* (quarterly)

Animal Research and Conservation Center, P.O. Box 5047, Church St. Station, N.Y., N.Y. 10242

Animal Welfare Institute, P.O. Box 3650, Washington, DC 20007; *Quarterly*; Reports & educational materials

Audubon Naturalists Society of the Central Atlantic States, 8940 Jones Mill Road, Washington, DC 20015; *Audubon Naturalist News* (monthly)

Bat Conservation International, c/o Dr. Merlin D. Tuttle, Milwaukee Public Museum, Milwaukee, WI 53233; *Bat Research News*

Center for Environmental Education, Inc., 1925 K St., N.W., Washington, DC 20006; see Teachers' Aids

Caribbean Conservation Association, P.O. Box 4187, St. Thomas, VI 00801

Committee for the Preservation of Tule Elk, P.O. Box 3696, San Diego, CA 92103

The Conservation Foundation, 1717 Massachusetts Ave., N.W., Washington, DC 20036; *Conservation Foundation Letter* (monthly)

Cooper Ornithological Society, c/o Dept. Zoology, University of California, Los Angeles, CA 90024; *The Condor* (quarterly)

Cousteau Society, Inc., 777 3rd Ave., N.Y., N.Y. 10017 & 8150 Beverly Blvd., Los Angeles, CA 90048; *The Log of the Calypso*

Defenders of Wildlife, 2000 N St., N.W., Washington, DC 20036; *Defenders* (bimonthly)

Desert Bighorn Council, 1500 N. Decatur Blvd., Las Vegas, NV 89109; *Proceedings* (annually)

Desert Fishes Council, 407 W. Line St., Bishop, CA 93514; *Proceedings* (annually)

Desert Tortoise Council, 5319 Cerritos Ave., Long Beach, CA 90805; *Proceedings* (annually)

Ecological Society of America, c/o Frank McCormick, University of Tennessee, Graduate Program in Ecology, Knoxville, TN 37916; *Ecology* (bimonthly)

Edward Ball Wildlife Foundation, P.O. Box 1792, Tallahassee, FL 32302

The Endangered Species Group, UMC 331-E, Campus Box 207, Boulder, CO 80309; *Share the Earth*

Environmental Action, Inc., 1346 Connecticut Ave., N.W., Washington, DC 20036; *Environmental Action* (biweekly)

Environmental Defense Fund, 475 Park Ave. South, N.Y., NY 10016; *EDF Letter* (bimonthly)

Environmental Law Institute, 1346 Connecticut Ave., N.W., Washington, DC 20036; *Environmental Law Reporter* (monthly)

Environmental Policy Center, 327 C St. S.E., Washington, DC 20003

Evergreen Wildlife Conservation Society, Inc., 23946 Sunset, Echo Lake, Lake Zurich, I 60047

Fauna and Flora Preservation Society, Regents Park, c/o The British Museum (Natural History) London, UK; *Oryx* (biannually)

Friends of Animals, Inc. 11 West 60th St., N.Y., NY 10023; *Actionline*

Friends of the Earth, 529 Commercial St., San Francisco, CA 94111 *Not Man Apart* (biweekly)

Friends of the Sea Otter, Box 221220, Carmel, CA 93922; *The Otter Raft* (quarterly)

The Fund for Animals, Inc., 140 West 57th St., N.Y., NY 10019; *The Washington Wildlife Newsletter*

Greenpeace USA, P.O. Box 4793, Santa Barbara, CA 93103; *The Greenpeace Examiner* (quarterly)

Hawk Mountain Sanctuary Association, R.D. 2, Kempton, PA 19529; *Newsletter* (annually)

Humane Society of the United States, 2100 L St., N.W., Washington, DC 20037; *HSUS News* and *Kind* (young people)

Institute for the Study of Animal Problems, 2100 L St., N.W., Washington, DC 20037; *International Journal for the Study of Animal Problems*

International Council for Bird Preservation, c/o British Museum (Natural History), Cromwell Road, London, UK; *Bulletin of the International Council for Bird Preservation* (annually); *Newsletter of the International Waterfowl Research Bureau* (biannually); *President's Letter*.

International Crane Foundation, City View Road, Baraboo, WI 53913; *The ICF Bugle*

International Fund for Animal Welfare, P.O. Box 193, Yarmouth Port, MA 02675

International Primate Protection League, P.O. Drawer X, Summerville, SC 29483; *Newsletter*

International Union for the Conservation of Nature and Natural Resources, 1196 Gland, Switzerland; *IUCN Bulletin* (bimonthly); *Red Data Books* (from Species Survival Commission); *TRAFFIC Bulletin* (from Wildlife Trade Monitoring Unit, 219c Huntingdon Rd., Cambridge CB3 ODL, U.K.)(bimonthly)

Jersey Wildlife Preservation Trust, U.S. address: 34th St. and Girard Ave., Philadelphia, PA 19104; *The Dodo* (annually)

National Audubon Society, 950 Third Ave., N.Y., NY 10022; *Audubon* (bimonthly); *American Birds* (bimonthly); *Nature Center News* (quarterly); *Audubon Action* (quarterly)

National Geographic Society, 1145 17th St., N.W., Washington, DC 20036; *National Geographic* (monthly); *Research Reports* (annually)

National Parks and Conservation Association, 1701 18th St., N.W., Washington, DC 20009; *National Parks & Conservation Association Magazine* (monthly)

Natural Resources Defense Council, Inc., 15 W. 44th St., N.Y., NY 10036; *Amicus* (quarterly); *NRDC News* (quarterly)

The Nature Conservancy, 1800 N. Kent St., Arlington, VA 22209; *News* (bimonthly)

New York Zoological Society, Bronx, NY 10460; *Animal Kingdom* (bimonthly)

North American Association for the Preservation of Predatory Animals, Box 161, Doyle, CA 96109

Oceanic Society, 240 Fort Mason, San Francisco, CA 94123; *Oceans* (bimonthly)

Raptor Research and Rehabilitation Program, Dept. Veterinary Biology, College of Veterinary Medicine, University of Minnesota, St. Paul, MN 55108

Rare and Endangered Native Plant Exchange, Department of Biology, Brooklyn College, Brooklyn, NY 11210

River Otter Fellowship, Box 20611, Irwindale, CA 91706; *Brightwater Journal*

Royal Society for the Protection of Birds, The Lodge, Sandy, Bedfordshire SG19 2DL England; *Birds* (quarterly)

Suncoast Sea Bird Sanctuary, 18328 Gulf Blvd., Indian Shores, Florida 33535; (rehabilitates injured wildlife)

Sierra Club, 530 Bush Street, San Francisco, CA 94108; *Sierra Club Bulletin* (monthly); *National News Report* (weekly)

Smithsonian Institution, Washington, DC 20560; *Research Reports* (quarterly); *Smithsonian* magazine (monthly)

The Society for Animal Protective Legislation, Post Office Box 3719, Washington, DC 20007; Letters to alert interested individuals when animal protective legislation needs support, primarily by grass roots-based letter writing. Sent out as issues arise.

Society for the Preservation of Birds of Prey, P.O. Box 891, Pacific Palisades, CA 90272; *The Raptor Report* (tri-annually)

Society of *Tympanuchus cupido pinnatus* Ltd., 611 E. Wisconsin Ave., P.O. Box 1156, Milwaukee, WI 53201; *Boom* (preservation of the Greater Prairie Chicken)

Trans-Species Unlimited, P.O. Box 1351, State College, PA 16801; *One World* (quarterly)

The Trumpeter Swan Society, P.O. Box 32, Maple Plain, MN 55359

Whooping Crane Conservation Association, Inc., 3000 Meadowlark Drive, Sierra Vista, AZ 83635

Wild Animal Infirmary for Nevada, 2920 Eagle St., Carson City, NV 89701; *Newsletter* (bimonthly)

Wild Canid Survival Research Center (Wolf Sanctuary), P.O. Box 20528, St. Louis, MO 63139; *Bulletin* (quarterly); *Alerts* (as needed)

Wild Horse Organized Assistance, P.O. Box 555, Reno, NV 89504

The Wilderness Society, 1901 Pennsylvania Ave., N.W., Washington, DC 20006; *The Living Wilderness* (quarterly); *Wilderness Report* (quarterly)

Wilson Ornithological Society, Secretary, Curtis S. Adkisson, Dept. Biology, VPI State Univ., Blacksburg, VA 24061; *The Wilson Bulletin* (quarterly)

World Society for the Protection of Animals, 29 Perkins St. P.O. Box 190 Boston, MA 02130; *Animals International*

World Wildlife Fund, 1196 Gland, Switzerland; WWF-US—1601 Connecticut Ave. N.W., Washington, DC 20009; *World Wildlife Fund Yearbook* (annually); WWF-US: Special Report (quarterly); *TRAFFIC (USA) Newsletter* (quarterly)

Worldwatch Institute, 1776 Massachusetts Ave. N.W., Washington, D.C. 20036; *Papers*

Xerces Society, Secretary, Teresa Clifford, 110 Biochemistry Bldg., University of Wyoming, Laramie, WY 82071; *Atala & Wings* newsletter (preservation of butterflies and moths)

This list includes North American and international organizations. See the *Sierra Club's World Dictionary* for foreign organizations.

Other sources for addresses of organizations:

The Sierra Club's World Directory of Environmental Organizations

Conservation Directory, National Wildlife Federation, 1412 16th St., Washington, DC 20036

Directory of Marine Education Resources, 1982. The Center for Environmental Education, Inc. Washington, D.C.

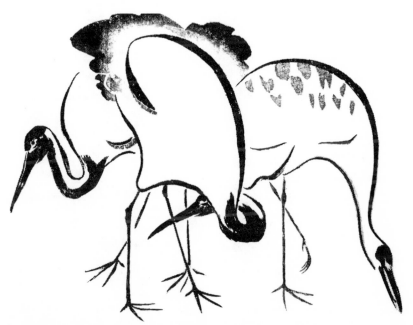

Cranes *by Korin, 17th century Japanese artist.*

Appendices

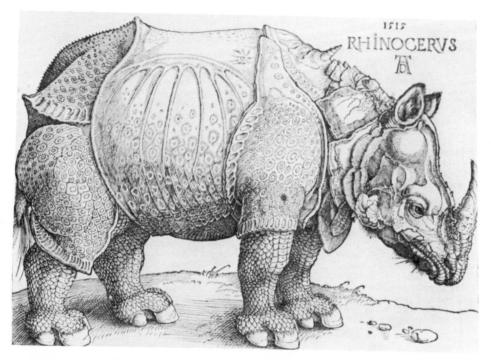

*An imaginary **rhinoceros** by Albrecht Dürer, 1515.*

Convention on International Trade in Endangered Species of Wild Fauna and Flora

Signed at Washington, D.C., on March 3, 1973

The Contracting States,

Recognizing that wild fauna and flora in their many beautiful and varied forms are an irreplaceable part of the natural systems of the earth which must be protected for this and the generations to come;

Conscious of the ever-growing value of wild fauna and flora from aesthetic, scientific, cultural, recreational and economic points of view;

Recognizing that peoples and States are and should be the best protectors of their own wild fauna and flora;

Recognizing, in addition, that international cooperation is essential for the protection of certain species of wild fauna and flora against over-exploitation through international trade;

Convinced of the urgency of taking appropriate measures to this end;

Have agreed as follows:

Article I

Definitions

For the purpose of the present Convention, unless the context otherwise requires:

(a) "Species" means any species, subspecies, or geographically separate population thereof;

(b) "Specimen" means:

(i) any animal or plant, whether alive or dead;

(ii) in the case of an animal: for species included in Appendices I and II, any readily recognizable part or derivative thereof; and for species included in Appendix III, any readily recognizable part or derivative thereof specified in Appendix III in relation to the species; and

(iii) in the case of a plant: for species included in Appendix I, any readily recognizable part or derivative thereof; and for species included in Appendices II and III, any readily recognizable part or derivative thereof specified in Appendices II and III in relation to the species;

(c) "Trade" means export, re-export, import and introduction from the sea;

(d) "Re-export" means export of any specimen that has previously been imported;

(e) "Introduction from the sea" means transportation into a State of specimens of any species which were taken in the marine environment not under the jurisdiction of any State;

(f) "Scientific Authority" means a national scientific authority designated in accordance with Article IX;

(g) "Management Authority" means a national management authority designated in accordance with Article IX;

(h) "Party" means a State for which the present Convention has entered into force.

Article II

Fundamental Principles

1. Appendix I shall include all species threatened with extinction which are or may be affected by trade. Trade in specimens of these species must be subject to particularly strict regulation in order not to endanger further their survival and must only be authorized in exceptional circumstances.

2. Appendix II shall include:

(a) all species which although not necessarily now threatened with extinction may become so unless trade in specimens of such species is subject to strict regulation in order to avoid utilization incompatible with their survival; and

(b) other species which must be subject to regulation in order that trade in specimens of certain species referred to in sub-paragraph (a) of this paragraph may be brought under effective control.

3. Appendix III shall include all species which any Party identified as being subject to regulation within its jurisdiction for the purpose of preventing or restricting exploitation, and as needing the cooperation of other parties in the control of trade.

4. The Parties shall not allow trade in specimens of species included in Appendices I, II and III except in accordance with the provisions of the present Convention.

Article III

Regulation of Trade in Specimens of Species included in Appendix I

1. All trade in specimens of species included in Appendix I shall be in accordance with the provisions of this Article.

2. The export of any specimen of a species included in Appendix I shall require the prior grant and presentation of an export permit. An export permit shall only be granted when the following conditions have been met:

(a) a Scientific Authority of the State of export has advised that such export will not be detrimental to the survival of that species;

(b) a Management Authority of the State of export is satisfied that the specimen was not obtained in contravention of the laws of that State for the protection of fauna and flora;

(c) a Management Authority of the State of export is satisfied that any living specimen will be so prepared and shipped as to minimize the risk of injury, damage to health or cruel treatment; and

(d) a Management Authority of the State of export is satisfied that an import permit has been granted for the specimen.

3. The import of any specimen of a species included in Appendix I shall require the prior grant and presentation of an import permit and either an export permit or a re-export certi-

ficate. An import permit shall only be granted when the following conditions have been met:

(a) a Scientific Authority of the State of import has advised that the import will be for purposes which are not detrimental to the survival of the species involved;

(b) a Scientific Authority of the State of import is satisfied that the proposed recipient of a living specimen is suitably equipped to house and care for it; and

(c) a Management Authority of the State of import is satisfied that the specimen is not to be used for primarily commercial purposes.

4. The re-export of any specimen of a species included in Appendix I shall require the prior grant and presentation of a re-export certificate. A re-export certificate shall only be granted when the following conditions have been met:

(a) a Management Authority of the State of re-export is satisfied that the specimen was imported into that State in accordance with the provisions of the present Convention;

(b) a Management Authority of the State of re-export is satisfied that any living specimen will be so prepared and shipped as to minimize the risk of injury, damage to health or cruel treatment; and

(c) a Management Authority of the State of re-export is satisfied that an import permit has been granted for any living specimen.

5. The introduction from the sea of any specimen of a species included in Appendix I shall require the prior grant of a certificate from a Management Authority of the State of introduction. A certificate shall only be granted when the following conditions have been met:

(a) a Scientific Authority of the State of introduction advises that the introduction will not be detrimental to the survival of the species involved;

(b) a Management Authority of the State of introduction is satisfied that the proposed recipient of a living specimen is suitably equipped to house and care for it; and

(c) a Management Authority of the State of introduction is satisfied that the specimen is not to be used for primarily commercial purposes.

Article IV

Regulation of Trade in Specimens of Species included in Appendix II

1. All trade in specimens of species included in Appendix II shall be in accordance with the provisions of this Article.

2. The export of any specimen of a species included in Appendix II shall require the prior grant and presentation of an export permit. An export permit shall only be granted when the following conditions have been met:

(a) a Scientific Authority of the State of export has advised that such export will not be detrimental to the survival of that species;

(b) a Management Authority of the State of export is satisfied that the specimen was not obtained in contravention of the laws of that State for the protection of fauna and flora; and

(c) a Management Authority of the State of export is satisfied that any living specimen will be so prepared and shipped as to minimize the risk of injury, damage to health or cruel treatment.

3. A Scientific Authority in each Party shall monitor both the export permits granted by that State for specimens of species included in Appendix II and the actual exports of such specimens. Whenever a Scientific Authority determines that the export of specimens of any such species should be limited in order to maintain that species throughout its range at a level consistent with its role in the ecosystems in which it occurs and well above the level at which that species might become eligible for inclusion in Appendix I, the Scientific Authority shall advise the appropriate Management Authority of suitable measures to be taken to limit the grant of export permits for specimens of that species.

4. The import of any specimen of a species included in Appendix II shall require the prior presentation of either an export permit or a re-export certificate.

5. The re-export of any specimen of a species included in Appendix II shall require the prior grant and presentation of a re-export certificate. A re-export certificate shall only be granted when the following conditions have been met:

(a) a Management Authority of the State of re-export is satisfied that the specimen was imported into that State in accordance with the provisions of the present Convention; and

(b) a Management Authority of the State of re-export is satisfied that any living specimen will be so prepared and shipped as to minimize the risk of injury, damage to health or cruel treatment.

6. The introduction from the sea of any specimen of a species included in Appendix II shall require the prior grant of a certificate from a Management Authority of the State of introduction. A certificate shall only be granted when the following conditions have been met:

(a) a Scientific Authority of the State of introduction advises that the introduction will not be detrimental to the survival of the species involved; and

(b) a Management Authority of the State of introduction is satisfied that any living specimen will be so handled as to minimize the risk of injury, damage to health or cruel treatment.

7. Certificates referred to in paragraph 6 of this Article may be granted on the advice of a Scientific Authority, in consultation with other national scientific authorities or, when appropriate, international scientific authorities, in respect of periods not exceeding one year for total numbers of specimens to be introduced in such periods.

Article V

Regulation of Trade in Specimens of Species included in Appendix III

1. All trade in specimens of species included in Appendix III shall be in accordance with the provisions of this Article.

2. The export of any specimen of a species included in Appendix III from any State which has included that species in Appendix III shall require the prior grant and presentation of an export permit. An export permit shall only be granted when the following conditions have been met:

(a) a Management Authority of the State of export is satisfied that the specimen was not obtained in contravention of the laws of that State for the protection of fauna and flora; and

(b) a Management Authority of the State of export is satisfied that any living specimen will be so prepared and shipped as to minimize the risk of injury, damage to health or cruel treatment.

3. The import of any specimen of a species included in Appendix III shall require, except in circumstances to which paragraph 4 of this Article applies, the prior presentation of a certificate of origin and, where the import is from a State which has included that species in Appendix III, an export permit.

4. In the case of re-export, a certificate granted by the Management Authority of the State of re-export that the specimen was processed in that State or is being re-exported shall be accepted by the State of import as evidence that the provisions of the present Convention have been complied with in respect of the specimen concerned.

Article VI

Permits and Certificates

1. Permits and certificates granted under the provisions of Articles III, IV, and V shall be in accordance with the provisions of this Article.

2. An export permit shall contain the information specified in the model set forth in Appendix IV, and may only be used for export within a period of six months from the date on which it was granted.

3. Each permit or certificate shall contain the title of the present Convention, the name and any identifying stamp of the Management Authority granting it and a control number assigned by the Management Authority.

4. Any copies of a permit or certificate issued by a Management Authority shall be clearly marked as copies only and no such copy may be used in place of the original, except to the extent endorsed thereon.

5. A separate permit or certificate shall be required for each consignment of specimens.

6. A Management Authority of the State of import of any specimen shall cancel and retain the export permit or re-export certificate and any corresponding import permit presented in respect of the import of that specimen.

7. Where appropriate and feasible a Management Authority may affix a mark upon any specimen to assist in identifying the specimen. For these purposes "mark" means any indelible imprint, lead seal or other suitable means of identifying a specimen, designed in such a way as to render its imitation by unauthorized persons as difficult as possible.

Article VII

Exemptions and Other Special Provisions Relating to Trade

1. The provisions of Articles III, IV and V shall not apply to the transit or trans-shipment of specimens through or in the territory of a Party while the specimens remain in Customs control.

2. Where a Management Authority of the State of export or re-export is satisfied that a specimen was acquired before the provisions of the present Convention applied to that specimen, the provisions of Articles III, IV and V shall not apply to that specimen where the Management Authority issues a certificate to that effect.

3. The provisions of Articles III, IV and V shall not apply to specimens that are personal or household effects. This exemption shall not apply where:

  (a) in the case of specimens of a species included in Appendix I, they were acquired by the owner outside his State of usual residence, and are being imported into that State; or

  (b) in the case of specimens of species included in Appendix II:

    (i) they were acquired by the owner outside his State of usual residence and in a State where removal from the wild occurred;

    (ii) they are being imported into the owner's State of usual residence; and

    (iii) the State where removal from the wild occurred requires the prior grant of export permits before any export of such specimens;

unless a Management Authority is satisfied that the specimens were acquired before the provisions of the present Convention applied to such specimens.

4. Specimens of an animal species included in Appendix I bred in captivity for commercial purpose, or of a plant species included in Appendix I artificially propagated for commercial purposes, shall be deemed to be specimens of species included in Appendix II

5. Where a Management Authority of the State of export is satisfied that any specimen of an animal species was bred in captivity or any specimen of a plant species was artificially propagated, or is a part of such an animal or plant or was derived therefrom, a certificate by that Management Authority to that effect shall be accepted in lieu of any of the permits or certificates required under the provisions of Articles III, IV or V.

6. The provisions of Articles III, IV and V shall not apply to the non-commercial loan, donation or exchange between scientists or scientific institutions registered by a Management Authority of their State, of herbarium specimens, other preserved, dried or embedded museum specimens, and live plant material which carry a label issued or approved by a Management Authority.

7. A Management Authority of any State may waive the requirements of Articles III, IV and V and alow the movement without permits or certificates of specimens which form part of a travelling zoo, circus, menagerie, plant exhibition or other travelling exhibition provided that:

  (a) the exporter or importer registers full details of such specimens with that Management Authority;

  (b) the specimens are in either of the categories specified in paragraphs 2 or 5 of this Article; and

  (c) the Management Authority is satisfied that any living specimen will be so transported and cared for as to minimize the risk of injury, damage to health or cruel treatment.

Article VIII

Measures to be Taken by the Parties

1. The Parties shall take appropriate measures to enforce the provisions of the present Convention and to prohibit trade in specimens in violation thereof. These shall include measures:

  (a) to penalize trade in, or possession of, such specimens, or both; and

  (b) to provide for the confiscation or return to the State of export of such specimens.

2. In addition to the measures taken under paragraph 1 of this Article, a Party may, when it deems it necessary, provide for any method of internal reimbursement for expenses incurred as a result of the confiscation of a specimen traded in violation of the measures taken in the application of the provisions of the present Convention.

3. As far as possible, the Parties shall ensure that specimens shall pass through any formalities required for trade with a minimum of delay. To facilitate such passage, a Party may designate ports of exit and ports of entry at which specimens must be presented for clearance. The Parties shall ensure further that all living specimens, during any period of transit, holding or shipment, are properly cared for so as to minimize the risk of injury, damage to health or cruel treatment.

4. Where a living specimen is confiscated as a result of measures referred to in paragraph 1 of this Article:

  (a) the specimen shall be entrusted to a Management Authority of the State of confiscation;

  (b) the Management Authority shall, after consultation with the State of export, return the specimen to that State at the expense of that State, or to a rescue centre or such other place as the Management Authority deems appropriate and consistent with the purposes of the present Convention; and

  (c) the Management Authority may obtain the advice of a Scientific Authority, or may, whenever it considers it desirable, consult the Secretariat in order to facilitate the decision under subparagraph (b) of this paragraph, including the choice of a rescue centre or other place.

5. A rescue centre as referred to in paragraph 4 of this Article means an institution designated by a Management Authority to look after the welfare of living specimens, particularly those that have been confiscated.

6. Each Party shall maintain records of trade in specimens of species included in Appendices I, II and III which shall cover:

  (a) the names and addresses of exporters and importers; and

  (b) the number and type of permits and certificates granted; the States with which such trade occurred; the numbers or quantities and types of specimens, names of species as included in Appendices I, II and III and, where applicable, the size and sex of the specimens in question.

7. Each Party shall prepare periodic reports on its implementation of the present Convention and shall transmit to the Secretariat:

  (a) an annual report containing a summary of the information specified in sub-paragraph (b) of paragraph 6 of this Article; and

  (b) a biennial report on legislative, regulatory and administrative measures taken to enforce the provisions of the present Convention.

8. The information referred to in paragraph 7 of this Article shall be available to the public where this is not inconsistent with the law of the Party concerned.

Article IX

Management and Scientific Authorities

1. Each Party shall designate for the purpose of the present Convention:

  (a) one or more Management Authorities competent to grant permits or certificates on behalf of that Party; and

  (b) one or more Scientific Authorities.

2. A State depositing an instrument of ratification, acceptance, approval or accession shall at that time inform the Depositary Government of the name and address of the Management Authority authorized to communicate with other Parties and with the Secretariat.

3. Any changes in the designations or authorizations under the provisions of this Article shall be communicated by the Party concerned to the Secretariat for transmission to all other Parties.

4. Any Management Authority referred to in paragraph 2 of this Article shall if so requested by the Secretariat or the Management Authority of another Party, communicate to it impression of stamps, seals or other devices used to authenticate permits or certificates.

Article X

Trade with States not Party to the Convention

Where export or re-export is to, or import is from, a State not a party to the present Convention, comparable documentation issued by the competent authorities in that State which substantially conforms with the requirements of the present Convention for permits and certificates may by accepted in lieu thereof by any Party.

Article XV

Amendments to Appendices I and II

1. The following provisions shall apply in relation to amendments to Appendices I and II at meetings of the Conference of the Parties:

(a) Any Party may propose an amendment to Appendix I or II for consideration at the next meeting. The text of the proposed amendment shall be communicated to the Secretariat at least 150 days before the meeting. The Secretariat shall consult the other Parties and interested bodies on the amendment in accordance with the provisions of sub-paragraph (b) and (c) of paragraph 2 of this Article and shall communicate the response to all Parties not later than 30 days before the meeting.

(b) Amendments shall be adopted by a two-thirds majority of Parties present and voting. For these purposes "Parties present and voting" means Parties present and casting an affirmative or negative vote. Parties abstaining from voting shall not be counted among the two-thirds required for adopting an amendment.

(c) Amendments adopted at a meeting shall enter into force 90 days after that meeting for all Parties except those which make a reservation in accordance with paragraph 3 of this Article.

2. The following provisions shall apply in relation to amendments to Appendices I and II between meetings of the Conference of the Parties:

(a) Any Party may propose an amendment to Appendix I or II for consideration between meetings by the postal procedures set forth in this paragraph.

(b) For marine species, the Secretariat shall, upon receiving the text of the proposed amendment, immediately communicate it to the Parties. It shall also consult inter-governmental bodies having a function in relation to those species especially with a view to obtaining scientific data these bodies may be able to provide and to ensuring coordination with any conservation measures enforced by such bodies. The Secretariat shall communicate the views expressed and data provided by these bodies and its own findings and recommendations to the Parties as soon as possible.

(c) For species other than marine species, the Secretariat shall, upon receiving the text of the proposed amendment, immediately communicate it to the Parties, and, as soon as possible thereafter, its own recommendations.

(d) Any Party may, within 60 days of the date on which the Secretariat communicated its recommendations to the Parties under sub-paragraphs (b) or (c) of this paragraph, transmit to the Secretariat any comments on the proposed amendment together with any relevant scintific data and information.

(e) The Secretariat shall communicate the replies received together with its own recommendations to the Parties as soon as possible.

(f) If no objection to the proposed amendment is received by the Secretariat within 30 days of the date the replies and recommendations were communicated under the provisions of sub-paragraph (e) of this paragraph, the amendment shall enter into force 90 days later for all Parties except those which make a reservation in accordance with paragraph 3 of this Article.

(g) If an objection by any Party is received by the Secretariat, the proposed amendment shall be submitted to a postal vote in accordance with the provisions of sub-paragraphs (h), (i) and (j) of this paragraph.

(h) The Secretariat shall notify the Parties that notification of objection has been received.

(i) Unless the Secretariat receives the votes for, against or in abstention from at least one-half of the Parties within 60 days of the date of notification under sub-paragraph (h) of this paragraph, the proposed amendment shall be referred to the next meeting of the Conference for further consideration.

(j) Provided that votes are received from one-half of the Parties, the amendment shall be adopted by a two-thirds majority of Parties casting an affirmative or negative vote.

(k) The Secretariat shall notify all Parties of the result of the vote.

(l) If the proposed amendment is adopted it shall enter into force 90 days after the date of the notification by the Secretariat of its acceptance for all Parties except those which make a reservation in accordance with paragraph 3 of this Article.

3. During the period of 90 days provided for by sub-paragraph (c) of paragraph 1 or sub-paragraph (l) of paragraph 2 of this Article any Party may by notification in writing to the Depositary Government make a reservation with respect to the amendment.

Until such reservation is withdrawn the Party shall be treated as a State not a Party to the present Convention with respect to trade in the species concerned.

Article XVI

Appendix III and Amendments thereto

1. Any party may at any time submit to the Secretariat a list of species which it identifies as being subject to regulation within its jurisdiction for the purpose mentioned in paragraph 3 of Article II. Appendix III shall include the names of the Parties submitting the species for inclusion therein, the scientific names of the species so submitted, and any parts or derivatives of the animals or plants concerned that are specified in relation to the species for the purposes of sub-paragraph (b) of Article I.

2. Each list submitted under the provisions of paragraph 1 of this Article shall be communicated to the Parties by the Secretariat as soon as possible after receiving it. The list shall take effect as part of Appendix III 90 days after the date of such communication. At any time after the communication of such list, any Party may by notification in writing to the Depositary Government enter a reservation with respect to any species or any parts or derivatives, and until such reservation is withdrawn, the State shall be treated as a State not a Party to the present Convention with respect to trade in the species or part or derivative concerned.

3. A Party which has submitted a species for inclusion in Appendix III may withdraw it at any time by notification to the Secretariat which shall communicate the withdrawal to all Parties. The withdrawal shall take effect 30 days after the date of such communication.

4. Any Party submitting a list under the provisions of paragraph 1 of this Article shall submit to the Secretariat a copy of all domestic laws and regulations applicable to the protection of such species, together with any interpretations which the Party may deem appropriate or the Secretariat may request. The Party shall, for as long as the species in questions is included in Appendix III, submit any amendment of such laws and regulations or any new interpretations as they are adopted.

Article XVII

Amendment of the Convention

1. An extraordinary meeting of the Conference of the Parties shall be convened by the Secretariat on the written request of at least one-third of the Parties to consider and adopt amendments to the present Convention. Such amendments shall be adopted by a two-thirds majority of Parties present and voting. For these purposes "Parties present and voting" means Parties present and casting an affirmative or negative vote. Parties abstaining from voting shall not be counted among the two-thirds required for adopting an amendment.

2. The text of any proposed amendment shall be communicated by the Secretariat to all Parties at least 90 days before the meeting.

3. An amendment shall enter into force for the Parties which have accepted it 60 days after two-thirds of the Parties have deposited an instrument of acceptance of the amendment with the Depositary Government. Thereafter, the amendment shall enter into force for any other Party 60 days after that Party deposits its instrument of acceptance of the amendment.

Article XVIII

Resolution of Disputes

1. Any dispute which may arise between two or more Parties with respect to the interpretation or application of the provisions of the present Convention shall be subject to negotiation between the Parties involved in the dispute.

2. If the dispute cannot be resolved in accordance with paragraph 1 of this Article, the Parties may, by mutual consent, submit the dispute to arbitration, in particular that of the Permanent Court of Arbitration at The Hague and the Parties submitting the dispute shall be bound by the arbitral decision.

Article XIX

Signature

The present Convention shall be open for signature at Washington until 30th April 1973 and thereafter at Berne until 31st December 1974.

Article XI

Conference of the Parties

1. The Secretariat shall call a meeting of the Conference of the Parties not later than two years after the entry into force of the present Convention.

2. Thereafter the Secretariat shall convene regular meetings at least once every two years, unless the Conference decides otherwise, and extraordinary meetings at any time on the written request of at least one-third of the Parties.

3. At meetings, whether regular or extraordinary, the Parties shall review the implementation of the present Convention and may:

(a) make such provision as may be necessary to enable the Secretariat to carry out its duties;

(b) consider and adopt amendements to Appendices I and II in accordance with Article XV;

(c) review the progress made towards the restoration and conservation of the species included in Appendices I, II and III;

(d) receive and consider any reports presented by the Secretariat or by any Party; and

(e) where appropriate, make recommendations for improving the effectiveness of the present Convention.

4. At each regular meeting, the Parties may determine the time and venue of the next regular meeting to be held in accordance with the provisions of paragraph 2 of this Article.

5. At any meeting, the Parties may determine and adopt rules of procedure for the meeting.

6. The United Nations, its Specialized Agencies and the International Atomic Energy Agency, as well as any State not a Party to the present Convention, may be represented at meetings of the Conference by observers, who shall have the right to participate but not to vote.

7. Any body or agency technically qualified in protection, conservation or management of wild fauna and flora, in the following catagories, which has informed the Secretariat of its desire to be represented at meetings of the Conference by observers, shall be admitted unless at least one-third of the Parties present object:

(a) international agencies or bodies, either governmental or non-governmental, and national governmental agencies and bodies; and

(b) national non-governmental agencies or bodies which have been approved for this purpose by the State in which they are located.

Once admitted, these observers shall have the right to participate but not to vote.

Article XII

The Secretariat

1. Upon entry into force of the present Convention, a Secretariat shall be provided by the Executive Director of the United Nations Environment Programme. To the extent and in the manner he considers appropriate, he may be assisted by suitable inter-governmental or non-governmental, international or national agencies and bodies technically qualified in protection, conservation and management of wild fauna and flora.

2. The functions of the Secretariat shall be:

(a) to arrange for and service meetings of the Parties;

(b) to perform the functions entrusted to it under the provisions of Articles XV and XVI of the present Convention;

(c) to undertake scientific and technical studies in accordance with programmes authorized by the Conference of the Parties as will contribute to the implementation of the present Convention, including studies concerning standards for appropriate preparation and shipment of living specimens and the means of identifying specimens;

(d) to study the reports of Parties and to request from Parties such further information with respect thereto as it deems necessary to ensure implementation of the present Convention;

(e) to invite the attention of the Parties to any matter pertaining to the aims of the present Convention;

(f) to publish periodically and distribute to the Parties current editions of Appendices I, II and III together with any information which will facilitate identification of specimens of species included in those Appendices.

(g) to prepare annual reports to the Parties on its work and on the implementation of the present Convention and such other reports as meetings of the Parties may request;

(h) to make recommendations for the implementation of the aims and provisions of the present Convention, including the exchange of information of a scientific or technical nature;

(i) to perform any other function as may be entrusted to it by the Parties.

Article XIII

International Measures

1. When the Secretariat in the light of information received is satisfied that any species included in Appendices I or II is being affected adversely by trade in specimens of that species or that the provisions of the present Convention are not being effectively implemented, it shall communicate such information to the authorized Management Authority of the Party or Parties concerned.

2. When any Party receives a communication as indicated in paragraph 1 of this Article, it shall, as soon as possible, inform the Secretariat of any relevant facts insofar as its laws permit and, where appropriate, propose remedial action. Where the Party considers that an inquiry is desirable, such inquiry may be carried out by one or more persons expressly authorized by the Party.

3. The information provided by the Party or resulting from any inquiry as specified in paragraph 2 of this Article shall be reviewed by the next Conference of the Parties which may make whatever recommendations it deems appropriate.

Article XIV

Effect on Domestic Legislation and International Conventions

1. The provisions of the present Convention shall in no way affect the right of Parties to adopt:

(a) stricter domestic measures regarding the conditions for trade, taking, possession or transport of specimens of species included in Appendices I, II and III, or the complete prohibition thereof; or

(b) domestic measures restricting or prohibiting trade, taking, possession, or transport of species not included in Appendices I, II or III.

2. The provisions of the present Convention shall in no way affect the provisions of any domestic measures or the obligations of Parties deriving from any treaty, convention, or international agreement relating to other aspects of trade, taking, possession, or transport of specimens which is in force or subsequently may enter into force for any Party including any measure pertaining to the Customs, public health, veterinary or plant quarantine fields.

3. The provisions of the present Convention shall in no way affect the provisions of, or the obligations deriving from, any treaty, convention or international agreement concluded or which may be concluded between States creating a union or regional trade agreement establishing or maintaining a common external customs control and removing customs control between the parties thereto insofar as they relate to trade among the States members of that union agreement.

4. A State Party to the present Convention, which is also a party to any other treaty, convention or international agreement which is in force at the time of the coming into force of the present Convention and under the provisions of which protection is afforded to marine species included in Appendix II, shall be relieved of the obligation imposed on it under the provisions of the present Convention with respect to trade in specimens of species included in Appendix II that are taken by ships registered in that State and in accordance with the provisions of such other treaty, convention or international agreement.

5. Notwithstanding the provisions of Articles III, IV and V, any export of a specimen taken in accordance with paragraph 4 of this Article shall only require a certificate from a Management Authority of the State of introduction to the effect that the specimen was taken in accordance with the provisions of the other treaty, convention or international agreement in question.

6. Nothing in the present Convention shall prejudice the codification and development of the law of the sea by the United Nations Conference on the Law of the Sea convened pursuant to Resolution 2750 C (XXV) of the General Assembly of the United Nations nor the present or future claims and legal views of any State concerning the law of the sea and the nature and extent of coastal and flag State jurisdiction.

Article XX

Ratification, Acceptance, Approval

The present Convention shall be subject to ratification, acceptance or approval. Instruments of ratification, acceptance or approval shall be deposited with the Government of the Swiss Confederation which shall be the Depositary Government.

Article XXI

Accession

The present Convention shall be open indefinitely for accession. Instruments of accession shall be deposited with the Depositary Government.

Article XXII

Entry into Force

1. The present Convention shall enter into force 90 days after the date of deposit of the tenth instrument of ratification, acceptance, approval or accession, with the Depositary Government.

2. For each State which ratifies, accepts or approves the present Convention or accedes thereto after the deposit of the tenth instrument of ratification, acceptance, approval or accession, the present Convention shall enter into force 90 days after the deposit by such State of its instrument of ratification, acceptance, approval or accession.

Article XXIII

Reservations

1. The provisions of the present Convention shall not be subject to general reservations. Specific reservations may be entered in accordance with the provisions of this Article and Articles XV and XVI.

2. Any State may, on depositing its instrument of ratification, acceptance, approval or accession, enter a specific reservation with regard to:

(a) any species included in Appendix I, II or III; or

(b) any parts or derivatives specified in relation to a species concluded in Appendix III.

3. Until a Party withdraws its reservation entered under the provisions of this Article, it shall be treated as a State not a party to the present Convention with respect to trade in the particular species or parts or derivatives specified in such reservation.

Article XXIV

Denunciation

Any Party may denounce the present Convention by written notification to the Depositary Government at any time. The denunciation shall take effect twelve months after the Depositary Government has received the notification.

Article XXV

Depositary

1. The original of the present Convention, in the Chinese, English, French, Russian and Spanish languages, each version being equally authentic, shall be deposited with the Depositary Government, which shall transmit certified copies thereof to all States that have signed it or deposited instruments of accession to it.

2. The Depositary Government shall inform all signatory and acceding States and the Secretariat of signatures, deposit of instruments of ratification, acceptance, approval or accession, entry into force of the present Convention, amendments thereto, entry and withdrawal of reservations and notifications of denunciation.

3. As soon as the present Convention enters into force, a certified copy thereof shall be transmitted by the Depositary Government to the Secretariat of the United Nations for registration and publication in accordance with Article 102 of the Charter of the United Nations.

In witness whereof the undersigned Plenipotentiaries, being duly authorized to that effect, have signed the present Convention.

Done at Washington this third day of March, One Thousand Nine Hundred and Seventy-three.

CITES Members (as of 1 June 1982)

GRAND TOTAL: 77 COUNTRIES

ASIA

Bangladesh
People's Republic of China
India
Indonesia
Japan
Malaysia
Nepal
Pakistan
Philippines
Sri Lanka
USSR

TOTAL: 11

OCEANIA

Australia
Papua New Guinea

TOTAL: 2

EUROPE

Austria
Denmark
Finland
France
East Germany
Italy

Liechtenstein
Monaco
Norway
Portugal
Sweden
Switzerland
United Kingdom
West Germany

TOTAL: 14

MIDDLE EAST

Cyprus
Egypt
Iran
Israel
Jordan
United Arab Emirates

TOTAL: 6

AFRICA

Botswana
Cameroon
Central African Republic
Gambia
Ghana

Guinea
Liberia
Kenya
Madagascar
Malawi
Mauritius
Morocco
Mozambique
Niger
Nigeria
Rwanda
Senegal
Seychelles
Republic of South Africa
Tanzania
Togo
Tunisia
Zaire
Zambia
Zimbabwe

TOTAL: 25

SOUTH AMERICA

Argentina
Bolivia
Brazil
Chile

Colombia
Ecuador
Guyana
Paraguay
Peru
Suriname
Uruguay
Venezuela

TOTAL: 12

CENTRAL AMERICA

Costa Rica
Guatemala
Nicaragua
Panama

TOTAL: 4

CARIBBEAN

Bahamas

TOTAL: 1

NORTH AMERICA

Canada
United States

TOTAL: 2

Extinct Species of Birds, Mammals, Reptiles and Amphibians, 1600-Present

This list is presented in chronological order so that the increase in number of extinctions is more readily apparent. Classes are identified under the column of that name with codes: Birds—B; Mammals—M; Reptiles—R; Amphibians—A. A "c" preceding year of extinction denotes *circa*, or about. This list includes only full species, not sub-species, although the latter represent a genetic loss.

The major sources for this list were the following: Allen, G.M. 1972. *Extinct and Vanishing Mammals of the Western Hemisphere.* Cooper Square Publishers, Inc.; HRH Prince Philip, and James Fisher. 1970. *Wildlife Crisis.* Cowles Book Co.; Day, David. 1981. *The Doomsday Book of Animals.* Viking, N.Y.; Honegger, Renê. 1981. List of amphibians and reptiles either known or thought to have become extinct since 1600. *Biological Conservation,* 19(2):141–158; Greenway, James C., Jr. 1967. *Extinct and Vanishing Birds of the World,* Dover; International Council for Bird Preservation. 1965. *List of Birds Either Known or Thought to Have Become Extinct since 1600.* ICBP. 1980. *Red Data Book of Endangered Birds.* Smithsonian Institution Press: (the latter publication omitted the Passenger Pigeon). Some species considered extinct in the *Red Data Books* but still included in endangered or other categories were also added.

Year of Extinction	Species	Where Found	Class
c. 1600	Puerto Rican Caviomorph *Heptaxodon bidens*	Puerto Rico	M
c. 1600	Hispaniolan Hexolobodon *Hexolobodon phenax*	Haiti-Dominican Republic	M
c. 1600	Hispaniolan Narrow-toothed Hutia *Aphaetraeus montanus*	Haiti-Dominican Republic	M
c. 1600	Barbuda Musk-Rat *Megalomys audreae*	Barbuda I., West Indies	M
c. 1600	Hispaniolan Spiny Rat *Brotomys contractus*	Haiti-Dominican Republic	M
c. 1600	Hispaniolan Spiny Rat *Brotomys voratus*	Haiti-Dominican Republic	M
c. 1600	Gadow's Giant Tortoise *Geochelone gadowi*	Mascarene Islands	R
1627	Auroch *Bos primigenius*	Europe	M
1638	Mauritius Broad-billed Parrot *Lophopsittacus mauritianus*	Mascarene Islands	B
c. 1640	Burley Lesser Moa *Eurapteryx gravis*	New Zealand	B
c. 1649	Great Elephant Bird *Aepyornis maximus*	Madagascar	B
c. 1650	Eastern Cuban Nesophontes *Nesophontes longirostris*	Cuba	M
c. 1650	Western Cuban Nesophontes *Nesophontes micrus*	Cuba	M
c. 1650	Puerto Rico Nesophontes *Nesophontes edithae*	Puerto Rico	M

Year of Extinction	Species	Where Found	Class
1650	Mauritian Giant Skink *Didosaurus mauritianus*	Mascarene Islands	R
1656	Ascension Flightless Crake *Atlantisia elpenor*	Ascension Island, Atlantic Ocean	B
1669	Bourbon Parrot *Necropsittacus borbonicus*	Mascarene Islands	B
1669	Bourbon Pink Pigeon *Columba duboisi*	Mascarene Islands	B
c. 1670	Brawny Great Moa *Dinornis torosus*	New Zealand	B
1675	Van den Broecke's Red Rail *Aphanapteryx bonasia*	Mascarene Islands	B
1681	Dodo *Raphus cucullatus*	Mascarene Islands	B
1590-1690	Chatham Island Swan *Cygnus sumnerensis*	Chatham Island, Pacific Ocean	B
1691-1693	Leguat's Owl *Bubo leguati*	Mascarene Islands	B
1693	Rodrigues Pigeon *Alectroenas rodericana*	Mascarene Islands	B
c. 1700	Puerto Rican Isolobodon *Isolobodon portoricensis*	Puerto Rico	M
c. 1700	Quemis *Quemisia gravis*	Puerto Rico	M
1700	Mauritius Owl *Strix sauzieri*	Mascarene Islands	B
1730	Rodrigues Little Owl *Athene murivora*	Mascarene Islands	·B
1730	Flightless Night Heron *Nycticorax megacephalus*	Mascarene Islands	B
1730	Rodrigues Blue Rail *Aphanapteryx leguati*	Mascarene Islands	B
1746	Reunion Solitaire *Raphus solitarius*	Mascarene Islands	B
c. 1750	Puerto Rican 'Agouti' *Heteropsomys insulans*	Puerto Rico	M
c. 1750	Puerto Rican 'Agouti' *Homopsomys antillensis*	Puerto Rico	M
c. 1750	Lesser Falcate-Winged Bat *Phyllops vetus*	Cuba	M
c. 1750	Hispaniolan Hutia *Plagiodontia spelaeum*	Haiti-Dominican Republic	M
1760	Rodrigues Parrot *Necropsittacus rodericanus*	Mascarene Islands	B
1768	Steller's Sea Cow *Hydrodamalis stelleri*	Bering Sea	M
1773-4	Raiatea Parakeet *Cyanoramphus ulietensis*	Society Islands	B
1773	Reunion Giant Tortoise *Geochelone indica*	Mascarene Islands	R

Year of Extinction	Species	Where Found	Class	Year of Extinction	Species	Where Found	Class
1774	Tanna Ground Dove *Gallicolumba ferruginea*	New Hebrides Is.	B	1852	Spectacled Cormorant *Phalacrocorax perspicillatus*	Bering Island	B
1774	Mysterious Starling *Aplonis mavornata*	Society Islands	B	1853	Macgillivray's Petrel *Pterodroma macgillivrayi*	Fiji	B
1774	Raiatea Thrush *Turdus ulietensis*	Society Islands	B	1859	Kioea *Chaetoptila angustipluma*	Hawaiian Islands	B
c. 1774	Sardinian Pika *Prolagus sardus*	Sardinia	M	1859	Jamaican Least Parauque *Siphonorhis americanus*	Jamaica	B
1775	St. Helena Blue Dove *Columba sp.*	St. Helena I., Atlantic Ocean	B	1860	New Caledonia Lorikeet *Charmosyna diadema*	New Caledonia	B
1777	Tahiti Sandpiper *Prosobonia leucoptera*	Society Islands	B	1862	Bourbon Crested Starling *Fregilupus varius*	Mascarene Islands	B
1785	South Island Tokoweka *Megalapteryx didinus*	New Zealand	B	1864	Hawaiian Brown Rail *Pennula millsi*	Hawaiian Islands	B
1791	Rodrigues Solitaire *Pezophaps solitaria*	Mascarene Islands	B	1867	Eastern Barred Bandicoot *Perameles fasciata*	Australia	M
1799	Blue Buck *Hippotragus leucophaeus*	South Africa	M	1868	Himalayan Mountain Quail *Ophrysia superciliosa*	Himalayas	B
c. 1800	Rodrigues Tortoise *Geochelone peltastes*	Mascarene Islands	R	c. 1870	Cuban Spiny Rat *Boromys torrei*	Cuba	M
c. 1800	Seychelles Island Giant Tortoise *Geochelone sumeirei*	Seychelle Islands	R	1870	Cherry-throated Tanager *Nemosia rourei*	Brazil	B
1828	Kusaie Starling *Aplonis corvina*	Caroline Islands	B	c. 1870	Cuban Spiny Rat *Boromys offella*	Cuba	M
1828	Kittlitz's Thrush *Zoothera terrestris*	Bonin Islands	B	1873	Samoan Wood Rail *Pareudiastes pacificus*	Samoan Islands	B
1838	Kusaie Crake *Aphanolimnas monasa*	Caroline Islands	B	1874	Rodrigues Gecko *Phelsuma gigas*	Mascarene Islands	R
1830	Mauritius Blue Pigeon *Alectroenas nitidissima*	Mascarene Islands	B	1875	Labrador Duck *Camptorhynchus labradorium*	North America	B
1832	Leguat's Starling *Fregilupus rodericanus*	Mascarene Islands	B	1875	Newton's Parakeet *Psittacula exsul*	Mascarene Islands	B
1834	Mascarene Parrot *Mascarinus mascarinus*	Mascarene Islands	B	1875	New Zealand Quail *Coturnix novaezelandiae*	New Zealand	B
1835	Chatham Rice Rat *Oryzomys galapagoensis*	Galapagos Islands	M	1876	Kermadec Island Megapode *Megapodius sp.*	Kermadec Islands, Pacific Ocean	B
1837	Oahu 'O' o *Moho apicalis*	Hawaiian Islands	B	1876	Falkland Fox *Dusicyon australis*	Falkland Islands	M
1837	Mauritius Scops Owl *Otus commersoni*	Mascarene Islands	B	1877	Jamaican Rice Rat *Oryzomys antillarum*	Jamaica	M
1837	Martinique Lizard *Leiocephalus herminieri*	Martinique	R	1880	New Caledonia Owlet Frogmouth *Aegotheles savesi*	New Caledonia	B
1840	Chatham Island Banded Rail *Rallus dieffenbachii*	Chatham I., Pacific Ocean	B	c. 1880	Jamaican Giant Galliwasp *Diploglossus occidus*	Jamaica	R
1840	Gilbert's Rat Kangaroo *Potorus gilberti*	Australia	M	1881	Seychelles Parakeet *Psittacula wardi*	Seychelles Islands	B
c. 1840	Vosmaer's Giant Tortoise *Geochelone vosmaeri*	Mascarene Islands	R	1881	St. Lucia Musk-Rat *Megalomys luciae*	St. Lucia, West Indies	M
1840	Mangareva Kingfisher *Halcyon gambieri*	Tuamotu Islands	B	1881	St. Lucia Rice Rat *Oryzomys luciae*	St. Lucia, West Indies	M
1844	Tahiti Parakeet *Cyanoramphus zealandicus*	Society Islands	B	1882	Quagga *Equus quagga*	South Africa	M
1844	Great Auk *Alca impennis*	Funk I., Newfoundland	B	1885	Cuban Red Macaw *Ara tricolor*	Cuba	B
c. 1850	Cuban Short-tailed Hutia *Geocapromys colombianus*	Cuba	M	1887	Ryukyu Kingfisher *Halcyon miyakoensis*	Ryukyu Islands	B
c. 1850	Puerto Rican Long-tongued Bat *Phyllonycteris major*	Puerto Rico	M	1888	Sao Tome Grosbeak Weaver *Neospiza concolor*	Africa	B
c. 1850	Cuban Yellow Bat *Natalus primus*	Cuba	M	1889	Bonin Wood Pigeon *Columba versicolor*	Bonin Islands	B
1851	Norfolk Island Kaka *Nestor productus*	Norfolk I., Pacific Ocean	B	1890	Bonin Grosbeak *Chaunoproctus ferreorostris*	Bonin Islands	B
1851	Tarpan *Equus gmelini*	Europe	M	1890	Brown Hare Wallaby *Lagorchestes leporides*	Australia	M

Year of Extinction	Species	Where Found	Class
1891	Lesser Kona Finch *Psittirostra flaviceps*	Hawaiian Islands	B
1892	Ula-ai-Hawane *Ciridops anna*	Hawaiian Islands	B
1893	Hawaiian Spotted Rail *Pennula sandwichensis*	Hawaiian Islands	B
1894	Kona Finch *Psittirostra kona*	Hawaiian Islands	B
1894	Stephen Island Wren *Xenicus lyalli*	New Zealand	B
1894	Sea Mink *Mustela macrodon*	North America	M
1894	Mauritius Tortoise *Geochelone inepta*	Mascarene Islands	R
1895	Akialoa *Hemignathus obscurus*	Hawaiian Islands	B
1896	Hopue, or Greater Kona Finch *Psittirostra palmeri*	Hawaiian Islands	B
1898	Mamo *Drepanis pacifica*	Hawaiian Islands	B
1898	Gull Island Vole *Microtus nesophilus*	Long Island, N.Y. United States	M
c. 1900	Glaucous Macaw *Anodorhynchus glaucus*	South America	B
1900	Greater 'Amakihi *Loxops sagittirostris*	Hawaiian Islands	B
1900	Guadalupe Caracara *Polyborus lutosus*	Guadalupe Island, Mexico	B
1900	Jerdon's Courser *Cursorius bitorguatus*	India	B
1900	Chatham Island Rail *Rallus modestus*	Chatham Island, Pacific Ocean	B
1900	Tahiti Rail *Rallus pacificus*	Society Islands	B
c. 1900	Bulldog Rat *Rattus nativitatus*	Christmas Island Indian Ocean	M
c. 1900	Maclear's Rat *Rattus macleari*	Christmas Island	M
c. 1900	St. Vincent Rice Rat *Oryzomys victus*	St. Vincent, West Indies	M
c. 1900	Haitian Long-tongued Bat *Phyllonycteris obtusa*	Haiti	M
c. 1900	Christmas Island Shrew *Crocidura trichura*	Christmas Island	M
c. 1900	Jamaican Long-tongued Bat *Reithronycteris aphylla*	Jamaica	M
c. 1900	St. Francis Island Potoroo *Porotous sp.*	Australia	M
1900	Navassa Island Lizard *Leiocephalus eremitus*	Navassa Island, West Indies	R
1902	Martinique Rice Rat *Oryzomys desmaresti*	Martinique, West Indies	M
1902	Martinique Musk-Rat *Megalomys desmaresti*	Martinique, West Indies	M
1902	Barbuda Rice Rat *Orzomys audreyae*	Barbuda, West Indies	M
1904	Choiseul Crested Pigeon *Microgoura meeki*	Solomon Islands	B
1904	New Caledonia Wood Rail *Tricholimnas lafresnayanus*	New Caledonia	B
1905	Auckland Island Merganser *Mergus australis*	Auckland Islands	B
1906	Four-colored Flowerpecker *Dicaeum quadricolor*	Philippine Islands	B
1906	James Rice Rat *Oryzomys swarthi*	Galapagos Islands	M
1907	Huia *Heteralocha acutirostris*	New Zealand	B
1907	Black Mamo *Drepanis funerea*	Hawaiian Islands	B
1908	Broadfaced Rat-Kangaroo *Potorus platyops*	Australia	M
1908	Dawson's Caribou *Rangifer dawsoni*	Canada	M
1910	Slender-billed Grackle *Cassidix palustris*	Mexico	B
c. 1911	Brown-banded Antpitta *Grallaria milleri*	Colombia, South America	B
c. 1911	Olive-headed Brush-Finch *Atlapetes flaviceps*	Colombia, South America	B
c. 1912	Tumaco Seedeater *Sporophila insulata*	Colombia, South America	B
1912	Guadalupe Storm Petrel *Oceanodroma macrodactyla*	Guadalupe Island, Mexico	B
1914	Passenger Pigeon *Ectopistes migratorius*	North America	B
1914	Carolina Parakeet *Conuropsis carolinensis*	North America	B
1917	Hispaniolan Fig-eating Bat *Phyllops haitiensis*	Dominican Republic—Haiti	M
1917	Newton's Day Gecko *Phelsuma edwardnewtoni*	Mascarene Islands	R
1920	Ameiva Lizard *Ameiva cineracea*	Guadeloupe, West Indies	R
1922	Red-moustached Fruit Dove *Ptilinopus mercierii*	Society Islands	B
1924	Crested Shelduck *Tadorna cristata*	Asia	B
c. 1925	Lord Howe & Norfolk Island Starling *Aplonis fuscus*	Lord Howe & Norfolk Islands, Pacific Ocean	B
c. 1927	Paradise Parakeet *Psephotus pulcherrimus*	Australia	B
1927	Pig-footed Bandicoot *Chaeropus ecaudatus*	Australia	M
1928	Lord Howe White-eye *Zosterops strenua*	Lord Howe Island, Pacific Ocean	B
c. 1930	Hispaniolan Nesophontes *Nesophontes zamicrus*	Dominican Republic—Haiti	M
1930	Madagascar Serpent Eagle *Eutriorchis astur*	Madagascar	B
1930	Madagascar Coucal *Coua delalandei*	Madagascar	B
1930	Atalaye Nesophontes *Nesophontes hypomicrus*	Haiti	M
c. 1930	St. Michel Nesophontes *Nesophontes paramicrus*	Haiti	M
c. 1930	Giant AyeAye *Daubentonia robusta*	Madagascar	M
1931	Fanovana Newtonia *Newtonia fanovanae*	Madagascar	B
1932	Schomburgk's Deer *Cervus schomburgki*	Thailand	M
c. 1933	Thylacine *Thylacinus cynocephalus*	Tasmania	M
c. 1934	Heinroth's Shearwater *Puffinus heinrothi*	Pacific Ocean	B
1934	Hawaii 'O'o *Moho nobilis*	Hawaiian Islands	B
1936	Ryukyu Wood Pigeon *Columba jouyi*	Ryukyu Islands, Pacific Ocean	B

Year of Extinction	Species	Where Found	Class
1938	Grand Cayman Thrush *Turdus ravidus*	Cayman Islands, West Indies	B
1938	Toulache Wallaby *Macropus greyi*	Australia	M
c. 1940	Rufous Gazelle *Gazella rufina*	North Africa	M
1943	Magdalena Tinamou *Crypturellus saltuarius*	Colombia, South America	B
1944	Pink-headed Duck *Rhodonessa caryophyllacea*	India	B
1944	Laysan Rail *Porzanula palmeri*	Hawaiian Islands	B
1945	Wake Island Rail *Rallus wakensis*	Wake Island, Pacific Ocean	B
1945	Darwin's Rice Rat *Oryzomys darwini*	Galapagos Islands	M
c. 1945	Indefatigable Rice Rat *Oryzomys indefessus*	Galapagos Islands	M
1950	New Zealand Laughing Owl *Sceloglaux albifacies*	New Zealand	B
c. 1950	St. Croix Racer *Alsophis sancticrucis*	Virgin Islands	R
1952	Caribbean Monk Seal *Monachus tropicalis*	Caribbean region	M

Year of Extinction	Species	Where Found	Class
c. 1954	Helmeted Woodpecker *Dryocopus galeatus*	South America	B
1940–1956	Israel Painted Frog *Discoglossus nigriventer*	Israel	A
c. 1957	Brasilia Tapaculo *Scytalopus novacapitalis*	Brazil	B
c. 1958	Imperial Woodpecker *Campephilus imperialis*	Mexico	B
1959	Hierro Giant Lizard *Gallotia simonyi*	Canary Islands	R
c. 1960	Martinique Giant Ameiva *Ameiva major*	Martinique, West Indies	R
c. 1960	Jamaica Tree Snake *Alsophis ater*	Jamaica, West Indies	R
1962	Martinique Racer *Dromicus cursor*	Martinique, West Indies	R
1963	Piopio *Turnagra capensis*	New Zealand	B
1968	Jamaica Iguana *Cyclura collei*	Jamaica, West Indies	R
1973	St. Lucia Racer *Dromicus ornatus*	St. Lucia, West Indies	R

Drawing from The Doomsday Book of Animals

The **Passenger Pigeon.**

Rare, Endangered and Threatened Species of Mammals, Birds, Reptiles and Amphibians

This list is a composite of the species in the IUCN *Red Data Books*, under which the categories are Endangered (E), Vulnerable (V), Rare (R), Indeterminate (I) and Out of danger (O); the United States Endangered Species Act of 1973 whose categories are Endangered (E) and Threatened (T); the CITES, whose categories are Appendix I, II and III (see Trade or International Legislation sections for definitions); and finally the species listed by the legislation of various U.S. states, whose categories Endangered (E), Threatened (T), Rare (R) were included, and other categories such as undetermined and peripheral were omitted. The latter species are only those actually protected by law, not species recommended for protection by various state or private publications. When a category is followed by an asterisk* it indicates that certain subspecies or populations are exempted and listed under other categories noted below. States which adopted the federal Endangered Species Act list but have not compiled a list of species endangered in their states were not included in the states list. The following 19 states protect species on the federal Endangered Species Act list: Alaska, Arkansas, Connecticut, Delaware, Idaho, Kentucky, Louisiana, Maine, Massachusetts, Minnesota, Montana, Nevada, North Carolina, Oklahoma, Pennsylvania, Rhode Island, Utah, Virginia, and Wyoming. If your state is listed above, refer to the U.S. list column to learn which native species it protects as endangered or threatened. *Sp.* indicates species, and *spp.* species plural.

An example of listings in which confusion could arise is the Brown Bear, *Ursus arctos*. This species occurs throughout Canada and Alaska, in a few U.S. states, Mexico (although probably extinct there), and in

scattered parts of Eurasia. The species as a whole is not listed by any of the above (*Red Data Book*, CITES, U.S. Endangered Species Act or states). All North American populations are listed by CITES Appendix II except the Mexican, which is Appendix I. The U.S. Act lists the Grizzly (a subspecies) as Threatened in the lower 48 states and Endangered in Mexico. The *Red Data Book* also lists the Mexican Grizzly as Endangered and the Barren-ground Grizzly subspecies of tundra areas as Rare. In Eurasia, the U.S. Act protects the Tibetan & Palearctic subspecies as Endangered, and the CITES lists the Tibetan, Italian and Himalayan subspecies or populations on Appendix II. Therefore, many populations such as those in Scandinavia, Russia and parts of Asia are unlisted. The *Red Data Book*, it should be stressed, does not confer legal protection, but is valuable as a guide for which species are endangered. Subspecies within a listing are abbreviated, e.g., Grizzly Bear listed under *Ursus arctos*, is *U.a.horribilis*.

Appendix III of CITES lists species protected by individual countries and this list notes the country in parentheses. For example, the African species, Aardwolf, *Proteles cristatus*, is listed under CITES, Appendix III with Botswana in parentheses, meaning that a permit is required for export of this species from Botswana. An example of the use of asterisks is the Asiatic Wild Ass, *Equus hemionus*. The species as a whole is considered vulnerable by the *Red Data Book*, and CITES lists it on Appendix II. However, three subspecies, the Indian (*E.h.khur*), Mongolian (*E.h.hemionus*) and Syrian (*E.h.hemippus*) are considered endangered by the *Red Data Book* and two of these are in Appendix I of CITES. The U.S. Endangered Species lists the species as endangered.

A Guide to the Following List

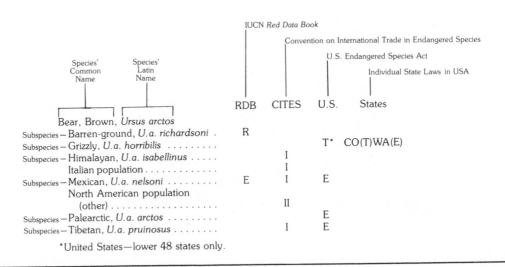

IUCN *Red Data Book*

Convention on International Trade in Endangered Species

U.S. Endangered Species Act

Individual State Laws in USA

Species' Common Name   Species' Latin Name

	RDB	CITES	U.S.	States
Bear, Brown, *Ursus arctos*				
Subspecies — Barren-ground, *U.a. richardsoni* .	R			
Subspecies — Grizzly, *U.a. horribilis*			T*	CO(T)WA(E)
Subspecies — Himalayan, *U.a. isabellinus*		I		
Italian population		I		
Subspecies — Mexican, *U.a. nelsoni*	E	I	E	
North American population (other)		II		
Subspecies — Palearctic, *U.a. arctos*			E	
Subspecies — Tibetan, *U.a. pruinosus*		I	E	

*United States—lower 48 states only.

MAMMALS	RDB	CITES	U.S.	States
Aardvark, *Orycteropus afer*		II		
Aardwolf, *Proteles cristatus*		III (Botswana)		
Addax, *Addax nasomaculatus*	V	II		
Anoa, Lowland, *Bubalus depressicornis*	E	I	E	
Anoa, Mountain, *Bubalus quarlesi*	E	I	E	
Anteater, Collared, *Tamandua tetradactyla*		III (Guatemala)		
Mato Grosso, *T.t. chapadensis*		II		
Anteater, Giant, *Myrmecophaga tridactyla*	V	II		
Anteater, Scaly, *Manis temmincki*		I	E	
Antelope, Beira, *Dorcatragus megalotis*	V			
Antelope, Bontebok, *Damaliscus dorcas dorcas*	O	II	E	
Antelope, Four-horned, *Tetracerus quadricornis*		III (Nepal)		
Antelope, Giant Sable, *Hippotragus niger variani*	E	I	E	
Antelope, Mongolian Saiga, *Saiga tatarica mongolica*			E	
Antelope, Roan, *Hippotragus equinus*		II		
Argali, see Moufflon				
Armadillo, Brazilian Three-banded, *Tolypeutes tricinctus*	I			
Armadillo, Central American Naked-tailed *Cabassous centralis*		III (Costa Rica)		
Armadillo, Giant, *Priodontes giganteus*	V	I	E	
Armadillo, Pink Fairy, or Lesser Pichiego *Chlamphorus truncatus*	V		E	
Armadillo, Uruguay Naked-tailed *Cabassous gymnurus* (tetouay)		III (Uruguay)		
Ass, African Wild, *Equus africanus*	E		E	
Ass, Asiatic Wild, *Equus hemionus*	V•	II•	E	
•Indian, *E.h. khur*	E	I		
•Mongolian, *E.h. hemionus*	E	I		
•Syrian, *E.h. hemippus*	E			
Avahis, *Avahi spp.*		I	E	
Avahi, Western Woolly, *Avahi laniger occidentalis*	V	I	E	
Ayeaye, *Daubentonia madagascariensis*	E	I	E	
Babirusa, *Babyrousa babyrussa*	V	I	E	
Badger, *Taxidea taxus*				IN(E)
Bandicoot, Desert, *Perameles eremiana*			E	
Bandicoot, Lesser Rabbit, *Macrotis leucura*		I	E	
Bandicoot, Pig-footed, *Chaeropus ecaudatus*	E	I	E	
Bandicoot, Rabbit-eared or Bilby, *Macrotis lagotis*	E	I	E	
Bandicoot, Western Barred, *Perameles bougainville*		I	E	
Banteng, *Bos javanicus*	V		E	
Bat, Evening, *Nycticeius humeralis*				IA(T)
Bat, Ghost, *Macroderma gigas*	E			
Bat, Gray, *Myotis grisescens*	E		E	FL(E)GA(E) IL(E)IN(E) KS(E)MO(E) TN(E)
Bat, Hawaiian Hoary, *Lasiurus cinereus semotus*	R		E	HI(E)
Bat, Indiana, *Myotis sodalis*	V		E	FL(E)GA(E) IL(E)IA(E) IN(E)MD(E) MI(E)MO(E) MS(E)NH(E) NY(E)OH(E) TN(E)
Bat, Keen's, *Myotis keenii*				IA(T)MO(R)
Bat, Singapore Roundleaf Horseshoe, *Hipposideros ridleyi*	E			
Bat, Southeastern Myotis, *Myotis austroriparius*				IN(E)
Bat, Spotted, *Euderma maculata*	R			
Bat, Western Big-eared, *Plecotus townsendi*				
Ozark, *P.t. ingens*	R		E	MO(R)
Virginia, *P.t. virginianus*	R		E	IN(E)MO(R)
Bat, Western Mastiff, *Eumops perotis*				NM(T)
Bat, White-lined, *Vampyrops lineatus*		III (Uruguay)		
Bat, Yellow, *Lasiurus ega xanthinus*				NM(T)

MAMMALS	RDB	CITES	U.S.	States
Bear, Asiatic, *Selenarctos thibetanus*		I		
Baluchistan, *S.t. gedrosianus*	E			
Bear, Black, *Ursus americanus*				FL(T)[1]IA(E) MS(T)MO(R) SD(T)
Bear, Brown, *Ursus arctos*				
Barren-ground, *U.a. richardsoni*	R			
Grizzly, *U.a. horribilis*			T[2]	CO(T)WA(E)
Himalayan, *U.a. isabellinus*		I		
Italian population		I		
Mexican, *U.a. nelsoni*	E	I	E	
North American populations (other)		II		
Palearctic, *U.a. arctos*			E	
Tibetan, *U.a. pruinosus*		I	E	
Bear, Polar, *Ursus maritima*	V	II		
Bear, Sloth, *Melursus ursinus*	I			
Bear, Spectacled, *Tremarctos ornatus*	V	I		
Bear, Sun, *Helarctos malayanus*		I		
Beaver, Mongolian, *Castor fiber birulai*			E	
Bison, European, *Bison bonasus*	O			
Bison, North American Wood, *Bison bison athabascae*		I		
Blackbuck, *Antilope cervicapra*		III (Nepal)		
Bobcat, *Felis rufus*		II*		IL(T)IA(E) IN(E)OH(E)
*Mexican, *F.r. escuinapae*		I	E	
Bongo, *Boocercus euryceros*		III (Ghana)		
Brocket, Guatemalan Red, *Mazama americana cerasina*		III (Guatemala)		
Buffalo, Asiatic, *Bubalus bubalis*	V	III (Nepal)·		
Bushbabies, *Galago spp.*		II		
Cacomistle, Central American, *Bassariscus sumichrasti*		III (Costa Rica)		
Camel, Bactrian, *Camelus bactrianus*	V		E	
Caracal, *Felis caracal*		II*		
*Asian populations		I		
Turkmenian, *F.c. michaelis*	R			
Caribou, *Rangifer tarandus montanus*				WA(T)
Cats, *Felidae*, all species not listed on App. I.		II		
Cat, Andean, *Felis jacobita*	R	I	E	
Cat, Black-footed, *Felis nigripes*		I	E	
Cat, Bornean Marbled, *Felis badia*	R	II		
Cat, Flat-headed, *Felis planiceps*	I	I	E	
Cat, Golden or Temminck's, *Felis temmincki*	I	I	E	
Cat, Iriomote, *Prionailurus iriomotensis*	E	II	E	
Cat, Leopard, *Felis bengalensis*		II*		
*Indian, *F.b. bengalensis*		I	E	
Cat, Little Spotted or Tiger, *Felis tigrina*		II*	E	
*Costa Rican, *F.t. oncilla*		I		
Cat, Marbled, *Felis marmorata*	I	I	E	
Cat, Rusty-spotted, *Felis rubiginosa*		II*		
*Indian population		I		
Cat, Sand, *Felis margarita*		II		
Pakistan, *F.m. scheffeli*	E			
Chamois, Abruzzi, *Rupicapra rupicapra ornata*		I	E	
Cheetah, *Acinonyx jubatus*	V*	I	E	
*Asiatic, *A.j. venaticus*	E			
Chevrotain, Water, *Hyemoschus aquaticus*		III (Ghana)		
Chimpanzee, *Pan troglodytes*	V	I	T	
Chimpanzee, Pygmy, *Pan paniscus*	V	I	T	

[1]except in Baker & Columbia counties and Apalachicola National Forest
[2]United States—lower 48 states only

MAMMALS	RDB	CITES	U.S.	States
Chinchillas, *Chinchillidae* (all species)		I		
Chinchilla, *Chinchilla brevicaudata boliviana*		I	E	
Chinchilla, *Chinchilla laniger*	V	I		
Chiru (Gazelle-Goat), *Pantholops hodgsoni*		I		
Civet, African, *Viverra civetta*		III (Botswana)		
Civet, Banded Palm, *Hemilagus derbyanus*		II		
Civet, Celebes Giant Palm, *Macrogalidia musschenbroeki*	R			
Civet, Malabar Large-spotted, *Viverra megaspila civettina*	R E		E	
Civet, Malagasy, *Fossa fossa*	V	II		
Coati, South Brazil, *Nasua nasua solitaria*		III (Uruguay)		
Coatimundi, *Nasua narica molaris*				NM(T)
Cochito (Baja California Dolphin) *Phocoena sinus*	V	I		
Colobus monkeys, all species not on App. I		II		
Colobus, Black, *Colobus satanus*	V	II	E	
Colobus, Olive, *Colobus verus*	R	II		
Colobus, Red, *Colobus badius*				
Preuss's, *C.b. preussi*	E	II		
Tana River, *C.b. rufomitratus*	E	I	E	
Uehe, *C.b. gordonorum*	R	II		
Zanzibar, *C.b.kirkii*	R	I	E	
Cougar, Puma or Mountain Lion, *Felis concolor*		II*		SD(T)
*Eastern, *F.c. cougar*	E	I	E	GA(E)MD(E) MS(E)MO(E) TN(E)
*Florida, *F.c. coryi*	E	I	E	FL(E)GA(E)
*Costa Rican, *F.c. costaricensis*		I	E	
Cuscus, Common Spotted, *Phalanger maculatus*		II		
Cuscus, Grey, *Phalanger orientalis*		II		
Deer, Brow-antlered, *Cervus eldi*		I	E	
Manipur, *C.e. eldi*	E			
Thailand, *C.e. siamensis*	E			
Deer, Calamian or Philippine, *Axis calamianensis*	V	I	E	
Deer, Cedros Island Black-tailed or Mule, *Odocoileus hemionus cerrosensis*	E		E	
Deer, Hog, *Axis porcinus annamiticus*		I	E	
Deer, Kuhl's, *Axis kuhli*	R	I	E	
Deer, Marsh, *Blastocerus dichotomus*	V	I	E	
Deer, Musk, all species not on App. I		II*		
*Deer, Musk, *Moshus moschiferus moschiferus*	V	I	E	
Deer, Pampas, *Ozotoceros bezoarticus*		I	E	
Argentine, *O.b. celer*	E			
Deer, Persian Fallow, *Dama mesopotamica*	E	I	E	
Deer, Red, *Cervus elaphus*				
Bactrian, *C.e. bactrianus*	E	II	E	
Barbary Stag, *C.e. barbarus*	E	III (Tunisia)	E	
Corsican, *C.e. corsicanus*	E		E	
Hangul, *C.e. hanglu*	E	I	E	
M'Neill's, *C.e. macneillii*	I		E	
Shou, *C.e. wallichi*	E		E	
Yarkand, *C.e. yarkandensis*	E		E	
Deer, Sika, *Cervus nippon*				
Formosan, *C.n. taiouanus*	E		E	
North China, *C.n. mandarinus*	E		E	
Ryukyu, *C.n. keramae*	E		E	
South China, *C.n. kopschi*	E		E	
Deer, Swamp, *Cervus duvauceli*	E	I	E	
Deer, Thorold's, *Cervus albirostris*		I		
Deer, White-tailed, *Odocoileus virginianus*		I		
Columbian, *O.v. leucurus*	E		E	OR(E)WA(E)
Guatemalan, *O.v. mayensis*		III (Guatemala)		
Key, *O.v. clavium*	O		E	FL(T)
Desman, Pyrenean, *Galemys pyrenaicus*	O R			
Desman, Russian, *Desmana moschata*	V			
Dibatag, or Clark's Gazelle, *Ammodorcas clarkei*	V		E	

MAMMALS	RDB	CITES	U.S.	States
Dibbler, *Antechinus apicalis*	R		E	
Dog, African Wild, *Lycaon pictus*	V			
Dog, Asiatic Wild, or Dhole, *Cuon alpinus*	V	II	E	
Dog, Bush, *Speothos venaticus*	R	I		
Dog, Small-eared, *Atelocynus microtis*	R			
Dolphins, all species not on App. I		II		
Dolphin, Ganges, *Platanista gangetica*		I		
Dolphins, Hump-backed, *Sousa spp.*		I		
Dolphin, Indus, *Platanista indi*	E	I		
Dolphin, Whitefin, *Lipotes vexillifer*	I	I		
Drill, *Papio leucophaeus*	E	I	E	
Dugong, *Dugong dugon*	V	I*	E	
*Australian population		II		
Duiker, Blue, *Cephalophus monticola*		II		
Duiker, Jentink's, *Cephalophus jentinki*	E		E	
Dunnart, see Marsupial—Mouse				
Echidnas, Long-beaked, *Zaglossus spp.*		II		
Echidna, Long-beaked, *Zaglossus bruijni*	I	II		
Eland, Western Giant, *Taurotragus derbianus derbianus*	E		E	
Elephant, African, *Loxodonta africana*	V	II	T	
Elephant, Asian, *Elaphas maximus*	E	I	E	
Elk, Tule, *Cervus canadensis nannodes*	O			
Fanalouc, *Eupleres goudotii*	V	II		
Fanalouc, Western, *Eupleres major*		II		
Ferret, Black-footed, *Mustela nigripes*	E	I	E	CO(E)KS(E) NE(E)NM(E) SD(E)TX(E)
Flying Fox, Guam, *Pteropus tokudae*	E			
Flying Fox, Marianas, *Pteropus mariannus*	V			
Flying Fox, Mauritian, *Pteropus niger*	R			
Flying Fox, Rodrigues, *Pteropus rodricensis*	E			
Fossa, *Cryptoprocta ferox*	V	II		
Fox, Argentine Grey, *Dusicyon griseus*		II		
Fox, Blanford's, *Vulpes cana*		II		
Fox, Chiloe Grey, *Dusicyon fulvipes*		II		
Fox, Colpeo, *Dusicyon culpaeus*		II		
Fox, Fennec, *Fennecus zerda*		III (Tunisia)		
Fox, Kit, *Vulpes macrotis*				
San Joaquin, *V.m. mutica*	E		E	CA(R) OR(T)
V.m. nevadensis				CA(R)
Fox, Island, *Urocyon littoralis*	E		E	
Fox, Northern Swift, *Vulpes velox hebes*		I		NE(E)SD(E)
Fox, Sierra Nevada Red, *Vulpes vulpes necator*	E		E	CA(R)
Fox, Simien, *Canis simensis*	V	I	E	
Gaur, *Bos gaurus*			E	
Gazelle, Arabian, *Gazella gazella*	E			
Arabian, *G.g. arabica*				
Edmi, *G.g. cuvieri*		III (Tunisia)		
Gazelle, Cuvier's *Gazella cuvieri*	E		E	
Gazelle, Dama, *Gazella dama*				
Mhorr, *G.d. mhorr*	E		E	
Rio de Oro, *G.d. lozanoi*	E		E	
Gazelle, Dorcas, *Gazella dorcas*		III (Tunisia)		
Moroccan, *G.d. massaesyla*	E		E	
Pelzeln's *G.d. pelzelni*	E		E	
Saudi Arabian, *G.d. saudiya*	E		E	
Gazelle, Sand, *Gazella subgutturosa marica*	E	III (Tunisia)	E	
Gazelle, Slender-horned, *Gazella leptoceros*	E		E	
Gazelle, Speke's, *Gazella spekei*	I			
Gelada, *Theropithecus gelada*			T	
Gibbons, *Hylobates spp.*		I	E	
Gibbon, Black, *Hylobates concolor*	I	I	E	
Gibbon, Kloss's, *Hylobates klossi*	V	I	E	

MAMMALS	RDB	CITES	U.S.	States
Gibbon, Javan, *Hylobates moloch*	E	I	E	
Gibbon, Pileated, *Hylobates pileatus*	E	I	E	
Gopher, Colonial Pocket, *Geomys colonus*				GA(E)
Gopher, Goff's Pocket, *Geomys pinetus goffi*				FL(E)
Gopher, Plains Pocket, *Geomys bursarius*				IN(E)
Gopher, Southern Pocket, *Thomomys umbrinus emotus*				NM(T)
Goral, Common, *Nemorhaedus goral*		I	E	
Gorilla, *Gorilla gorilla*	V*	I	E	
*Mountain, *G.g. beringei*	E			
Grison, Central American, *Galictus allamandi*		III (Costa Rica)		
Guanaco, *Lama guanicoe*		II		
Gymnure, Mindanao, *Podogymnura truei*	V			
Hangul, see Deer, Red				
Hare-Wallaby, Banded, see under Wallaby				
Hare-Wallaby, Rufous, see under Wallaby				
Hartebeest, *Alcelaphus buselaphus*				
Swayne's *A.b. swaynei*	E		E	
Tora, *A.b. tora*	E		E	
Hartebeest, Hunter's, *Damaliscus hunteri*	R			
Hedge-hog, South African, *Erinaceus frontalis*		II		
Hippopotamus, *Hippopotamus amphibius*		III (Ghana)		
Hippopotamus, Pygmy, *Choeropsis liberiensis*	V	II		
Hog, Pygmy, *Sus salvanius*	E	I	E	
Hopping-mice, see Mice, Australian				
Horse, Przewalski's, *Equus przewalskii*	E	I	E	
Huemul, North Andean, *Hippocamelus antisensis*	V	I	E	
Huemul, South Andean, *Hippocamelus bisulcus*	I	I	E	
Hutia, Bahaman, *Geocapromys ingrahami*	R			
Hutia, Bushy-tailed, *Capromys melanurus*	R			
Hutia, Cuvier's, *Plagiodontia aedium*	R			
Hutia, Dominican, *Plagiodontia hylaeum*	R			
Hutia, Dwarf, *Capromys nanus*	R			
Hutia, Jamaica, *Geocapromys brownii*	V			
Hyaena, Barbary, *Hyaena hyaena barbara*	E		E	
Hyaena, Brown, *Hyaena brunnea*	V	I	E	
Ibex, Pyrenean, *Capra pyrenaica pyrenaica*	E		E	
Ibex, Walia, *Capra walie*	E		E	
Impala, Black-faced, *Aepyceros melampus petersi*	E		E	
Indri, *Indri indri*	E	I	E	
Jackrabbit, Black-tailed, *Lepus californicus*				MO(R)
Jackrabbit, White-sided, *Lepus callotis gaillardi*				NM(E)
Jackrabbit, White-tailed, *Lepus townsendii*				IL(E)MO(E)
Jaguar, *Panthera onca*	V	I	E	TX(E)
Jaguarundi, *Felis yagouaroundi*		II*		
*Guatemalan, *F.y. fossata*		I	E	
*Panamanian, *F.y. panamensis*		I	E	
*Sinaloan, *F.y. tolteca*		I	E	
*Tamaulipas, *F.y. cacomitli*		I	E	TX(E)
Kangaroo, Eastern Gray, *Macropus giganteus*			T*	
*Tasmanian, *M.g. tasmaniensis*			E	
Kangaroo, Red, *Megeleia rufa*			T	
Kangaroo, Western Gray, *Macropus fulginosus*			T	
Kangaroo Rat, Big-eared, *Dipodomys elephantinus*	R			
Kangaroo Rat, Fresno, *Dipodomys nitratoides exilis*				CA(E)
Kangaroo Rat, Giant, *Dipodomys ingens*				CA(E)
Kangaroo Rat, Morro Bay, *Dipodomys heermanni morroensis*	E		E	CA(E)
Kangaroo Rat, Phillip's, *Dipodomys phillipsii phillipsii*		II		
Kangaroo Rat, Stephen's *Dipodomys stephensi*				CA(R)
Kangaroo Rat, Texas, *Dipodomys elator*	R			
Kouprey, *Bos sauveli*	E	I	E	
Langur, Capped, *Presbytis pileatus*		I	E	
Langur, Douc, *Pygathrix nemaeus*	E	I	E	
Langur, Entellus, *Presbytis entellus*		I	E	
Langur, Golden, *Presbytis geei*	R	I	E	
Langur, Mentawai Islands or Long-tailed *Presbytis potenziani*	I	I	T	

MAMMALS	RDB	CITES	U.S.	States
Langur, Nilgiri, *Presbytis johni*	V	II		
Langur, Pig-tailed, *Simias concolor*	E	I	E	
Langur, Purple-faced, *Presbytis senex*		II	T	
Langur, Snub-nosed, *Rhinopithecus roxellana*	R	II		
Langur, Snub-nosed, *Rhinopithecus roxellana*	V	II	T	
Lechwe, *Kobus leche*				MI(T)
Lemming, Southern Bog, *Synaptomys cooperi*		I	E	
Lemurs, all species, *Lemuridae*		I	E	
Lemur, Black, *Lemur macao*				
Black, *L.m. macao*	E			
Red-fronted, *L.m. rufus*	E			
Sanford's, *L.m. sanfordi*	E			
Sclater's, *L.m. flavifrons*	E			
Lemur, Broad-nosed Gentle, *Hapalemur simus*	R	I	E	
Lemur, Coquerel's Mouse, *Microcebus coquereli*	V	I	E	
Lemur, Fat-tailed Dwarf, *Cheirogaleus medius*	V	I	E	
Lemur, Fork-marked Mouse, *Phaner furcifer*	I	I	E	
Lemur, Grey Gentle, *Hapalemur griseus*	V	I	E	
Lemur, Hairy-eared Dwarf, *Allocebus trichotis*	R	I	E	
Lemur, Mongoose, *Lemur mongoz*	V	I	E	
Lemur, Sportive, *Lepilemur mustelinus*		I	E	
Nossi-be, *L.m. dorsalis*	R			
Red-tailed, *L.m. ruficaudatus*	E			
White-footed, *L.m. leucopus*	E			
Leopard, *Panthera pardus*	V*	I	E**	
**Africa, Gabon, Congo, Zaire, Uganda, Kenya & countries south of these			T	
*Amur, *P.p. orientalis*	E			
*Anatolian, *P.p. tulliana*	E			
*Barbary, *P.p. panthera*	E			
*Sinai, *P.p. jarvisi*	E			
*South Arabian, *P.p. nimr*	V			
Leopard, Clouded, *Neofelis nebulosa*	E	I	E	
Leopard, Snow, *Panthera uncia*		I	E	
Linsang, Banded, *Prionodon linsang*		II		
Linsang, Spotted, *Prionodon pardicolor*		I	E	
Lion, *Panthera leo*		II*		
*Asiatic, *P.l. persica*	E	I	E	
Loris, Lesser Slow, *Nycticebus pygmaeus*		II	T	
Lynx, *Lynx canadensis*		II		CO(E)NH(E) WI(E)
Lynx, Spanish, *Felis pardina*	E	II	E	
Macaque, Barbary, *Macaca sylvana*	V	II		
Macaque, Formosan Rock, *Macaca cyclopis*		II	T	
Macaque, Japanese, *Macaca fuscata*		II	T	
Macaque, Lion-tailed, *Macaca silenus*	E	I	E	
Macaque, Mentawai Islands, *Macaca pagensis*	I	II		
Macaque, Stump-tailed, *Macaca arctoides*		II	T	
Macaque, Toque, *Macaca sinica*		II	T	
Manatee, Amazonian, *Trichechus inunguis*	E	I	E	
Manatee, Caribbean, *Trichechus manatus*	V	I	E	FL(E)GA(E) TX(E)
Manatee, West African, *Trichechus senegalensis*	V	II	T	
Mandrill, *Papio sphinx*		I	E	
Mangabey, Tana River, *Cercocebus galeritus*			E	
C.g. galeritus	E	I		
Mangabey, White-collared, *Cerococebus torquatus*		II	E	
Margay, *Felis wiedii*		II*	E	TX(E)
*Central American, *F.w. nicaraguae*		I		
*Guatemalan, *F.w. salvinia*		I		
Markhor, *Capra falconeri*	V*	II*		
*Chiltan, *C.f. chiltanensis*		I	E	
*Kabul or Straight-horned, *C.f. megaceros*	E	I	E	
*Suleman, *C.f. jerdoni*		I	E	
Marmoset, Buff-headed, *Callithrix flaviceps*	R	I		
Marmoset, Cotton-top, *Saguinus oedipus*		I		
S.o. oedipus	E		E	
Marmoset, Goeldi's, *Callimico goeldii*	I	I	E	

MAMMALS	RDB	CITES	U.S.	States
Marmoset, Golden Lion, *Leontopithecus rosalia*	E	I	E	
Marmoset, Golden-rumped, *Leontopithecus chrysopygus*	E	I	E	
Marmoset, Golden-headed, *Leontopithecus chrysomelas*	E	I	E	
Marmoset, Tassel-eared, *Callithrix humeralifer*	I	II		
Marmoset, White, *Callithrix argentata leucippe*	V	II		
Marmoset, White-eared, *Callithrix aurita*	V	I		
Marmot, Menzbier's, *Marmota menzbieri*	V			
Marmot, Vancouver Island, *Marmota vancouverensis*	I			
Marsupial, Eastern Jerboa, *Antechinomys laniger*	E		E	
Marsupial-mouse, Large Desert, *Sminthopsis psammophila*		I	E	
Marsupial-mouse, Long-tailed, *Sminthopsis longicaudata*	I	I	E	
Marten, Formosan Yellow-throated, *Martes flavigula chrysospila*			E	
Marten, Pine, *Martes americana*				MI(T)NH(T) NM(T)WI(E)
Mice, Australian, *Notomys spp.*		II		
Mink, *Mustela vison*				
M.v. energumenos				NM(T)
Everglades, *M.v. evergladensis*				FL(T)
Mole, Giant Golden, *Chrysoplax trevelyani*	R			
Mole, Juliana's Golden, *Amblysomus julianae*	R			
Mole, Star-nosed, *Condylura cristata*				IN(E)
Monkeys, All species not on Appendix I		II		
Monkey, Black Howler, *Alouatta pigra*	I	II	T	
Monkey, Brown Howler, *Alouatta fusca*	I	II		
Monkey, Central American Squirrel or Red-backed, *Saimiri oerstedi* ...	E	I	E	
Monkey, Diana, *Cercopithecus diana*		I	E	
Monkey, Francois Leaf, *Presbytis francoisi*		II	E	
Monkey, Howler, *Alouatta villosa*		II	E	
Monkey, L'hoest's, *Cercopithecus lhoesti*		II	E	
Monkey, Proboscis, *Nasalis larvatus*	V	I	E	
Monkey, Red-bellied, *Cercopithecus erythrogaster*		II	E	
Monkey, Red-eared Nose-spotted, *Cercopithecus erythrotis*		II	E	
Monkey, Spider, *Ateles geoffroyi*		II		
A.g. frontatus			E	
A.g. panamensis			E	
Monkey, Tonkin Snub-nosed, *Rhinopithecus avunculus*		II	T	
Monkey, Woolly, *Lagothrix lagothicha*	V	II		
Monkey, Woolly Spider, *Brachyteles arachnoides*	E	I	E	
Monkey, Yellow-tailed Woolly, *Lagothrix flavicauda*	E	II	E	
Moufflon, Argali, *Ovis ammon*		II*		
*Cyprus Moufflon, *O.a. ophion*		I		
Mediterranean Moufflon, *O.a. musimon*	E			
*Tibetan Argali, *O.a. hodgsoni*		I	E	
Mouse, Australian Native, *Notomys aquilo*		II	E	
Mouse, Australian Native, *Notomys pedunculatus*		II	E	
Mouse, Beach, *Peromyscus polionotus*				
Choctawhatchee, *P.p. allophrys*				FL(T)
Pallid, *P.p. decoloratus*				FL(E)
Perdido Bay, *P.p. trissyllepsis*				FL(T)
Mouse, Field's, *Pseudomys fieldi*			E	
Mouse, Florida, *Peromyscus floridanus*				FL(T)
Mouse, Golden, *Peromyscus nuttalli*				IL(T)
Mouse, Gould's, *Pseudomys gouldii*			E	
Mouse, Grasshopper, *Onychomys leucogaster*				IA(E)
Mouse, Heath, see Mouse, Shortridge's				
Mouse, Key Largo Cotton, *Peromyscus gossypinus restrictus*				FL(E)
Mouse, Nelson's Pocket, *Perognathus nelsoni canescens*				NM(T)
Mouse, New Holland, *Pseudomys novaehollandiae*			E	
Mouse, Plains Pocket, *Perognathus flavescens*				IA(E)
Mouse, Salt Marsh Harvest, *Reithrodontomys raviventris*	E		E	CA(E)
Mouse, Shark Bay, *Pseudomys praeconis*		I	E	
Mouse, Shortridge's, *Pseudomys shortridgei*		II	E	
Mouse, Smoky, *Pseudomys fumeus*		I	E	
Mouse, Western, *Pseudomys occidentalis*			E	
Mouse, Western Harvest, *Reithrodontomys megalotis*				IN(E)
Muntjac, Black, *Muntiacus crinifrons*	I			
Muntjac, Fea's, *Muntiacus feae*	E		E	

MAMMALS	RDB	CITES	U.S.	States
Musk-shrew, Maquassi, *Crocidura maguassiensis*	R			
Narwhal, *Monodon monocerus*		II		
Native-cat, Eastern, *Dasyurus viverrinus*			E	
Numbat, *Myrmecobius fasciatus*			E	
Olingo, Bushy-tailed, *Bassaricyon gabbii*		III (Costa Rica)		
Ocelot, *Felis pardalis*	V	II*	E	TX(E)
*Brazilian, *F.p. mitis*		I		
*Costa Rican, *F.p. mearnsi*		I		
Orangutan, *Pongo pygmaeus*	E	I	E	
Oryx, Arabian, *Oryx leucoryx*	E	I	E	
Oryx, Scimitar-horned, *Oryx dammah*	V	II		
Otters, all species not on Appendix I		II		
Otter, Cameroon Clawless, *Aonyx microdon*	R	I	E	
Otter, European, *Lutra lutra*		I		
Lutra l. lutra	V			
Otter, Giant, *Pteronura brasiliensis*	E	I	E	
Otter, La Plata or Long-tailed, *Lutra platensis (longicaudis)*	E	I	E	
Otter, Marine, *Lutra felina*	E	I	E	
Otter, River, *Lutra canadensis*		II		CO(E)IL(T) IN(E)IA(T) MO(E)NM(E) OH(E)SD(T) TN(T) OR(T)WA(E)
Otter, Southern Sea, *Enhydra lutris nereis*		I	T	
Otter, Southern River, *Lutra provocax*	E	I	E	
Otter-civet, *Cynogale bennetti*		II		
Panda, Giant, *Ailuropoda melanoleuca*	R			
Panda, Lesser, *Ailurus fulgens*		II		
Pangolin, Chinese, *Manis pentadactyla*		II		
Pangolin, Giant, *Manis gigantea*		III (Ghana)		
Pangolin, Indian, *Manis crassicaudata*		II		
Pangolin, Long-tailed, *Manis longicaudata*		III (Ghana)		
Pangolin, Malayan, *Manis javanica*		II		
Pangolin, Temminck's, see Anteater, Scaly				
Pangolin, Tree, *Manis tricuspis*		III (Ghana)		
Peccary, Chacoan, *Catagonus wagneri*	V			
Peccary, Collared, *Tayassu tajacu*		III (Guatemala)		
Phascogale, Red-tailed, *Phascogale calura*	R			
Pichiciego, Greater, *Burmeisteria retusa*	R			
Pichiciego, Lesser, see Armadillo, Pink Fairy				
Planigale, Kimberley, or Little, *Planigale subtilissima*	R		E	
Planigale, Narrow-nosed or Southern, *Planigale tenuirostris*	R		E	
Porcupines, Crested, *Hystrix spp.*		III (Ghana)		
Porcupine, Thin-spined, *Chaetomys subspinosus*	R		E	
Porcupine, Spiny Tree, *Coendou spinosus*		III (Uruguay)		
Porpoises, all species not on Appendix I		II		
Porpoise, Finless, *Neophocaena phocaenoides*		I		
Possum, Leadbeater's, *Gymnobelideus leadbeateri*	E			
Possum, Mountain Pigmy, *Burramys parvus*		II	E	
Possum, Scaly-Tailed, *Wyulda squamicaudata*	R		E	
Potto, *Perodicticus potto*		II		
Prairie Dog, Black-tailed, *Cynomys ludovicanus*				NM(T)
Prairie Dog, Mexican, *Cynomys mexicanus*	V	I	E	
Prairie Dog, Utah, *Cynomys parvidens*	R		E	
Primates, all species not on Appendix I		II		
Pronghorn, *Antilocapra americana*				
Lower California, *A.a. peninsularis*	E	I	E	
Mexican, *A.a. mexicana*		II		
Sonoran, *A.a. sonoriensis*	E	I	E	
Pudu, Northern, *Pudu mephistophiles*	I	II		

MAMMALS	RDB	CITES	U.S.	States
Pudu, Southern, *Pudu pudu*		I	E	
Quokka, *Setonix brachyurus*			E	
Rabbit, Assam or Hispid Hare, *Caprolagus hispidus*	E	I	E	
Rabbit, Pigmy, *Sylvilagus idahoensis*				WA(T)
Rabbit, Ryukyu, *Pentalagus furnessi*	E		E	
Rabbit, Sumatra Short-eared, *Nesolagus netscheri*	R	II		
Rabbit, Swamp, *Sylvilagus aquaticus*				IN(E)MO(R)
Rabbit, Volcano, *Romerolagus diazi*	E	I	E	
Raccoon, Key Vaca, *Procyon lotor auspicatus*				FL(T)
Rat, False Water, see Water-Rat, False				
Rat, Greater Stick-nest, *Leporillus conditor*		I	E	
Rat, Rice, *Oryzomys palustris*				IL(T)
Rat, Ryukyu Spiny, *Tokudaia osimensis muenninki*	I			
Rat, Silver Rice, *Oryzomys argentatus*				FL(E)
Rat-Kangaroos, *Bettongia spp.*		I		
Rat-Kangaroo, Brush-tailed, *Bettongia penicillata*		I	E	
Rat-Kangaroo, Desert or Plain, *Caloprymnus campestris*	R	I	E	
Rat-Kangaroo, Gaimard's, *Bettongia gaimardi*			E	
Rat-Kangaroo, Lesueur's, *Bettongia lesueur*	R	I	E	
Rat-Kangaroo, Northern or Queensland, *Bettongia tropica*	R	I	E	
Ratel, *Mellivora capensis*		III (Ghana)		
Rhinoceros, Black, *Diceros bicornis*	V	I	E	
Rhinoceros, Great Indian, *Rhinoceros unicornis*	E	I	E	
Rhinoceros, Javan, *Rhinoceros sondaicus*	E	I	E	
Rhinoceros, Sumatran, *Didermocerus sumatrensis*	E	I	E	
Rhinoceros, White, *Ceratotherium simum*		I		
Northern, *C.s. cottoni*	E		E	
Rock-rat, Central, *Zyzomys pedunculatus*		I		
Saki, White-nosed, *Chiropotes albinasus*	V	I	E	
Sea Lion, Japanese, *Zalophus californianus japonicus*	E			
Seal, Caribbean Monk, *Monachus tropicalis*	E	I	E	
Seals, Fur all species not on App. I		II		
Seal, Galapagos Fur, *Arctocephalus galapagoensis*	V	II		
Seal, Guadalupe Fur, *Arctocephalus townsendi*	V	I	E	CA(R)
Seal, Hawaiian Monk, *Monachus schauinslandi*	E	I	E	HI(E)
Seal, Juan Fernandez Fur, *Arctocephalus philippi*	V	II		
Seal, Kurile Harbor, *Phoca kurilensis*	I			
Seal, Mediterranean Monk, *Monachus monachus*	E	I	E	
Seal, Northern Elephant, *Mirounga angustirostris*		II		
Seal, Saimaa, *Phoca hispida saimensis*	R			
Seal, Southern Elephant, *Mirounga leonina*		II		
Serow, Sumatran, *Capricornis sumatraensis*		I		
C.s. sumatraensis	E		E	
Serval, Barbary, *Felis serval constantina*			E	
Shapo, see Urial				
Sheep, Barbary, *Ammotragus lervia*		III (Tunisia)		
Sheep, Bighorn, *Ovis canadensis*	V	II		
California, *O.c. californiana*				CA(R)
Desert, *O.c. mexicana*				NM(E)TX(E)
Peninsular, *O.c. cremnobates*				CA(R)
Shou, see Deer, Red				
Shrew, Arizona, *Sorex arizonae*				NM(E)
Shrew, Pigmy, *Microsorex hoyi thompsoni*				MI(T)
Siamang, *Symphalangus syndactylus*		I	E	
Sifakas, *Propithecus spp.*		I	E	
Sifaka, Perrier's *Propithecus diadema perrieri*	R	I		
Sifaka, Verreaux's, *Propithecus verreauxi*	E	I		
Sitatunga, *Tragelaphus spekei*		III (Ghana)		
Skunk, Patagonian, *Conepatus humboldti*		II		
Sloth, Bolivian Three-toed, *Bradypus boliviensis*		II		
Sloth, Grey Three-toed, *Bradypus griseus*		III (Costa Rica)		
Sloth, Hoffman's, *Choloepus hoffmanni*		III (Costa Rica)		

223

MAMMALS	RDB	CITES	U.S.	States
Sloth, Maned or Three-toed Brazilian, *Bradypus torquatus*	R		E	
Solenodon, Cuban, *Atopogale cubana*	R		E	
Solenodon, Haitian, *Solenodon paradoxus*	E		E	
Squirrel, Deppe's, *Sciurus deppei*		III (Costa Rica)		
Squirrel, Four-striped Ground, *Lariscus hosei*	R	II		
Squirrel, Fox, *Sciurus niger*				
Delmarva Peninsula, *S.n. cinereus*	E		E	MD(E)
Mangrove, *S.n. avicennia*				FL(T)
Squirrel, Franklin's Ground, *Spermophilus franklini*				IN(E)
Squirrel, Mohave Ground, *Spermophilus mohavensis*				CA(R)
Squirrels, Oriental Giant, *Ratufa spp.*		II		
Squirrels, Pygmy Scaly-tailed, *Idiurus spp.*		III (Costa Rica)		
Squirrel, San Joaquin Antelope, *Ammospermophilus nelsoni*				CA(R)
Squirrels, Scaly-tailed, *Anomalurus spp.*		III (Ghana)		
Squirrel, Southern Flying, *Glaucomys volans*				NE(T)
Squirrel, Temminck's Giant, *Epixerus ebii*		III (Ghana)		
Stag, Barbary, see Deer, Red				
Stick-nest Rat, Greater, see Rat, Greater Stick-nest				
Suni, Zanzibar, *Neotragus moschatus moschatus*	E		E	
Tahr, Arabian, *Hemitragus jayakari*	E		E	
Tahr, Nilgiri, *Hemitragus hylocrius*	V			
Takin, *Budorcas taxicolor*				
Golden, *B.t. bedfordi*	R			
Szechwan, *B.t. tibetana*	I			
Tamaraw, *Bubalus mindorensis*	E	I	E	
Tamarin, Emperor, *Saguinus imperator*	I	II		
Tamarin, Pied, *Saguinus bicolor*	I	I	E	
Tamarin, White-footed, *Saguinus leucopus*	I	I	T	
Tapir, Brazilian, *Tapirus terrestris*		II	E	
Tapir, Central American, *Tapirus bairdii*	E	I	E	
Tapir, Malayan, *Tapirus indicus*	E	I	E	
Tapir, Mountain, *Tapirus pinchaque*		I	E	
Tarsier, Bornean, *Tarsius bancanus borneanus*	I	II		
Tarsier, Eastern, *Tarsius spectrum*	I	II		
Tarsier, Philippine, *Tarsius syrichta*	E	II	T	
Thylacine, *Thylacinus cynocephalus*	E	I	E	
Tiger, *Panthera tigris*	E	I*	E	
*Siberian, *P.t. altaica (amurensis)*		II		
Titi, Masked, *Callicebus personatus*	I	II		
Tree-Kangaroo, Bennett's *Dendrolagus bennettianus*		II		
Tree-Kangaroo, Black, *Dendrolagus ursinus*		II		
Tree-Kangaroo, Grizzled, *Dendrolagus inustus*		II		
Tree-Kangaroo, Lumholtz', *Dendrolagus lumholtzi*		II		
Tsessebi, *Damaliscus lunatus*		III (Ghana)		
Uakari, *Cacajao calvus*	I*	I	E	
White, *C.c. calvus*	E			
Red, *C.c. rubicundus*	E			
Uakari, Black-headed, *Cacajao melanocephalus*	V	I	E	
Urial, Shapo, *Ovis (orientalis) vignei*		I	E	
O. orientalis ophion			E	
Vicuna, *Lama vicugna*	V	I	E	
Vole, Amargosa, *Microtus californicus scirpensis*				CA(E)
Vole, Arizona Montane, *Microtus montanus arizonensis*				NM(T)
Vole, Beach Meadow, *Microtus breweri*	R			
Vole, Block Island Meadow, *Microtus pennsylvanicus provectus*	R			
Vole, Pine, *Microtus pinetorum*				IA(E)
Vole, Red-backed, *Clethrionomys gapperi*				IA(E)
Wallaby, Banded Hare, *Lagostrophus fasciatus*	R	I	E	
Wallaby, Brindled Nail-tailed, *Onychogalea frenata*	E	I	E	
Wallaby, Crescent Nail-tailed, *Onychogalea lunata*	E	I	E	
Wallaby, Parma, *Macropus parma*	R		E	
Wallaby, Western Hare, *Lagorchestes hirsutus*	R	I	E	

MAMMALS	RDB	CITES	U.S.	States
Wallaby, Yellow-footed Rock, *Petrogale xanthopus*	V		E	
Walrus, *Odobenus rosmarus*		III (Canada)		
Laptev, *O.r. laptevi*	I			
Water-rat, False, *Xeromys myoides*		I	E	
Weasel, Least, *Mustela nivalis*				MO(R)
Weasel, Long-tailed, *Mustela frenata*				MO(R)
Whales, all species not on Appendix I		II		
Whale, Blue, *Balaenoptera musculus*	E	I	E	MD(E)NJ(E) TX(E)WA(E)
Whale, Bowhead, *Balaena mysticetus*	E	I	E	
Whale, Finback, *Balaenoptera physalus*	V	I	E	HI(E)MD(E) NJ(E)TX(E) WA(E)
Whale, Gray, *Eschrictius robustus*		I	E	WA(E)
Whale, Humpback, *Megaptera novaengliae*	E	I	E	GA(E)HI(E) MD(E)NJ(E) WA(E)
Whale, Northern Bottlenose, *Hyperoodon ampullatus*	V	II		
Whale, Right, *Eubalaena glacialis*	E	I	E	GA(E)MD(E) NJ(E)TX(E) WA(E)
Whale, Sei, *Balaenoptera borealis*		I	E	MD(E)NJ(E) WA(E)
Whale, Sperm, *Physeter catodon*		I	E	HI(E)MD(E) NJ(E)TX(E) WA(E)
Wildebeest, Black, *Connochaetes gnou*	O			
Wolf, Gray, *Canis lupus*	V	II*		
*Indian Populations in Bhutan, India, Nepal and Pakistan		I		
Minnesota, U.S.A.			T	
U.S.A.—lower 48 states except Minnesota			E	CO(E)MI(E) IN(E)NY(E) NM(E)TX(E) WA(E)WI(E)
Wolf, Maned, *Chrysocyon brachyurus*	V	II	E	
Wolf, Red, *Canis rufus*	E		E	MS(E)TX(E)
Wolverine, *Gulo gulo*				CA(R)CO(E) OR(T)
Wombat, Barnard's, *Lasiorhinus barnardi*			E	
Wombat, Northern Hairy-nosed, *Lasiorhinus krefftii*		I		
Wombat, Queensland Hairy-nosed, *Lasiorhinus gillespiei*			E	
Woodrat, Eastern, *Neotoma floridana*				IL(E)
Allegheny, *N.f. magister*				IN(E)OH(E)
Key Largo, *N.f. smalli*				FL(E)
Yak, Wild, *Bos (grunniens) mutus*	E	I	E	
Zebra, Grevy's, *Equus grevyi*	E	I	T	
Zebra, Mountain, *Equus zebra*	V			
Cape Mountain, *E.z. zebra*		I	E	
Hartmann's, *E.z. hartmannae*		II	T	

BIRDS	RDB	CITES	U.S.	States
'Akepa, *Loxops coccinea*				
Hawaii, *L.c. coccinea*	V		E	HI(E)
Maui, *L.c. ochracea*	E		E	HI(E)
'Akialoa, Kauai, *Hemignathus procerus*	E		E	HI(E)
'Akiapola'au, *Hemignathus wilsoni*	E		E	HI(E)
Albatross, Short-tailed, or Steller's, *Diomedea albatrus*	E	I	E	
Amakihi, Maui, *Loxops virens wilsoni*				HI(E)
Antbird, Slender, *Rhopornis ardesiaca*	V			
Antpitta, Brown-banded, *Grallaria milleri*	I			
Antwren, Black-hooded, *Myrmotherula erythronotos*	E			
Antwren, Narrow-billed, *Formicivora iheringi*	V			
Barbet, Ngoye Green, *Stactolaema olivacea woodwardi*	R			
Barbet, Toucan, *Semnornis ramphastinus*	V			
Bellbird, Marcgrave's Bearded, *Procnias averano averano*	V			

BIRDS	RDB	CITES	U.S.	States
Bird, Secretary, *Sagittarius serpentarius*		II		
Birds of Paradise, *Paradisaeidae spp.*		II		
Birds of Prey, *Falconiformes*		II*		
*New World Vultures excepted and App. I species				
Bittern, American, *Botaurus lentiginosus*				IL(E)
Blackbird, Brewer's, *Euphagus cyanocephalus*				IL(T)
Blackbird, Grey-headed Mountain, *Turdus poliocephalus poliocephalus*	E			
Blackbird, Saffron-cowled, *Xanthopsar flavus*		III		
		(Uruguay)		
Blackbird, Yellow-headed, *Xanthocephalus xanthocephalus*				IL(E)
Blackbird, Yellow-shouldered, *Agelaius xanthomus*			E	
Mona Island, *A.x. monensis*	V			
Puerto Rico, *A.x. xanthomus*	V			
Bluebird, Eastern, *Sialia sialis*				NH(T)
Bobolink, *Dolichonyx oryzivorus*				NJ(T)
Bobwhite, Masked, see Quail, Bobwhite				
Booby, Abbott's, *Sula abbotti*	E	I	E	
Bristlebird, Western, *Dasyornis brachypterus longirostris*	R	I	E	
Bristlebird, Western Rufous, *Dasyornis broadbenti littoralis*	E	I	E	
Bristlefront, Stresemann's, *Merulaxis stresemanni*	I			
Brush-finch, Olive-headed, *Atlapetes flaviceps*	I			
Bulbul, Mauritius Olivaceous, *Hysipetes borbonicus olivaceous*			E	
Bullfinch, Sao Miguel, *Pyrrhula pyrrhula murina*	E		E	
Bunting, Grosbeak, *Neospiza wilkinski*	R			
Bunting, Varied, *Passerina versicolor*				NM(T)
Bush-shrike, Black-capped, *Malaconotus alius*	E			
Bush-shrike, Kupe Mountain, *Malaconotus kupeensis*	R			
Bustard, Great, *Otis tarda*		II		
Bustard, Great Indian, *Choriotis nigriceps*	E	I	E	
Bustard, Houbara, *Chlamydotis undulata*		I		
Buttonquail, Black-breasted, *Turnix melanogaster*		II		
Cahow, see Petrel, Bermuda				
Calyptura, Kinglet, *Calyptura cristata*	I			
Capercaillie, Cantabrian, *Tetrao urugallus cantabricus*	E			
Caracara, *Polyborus cheriway*				FL(E)NM(E)
Cardinal, Yellow, *Gubernatrix cristata*		III		
		(Uruguay)		
Chachalaca, Plain, *Ortalis vetula*		III		
		(Guatemala)		
Utila, *O.v. deschauenseei*	E			
Cockatoos, all species		II		
Cock-of-the-Rock, Andean, *Rupicola peruviana*		II		
Cock-of-the-Rock, Guianan, *Rupicola rupicola*		II		
Condor, Andean, *Vultur gryphus*		I	E	
Condor, California, *Gymnogyps californianus*	E	I	E	CA(E)
Conure, Blue-throated, see Parakeet, Ochre-marked				
Conure, Yellow-eared, *Ognorhynchus icterotis*	V	II		
Coot, Hawaiian, *Fulica americana alai*	R R		E	H(E)
Coot, Horned, *Fulica cornuta*	R			
Cormorant, Double-crested, *Phalacrorax auritus*				IL(E)MI(E)
				MO(E)WI(E)
Cormorant, Galapagos Flightless, *Nannopterum harrisi*	R			
Cormorant, Olivaceous, *Phalacrorax olivaceus*				NM(T)
Cotinga, Banded, *Cotinga maculata*	V	I	E	
Cotinga, White-winged, *Xipholena atropurpurea*	V	I	E	
Crane, Black-necked, *Grus nigricollis*	I	I	E	
Crane, Hooded, *Grus monacha*	V	I	E	
Crane, Japanese or Red-crowned, *Grus japonensis*	V	I	E	
Crane, Sandhill, *Grus canadensis*				WA(E)
Cuban, *G.c. nesiotes*	R	I	E	
Florida, *G.c. pratensis*		II		FL(T)
Greater, *G.c. tabida*				CO(E)
Mississippi, *G.c. pulla*	E	I	E	MS(E)
Crane, Siberian White, *Grus leucogeranus*	E	I	E	
Crane, Southern Crowned, *Balearica regulorum*		II		
Crane, White-naped, *Grus vipio*	V	I	E	

BIRDS	RDB	CITES	U.S.	States
Crane, Whooping, *Grus americanus*	E	I	E	CO(E)KS(E) NE(E)NM(T) SD(E)TX(E)
Creeper, Brown, *Certhia familiaris*				IL(E)
Creeper, Hawaiian, *Loxops maculata*				
Hawaii, *L.m. mana*			E	HI(E)
Kauai, *L.m. bairdi*	R			
Molokai, *L.m. flammea*	E		E	HI(E)
Oahu, *L.m. maculata*	E		E	HI(E)
Crow, Hawaiian, *Corvus tropicus*	E		E	HI(E)
Crow, Marianas, *Corvus kubaryi*	E			
Crow-tit, Lower Yangtze, *Paradoxornis heudei heudei*	I			
Cuckoo, California Yellow-billed, *Coccyzus americanus occidentalis* . . .				CA(R)
Cuckoo, Madagascar Thick-billed, *Pachycoccyx audeberti audeberti* . . .	I			
Cuckoo-Shrike, Mauritius, *Coracina typica*	V		E	
Cuckoo-Shrike, Reunion, *Coracina newtoni*	R		E	
Curassow, Bare-faced, *Crax fasciolata pinima*	I			
Curassow, Blue-billed, *Crax alberti*	V			
Curassow, Eastern Razor-billed, *Crax mitu mitu*	E	I	E	
Curassow, Great, *Crax rubra*		III (Costa Rica, Guatemala)		
Cozumel, *C.r. griscomi*	R			
Curassow, Red-billed, *Crax blumenbachii*	E	I	E	
Curlew, Eskimo, *Numenius borealis*	E	I	E	IL(E)KS(E) MD(E)NE(E) NY(E)SD(E) TX(E)
Curlew, Little, *Numenius minutus*		II		
Curlew, Slender-billed, *Numenius tenuirostris*		II		
Currawong, Lord Howe Pied, *Strepera graculina crissalis*	E			
Dipper, Rufous-throated, *Cinclus schultzi*	I			
Doves and Pigeons, *Columbidae spp.*		III (Ghana)		
Dove, Cloven-feathered, *Drepanoptila holosericea*	V		E	
Dove, Grenada, *Leptotila wellsi*	I		E	
Dove, Marianas Fruit, *Ptilinopus roseicapillus*	V			
Dove, Marquesas Ground, *Gallicolumba rubescens*	I			
Dove, Palau Ground, *Gallicolumba canifrons*			E	
Dove, Rapa Fruit, *Ptilinopus huttoni*	R			
Dove, Seychelles Turtle, *Streptopelia picturata rostrata*	E			
Dove, Society Islands Ground, *Gallicolumba erythroptera*	I			
Dove, Tolima, *Leptotila conoveri*	I			
Dowitcher, Asian, *Limnodromus semipalmatus*	R			
Ducks and Geese, *Anatidae spp.*		III (Ghana)		
Duck, Comb, *Sarkidiornis melanotos*		II		
Duck, Hawaiian or Koloa, *Anas wyvilliana*	V		E	HI(E)
Duck, Marianas, *Anas oustaleti*	E	I	E	
Duck, Pink-headed, *Rhodonessa caryophyllacea*		I	E	
Duck, West Indian Tree, *Dendrocygna arborea*	V	II		
Duck, White-winged Wood, *Cairina scutulata*	V	II	E	
Eagles, *Aquila spp.* all species not on App. I		II		
Eagle, Bald, *Haliaeetus leucocephalus*		I		
Southern, *H.l. leucocephalus*	E			
U.S.A.-lower 48 states			E*	CA(E)CO(E) FL(E)GA(E) IL(E)IN(E) KS(E)MD(E) MS(E)MO(R) NH(E)NJ(E) NE(E)NM(T) NY(E)OH(E) SC(E)SD(E) TN(E)TX(E)
*U.S.A.—Michigan, Minnesota, Oregon, Washington, Wisconsin			T	MI(T)MN(T) OR(E)WA(T) WI(E)

BIRDS	RDB	CITES	U.S.	States
Eagle, Crested, *Morphnus guianensis*	R	II		
Eagle, Golden, *Aquila chrysaetos*		II		TN(E)
Eagle, Harpy, *Harpia harpyia*	R	I	E	
Eagle, Imperial, *Aquila heliaca*		I		
Spanish, *A.h. adalberti*	E		E	
Eagle, Madagascar Sea, *Haliaeetus vociferoides*	E	II		
Eagle, Madagascar Serpent, *Eutriorchis astur*	E	II		
Eagle, Philippine, *Pithecophaga jefferyi*	E	I	E	
Eagle, White-tailed, *Haliaetus albicilla*	V	I		
Greenland, *H.a. groenlandicus*			E	
Egret, Cattle, *Bubulcus ibis*		III (Ghana)		
Egret, Chinese, *Egretta eulophotes*	V		E	
Egret, Great, *Casmerodius albus*		III (Ghana)		IL(E)WI(T)
Egret, Little, *Egretta garzetta*		III (Ghana)		
Egret, Snowy, *Egretta thula*				IL(E)
Falcon, Aplomado, *Falco femoralis septentrionalis*				NM(E)
Falcon, Kleinschmidt's, *Falco kreyenborgi*	I	II		
Falcon, Peregrine, *Falco peregrinus*	V*	I		IL(E)IA(E) KS(E)MI(E) MO(E)MS(E) NH(E)NJ(E) TN(E)WI(E)
*American, *F.p. anatum*	E		E	AK(E)CA(E) CO(E)FL(E) GA(E)IN(E) MD(E)NE(E) NM(E)NY(E) OH(E)OR(E) SC(E)SD(E) TX(E)WA(E)
*Arctic, *F.p. tundrius*	E		E	CO(E)GA(E) IN(E)MD(E) NE(E)NJ(E) OR(E)SC(E) TX(E)WA(E)
*Cape Verde, *F.p. madens*	R			
Eurasian, *F.p. peregrinus*			E	
*Iwo, *F.p. fruitii*	R			
Peale's, *F.p. pealei*				WA(T)
Falcon, Prairie, *Falco mexicanus*		II		KS(T)
Fernbird, Codfish Island, *Bowdleria punctata wilsoni*	E			
Finches, *Fringillidae spp.*		III (Ghana)		
Finch, Floreana Large Ground, *Geospiza magnirostris magnirostris*	I			
Finch, Laysan, Nihoa				
Laysan, *Psittirostra cantans cantans*			E	HI(E)
Nihoa, *P.c. ultima*			E	HI(E)
Finch, Mangrove, *Camarhynchus heliobates*	R			
Finch, Southern Black-throated, *Poephila cincta cincta*		II		
Fire-eye, Fringe-backed, *Pyriglena atra*	E			
Firetail, Red-eared, *Emblema oculata*		II		
Flamingo, Andean, *Phoenicoparrus andinus*		II		
Flamingo, Greater, *Phoenicopterus ruber*				
Caribbean, *P.r. ruber*		II		
Chilean, *P.r. chilensis*		II		
Flamingo, James', *Phoenicoparrus jamesi*		II		
Florican, Bengal, *Eupodotis bengalensis*		I		
Flycatcher, Beardless, *Camptostoma imberbe ridgwayi*				NM(E)
Flycatcher, Buff-breasted, *Empidonax fulvifrons pygmaeus*				NM(E)
Flycatcher, Eiao, *Pomarea iphis fluxa*	I			
Flycatcher, Euler's *Empidonax euleri johnstonei*			E	
Flycatcher, Marquesas, *Pomarea mendozae*				
Hivoa, *P.m. mendozae*	E			
Nukuhiva, *P.m. nukuhivae*	E			
Uapou, *P.m. mira*	R			

BIRDS	RDB	CITES	U.S.	States
Flycatcher, Mauritius Paradise, *Terpsiphone bourbonnensis desolata*	R	III (Mauritius)		
Flycatcher, Palau Fantail, *Rhipidura lepida*			E	
Flycatcher, Rarotonga, *Pomarea dimidiata*	V			
Flycatcher, Rueck's Blue, *Muscicapa ruecki*		II		
Flycatcher, Seychelles Paradise, *Terpsiphone corvina*	E		E	
Flycatcher, Sulphur-bellied, *Myiodynastes luteiventris swarthi*				NM(E)
Flycatcher, Tahiti, *Pomarea nigra*	E		E	
Flycatcher, Tinian Monarch, *Monarcha takatsukasae*			E	
Fody, Mauritius, *Foudia rubra*	E			
Fody, Rodrigues, *Foudia flavicans*	E			
Fody, Seychelles, *Foudia sechellarum*	R		E	
Francolin, Swierstra's, *Francolinus swierstrai*	I	II		
Francolin, Tadjoura or Pale-bellied, *Francolinus ochropectus*	R	II		
Frigatebird, Ascension Island, *Fregata aquila*	R			
Frigatebird, Christmas Island, *Fregata andrewsi*	V	I	E	
Gallinule, Common, *Gallinula chloropus*				IL(T)
Hawaiian, *G.c. sandvicensis*	E		E	
Marianas, *G.C. guami*	R			
Gallinule, Purple, *Porphyrula martinica*				IL(E)
Goose, Aleutian Canada, *Branta canadensis leucopareia*	R	I	E	OR(E)WA(E)
Goose, Hawaiian (Nene), *Branta sandvicensis*	V	I	E	HI(E)
Goose, Red-breasted, *Branta ruficollis*		II		
Goose, Ruddy-headed, *Chloephaga rubidiceps*	V			
Goose, Tule White-fronted, *Anser albifrons elgasi*	R	II		
Goshawk, Christmas Island Brown, *Accipiter fasciatus natalis*	R	II	E	
Goshawk, Northern, *Accipiter gentilis*		II		
Grackle, Slender-billed, *Cassidix palustris*			E	
Grebe, Atitlan, *Podilymbus gigas*	E	I	E	
Grebe, Colombian, *Podiceps andinus*	E			
Grebe, Eared, *Podiceps caspicus*				IA(T)
Grebe, Hooded, *Podiceps gallardoi*	R			
Grebe, Junin, *Podiceps taczanowskii*	R			
Grebe, Madagascar Red-necked, *Tachybaptus rufolavatus*	V			
Grebe, Pied-billed, *Podilymbus podiceps*				NJ(T)
Greenshank, Nordmann's or Spotted, *Tringa guttifer*	I	I	E	
Ground-Cuckoo, Rufous-Vented, *Neomorphus geoffroyi*				
Bahia, *N.g. maximiliani*	I			
Southeastern, *N.g. dulcia*	E			
Ground-Dove, Purple-winged, *Claravis godefrida*	V			
Grouse, Caucasian Black, *Lyrurus mloksiewiczi*		II		
Grouse, Ruffed, *Bonasa umbellus*				MO(R)
Grouse, Sage, *Centrocercus urophasianus*				NM(E)
Grouse, Sharp-tailed, *Pediocetes phasianellus*				
P.p. columbianus				NM(E)
Prairie, *P.p. jamesii*				CO(E)
Guan, Black-fronted Piping, *Aburria jacutinga*	E	I	E	
Guan, Cauca, *Penelope perspicax*	E			
Guan, Highland, *Penelopina nigra*		III (Guatemala)		
Guan, Horned, *Oreophasis derbianus*	E	I	E	
Guan, Trinidad Piping, *Pipile pipile pipile*	E	I	E	
Guan, White-winged, *Penelope albipennis*	E	I		
Guineafowl, White-breasted, *Agelastes meleagrides*		III (Ghana)		
Gull, Audouin's, *Larus audouinii*	R		E	
Gull, Brown-headed, *Larus brunneicephalus*		II		
Gull, Relict, *Larus relictus*	R	I	E	
Gyrfalcon, *Falco rusticolus*		I*		
*North American population		II		
Hawk, Black, *Buteogallus anthracinus anthracinus*		II		NM(E)
Hawk, Broad-winged, *Buteo platypterus*		II		IA(T)
Puerto Rican, *B.p. brunnescens*	R			

BIRDS	RDB	CITES	US	States
Hawk, Cooper's, *Accipiter cooperi*		II		IL(E)IA(T) MI(T) MO(E)NH(T) NJ(E)TN(T) WI(T) WA(T)
Hawk, Ferruginous, *Buteo regalis*		II		
Hawk, Galapagos, *Buteo galapagoensis*	R	II	E	
Hawk, Gray, *Buteo nitidus maximus*		II		NM(E)
Hawk, Grey-backed, *Leucopternis occidentalis*	I R	II		
Hawk, Hawaiian, *Buteo solitarius*	R	II	E	HI(E)
Hawk, Mantled, *Leucopternis polionota*	I	II		
Hawk, Marsh, or Northern Harrier, *Circus cyaneus*		II		IL(E)IA(E) MI(T)MO(E) NH(T)NJ(T) TN(T)
Hawk, Red-shouldered, *Buteo lineatus*		II		IL(E)IA(E) MI(T)MO(E) NH(T)NJ(T) WI(T)
Hawk, Sharp-shinned, *Accipiter striatus*		II		MO(E)TN(T) OH(E)
A.s. velox	R			
Cuban, *A.s. fringilloides*	R			
Puerto Rican, *A.s. venator*		II		IL(E)
Hawk, Swainson's, *Buteo swainsoni*		II		IL(E)TN(T)
Heron, Black-crowned Night, *Nycticorax nycticorax*				
Heron, Goliath, *Ardea goliath*		III (Ghana)		
Heron, Great Blue, *Ardea herodias*				NJ(T)
Heron, Little Blue, *Florida caerulea*				IL(E)
Honeyeater, Helmeted, *Meliphaga (melanops) cassidix*	E	I		
Honeyeater, Mukojima Bonin, *Apalopteron familiare familiare*	E			
Honeycreeper, Crested, *Palmeria dolei*	V		E	HI(E)
Hornbill, Great Pied, *Buceros bicornis*		II*		
Northern, B.b. homrai		I		
Hornbill, Helmeted, *Rhinoplax vigil*	I	I	E	
Hornbill, Narcondam, *Aceros narcondami*		II		
Hornbill, Rufous, *Buceros hydrocorax*				
Luzon, *B.h. hydrocorax*		II		
Malayan, *B.h. rhinoceros*		II		
[Hummingbird] Black Barbthroat, *Threnetes grzimeki*	E			
[Hummingbird] Black-billed Hermit, *Phaethornis nigrirostris*	R			
Hummingbird, Black Inca, *Coeligena prunellei*	I			
Hummingbird, Broad-billed, *Cynanthus latirostris*				NM(T)
[Hummingbird] Chilean Woodstar, *Eulidia yarrellii*	E			
[Hummingbird] Hook-billed Hermit, *Glaucis dohrnii*	E	I	E	
[Hummingbird] Klabin Farm Long-tailed Hermit, *Phaethornis margarettae*	E			
Hummingbird, Violet-crowned, *Amazilia violiceps ellioti*				NM(T)
Hummingbird, White-eared, *Hylocharis leucotis*				NM(E)
Ibis, Giant, *Thaumatibis gigantea*	R			
Ibis, Hadada, *Hagedashia hagedash*		II		
Ibis, Hermit, *Geronticus eremita*	E	I		
Ibis, Japanese Crested, *Nipponia nippon*	E V	I	E	
Ibis, Madagascar Crested, *Lophotibis cristata*				
Ibis, Sacred, *Threskionis aethiopica*		III (Ghana)		
Aldabra, *T.a. abbotti*	R			
Ibis, Southern Bald, *Geronticus calvus*	R	II		
Ibis, Spot-breasted, *Lampribis rara*		III (Ghana)		
Ibis, White-shouldered, *Pseudibis davisoni*	I			
I'iwi, *Vestiaria coccinea*				HI(E)
Jay, Florida Scrub, *Aphelocoma coerulescens coerulescens*				FL(T)
Junco, Yellow-eyed, *Junco phaenotus palliatus*				NM(T)
Junglefowl, Grey, *Gallus sonneratii*		II		
Kagu, *Rhynochetos jubatus*	E E	I	E	
Kakapo, *Strigops habroptilus*	E R	I	E	
Kestrel, Aldabra, *Falco newtoni aldabranus*	R	I		

BIRDS	RDB	CITES	U.S.	States
Kestrel, Mauritius, *Falco punctatus*	E	I	E	
Kestrel, Seychelles, *Falco araea*	R	I	E	
Kestrel, Southeastern, *Falco sparverius sparverius*		II		FL(T) NM(T)
Kingbird, Thickbilled, *Tyrannus crassirostris pompalis*				
Kingfisher, Guam, *Halcyon cinnamomina cinnamomina*	E			
Kinglet, Guadalupe, *Regulus calendula obscura*	I			
Kite, Everglades Snail, *Rostrhamus sociabilis sociabilis*	R	II	E	FL(E)
Kite, Hook-billed, *Chondrohierax uncinatus*		II*		
*Cuban, *C.u. wilsonii*	RE	I	E	
Grenada, *C.u. mirus*	E		E	
Kite, Mississippi, *Ictinia mississippiensis*		II		IL(E)MO(R) NM(T)TN(E)
Kokako (Wattlebird), *Callaeas cinerea*			E	
North Island, *C.c. wilsoni*	V			
South Island, *C.c. cinerea*	E			
Lammergeier, *Gypaetus barbatus*		II		
Lapwing, Javanese Wattled, *Vanellus macropterus*	I			
Lark, Razo, *Alaudo razae*	R			
Longspur, McCown's, *Calcarius mccownii*				NM(T)
Loon, Common, *Gavia immer*				NH(T)
Lorikeet, Tahiti, *Vini peruviana*	R			
Lorikeet, Ultramarine, *Vini ultramarina*	R			
Lourie, Zanzibar, *Tauraco fischeri zanzibaricus*	R			
Macaw, Caninde, *Ara caninde*	I	II		
Macaw, Glaucous, *Anodorhynchus glaucus*	E	I	E	
Macaw, Guayaquil Great Green, *Ara ambigua guayaguilensis*	I	II		
Macaw, Lears, or Indigo, *Anodorhynchus leari*	E	I	E	
Macaw, Spix's, *Cyanopsitta spixii*	V	I	E	
Malkoha, Red-faced (Cuckoo), *Phaenicophaeus pyrrhocephalus*			E	
Martin, Purple, *Progne subis*				NH(T)
Martin, White-eyed River, *Pseudochelidon sirintarae*	I	II		
Megapode, La Perouse, *Megapodius laperouse*			E	
M.l. laperouse	R			
Palau, *M.l. senex*	R			
Megapode, Maleo, *Macrocephalon maleo*	V	I	E	
Merganser, Brazilian, *Mergus octosetaceus*	I			
Merganser, Chinese, *Mergus squamatus*	I			
Merlin, *Falco columbarius*		II		NJ(T)
Mesite, Brown, *Mesoenas unicolor*	R			
Mesite, White-breasted, *Mesoenas variegata*	R			
Millerbird, Nihoa, *Acrocephalus familiaris kingi*	R		E	HI(E)
Mockingbird, Galapagos, *Nesomimus trifasciatus trifasciatus*	R			
Monarch, Truk, *Metabolus rugensis*	R			
Monia, Bensch's, *Monias benschi*	R			
Mountain-Robin, Dappled, *Modulatrix orostruthus*				
M.o. orostruthus	E			
M.o. amani	E			
Newtonia, Fanovana, *Newtonia fanovanae*	I			
Nukupu'u, *Hemignathus lucidus*			E	
Kauai, *H.l. hanapepe*	E			HI(E)
Maui, *H.l. affinis*	E			HI(E)
Nuthatch, Kabylian, *Sitta ledanti*	R			
'O'o, Kauai, *Moho braccatus*	E		E	HI(E)
Osprey, *Pandion haliaetus*		II		IL(E)MI(T) NH(T)NJ(E) NY(E)SD(T) TN(E)WI(E)
Ostrich, *Struthio camelus*				
Arabian, *S.c. syriacus*			E	
West African, *S.c. spatzi*			E	
O'u, *Psittirostra psittacea*	E		E	HI(E)
Owls, all species not on Appendix I		II		
Owl, Anjouan Scops, *Otus rutilus capnodes*	E	II	E	
Owl, Barn, *Tyto alba*		II		IL(E)IA(E) MI(T)MO(E) WI(E)
Owl, Barred, *Strix varia*		II		NJ(T)

BIRDS	RDB	CITES	U.S.	States
Owl, Norfolk I. Boobook, *Ninox novaeseelandiae undulata*	I	I		
Owl, Burrowing, *Athene cunicularia*		II		IA(E)
Owl, Elf, *Micrathene whitneyi*		II		CA(E)
Owl, Forest Little, *Athene blewitti*	I	I		
Owl, Giant Scops, *Otus gurneyi*		I	E	
Owl, Great Gray, *Strix nebulosa*		II		CA(E)
Owl, Indonesian Hawk, *Ninox squamipila*		II*		
*Christmas Island, *N.s. natalis*	R	I		
Owl, Long-eared, *Asio otus*		II		IL(E)IA(T)
Owl, Morden's Scops, *Otus ireneae*	R	II	E	
Owl, Nduk Eagle, *Bubo poensis vosseleri*	R	II		
Owl, Palau, *Otus podargina*			E	
Owl, Papuan Scops, *Otus beccarii*	I	II		
Owl, Scops, *Otus elegans botelensis*	E	II		
Owl, Seychelles, *Otus insularis*	R	II	E	
Owl, Short-eared, *Asio flammeus*		II		IL(E)NJ(T)
Hawaiian, *A.f. sandwichensis*				HI(E)
Ponape, *A.f. ponapensis*	R			
Owl, Soumagne's, *Tyto soumagnei*	E	I		
Owl, Spotted, *Strix occidentalis caurina*		II		OR(T)WA(T)
Owl, Tobago Striped, *Asia clamator oberi*	R	II		
Owl, Virgin Islands Screech, *Otus nudipes newtoni*	R	II		
Oystercatcher, Canarian Black, *Haematopus moguini meadewaldoi*	E			
Oystercatcher, Chatham Island, *Haematopus chathamensis*	E			
Palila, *Psittirostra bailleui*	E		E	HI(E)
Parakeet, Golden, *Aratinga guarouba*	V	I	E	
Parakeet, Golden-shouldered, *Psephotus chrysopterygius chrysopterygius*	R	I	E	
Hooded, *P.c. dissimilis*	R	I	E	
Parakeet, Uvea Horned, *Eunymphicus cornutus uvaeensis*	E	II		
Parakeet, Mauritius, *Psittacula echo*	E	I	E	
Parakeet, Ochre-marked, *Pyrrhura cruentata*	R	I	E	
Parakeet, Orange-bellied, *Neophema chrysogaster*	R	I	E	
Parakeet, Orange-fronted, *Cyanoramphus malherbi*	E	II		
Parakeet, Paradise, *Psephotus pulcherrimus*	E	I	E	
Parakeet, Red-fronted, *Cyanoramphus novaezelandiae*		I		
Norfolk Island, *C.n. cookii*	E			
Parakeet, Rose-ringed, *Psittacula krameri*		III		
		(Ghana)		
Parakeet, Rufous-fronted, *Bolborhynchus ferrugineifrons*	I	II		
Parakeet, Splendid or Scarlet-chested, *Neophema splendida*	R	II	E	
Parakeet, Turquoise, *Neophema pulchella*	O	II	E	
Parakeet, Yellow-crowned, *Cyanoramphus auriceps*		II*		
*Forbes', *C.a. forbesi*	E	I	E	
Parrots, Parakeets, *Psittaciformes* all species not on Appendix I		II*		
*except Budgerigar, Cockatiel and Rose-ringed Parakeet				
Parrot, Coxen's Double-eyed Fig, *Cyclopsitta diophthalma coxeni*		I		
Parrot, Cuban, *Amazona leucocephala*		I	E	
Bahamas, *A.l. bahamensis*	R			
Cayman Brac, *A.l. hesterna*	R			
Parrot, Gray, *Psittacus erithacus*		II*		
*Principe, *P.e. princeps*		I		
Parrot, Ground, *Pezoporus wallicus*		I	E	
Eastern, *P.w. wallicus*	V			
Western, *P.w. flaviventris*	E			
Parrot, Imperial, *Amazona imperialis*	E	I	E	
Parrot, Indigo-winged, *Halalopsittaca amazonina fuertisi*	I	II		
Parrot, Maroon-fronted, *Rhynchopsitta terrisi*	E	I		
Parrot, Night, *Geopsittacus occidentalis*	I	I	E	
Parrot, Pileated, *Pionopsitta pileata*		I	E	
Parrot, Puerto Rican, *Amazona vittata*	E	I	E	
Parrot, Red-crowned, *Amazona rhodocorytha*		I	E	
Parrot, Red-necked, *Amazona arausiaca*	E	I		
Parrot, Red-spectacled, *Amazona pretrei*	V	II*		
A.p. pretrei		I	E	
Parrot, Red-tailed, *Amazona brasiliensis*	E	I		
Parrot, St. Lucia, *Amazona versicolor*	E	I	E	
Parrot, St. Vincent, *Amazona guildingii*	E	I	E	

BIRDS

BIRDS	RDB	CITES	U.S.	States
Parrot, Thick-billed, *Rhynchopsitta pachyrhyncha*	V	I	E	
Parrot, Vasa, *Coracopsis nigra barklyi* (Seychelles)	E	II		
Parrot, Vinaceous, *Amazona vinacea*		I	E	
Parrot, Yellow-shouldered, *Amazona barbadensis*		I		
Parrotbill, Maui, *Pseudonestor xanthophrys*	V		E	HI(E)
Parrotfinch, Palau Blue-faced, *Erythrura trichroa pelewensis*	I			
Parrotfinch, Pink-billed, *Erythrura kleinschmidti*	R			
Parrotlet, Black-eared, *Touit melanonota*	R	II		
Parrotlet, Golden-tailed, *Touit surda*	I	II		
Partridge, Italian Gray, *Perdix perdix italica*	E			
Peafowl, Green, *Pavo muticus*	V	II		
Pelican, Brown, *Pelecanus occidentalis*			E	CA(E)FL(T) GA(E)MS(E) OR(E)SC(E) TX(E)WA(E)
Pelican, Dalmatian, *Pelecanus crispus*	V	II	E	
Pelican, White, *Pelecanus erythrorhynchos*				CO(T)WA(E)
Penguin, Galapagos, *Spheniscus mendiculus*			E	
Penguin, Humboldt, *Spheniscus humboldti*		I		
Penguin, Jackass, *Spheniscus demersus*	V	II		
Petrel, Beck's Tahiti, *Pterodroma rostrata becki*	I			
Petrel, Bermuda, or Cahow, *Pterodroma cahow*	E		E	
Petrel, Black, *Procellaria parkinsoni*	E			
Petrel, Black-capped, *Pterodroma hasitata*	V			
Petrel, Chatham Island, *Pterodroma hypoleuca axillaris*	E			
Petrel, Cook's, *Pterodroma cookii cookii*	E			
Petrel, Dark-rumped, *Pterodroma phaepygia*				
Galapagos, *P.p. phaepygia*	E			
Hawaiian, *P.p. sandwichensis*	E		E	HI(E)
Petrel, Gould's, *Pterodroma leucoptera leucoptera*	R			
Petrel, MacGillivray's, *Pterodroma macgillivrayi*	I			
Petrel, Madeira Soft-plumaged, *Pterodroma mollis madeira*	R			
Petrel, Magenta, *Pterodroma magentae*	E			
Petrel, Reunion, *Pterodroma aterrima*	E			
Petrel, Westland Black, *Procellaria westlandica*	V			
Phalarope, Wilson's, *Phalaropus tricolor*				IL(E)
Pheasant, Blood, *Ithaginus cruentus*		II		
Pheasant, Brown-eared, *Crossoptilon mantchuricum*	E	I	E	
Pheasant, Bulwer's Wattled, *Lophura bulweri*	V			
Pheasant, Cheer, *Catreus wallichii*	E	I		
Pheasant, Chinese Monal, *Lophophorus lhuysii*	E	I	E	
Pheasant, Crested Argus, *Rheinardia ocellata*				
R.o. ocellata	R			
R.o. nigrescens	R			
Pheasant, Edward's, *Lophura edwardsi*	V	I	E	
Pheasant, Elliot's, *Syrmaticus ellioti*	E	I	E	
Pheasant, Germain's Peacock, *Polyplectron germaini*		II		
Pheasant, Great Argus, *Argusianus argus*		II		
Pheasant, Grey Peacock, *Polyplectron bicalcaratum*		II		
Pheasant, Himalayan Monal, *Lophophorus impejanus*		I		
Pheasant, Hume's Bar-tailed, *Syrmaticus humiae*		I	E	
S.h. humiae	R			
S.h. burmanicus	R			
Pheasant, Imperial, *Lophura imperialis*	V	I	E	
Pheasant, Malay Peacock, *Polyplectron malacense*		II		
Pheasant, Mikado, *Syrmaticus mikado*	V	I	E	
Pheasant, Palawan Peacock, *Polyplectron emphanum*	V	I	E	
Pheasant, Sclater's Monal, *Lophophorus sclateri*	R	I	E	
Pheasant, Swinhoe's, *Lophura swinhoii*	V	I	E	
Pheasant, White-eared, *Crossoptilon crossoptilon*	V	I	E	
Phoebe, Say's, *Sayornis saya*				IA(T)
Pigeon, Azores Wood, *Columba palumbus azorica*	R			
Pigeon, Bleeding-heart, *Gallicolumba luzonica*		II		
Pigeon, Blue crowned, *Goura cristata*		II		
Pigeon, Chatham Island, *Hemiphaga novaeseelandiae chathamensis*	E		E	
Pigeon, Christmas Imperial, *Ducula whartoni*	V			
Pigeon, Giant Imperial, *Cucula goliath*	V			

BIRDS	RDB	CITES	U.S.	States
Pigeon, Laurel, *Columba junoniae*	E			
Pigeon, Long-toed, *Columba trocaz*				
C.t. trocaz	V			
C.t. bollii	V			
Pigeon, Maroon-breasted, *Goura scheepmakeri*		II		
Pigeon, Marquesas, *Ducula galeata*	E			
Pigeon, Micronesian, *Ducula oceanica*				
Radak, *D.o. ratakensis*	I			
Truk, *D.o. teraokai*	E			
Pigeon, Mindoro Imperial, *Ducula mindorensis*		I	E	
Pigeon, Moheli Green, *Treron australis griveaudi*	R			
Pigeon, Nicobar, *Caloenas nicobarica*		I		
Palau, *C.n. pelewensis*	E			
Pigeon, Pink, *Nesoenas mayeri*	E	III (Mauritius)		
Pigeon, Plain, *Columba inornata*				
Jamaican, *C.i. exigua*	I			
Puerto Rican, *C.i. wetmorei*	E		E	
Pigeon, Society Islands, *Ducula aurorae*	V			
Pigeon, Tooth-billed, *Didunculus strigirostris*	V			
Pigeon, Victoria crowned, *Goura victoria*		II		
Pigeon, White-crowned, *Columba leucocephala*				FL(T)
Pipit, Sokoke, *Anthus sokokensis*	R			
Pitta, Fairy, *Pitta brachyura nympha*		II		
Pitta, Gurney's, *Pitta gurneyi*	I			
Pitta, Koch's, *Pitta kochi*		I	E	
Plover, Mountain, *Charadrius montanus*				NE(T)
Plover, New Zealand Shore, *Thinornis novaeseelandiae*	E		E	
Plover, Piping, *Charadrius melodus*				IL(E)IA(E) MI(T)WI(E)
Plover, Snowy, *Charadrius alexandrinus*				
C.a. tenuirostris				FL(E)
Western, *C.a. nivosus*				OR(T)WA(E)
Pochard, Madagascar, *Aythya innotata*	V			
Pochard, South American, *Netta erythrophthalma erythrophthalma*	I			
Po'ouli, *Melamprosops phaeosoma*	R		E	HI(E)
Prairie Chicken, Greater, *Tympanuchus cupido*				CO(E)IL(E) MI(T)MO(R) WI(T)
Attwater's, *T.c. attwateri*	R	I	E	TX(E)
Prairie Chicken, Lesser, *Tympanuchus pallidicinctus*				CO(T)
Ptarmigan, White-tailed, *Lagopus leucurus altipetens*				NM(E)
Quail, Masked Bobwhite, *Colinus virginianus ridgwayi*	E	I	E	
Quail, Montezuma, *Cyrtonyx montezumae*				
Merriam's, *C.m. merriami*			E	
Mexican Mearns' *C.m. mearnsi* (except U.S. population)		II		
Southern, *C.m. montezumae*		II		
Quetzal, Resplendent, *Pharomacrus mocinno*			E	
P.m. mocinno	V	I		
P.m. costaricensis	V	I		
Rail, Aldabra White-throated, *Dryolimnas cuvieri aldabranus*	R			
Rail, Auckland Island, *Rallus pectoralis meulleri*	I			
Rail, Barred-wing, *Rallus poecilopterus*	E			
Rail, Black, *Latorallus jamaicensis*				IL(E)
California, *L.j. coturniculus*	V			CA(R)
Rail, Bogata, *Rallus semiplumbeus*				
Rail, Clapper, *Rallus longirostris*				
California, *R.l. obsoletus*	V		E	CA(E)
Light-footed, *R.l. levipes*	E		E	CA(E)
Yuma, *R.l. yumanensis*				CA(R)
Rail, Guam, *Rallus owstoni*	V			
Rail, King, *Rallus elegans elegans*				OH(E)
Rail, Lord Howe Wood, *Tricholimnas sylvestris*	E	I	E	
Rail, San Cristobal Mountain, *Pareudiastes sylvestris*	I			
Rail, Yellow, *Coturnicops noveboracensis*				IL(E)
Goldman's, *C.n. goldmani*	I			
Rail, Zapata, *Cyanolimnas cererai*	R			

BIRDS	RDB	CITES	U.S.	States
Raven, *Corvus corax*				TN(E)
Rhea, Greater, *Rhea americana*		III (Uruguay)		
Argentine, *R.a. albescens*		II		
Rhea, Lesser or Darwin's, *Pterocnemia pennata*		I	E	
Puna, *P.p. tarapacensis*	E			
Robin, Chatham Island Black, *Petroica traversi*	E		E	
Robin, Ryukyu, *Erithacus komadori subrufa*	E			
Robin, Scarlet-breasted, *Petroica multicolor multicolor*			E	
Robin, Seychelles Magpie, *Copsychus sechellarum*	E		E	
Robin-chat, Usambara, *Alethe montana*	R			
Rock-fowl, Grey-necked, *Picathartes oreas*	V	I	E	
Rock-fowl, White-necked, *Picathartes gymnocephalus*	V	I	E	
Roller, Ceylon Broad-billed, *Eurystomus orientalis irisi*	I			
Roller, Crossley's Ground, *Atelornis crossleyi*	R			
Roller, Long-tailed Ground, *Uratelornis chimaera*	V		E	
Roller, Pitta-like Ground, *Atelornis pittoides*	R			
Roller, Scaled Ground, *Brachyptercias squamigera*	R			
Roller, Short-legged Ground, *Brachypteracias leptosomus*	R	O		
Saddleback, *Creadion carunculatus*	O			
Sandpiper, Buff-breasted, *Tryngites subruficollis*				SD(T)
Sandpiper, Tuamotu, *Prosobonia cancellatus*	V			
Sandpiper, Upland, *Bartramia longicuada*				IL(E)IA(E) MO(R)NH(T) OH(E)WA(E)
Scrub-bird, Noisy, *Atrichornis clamosus*	E	I	E	
Scrub-bird, Rufous, *Atrichornis rufescens*	R			
Scrub Fowl, Common, *Megapodius freycinet*				
Abbott's, *M.f. abbotti*		II		
Nicobar, *M.f. nicobariensis*		II		
Seedeater, Tumaco, *Sporophila insulata*	I			
Shag, New Zealand King, *Phalacrorax carunculatus carunculatus*	R			
Shama, Cebu Black, *Copsychus niger cebuensis*			E	
Shearwater, Newell's Manx, *Puffinus puffinus newelli*	V		T	HI(T)
Shrike, Loggerhead, *Lanius ludovicianus*				IL(T)IA(T) MI(T)WI(T)
San Clemente, *L.l. mearnsi*	E		E	
Silver-eye, White-breasted, *Zosterops albogularis*	E	I	E	
Siskin, Red, *Spinus cucullatus*	E	I	E	
Siskin, Yellow-faced, *Spinus yarrellii*		II		
Skimmer, Black, *Rynchops niger*				NJ(E)
Snipe, New Zealand, *Coenocorypha aucklandica*	R			
Snowcock, Caspian, *Tetraogallus caspius*		I		
Snowcock, Tibetan, *Tetraogallus tibetanus*		I		
Solitaire, St. Vincent, *Myadestes genibarbis sibilans*	R			
Sparrow, Bachman's, *Aimophila aestivalis*				IL(E)MO(R)
A.a. bachmanii				TN(E)
Sparrow, Baird's, *Ammodramus bairdii*				NM(T)
Sparrow, Grasshopper, *Ammodramus savannarum*				FL(E)NJ(T) TN(T)
Sparrow, Henslow's, *Ammodramus henslowii*				IL(T)MO(R) NJ(T)
Sparrow, San Clemente Sage, *Amphispiza belli clementeae*	E		E	
Sparrow, Savannah, *Passerculus sandwichensis*				NJ(T)
Belding's, *P.s. beldingi*				CA(E)
Ipswich, *P.s. princeps*				NJ(T)
Sparrow, Seaside, *Ammospiza maritima*				
Cape Sable, *A.m. mirabilis*	E		E	FL(E)
Dusky, *A.m. nigriscens*	E		E	FL(E)
Sparrow, Song, *Melospiza melodia*				
Amak, *M.m. amaka*	E			
Santa Barbara, *M.m. graminea*			E	
Sparrow, Vesper, *Pooecetes gramineus*				NJ(T)
Sparrow, Zapata, *Torreornis inexpectata*	R			
Sparrowhawk, Anjouan Island, *Accipiter francesii pusillus*	E	II		
Spoonbill, White, *Platalea leucorodia*		II		
Starling, Ponape Mountain, *Aplonis pelzelni*	V		E	

BIRDS	RDB	CITES	U.S.	States
Starling, Rothschild's, *Leucopsar rothschildi*	E	I	E	
Starling, Santo Mountain, *Aplonis santovestris*	R			
Stilt, Black, *Himantopus novaezealandiae*	E			
Stilt, Hawaiian, *Himantopus mexicanus knudseni*	R		E	HI(E)
Stitchbird, *Notiomystis cincta*	V			
Stork, Black, *Ciconia nigra*		II		
Stork, Marabou, *Leptoptilos crumeniferus*		III (Ghana)		
Stork, Milky, *Mycteria cinerea*	V			
Stork, Oriental White, *Ciconia ciconia boyciana*	E	I	E	
Stork, Saddlebill, *Ephippiorhynchus senegalensis*		III (Ghana)		
Stork, Storm's White-necked, *Ciconia episcopus stormi*	I			
Stork, Wood, *Mycteria americana*				FL(E)
Storm-Petrel, Hawaiian, *Oceanodroma castro cryptoleucura*				HI(E)
Sunbird, Amani, *Anthreptes pallidigaster*	R			
Sunbird, Small-billed Wattled, *Neodrepanis hypoxantha*	I			
Swallow, Cliff, *Petrochelidon pyrrhonata*				MS(T)NJ(T)
Swallow, Jamaican Golden, *Kalochelidon euchrysea euchrysea*	I			
Swan, Black-necked, *Cygnus melancoryphus*		II		
Swan, Coscoroba, *Coscoroba coscoroba*		II		
Swan, Jankowski's Bewick, *Cygnus bewickii jankowskii*		II		
Tachuri, Bogota Bearded, *Polystictus pectoralis bogotensis*	I			
Takahe, *Notornis montelli*	E			
Tanager, Azure-rumped, *Tangara cabanisi*	I			
Tanager, Cherry-throated, *Nemosia rourei*	E			
Tanager, Seven-colored, *Tangara fastuosa*	V			
Tapaculo, Brasilia, *Scytalopus novacapitalis*	I			
Teal, Laysan, *Anas laysanensis*	R	I	E	HI(E)
Teal, Madagascar, *Anas bernieri*	V	II		
Teal, New Zealand Brown, *Anas aucklandica*	V			
Auckland Island, *A.a. aucklandica*		II		
Campbell Island, *A.a. nesiotis*		I	E	
New Zealand, *A.a. chlorotis*		II		
Tern, Arctic, *Sterna paradisaea*				NH(T)
Tern, Black, *Chlidonias nigra*				IL(E)
Tern, Caspian, *Hydroprogne caspia*				MI(T)
Tern, Chinese Crested, *Sterna zimmermanni*	I			
Tern, Common, *Sterna hirundo*				IL(E)MI(E) NH(T)WI(E) OH(E)
S.h. hirundo				
Tern, Damara, *Sterna balaenarum*	R			
Tern, Forster's, *Sterna foresteri*				IL(E)WI(E)
Tern, Least, *Sterna albifrons*				FL(T)IL(E) IA(E)KS(T) MO(E)NJ(E)
California, *S.a. browni*	E		E	CA(E)
Interior, *S.a. athalassos*				NE(T)NM(T) SD(E)TX(E)
Tern, Roseate, *Sterna dougallii*				FL(T)NH(T) NJ(T)
Tern, White, *Gygis alba*				HI(E)
Thick-knee, Double-striped, *Burhinus bistriatus*		III (Guatemala)		
Thrasher, White-breasted, *Ramphocinclus brachyurus*			E	
Martinique, *R.b. brachyurus*	E			
St. Lucia, *R.b. sanctaeluciae*	E			
Thrush, Amani Ground, *Zoothera daurna major*	I			
Thrush, Kauai, *Phaeornis obscurus myadestina*	E		E	HI(E)
Thrush, Molokai, *Phaeornis obscurus rutha*	E		E	HI(E)
Thrush, New Zealand, *Tumagra capensis*			E	
Thrush, Small Kauai or Puaiohi, *Phaeornis palmeri*	E		E	HI(E)
Thrush, St. Lucia Forest, *Cichlherminia lherminieri sanctaeluciae*	E			
Tiger-Heron, Fasciated, *Tigrisoma fasciatum fasciatum*	I			
Tinamou, Magdalena, *Crypturellus saltuarius*	I			

BIRDS	RDB	CITES	U.S.	States
Tinamou, Rufous, *Rhynchotus rufescens*				
Argentine, *R.r. pallescens*		II		
Bolivian, *R.r. maculicollis*		II		
Brazilian, *R.r. rufescens*		II		
Tinamou, Solitary, *Tinamus solitarius*		I	E	
Pernambuco, *T.s. pernambucensis*	E			
Toucan, Keel-billed, *Rhamphastos sulphuratus*		III (Guatemala)		
Towhee, Inyo Brown, *Pipilo fuscus eremophilus*				CA(E)
Tragopan, Blyth's, *Tragopan blythii*		I	E	
T.b. blythii	R			
T.b.. molesworthi	R			
Tragopan, Cabot's, *Tragopan caboti*	E	I	E	
Tragopan, Satyr, *Tragopan satyra*		III (Nepal)		
Tragopan, Western, *Tragopan melanocephalus*	E	I	E	
Trembler, Martinique Brown, *Cinclocerthia ruficauda gutturalis*	E		E	
Trogon, Coppery-tailed, *Trogon elegans canescens*				NM(E)
Turacos, *Musophagidae spp.*		III (Ghana)		
Turaco, Knysna, *Tauraco corythaix*		II		
Turaco, Purple-crested, *Gallirex prophyreolophus*		II		
Turkey, Mexican, *Meleagris gallopavo mexicana*				NM(T)
Turkey, Ocellated, *Agriocharis ocellata*		III (Guatemala)		
Umbrellabird, Long-wattled, *Cephalopterius penduliger*	V			
Vanga, Bernier's, *Oriolia bernieri*	I			
Vanga, Pollen's, *Xenopirostris polleni*	E			
Vanga, Van Dam's, *Xenopirostris damii*	E			
Veery, *Catharus fuscescens*				IL(T)
Vireo, Bell's, *Vireo bellii pusillus*				CA(E)NM(T)
Vultures, all spp. except New World and App. I		II		
Vulture, Cape, *Gyps coprotheres*	V	II		
Wanderer, Plains, *Pedionomus torquatus*		II	E	
Warbler, Aldabra Brush, *Nesillas aldabranus*	R			
Warbler, Bachman's, *Vermivora bachmanii*	E		E	FL(E)GA(E) IL(E)MS(E) SC(E)TX(E) IA(T)
Warbler, Blue-winged, *Vermivora pinus*				
Warbler, Kirtland's, *Dendroica kirtlandii*	E		E	GA(E)IN(E) MI(E)OH(E) SC(E)
Warbler, Japanese Marsh, *Megalurus pryeri pryeri*	R			
Warbler, Long-legged, *Trichocicha rufa*	E			
Warbler, Polynesian, *Acrocephalus caffra*				
Eiao, *A.c. aquilonis*	E			
Moorea, *A.c. longirostris*	E			
Hatutu, *A.c. postremus*	R			
Warbler, Reed, *Acrocephalus luscinia*			E	
Warbler, Rodrigues Brush, *Bebrornis rodericana*	E	III (Mauritius)	E	
Warbler, Semper's, *Leucopeza semperi*	E		E	
Warbler, Seychelles Brush, *Bebrornis sechellensis*	O		E	
Warbler, Swainson's, *Limnothlypis swainsonii*				IL(T)MO(E)
Warbler, Barbados Yellow, *Dendroica petechia petechia*	E		E	
Weavers, *Ploceidae spp.*		III (Ghana)		
Weaver, Clarke's, *Ploceus golandi*	R			
Weaver, Usambara Olive-headed, *Ploceus olivaceiceps nicolli*	R			
Weka, Eastern, *Gallirallus australis hectori*		II		
Whipbird, Western *Psephodes nigrogularis*	O	II	E	
Whippoorwill, *Caprimulgus vociferus*				NH(T)
Whippoorwill, Puerto Rican, *Caprimulgus noctitherus*	R		E	
Whippoorwill, Ridgway's, *Caprimulgus ridgwayi*				NM(T)
White-eye, Gizo, *Zosterops luteirostris luteirostris*	E			
White-eye, Mauritius, *Zosterops olivacea chloronothos*	V			
White-eye, Ponape Greater, *Rukia longirostris*	R		E	

BIRDS	RDB	CITES	U.S.	States
White-eye, Rota Bridled, *Zosterops conspicillata rotensis*	I			
White-eye, Seychelles, *Zosterops modesta*	R		E	
White-eye, Truk Greater, *Rukia rukia*	I			
Woodcreeper, Trinidad, *Xiphorhynchus picus altirostris*	R			
Woodpecker, Gila, *Melanerpes uropygiallis uropygiallis*				NM(T)
Woodpecker, Helmeted, *Dryocopus galeatus*	I			
Woodpecker, Inouye's, *Picoides tridactylus inouyei*	R			
Woodpecker, Imperial, *Campephilus imperialis*	E	I	E	
Woodpecker, Ivory-billed, *Campephilus principalis*			E	
American, *C.p. principalis*	E			FL(E)GA(E) MS(E)SC(E) TX(E)
Cuban, *C.p. bairdii*	E			
Woodpecker, Okinawa, *Sapheopipo noguchii*	E			
Woodpecker, Red-bellied, *Melanerpes superciliaris*				
Grand Bahama, *M.s. bahamensis*	I			
San Salvador, *M.s. nyeanus*	R			
Woodpecker, Red-cockaded, *Picoides borealis*	V		E	FL(E)GA(E) MD(E)MS(E) SC(E)TN(E) TX(E) NJ(T)
Woodpecker, Red-headed, *Melanerpes erythrocephalus*				NM(T)
M.e. caurinus				
Woodpecker, Takatsukasa's Green, *Picus awokera takatsukasae*	R			
Woodpecker, Tristam's, *Dryocopus javensis richardsi*	E	I	E	
Woodpecker, Western Scaly-bellied, *Picus squamatus flavirostris*		II		
Woodpecker, White-backed, *Dendrocopos leucotos owstoni*	R			
Wood-quail, Gorgeted, *Odontophorus strophium*	E			
Wood-Swallow, Palau White-breasted, *Artamus leucorhynchus pelewensis*	R			
Wren, Apolinar's Marsh, *Cistothorus apolinari*	V			
Wren, Bewick's, *Thyromanes bewickii*				IL(T)TN(T)
Wren, Eyrean Grass, *Amytornis goyderi*	I		E	
Wren, Fair Island, *Troglodytes troglodytes fridariensis*	R			
Wren, House, *Troglodytes aedon*				
Guadeloupe, *T.a. guadeloupensis*	E		E	
St. Lucia, *T.a. mesoleucus*	E		E	
Wren, New Zealand Bush, *Xenicus longipes*	E			
Wren, Short-billed Marsh, *Cistothorus platensis*				NJ(T)
Wren, Zapata, *Ferminia ceverai*	R			
Yellowthroat, New Providence, *Geothlypis rostrata rostrata*	I			

REPTILES	RDB	CITES	U.S.	States
Alligator, American, *Alligator mississippiensis*	O	II	E*	GA(E)MS(E) SC(E)TX(E)
Florida, parts of Georgia			T*	
Lousiana			T	
			(S/A)[1]	
Alligator, Chinese, *Alligator sinensis*	E	I	E	
Anaconda, Yellow, *Eunectes notaeus*		II		
Anole, Giant, *Anolis roosevelti*	E		E	
Boas, *Boidae,* all species not on App. I		II		
Boa, Bimini, *Epicrates striatus fosteri*	R	II		
Boa, Cuban, *Epicrates angulifer angulifer*	I	II		
Boa, Jamaican, *Epicrates subflavus*	V	I	E	
Boas, Keel-scaled, *Casarea spp.*		I		
Boas, Madagascar, *Acrantophis spp.*		I		
Boa, Mona, *Epicrates monensis monensis*	R	II	T	
Boa, Puerto Rican, *Epicrates inornatus*	E	I	E	
Boa, Round Island, *Casarea dussumieri*	E	I	E	
Boas, Round Island, *Bolyeria spp.*		I		
Boa, Round Island, *Bolyeria multocarinata*	E	I	E	
Boa, Rubber, *Charina bottae*		II		
Southern, *C.b. umbratica*	R			CA(R)
Boa, Virgin Islands Tree, *Epicrates monensis granti*			E	

[1]S/A = Similarity of Appearance (to other populations)

REPTILES	RDB	CITES	U.S.	States
Caiman, Black, *Melanosuchus niger*	E	I	E	
Caiman, Broad-nosed, *Caiman latirostris*	E	I	E	
Caiman, Dwarf, *Palaeosuchus palpebrosus*	V	II		
Caiman, Smooth-fronted, *Palaeosuchus trigonatus*	V	II		
Caiman, Spectacled, *Caiman crocodilus*				
Magdalena or Brown, *C.c. fuscus*	E	II		
Rio Apaporia, *C.c. apaporiensis*	E	I	E	
South American, *C.c. crocodilus*	E	II		
Yacare, *C.c. yacare*	E	II	E	
Chameleons, *Chamaeleo spp.*		II		
Chuckwalla, San Esteban Island, *Sauromalus varius*		I	E	
Cobra, Central Asia, *Naja oxiana*	E			
Cobra, False, *Cyclagras gigas*		II		
Constrictor, Boa, *Constrictor constrictor*		II		
Copperhead, Northern, *Agkistrodon contortrix*				IA(E)
Crocodiles, *Crocodylidae,* all species not on App. I		II		
Crocodile, African Slender-snouted or Sharp-nosed, *Crocodylus cataphractus*	E	I	E	
Crocodile, American, *Crocodylus acutus*	E	I	E	FL(E)
Crocodile, Cuban, *Crocodylus rhombifer*	E	I	E	
Crocodile, Estuarine or Saltwater, *Crocodylus porosus*	V	I*	E*	
*Papua New Guinea population		II	unlisted	
Crocodile, Johnson's, *Crocodylus johnsoni*	V	II		
Crocodile, Morelet's, *Crocodylus moreleti*	E	I	E	
Crocodile, Mugger, *Crocodylus palustris*	E*	I		
*Ceylon, *C.p. kimbula*	V			
C.p. palustris			E	
Crocodile, New Guinea, *Crocodylus novaeguineae*				
Mindoro, *C.n. mindorensis*	I	I	E	
New Guinea, *C.n. novaeguineae*	V	II		
Crocodile, Nile, *Crocodylus niloticus*	V	I	E	
Crocodile, Orinoco, *Crocodylus intermedius*	E	I	E	
Crocodile, Siamese, *Crocodylus siamensis*	E	I	E	
Crocodile, West African Dwarf, *Osteolaemus tetraspis*	E	I		
Congo, *O.t. osborni*			E	
O.t. tetraspis			E	
Dragon, Komodo, *Varanus komodensis*	R	I	E	
Gavial, *Gavialis gangeticus*	E	I	E	
Gavial, False, *Tomistoma schlegelii*	E	I	E	
Geckos, Day, *Phelsuma spp.*		II		
Gecko, Day, *Phelsuma newtoni*			E	
Gecko, Magic, *Anarbylus switaki*				CA(R)
Gecko, Reticulated Velvet, *Oedura reticulata*	V			
Gecko, Round Island Day, *Phelsuma guentheri*	R	II	E	
Gecko, Serpent Island, *Cyrtodactylus serpeninsula*	R	II		
Iguana, Andros Island Ground, *Cyclura baeolopha*	R	I		
Iguana, Anegada Ground, *Cyclura pinguis*	R	I	E	
Iguana, Barrington Land, *Conolophus pallidus*	R	V	E	
Iguana, Cuban Ground, *Cyclura nubila*	V	I		
Iguanas, Fiji, *Brachylophus spp.*		I	E	
Iguana, Fiji Banded, *Brachylophus fasciatus*	E	I	E	
Iguana, Galapagos Land, *Conolophus subcristatus*	V			
Iguana, Galapagos Marine, *Amblyrhynchus cristatus*	R	II		
Iguanas, Green, *Iguana spp.*		II		
Iguana, Ground, *Cyclura cychlura*		I		
Allen Cays, *C.c. inornata*	R			
Andros Island, *C.c. cyclura*	R			
Exuma Island, *C.c. figginsi*	R			
Iguana, Ground, *Cyclura carinata*		I		
Mayaguana, *C.c. bartschi*	R			
Turks & Caicos, *C.c. carinata*	R			
Iguana, Mona Ground, *Cyclura stejnegeri*	V	I	T	
Iguana, Rhinoceros, *Cyclura cornuta*		I		
Iguana, Rock, *Cyclura rileyi*		I		
Acklin's Ground, *C.r. nuchalis*	R			
Watling Island, *C.r. rileyi*	E			
White Cay, *C.r. cristata*	R			
Iguanas, West Indian Rock, *Cyclura spp.*		I		

REPTILES	RDB	CITES	U.S.	States
Kingsnake, Sonora Mountain, *Lampropeltis pyromelana pyromelana*				NM(T)
Kingsnake, Speckled, *Lampropeltis getulus*				IA(E)
Lizard, Beaded, *Heloderma horridum*	I	II		
Lizard, Black, or California Legless, *Anniella pulchra nigra*	E			
Lizard, Blunt-nosed Leopard, *Gambelia silus*	E		E	CA(E)
Lizard, Bunchgrass, *Sceloporus scalaris*				NM(T)
Lizard, Caiman, *Dracaena guianensis*		II		
Lizard, Coachella Fringe-toed, *Uma inornata*			T	CA(E)
Lizards, Crag, *Pseudocordylus spp.*		II		
Lizard, Dixon's Whiptail, *Cnemidophoros dixoni*				NM(T)
Lizard, Filfola, *Lacerta filfolensis filfolensis*	R			
Lizard, Giant Spotted Whiptail, *Cnemidophorus burti stictogrammus*				NM(T)
Lizards, Girdled, *Cordylus spp.*		II		
Lizard, Glass, *Ophisaurus attenuatus*	R		T	IA(E)WI(T)
Lizard, Island Night, *Klauberina riversiana*	V	II		
Lizard, Orange-throated Whiptail, *Cnemidophorus hyperythrus*	V			
Lizard, Sail-fin, *Hydrosaurus pustulatus*		II		
Lizard, San Diego Horned, *Phrynosoma coronatum blainvillei*		II		
Lizard, Sanddune Sagebrush, *Sceloporus graciosus arenicolous*				NM(T)
Lizards, Spiny-tailed, *Uromastys spp.*		II	E	
Lizard, St. Croix Ground, *Ameiva polops*	E		E	
Lizardet, Dragon, *Crocodilurus lacertinus*		II		
Massasauga, *Sistrurus catenatus*				IN(E)IA(T) MO(R)WI(E)
Monitors, *Varanus spp.* all species not on App. I		II		
Monitor, Bengal, *Varanus bengalensis*		I	E	
Monitor, Desert, *Varanus griseus*		I	E	
Central Asian, *V.g. caspius*	V			
Monitor, Yellow, *Varanus flavescens*		I	E	
Monster, Gila, *Heloderma suspectum*	V	II		
H.s. suspectum				NM(E)
Mussurana, *Pseudoboa cloelia*		II		
Pythons, *Python spp.*		II		
Python, Indian, *Python molurus*	V	II		
P. molurus molurus			E	
Racer, Alameda Striped, *Masticophis lateralis euryxanthus*				CA(R)
Racer, Speckled, *Drymobius margaritiferus margaritiferus*				TX(E)
Rattlesnake, Aruba Island, *Crotalus unicolor*	R			
Rattlesnake, Mottled Rock, *Crotalus lepidus lepidus*				NM(T)
Rattlesnake, New Mexico Ridge-nosed, *Crotalus willardi obscurus*	E		T	NM(E)
Rattlesnake, Timber, *Crotalus horridus*				
Eastern, *C.h. horridus*				NJ(E)
Canebrake, *C.h. atricaudatus*				MO(E)
Rattlesnake, Western, *Crotalus viridis*				
Arizona Black, *C.v. cerberus*				NM(T)
Prairie, *C.v. viridus*				IA(E)
Rattlesnake, Western Pigmy, *Sistrurus miliarius streckeri*				TN(T)
Skink, Blue-tailed Mole, *Eumeces egregius lividus*				FL(T)
Skink, Cape Verde Giant, *Macroscincus coctaei*	I			
Skink, Coal, *Eumeces anthracinus*				MD(E)
Southern, *E.a. pluvialis*				MS(T)
Skink, Five-lined, *Eumeces fasciatus*				IA(T)
Skink, Great Plains, *Eumeces obsoletus*				IA(E)MO(R)
Skink, Macabe Forest, *Gonglomorphus bojerii fontenayi*	R			
Skink, Mountain, *Eumeces callicephalus*				NM(T)
Skink, Round Island, *Leiolopisma telfairii*	R			
Skink, Sand, *Neoseps reynoldsi*	R			FL(T)
Snake, Atlantic Saltmarsh Water, *Merodia fasciata fasciata*	R		T	FL(E)
Snake, Big Pine Key Ringneck, *Diadophis punctatus acricus*				FL(T)
Snake, Black Pine, see Snake, Pine-Gopher				
Snake, Brown, *Storeria dekayi*				SD(T)
Florida, *S.d. victa*				FL(T)
Snake, Butler's Garter, *Thamnophis butleri*				IN(E)
Snake, Coachwhip, *Masticophis flagellum*				
Eastern, *M.f. flagellum*				IL(T)
San Joaquin, *M.f. ruddocki*	R			
Sonora, *M.f. cingulum*				NM(T)

REPTILES	RDB	CITES	U.S.	States
Snake, Corn, *Elaphe guttata*				NJ(T)
Snake, Diamondback Water, *Nerodia rhombifera*				IA(T)
Snake, Eastern Fox, *Elaphe vulpina gloyote*				MI(T)
Snake, Eastern Hognose, *Heterodon platyrhinos*				SD(T)
Snake, Eastern Indigo, *Drymarchon corais couperi*	V		T	FL(T)GA(T)
				MS(E)SC(T)
Snake, Eastern Ribbon, *Thamnophis sauritus*				
Eastern, *T.s. sauritus*				IL(E)
Northern, *T.s. septentrionalis*				WI(E)
Peninsula, *T.s. sackeni*				FL(T)
Snake, Fiji, *Ogmodon vitianus*	V			
Snake, Giant Garter, see Snake, Western Aquatic Garter				
Snake, Graham's Water, *Nerodia grahami*				IA(T)
Snake, Green Water, *Nerodia cyclopion*				MO(R)
Snake, Harter's Water, *Nerodia harteri*				TX(E)
Snake, Indian Egg-eating, *Elachistodon westermanni*		II		
Snake, Kirtland's Water, *Clonophis kirtlandi*				MI(E)
Snake, Miami Black-headed, *Tantilla oolitica*				FL(T)
Snake, Mona Blind, *Typhlops monensis*	R			
Snake, Narrow-headed Garter, *Thamnophis rufipunctatus*				NM(T)
Snake, Northern Red-bellied, *Storeria occipitomaculata*				SD(T)
Snake, Pine-Gopher, *Pituophis melanoleucus*				
Black Pine, *P.m. lodingi*				MS(E)
Northern, *P.m. melanoleucus*				NJ(T)TN(T)
Snake, Plain-bellied Water, *Nerodia erythrogaster*				
Blotched, *N.e. transversa*				NM(T)
Copper-bellied, *N.e. neglecta*				IN(E)MI(T)
				OH(E)
Yellow-bellied, *N.e. flavigaster*				IA(T)
Snake, Plains Garter, *Thamnophis radix radix*				OH(E)
Snake, Queen, *Nerodia septemvittata*				MO(E)WI(E)
Snake, Rainbow, *Farancia erytrogramma*				MD(E)MS(E)
Snake, Rat, *Elaphe obsoleta*				IL(T)
Black, *E.o. obsoleta*				IA(T)MI(T)
Snake, San Francisco Garter, *Thamnophis sirtalis tetrataenia*	E		E	CA(E)
Snake, Scarlet, *Cemophora coccinea copei*				IN(E)
Snake, Short-tailed, *Stilosoma extenuatum*				FL(T)
Snake, Smooth Earth, *Virginia valeriae*				
Mountain, *V.v. pulchra*				MD(E)
Western, *V.v. elegans*				IA(T)
Snake, Smooth Green, *Opheodrys vernalis*				MO(R)
O.v. blanchardi				IN(E)
Snake, Southern Hognosed, *Heterodon simus*				MS(E)
Snake, Three-lined, *Tropidoclonion lineatum*				SD(T)
Snake, Trans-Pecos Rat, *Elaphe subocularis*				NM(T)
Snake, Two-striped, see Snake, Western Aquatic Garter				
Snake, Western Aquatic Garter, *Thamnophis couchi*				
Giant, *T.c. gigas*	R			CA(R)
Two-striped, *T.c. hammondi*	R	II		
Snake, Western Hognosed, *Heterodon nasicus*				IL(T)MO(R)
Snake, Western Ribbon, *Thamnophis proximus*				
Pecos, *T.p. diabolicus*				NM(T)
Western, *T.p. proximus*				WI(E)
Snake-Lizard, Queensland, *Paradelma orientalis*		II		
Tegus, *Tupinambis spp.*		II		
Terrapin, River, *Batagur baska*	E	I	E	
Tomistoma, see Gavial, False				
Tortoises, *Testudinidae*, all species not on App. I		II		
Tortoise, Angulated, See Tortoise, Madagascar				
Tortoise, Argentine Land, *Geochelone chilensis*	R	II		
Tortoise, Berlandier's, *Gopherus berlandieri*	R			
Tortoise, Bolson, *Gopherus flavomarginatus*	I	I	E	
Tortoise, Desert, *Gopherus agassizi*	R			
Beaver Dam Slope, Utah population			T	
Tortoise, Galapagos Giant, *Geochelone elephantopus*	E	I	E	
Tortoise, Geometric, *Geochelone geometrica*	R	I	E	
Tortoise, Gopher, *Gopherus polyphemus*		II		

REPTILES	RDB	CITES	U.S.	States
Tortoise, Indian Flap-Shell, see Turtle, Indian Flap-Shell				
Tortoise, Madagascar, *Geochelone yniphora*	V	I	E	
Tortoise, Madagascar Spider, *Pyxis arachnoides*	R	II		
Tortoise, Mediterranean Spur-thighed, *Testudo graeca graeca*	V	II		
Tortoise, Pancake, *Malacochersus tornieri*	I	II		
Tortoise, Radiated, *Geochelone radiata*	V	I	E	
Tuatara, *Sphenodon punctatus*	O	I	E	
Turtle, Alligator Snapping, *Macroclemys temmincki*				KS(T)MO(R)
Turtle, Aquatic Box, *Terrapene coahuila*	V	I	E	
Turtle, Black or Cuatra Cienegas Soft-Shell, *Trionyx ater*		I	E	
Turtle, Black Pond, *Geoclemys hamiltoni*		I	E	
Turtle, Black-knobbed Sawback, *Graptemys nigrinoda*				MS(E)
Turtle, Blanding's, *Emydoidea blandingii*				IA(T)MO(E) SD(T)WI(T)
Turtle, Bog, *Clemmys muhlenbergii*	V			MD(E)NJ(E) NY(E)
Turtle, Burmese Swamp, *Morenia ocellata*		I	E	
Turtle, Central American River, *Dermatemys mawii*	V	II		
Turtle, Dark Soft-shell, *Trionyx nigricans*		I	E	
Turtle, Eastern Box, *Terrapene carolina carolina*				MI(T)
Turtle, Eastern Mud, *Kinosternon subrubrum subrubrum*				IN(E)
Turtle, False Map, *Graptemys pseudogeographica*				SD(T)
Turtle, Flatback, *Chelonia depressa*	R	I		
Turtle, Ganges Soft-shell, *Trionyx gangeticus*		I		
Turtle, Green Sea, *Chelonia mydas*	E*	I**	T***	FL(E)HI(T) MD(E)MS(E) WA(T)
*East Pacific, *C.m. agassizi*	V			
**Australian population		II		
***Florida and Pacific coast of Mexico population			E	
Turtle, Hawksbill, *Eretmochelys imbricata*	E	I	E	FL(E)GA(E) HI(E)MD(E) NJ(E)SC(E) TX(E)
Turtle, Helmeted, *Pelomedusa subrufa*		III (Ghana)		
Turtle, Hieroglyphic, *Chrysemys concinna hieroglyphica*				IN(E)
Turtle, Illinois Mud, *Kinosternon flavescens spooneri*				IL(E)IA(E) MO(R)
Turtle, Inagua Island, *Chrysemys malonei*	R			
Turtle, Indian Flap-Shell, *Lissemys punctata punctata*		I	E	
Turtle, Indian Tent or Sawback, *Kachuga tecta tecta*		I	E	
Turtle, Kemp's Ridley, *Lepidochelys kempi*	E	I	E	FL(E)GA(E) MD(E)NJ(E) SC(E)TX(E) FL(T)
Turtle, Key Mud, *Kinosternon bauri bauri*				
Turtle, Leatherback, *Dermochelys coriacea*	E	I	E	FL(E)GA(E) HI(E)MD(E) NJ(E)SC(E) TX(E)WA(E)
Turtle, Loggerhead, *Caretta caretta*	V	I	T	FL(T)MD(E) MS(E)NJ(E) SC(T)
Turtles, Marine, *Cheloniidae spp.*		I		
Turtle, Nile Soft-Shell, *Trionyx triunguis*		III (Tunisia)		
Turtle, Olive Ridley, *Lepidochelys olivacea*	E	I	T*	
*breeding populations on Pacific coast of Mexico			E	
Turtle, Ornate Box, *Terrapene ornata*				IA(T)WI(E)
Turtle, Peacock-marked Soft-Shell, *Trionyx hurum*		I	E	
Turtle, Plymouth Red-Bellied, *Chrysemys rubriventris bangsi*			E	
Turtle, Red-eared, *Chrysemys scripta*				IA(T)
Turtle, Ringed-Sawback, *Graptemys oculifera*				MS(T)
Turtle, Short-necked, *Pseudemydura umbrina*	E	I	E	
Turtle, Side-necked, *Pelusios spp.*		III (Ghana)		
Turtle, Smooth Softshell, *Trionyx muticus muticus*				NM(T)

REPTILES

	RDB	CITES	U.S.	States
Turtle, South American Red-lined, *Pseudemys (Chrysemys) ornata callirostris*	E			
Turtles, South American River, *Podocnemis spp.*		II		
Turtle, South American River, *Podocnemis expansa*	E	II	E	
Turtle, Spotted, *Clemmys guttata*				IL(E)IN(E) OH(E)
Turtle, Spotted Pond, see Turtle, Black Pond				
Turtle, Stinkpot, *Sternotherus odoratus*				IA(T)
Turtle, Terecay, *Podocnemis unifilis*	V	II	E	
Turtle, Texas Slider, *Chrysemys concinna texana*				NM(T)
Turtle, Three-keeled Land, *Geoemyda tricarinata*		I	E	
Turtle, Western Pond, *Clemmys marmorata*				WA(T)
Turtle, Western Spiny Softshell, *Trionyx spiniferus hartwegi*				NM(T)SD(T)
Turtle, Wood, *Clemmys insulpta*				IA(E)NJ(T) WI(E) MS(T)
Turtle, Yellow-blotched Map, *Graptemys flavimaculata*				
Viper, Armenian, *Vipera xanthina raddei*	R			
Viper, Latifi's, *Vipera latifii*	E			
Viper, Lebetina, *Vipera lebetina schweizeri*	V			
Viper, Transcaucasian Long-nosed, *Vipera ammodytes transcaucasiana*	R			
Whipsnake, San Joaquin, see Snake, Coachwhip				

AMPHIBIANS

	RDB	CITES	U.S.	States
Axolotl, *Ambystoma mexicanum*	R	II		
Coqui, Golden, *Eleutherodactylus jasperi*	R		T	
Frog, Archey's, *Leiopelma archeyi*	R			
Frog, BawBaw, *Philoria frosti*	R			
Frog, Blanchard's Cricket, *Acris crepitans blanchardi*				NM(T)
Frog, Burns' Leopard, *Rana pipiens burnsii*				WI(T)
Frog, Eastern Barking, *Hylactophryne augusti latrans*				NM(T)
Frog, Eastern Narrow-mouthed, *Gastrophryne carolinensis*				MD(E)
Frog, Golden, see Frog, Panamanian Golden				
Frog, Goliath, *Conrana goliath*	V			
Frog, Hamilton's, *Leiopelma hamiltoni*	R		E	
Frog, Hochstetter's, *Leiopelma hochstetteri*	R			
Frog, Illinois Chorus, *Pseudaoris streckeri illinoensis*	I			IL(T)IN(E)
Frog, Israel Painted, *Discoglossus nigriventer*			E	
Frog, Northern Crawfish, *Rana arealata circulosa*				KS(T)
Frog, Panamanian Gold, *Atelopus varius zeteki*		I	E	
Frog, Pickerel, *Rana palustris*				WI(T)
Frog, Pine Barrens Tree, *Hyla andersoni*	R		E	NJ(E)
Frog, Platypus, *Rheobatrachus silus*	V			
Frog, Seychelle Islands, *Nesomantis thomasseti*	I			
Frog, Seychelle Islands, *Sooglossus gardinieri*	I			
Frog, Seychelle Islands, *Sooglossus sechellensis*	I			
Frog, Southern Gray Tree, *Hyla chrysoscelis*				NJ(E)
Frog, Stephen Island, see Frog, Hamilton's				
Frog, Western Spotted, *Rana pretiosa*				OR(T)
Frog, Wood, *Rana sylvatica*				MO(E)
Hellbender, *Cryptobranchus alleganiensis alleganiensis*				IN(E)MD(E)
Newt, Central, *Notophthalmus viridescens louisianensis*				IA(E)KS(E)
Olm, *Proteus anguinus*	V			
Peeper, Spring, *Hyla crucifer*				IA(T)
Platana, Cape, *Xenopus gilli*	V			
Salamander, Blue-spotted, *Ambystoma laterale*				IA(E)NJ(E) OH(E)
Salamander, Cascade Cavern, *Eurycea latitans*				TX(E)
Salamander, Cave, *Eurycea lucifuga*				KS(E)MS(E) OH(E)
Salamander, Chinese Giant, *Andrias davidianus*	I	I	E	
Salamander, Desert Slender, *Batrachoseps aridus*	E		E	CA(E)
Salamander, Dusky, *Desmognathus fuscus*				IL(E)
Salamander, Dwarf, *Eurycea quadridigitatus*				MO(E)
Salamander, Eastern Mud, *Pseudotriton montanus*				NJ(T)
Salamander, Four-toed, *Hemidactylium scutatum*				IN(E)MO(R) OH(E)

AMPHIBIANS	RDB	CITES	U.S.	States
Salamander, Gold-striped, *Chioglossa lusitanica*	V			
Salamander, Gray-bellied, *Eurycea multiplicata griseogaster*				KS(E)
Salamander, Green, *Aneides aeneus*				MD(E)MS(E)
				OH(E)
Salamander, Grotto, *Typhlotriton spelaeus*				KS(E)
Salamander, Japanese Giant, *Andrias japonicus*	R	I	E	
Salamander, Jefferson, *Ambystoma jeffersonianum*				MD(E)
Salamander, Jemez Mountain, *Plethodon neomexicanus*	V			NM(T)
Salamander, Kern Canyon Slender, *Batrachoseps simatus*	R			CA(R)
Salamander, Lake Lerma, *Ambystoma lermaensis*	R	II		
Salamander, Lake Patzcuaro, *Ambystoma dumerili*		II		
A.d. dumerili	R			
	I			
Salamander, Larch Mountain, *Plethodon larselli*	R			CA(R)
Salamander, Limestone, *Hydromantes brunus*				NJ(T)
Salamander, Long-tailed, *Eurycea longicauda*				MI(T)
Salamander, Marbled, *Ambystoma opacum*				IN(E)
Salamander, Northern Red, *Pseudotriton ruber ruber*				MO(R)
Salmander, Oklahoma, *Eurycea tynerensis*				
Salamander, Red Hills, *Phaeognathus hubrichti*	R		T	NM(T)
Salamander, Sacramento Mountain, *Aneides hardyi*				
Salamander, San Marcos, *Eurycea nana*	R		T	CA(E)
Salamander, Santa Cruz Long-toed, *Ambystoma macrodactylum croceum*	E		E	CA(R)
Salamander, Shasta, *Hydromantes shastae*	R			IL(E)IN(E)
Salamander, Silvery, *Ambystoma platineum*				CA(E)
Salamander, Siskiyou Mountain, *Plethodon stormi*				IA(T)MI(T)
Salamander, Small-mouthed, *Ambystoma texanum*				WI(T)
Salamander, Spotted, *Ambystoma maculatum*				CA(R)
Salamander, Tehachapi Slender, *Batrachoseps stebbinsi*	R			TN(T)
Salamander, Tennessee Cave, *Gyrinophilus palleucus*				TX(E)
Salamander, Texas Blind, *Typhlomolge rathbuni*	E		E	MD(E)NJ(E)
Salamander, Tiger, *Ambystoma tigrinum*	V			
California, *A.t. californiense*				NJ(E)WI(T)
Salamander, Tremblay's, *Ambystomà tremblayi*				OH(E)
Salamander, Wehrle's, *Plethodon wehrlei*				MI(T)
Siren, Western Lesser, *Siren intermedia nettingi*		I	E	
Toads, African Viviparous, *Nectophrynoides spp.*				
Toad, Amargosa, see Toad, Boreal				
Toad, Black, *Bufo exsul*	V			CA(R)
Toad, Boreal, *Bufo boreas*				
Amargosa, *B.b. nelsoni*	I			
Western, *B.b. boreas*				NM(T)
Toad, Cameroon, *Bufo superciliaris*		I	E	
Toad, Colorado River, *Bufo alvarius*				NM(T)
Toad, Houston, *Bufo houstonensis*	E		E	TX(E)
Toad, Italian Spade-foot, *Pelobates fuscus fuscus*	E			
Toad, Monte Verde or Orange, *Bufo periglenes*	E	I	E	
Toad, Mount Nimba Viviparous, *Nectophrynoides occidentalis*	V	I	E	
Toad, Plains Spadefoot, *Scaphiopus bombifrons*				IA(T)
Toad, Sonoran Green, *Bufo retiformis*	V	II		

Wildlife Rescue Centers

Alliance for Wildlife
  Rehabilitation & Education
P.O. Box 4572
North Hollywood, CA 91607

Lake Tahoe Wildlife Care
P.O. Box 7586
South Lake Tahoe, CA 95731

Wildlife Care Assn.
3615 Auburn Blvd.
Sacramento, CA 95821

Wildlife Rehabilitation Council
P.O. Box 3007
Walnut Creek, CA 94598

North American Wildlife Center, Inc.
Rt. 1 Box 580
Golden, CO 80401

Tri-State Bird Rescue
P.O. Box 1713
Wilmington, DE 19899

Suncoast Seabird Sanctuary
18328 Gulf Blvd.
Indian Shores, FL 33535

Treehouse Wildlife Center
RRI, Box 125 E
Brighton, IL 62012

The Orphan Animal Care Facility, Inc.
4643 S. Main St.
South Bend, IN 46614

Wild Bird Rehabilitation
Audubon Park Zoo
New Orleans, LA 70178

Chesapeake Bird Sanctuary
10305 King Richard Place
Upper Marlboro, MD 20772

Kalamazoo Nature Center
7000 N. Westnedge
Kalamazoo, MI 49007

Carpenter St. Croix
  Valley Nature Center
12805 St. Croix Trail
Hastings, MN 55033

Minnesota Wildlife Assistance
  Coop.
Rt. #2
St. Cloud, MN 56301

Raptor Research and Rehabilitation
  Program
College of Veterinary Medicine
University of Minnesota
St. Paul, MN 55108

Raptor Rehabilitation and
  Propagation Project
Tyson Research Center
Box 193
Eureka, MO 63025

Wildlife Rescue Team
Rt. #1
Walton, NE 68461

The Wild Animal Infirmary for Nevada
2929 Eagle St.
Carson City, NV 89701

Wild Birds Rehabilitation
  Research Center
325 S. First St.
Surf City, NJ 08008

Woodford Cedar Run
  Wildlife Refuge
R.D.2
Marlton, NJ 08053

Hawk Hideaway Rehabilitation Lab
3086 Haskell Rd., RD #2
Cuba, NY 14727

Lifeline for Wildlife, Inc.
RD #104
Ulster Heights Rd
Ellenville, NY 12428

Carolina Raptor Rehabilitation
  and Research Center
Department of Biology
University of North Carolina
at Charlotte
Charlotte, NC 28223

Felicidades Wildlife Foundation, Inc.
P.O. Box 490
Waynesville, NC 28786

Brukner Nature Center
5995 Horseshoe Bend Rd.
Troy, OH 45373

Hawk Mountain Sanctuary
Rt. #2
Kempton, PA 19529

Richland Veterinary Hospital
1003 Eisenhower Blvd.
Johnstown, PA 15905

Texas Wildlife Rehabilitation
  Coalition, Inc.
11506 Chariot
Stafford, TX 77477

Wildlife Rescue, Inc.
c/o Austin Nature Center
8411 Adirondack Trail
Austin, TX 78750

Northwoods Wildlife Center
P.O. Box 358
Minocqua, WI 54548